Uncertainty, information, and communication
Essays in honor of Kenneth J. Arrow, Volume III

Uncertainty, information, and communication

Essays in honor of Kenneth J. Arrow, Volume III

Edited by

WALTER P. HELLER
University of California, San Diego

ROSS M. STARR
University of California, San Diego

DAVID A. STARRETT
Stanford University

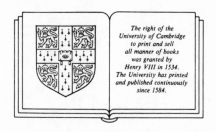

The right of the
University of Cambridge
to print and sell
all manner of books
was granted by
Henry VIII in 1534.
The University has printed
and published continuously
since 1584.

CAMBRIDGE UNIVERSITY PRESS
Cambridge
London   New York   New Rochelle
Melbourne   Sydney

Published by the Press Syndicate of the University of Cambridge
The Pitt Building, Trumpington Street, Cambridge CB2 1RP
32 East 57th Street, New York, NY 10022, USA
10 Stamford Road, Oakleigh, Melbourne 3166, Australia

First published 1986

Printed in the United States of America

Library of Congress Cataloging in Publication Data
Uncertainty, information, and communication.
√ (Essays in honor of Kenneth J. Arrow ; v. 3)
Bibliography: p.
1. Social choice. 2. Decision-making.
3. Equilibrium (Economics) 4. Uncertainty. 5. Arrow,
Kenneth Joseph, 1921– . I. Heller, Walter P.
II. Starr, Ross M. III. Starrett, David A.
IV. Arrow, Kenneth Joseph, 1921– . V. Series.
HB846.8.U53 1986   330   86–11756

British Library Cataloguing in Publication Data
Uncertainty, information, and communication :
essays in honor of Kenneth J. Arrow, volume III.

1. Uncertainty
I. Heller, Walter P. II. Starr, Ross M.
III. Starrett, David A. IV. Arrow,
Kenneth J.
330.15′4   HB615

ISBN 0 521 32704 0

Contents

Essays in honor of Kenneth J. Arrow, Volumes I, II, III

Contributors

Yves Balasko
Université de Genève

Theodore Bergstrom
University of Michigan

David F. Bradford
Woodrow Wilson School of Public
and International Affairs
Princeton University

Graciela Chichilnisky
Columbia University

John D. Geanakoplos*
Yale University

Louis Gevers
Faculté Notre Dame de la Paix
Namur, Belgium

W. M. Gorman*
Nuffield College
Oxford

Jerry R. Green*
Harvard University

Frank Hahn
Churchill College
Cambridge

Peter J. Hammond
Stanford University

John C. Harsanyi
University of California, Berkeley

Walter P. Heller
University of California, San Diego

Leonid Hurwicz
University of Minnesota

Michael D. Intriligator
University of California, Los Angeles

Takatoshi Ito
University of Minnesota

Heinz Koenig
University of Mannheim

Mordecai Kurz
Stanford University

Jean-Jacques Laffont*
Université des Sciences Sociales
Toulouse

Robert C. Lind
Cornell University

Thomas Marschak*
University of California, Berkeley

Eric S. Maskin*
Harvard University

Roger B. Myerson*
Northwestern University

Marc Nerlove
University of Pennsylvania

Hajime Oniki*
Osaka University

Heraklis M. Polemarchakis*
Columbia University

Roy Radner*
AT&T Bell Laboratories

Michael Rothschild*
University of California, San Diego

Herbert E. Scarf
Yale University

Amartya Sen
All Souls College
Oxford

*Contributors to Volume III.

Karl Shell
University of Pennsylvania

Eytan Sheshinski
Hebrew University
Jerusalem

Robert M. Solow
Massachusetts Institute of Technology

Ross M. Starr
University of California, San Diego

David A. Starrett
Stanford University

Nancy L. Stokey
Northwestern University

Laurence Weiss
University of California, San Diego

Menahem E. Yaari*
Hebrew University
Jerusalem

Editors' preface

This three-volume work is composed of essays written by many of Kenneth Arrow's students and collaborators. Although it is impossible to cover the entire range of his contributions to economics, we have organized the presentation around the major topics of his research career: Volume I treats "Social Choice and Public Decision Making," Volume II covers "Equilibrium Analysis," and Volume III deals with "Uncertainty, Information, and Communication."

We would like to thank all contributors to these volumes not only for their cooperation in helping expedite on-time production but also for voluntary efforts contributed in reading and commenting on each other's essays. In addition, we acknowledge with thanks the help of the following outside referees: Chuck Blackorby, Mark Johnson, Mark Machina, John McMillan, and Joel Sobel.

Special thanks go to Deborah Bailey who coordinated our (sometimes chaotic) correspondence among authors, editors, and publisher; she cheerfully dealt with potential disasters and enabled us to deliver the completed manuscript as scheduled. Also, we would like to thank Colin Day and his staff at Cambridge University Press for a highly professional effort at their end.

Finally, and most importantly, we speak for all contributors in thanking Kenneth Arrow for being an inspirational teacher and colleague over the years. The intellectual standards he set and the enthusiasm with which he approaches our subject are surely part of all of us. We can only hope that these essays convey some sense of our appreciation and esteem.

Kenneth J. Arrow

The impact of Kenneth Arrow's work on twentieth century economics has been to change fundamentally economists' understanding of their discipline and their view of several major classes of problems.[1] Arrow was a leader in the post-World War II push to bring the full power of mathematics and statistics to bear on economic analysis. The fields of general equilibrium, social choice and welfare economics, mathematical programming, and economics of uncertainty have been fundamentally altered by his contributions. In addition, Arrow is a man of wide learning, refreshing spontaneity, personal warmth, and remarkable absence of pretension.

Born in 1921 to Harry and Lillian Arrow of New York City, Kenneth Arrow was raised in and around New York. He pursued his undergraduate studies at City College of New York. On graduation from CCNY in 1940, he was awarded the Gold Pell Medal for highest grades in the graduating class. He studied then at Columbia, in particular with Harold Hotelling, and received an M.A. in mathematics in 1941.

Arrow's studies were interrupted by World War II. He served with the Weather Division of the Army Air Force and there wrote his first scientific paper ("On the use of winds in flight planning"). However, his other professional activities in the division almost prevented this line of research. The new young group of statisticians in the Weather Division subjected the prevailing prediction techniques to statistical test against a simple null hypothesis based on historical averages for the date in question. Finding that prevailing techniques were not significantly more reliable, several junior officers sent a memo to the general in charge suggesting that the unit be disbanded and the manpower reallocated. After a succession of such memos, the general's secretary is reported to have replied brusquely on his behalf, "The general is well aware that your division's forecasts are worthless. However, they are required for planning purposes." The division remained intact.

---

[1] Arrow has a rich personal intellectual history. This is best summarized in the headnotes to his research papers in the *Collected papers of Kenneth J. Arrow*. We have borrowed freely from this material. Discussions of Arrow's contributions to each of the topics treated in this collection appear in the introductions to the individual sections.

In 1946, Arrow returned to Columbia for doctoral study with Hotelling. In 1947, he joined the Cowles Commission at the University of Chicago, then under the direction of Jacob Marschak. Cowles was then virtually synonymous with mathematical economics and econometrics in North America. With Hurwicz, Klein, Koopmans, and Marschak there, it formed an active research environment. Arrow was unsure then of his vocation. He considered the possibility of pursuing a nonacademic career as an actuary. Tjalling Koopmans advised him that actuarial statistics would prove unrewarding, saying, with characteristic reticence, "There is no music in it." Fortunately for economic science, Arrow followed this advice and decided to continue a research career.

In 1947, Arrow married Selma Schweitzer, then a graduate student in economics at the University of Chicago. Jacob Marschak, in his capacity as Cowles Commission Research Director, had arranged for the Commission to administer the Sarah Frances Hutchinson Fellowship. This fellowship was held by Sonia Adelson (subsequently married to Lawrence Klein) and then by Selma Schweitzer. The succession of fellows generated some administrative scrutiny. Upon review, it was determined that the terms of the bequest establishing the fellowship required the fellows to be women of the Episcopal Church of Seneca Falls, New York, and the fellowship was withdrawn from Cowles' administration. Nevertheless, the fellowship was clearly a great social success while at Cowles.

In 1948, Arrow joined the recently formed RAND Corporation in Santa Monica, California. RAND was then an active center for fundamental research, particularly in the fast-developing area of mathematical game theory. He returned to RAND during several subsequent summers. There, in the summers of 1950 and 1951, the collaboration with Leonid Hurwicz was initiated.

In 1949, Arrow accepted an assistant professorial appointment in economics and statistics at Stanford University. The research work and publications of the next decade represent an extraordinary burst of creativity and scientific progress. In the space of four years, 1951–4, three of Arrow's most important works of economic theory appeared: *Social choice and individual values* (1951), "An extension of the basic theorems of classical welfare economics" (1951), and "Existence of equilibrium for a competitive economy" (with G. Debreu, 1954). Work on the theory of social choice, started at RAND, was a particularly distinctive act of creation, since the theory was developed with very few antecedents. Arrow describes it as "a concept that took possession of [him]... development of the theorems and their proofs... required only about three weeks, although writing them as a monograph... took many months" (Arrow, *Collected papers*).

The Ph.D. from Columbia was awarded in 1950; and the dissertation, *Social choice and individual values,* was published in 1951. "Extension of the basic theorems of classical welfare economics" was developed for the Second Berkeley Symposium on Mathematical Statistics and Probability to which Arrow was invited in his capacity as a statistician.

In the early 1950s, Arrow pursued – largely by correspondence – joint work on general equilibrium theory with Gerard Debreu, who was then at the Cowles Commission in Chicago. Abraham Wald, with whom Arrow had studied at Columbia, had written several papers in the field but had run up against fundamental mathematical difficulties. It was the recognition by Arrow and Debreu of the importance of using a fixed point theorem that led to major progress in this area.[2] Publication of Arrow and Debreu's "Existence of equilibrium for a competitive economy" represented a fundamental step in the revision of economic analysis and modeling, demonstrating the power of a formal axiomatic approach with relatively advanced mathematical techniques.

During the mid-1950s, Leonid Hurwicz was a frequent academic visitor to Stanford. In 1955–6, Hurwicz was at the Center for Advanced Study in the Behavioral Sciences at Stanford, and in 1957–8 he was a visiting faculty member in the economics department. Collaboration with Hurwicz led to papers in mathematical programming, decentralization, and classic work on the stability of competitive equilibrium. The research faculty in mathematical economics was housed in a converted residence, Serra House. Colleagues there included Herbert Scarf and Hirofumi Uzawa. The informal, quiet, and somewhat isolated setting resulted in a particularly friendly atmosphere and esprit de corps.

Arrow was rapidly promoted at Stanford: to associate professor in 1950 and to full professor in 1953. The full professorship included appointment to the new Department of Operations Research, in addition to economics and statistics. Mathematical programming is a recurrent area of Arrow's research interest, and the new department was founded with Arrow's vigorous support. Although the profession is used to it now, the mathematical complexity of the body of work was then regarded as a bit forbidding. This reputation was a source of some humor when Arrow received the 1957 John Bates Clark Award of the American Economic Association. At the presentation ceremony, introductory remarks were made by George Stigler, who reportedly advised Arrow, in a loud stage-whisper, "You should probably say, 'Symbols fail me.'"

---

[2] Credit for independent discovery of the importance of fixed point theorems in this context is due to Lionel McKenzie ["On equilibrium in Graham's model of world trade and other competitive systems," *Econometrica,* 22: 147–61 (1954)].

In 1962, Arrow served on the research staff of the Council of Economic Advisers. In 1963-4, he was visiting fellow at Churchill College, Cambridge. The collaboration with Frank Hahn on *General competitive analysis* was pursued there and continued at Stanford in 1967. During the late 1960s, Arrow took up a research program in continuous-time optimal control (a topic touched on twenty years earlier in his Army Air Force service). In collaboration with Mordecai Kurz of Stanford, the result was *Public investment, the rate of return, and optimal fiscal policy.*

In 1968, Arrow accepted a professorship at Harvard and moved to Cambridge, Massachusetts. For the next decade, Harvard was the center of his activity, though he returned to Stanford annually for summer-long seminar series.

When the Nobel Prize in Economics was created in the mid-1960s, a common parlor game among professional economists was to forecast the next recipient. Arrow was on virtually everyone's short list. It was hence no surprise when the 1972 Nobel Prize in Economic Sciences was announced. Arrow was the laureate, jointly with the distinguished British economic theorist, John Hicks of Oxford. Age 51 at the time of the award, he is (at this writing) by far the youngest recipient of the Nobel Prize in Economics.

In 1979, Arrow returned to Stanford; he has been on the faculty there continually since then. Arrow lives on the Stanford campus with his wife, Selma. They have two sons, David and Andrew.

At both Stanford and Harvard, Arrow has been active in the affairs of the faculty and institution. Indeed, he has sometimes advised students, "true academic freedom is freedom from committee assignments." At both institutions and within the profession at large, he has been a source of intellectual excitement and ferment. He holds honorary doctorates from a variety of universities around the globe, including his alma mater, CCNY. He is a fellow of the Econometric Society, Institute of Mathematical Statistics, and American Statistical Association and a distinguished fellow of the American Economic Association. He is past president of the Econometric Society, American Economic Association, Institute of Management Sciences, and Western Economic Association. He holds the distinction, particularly rare among non-Japanese, of membership in the Second Class Order of the Rising Sun, an award presented by the Emperor of Japan.

Arrow is personally accessible and unpretentious, addressed as Ken by students, colleagues, and staff. The student, however junior, who steels his nerve to talk with the distinguished professor discovers that he has Arrow's undivided attention. To devoted students and colleagues, Arrow is a legendary figure, larger than life. Stories abound, highlighting his abilities:

- Arrow thinks faster than he – or anyone else – can talk. Hence conversation tends to take place at an extremely rapid pace; no sentence is ever actually completed.
- The breadth of Arrow's knowledge is repeatedly a surprise, even to his friends. By the end of an evening's dinner party whose guests included a professor of art specializing in the art of China, it seemed clear to the host that Arrow was as well versed as the specialist in this subject.
- Arrow can quote passages of Shakespeare and facts of English history accurately and at length.
- Arrow's presence in seminars is legendary. He may open his (abundant) mail, juggle a pencil, or give every evidence of inattention. He will then make a comment demonstrating that he is several steps ahead of the speaker.

Those of us who have had the chance to know him well are particularly fortunate. We are far richer for the experience.

Contents

xix

PART I

Uncertainty

Any review of Kenneth Arrow's contributions to the economics of uncertainty is likely to focus on two topics: *Arrow securities* and *measures of risk aversion,* the first relating to allocation of risk in a general equilibrium setting and the second to characterizing behavior toward risk at the individual level. Arrow recognized early on that uncertainty could be incorporated in a general equilibrium setting through the introduction of contingent commodity markets (markets for trading goods contingent on the state of the world); the presence of such markets, together with other standard assumptions of the competitive model, would assure the first best allocation of risk for the same reasons that competitive equilibrium is Pareto efficient in the certainty model.

Since the set of contingent commodity markets would be absurdly large, Arrow explored the question: What is the minimal set of financial assets that, together with spot markets, would generate a first best allocation? The minimal set he identified is appropriately termed Arrow securities. The Arrow security model became the benchmark against which other market structures could be compared. It led naturally to analysis of the properties and performance of models in which the asset markets were incomplete (in that they provided fewer risk sharing opportunities than Arrow securities).

One line of research sought to explain why markets were in fact incomplete. Although some pointed to setup costs in operating the contingent markets, others focused on the presence of private information concerning the correct state of the world. The presence of such monopoly elements naturally entails a breakdown of perfectly competitive processes and leads to the consideration of bargaining games. Meyerson surveys the theory of bargaining in the presence of private information and suggests general principles that determine the nature and type of private information that generally will be revealed. Radner looks at a restricted class of problems involving two agents, one of which has private information. He shows that first best allocations will be achieved (at least approximately) if the relationship between these agents is of a sufficiently "important" repetitive nature.

1

Another strand of research took incomplete markets as given and sought to study their properties. The chapter by Geanakoplos and Polemarchakis falls in this category. Earlier authors had demonstrated that equilibria might not exist when asset markets are incomplete, and important questions were raised concerning the efficiency properties of equilibria when they are reached. Geanakoplos and Polemarchakis show that equilibria will exist as long as assets are denominated in a common *numéraire* unit. However, they find that such equilibria are generically inefficient even within the class of risk distributions the existing set of markets could reasonably be expected to handle.

When markets are complete, asset pricing problems are trivial. Each asset will be priced as if it were a bundle of Arrow securities. However, as soon as markets are effectively incomplete, the asset pricing problem becomes formidable. Much research has focused on finding useful restrictions on models that will render this problem tractable. Rothschild summarizes the most promising approaches and argues that the so-called factor risk structure is the only one flexible enough to serve in a variety of settings.

The other chapters in this volume relate closely to Arrow's work on measuring behavior toward risk. Adopting the expected utility framework, Arrow derived simple measures of risk aversion (or preference) in terms of properties of the underlying von Neumann–Morgenstern utility function. These measures proved enormously useful in later work, both theoretically and empirically. Unfortunately, evidence against the expected utility hypothesis has mounted in recent years, calling into question the positive validity of some of this work. Marschak reviews some of the arguments and shows that much of the edifice constructed by Arrow and his followers will stand against them. Yaari develops an alternative to the expected utility model and shows how to develop corresponding measures of risk aversion that will parallel those of Arrow.

CHAPTER 1

Negotiation in games: a theoretical overview

Roger B. Myerson

1   The perspective of cooperative game theory

This chapter offers a general perspective on what the methods of cooperative game theory can tell us about bargaining and negotiation between individuals who have different private information. The logical foundations and methodology of cooperative game theory may not be as clearcut as those of noncooperative game theory, but cooperative game theory does provide a conceptual structure that can give important insights into the practical problems of negotiation. In particular, the analysis of cooperative games with incomplete information can explain how regrettable (or ex post inefficient) outcomes, such as strikes, costly delays, and litigation, can occur in an efficiently designed social system, which older theories of cooperative games with complete information could not explain. This chapter surveys the basic ideas and results of the theory of cooperative games with incomplete information at a conceptual level, without getting deeply into the technical detail. For a more detailed and broader introduction to game theory, see Myerson (1985a, 1986b).

The fundamental principle of game theory is that any definite theory or social plan that predicts or prescribes behavior for all players in a game must designate a Nash equilibrium (or, more precisely, a sequentially rational Nash equilibrium), if this theory or plan is to be understood by all the players and is not to impute irrational behavior to any player at any point in time. [By "sequentially rational" we mean that the equilibrium should satisfy some conditions similar to those discussed by Kreps and Wilson (1982) or Myerson (1986a), or at least the subgame perfectness

This contribution was written with the support of a grant from the Alfred P. Sloan Foundation. Helpful suggestions by Peter Cramton are also gratefully acknowledged.

This essay was prepared for presentation at the I.M.S.S.S. summer workshop at Stanford University.

3

condition of Selten (1975).] Thus, the basic method of "noncooperative" game-theoretic analysis is to formulate an extensive or strategic form model for the social situation in question, and then identify all (sequentially rational) equilibria of this model.

There are two general problems with such analysis: There may only be dismal equilibria (as in the well-known Prisoners' Dilemma example) or there may be multiple equilibria [as in the well-known battle of sexes example, see Luce and Raiffa (1957)].

The general response to the dismal-equilibrium problem is, if possible, to make a *cooperative transformation* of the game, by adding communication or contract signing options, or by repeating the game so as to create a new game that may have equilibria with better welfare properties. Mediators, regulators, and auditors are outside interveners who assist in such cooperative transformations. A mediator is any person or machine that can help the players to communicate. The *revelation principle* asserts that a central mediator subject to incentive constraints can simulate any equilibrium of any communication-transformed game. The effect of a regulator or auditor is to relax some of these incentive constraints. A regulator helps the players to precommit to do some future action that they might not actually want to do when the time of action comes, and an auditor helps the players to avoid the temptation to lie about their private information.

Nash's (1951) program for the analysis of bargaining is to formulate and analyze the cooperatively transformed game by noncooperative methods. However, these cooperative transformations usually exacerbate the multiple-equilibrium problem. For example, in the demand game formulated by Nash (1953), every physically feasible allocation that gives each player more than his disagreement payoff is the outcome in some equilibrium. For the purposes of a social planner or arbitrator who can select among the available equilibria, such multiplicity may be good news, but for the purposes of a theorist who wants to make tight predictions, such multiplicity is very bad.

The basic response to the multiple-equilibrium problem is Schelling's (1960) *focal point* effect. This asserts that, in a game with multiple equilibria, anything that tends to focus the players' attention on one particular equilibrium, in a way that is commonly recognized, will tend (like a self-fulfilling prophecy) to make this the equilibrium that the players actually implement. Criteria for determining a focal equilibrium may be grouped into seven general categories as follows.

(1) *Environmental factors* and historical precedent may determine the focal equilibrium that the players implement. To the extent that such factors are important and depend on structures that are ignored in the basic models of game theory, their effect is to limit the power of game-theoretic analysis.

(2) *Strategic properties* such as simplicity or stationarity may make some equilibria seem more natural and hence focal.

(3) Because the *limit of equilibria* of some sequence of perturbed games converges to the actual game may make some equilibrium focal. A basic difficulty with this kind of criterion is that the limits of equilibria may depend on which sequence of perturbed games is considered. Nevertheless, this idea was used in various forms by Nash (1953) and Binmore (1981) to provide one justification of Nash's bargaining solution. This idea is also part of the motivation for concepts of stable equilibria defined by Kohlberg and Mertens (1983) and for Harsanyi's (1975) tracing procedure.

(4) Judgment of an outside *arbitrator* or social planner may determine the focal equilibrium. That is, we may say that an arbitrator is any outside individual who has the authority or power of persuasion to make an equilibrium focal by advocating it in some preplay communication.

(5) Objective standards of *equity* and *efficiency,* which might be the basis of an impartial arbitrator's judgment, may determine the focal equilibrium even when no arbitrator is present, if the players all understand these standards and can therefore predict the equilibrium that such an impartial arbitrator would have selected.

(6) There may be one player in the game, whom we may call the *principal,* who has the arbitrative power to make an equilibrium focal by advocating it in preplay communication.

(7) The focal equilibrium may be determined by a consensus reached in *negotiations* that involve some or all of the players. That is, for a given game, we may define a negotiation to be any process of preplay communication among the players that involves no actions that are intrinsically relevant to payoffs but that can influence the outcome of the game by determining a focal equilibrium.

To relate categories (4), (6), and (7) above, we could say that a principal, in our terminology, is a player who can act like an arbitrator, or, equivalently, is a player who has all of the negotiating ability.

One could try to analyze processes of arbitration and negotiation by making them an explicit part of an (augmented) extensive form model of the game. To do so, however, is to represent a process for selecting equilibria in one game as a part of an equilibrium in a larger game, which generally may have an even larger set of equilibria, so that we are still left with an equilibrium selection problem. For example, preplay announcements by an arbitrator or principal could be included as the first stage in the augmented game model (where the set of permissible announcements may be identified with the set of sequentially rational equilibria of the original game), but there would always be sequential equilibria of this augmented game in which the players all ignore this initial announcement. Of course, there will also be sequential equilibria in this augmented game in which the players always implement the announced equilibrium, but the traditional methods of noncooperative game theory have not offered any criterion to lead theorists to focus on these.

Thus, our analysis of category (4), (6), or (7) must be directly based on some further assumption that expresses the idea that the arbitration or negotiation process will effectively influence the equilibrium perceptions of all players in the direction that the arbitrator, principal, or negotiating players desire. The significance of such an *effectiveness* assumption must be that the selected equilibrium will systematically depend on the preferences of the relevant individuals (arbitrator, principal, or all the negotiating players) over the set of all equilibria, in some way such that the more preferred equilibria are more likely to occur. If players can negotiate effectively, then they should be expected to play an equilibrium that is not Pareto dominated for them within the set of possible equilibria. Furthermore, an effectively negotiated equilibrium should give to each player an expected payoff that is in some sense commensurate with the relative strength of that player's position in the game (what the player has to offer others and what he can guarantee) and negotiating ability.

Criteria (5), (6), and (7) all depend on some kind of comparison of the welfare properties (that is, the players' expected payoff allocations) of the various equilibria. The basic goal of cooperative game theory is to develop a formal theory to predict the outcome of cooperatively transformed games in which any of these welfare-based focal criteria are effective.

2   Complications in extending the theory of equilibrium selection

The idea that the focal equilibrium may be selected by one individual, or negotiated by several individuals, is important and relevant to many real situations. However, it also creates some subtle theoretical difficulties that any general theory of equilibrium selection will need to resolve.

The significance of assuming that some principal player can select the focal equilibrium seems clear, provided the selection is made before any private information is learned. In this case, the (sequentially rational) equilibrium that gives the highest expected utility to the principal should be implemented. However, if the principal has private information at the time of equilibrium selection, then he may face a dilemma. The preferred equilibrium may depend on the principal's information, but may cease to be an equilibrium if its selection depends on (and thus reveals) this information. To resolve this dilemma, the principal's selection must reflect an *inscrutable compromise* between possible preferences. We will discuss this issue further in Section 4.

There is also some conceptual difficulty if a principal has arbitrative power only over a subset of the players or stages of the game. To see this, for example, let us consider the following two two-stage games. In the first game, at stage 1, there is a chance move that chooses H or T with equal probability, and then, at stage 2, player 1 chooses h or t without observing the move from stage 1. Player 1 gets a payoff of $+1$ if the chance move is matched and -1 if it is not. Player 2 has no intrinsically payoff-relevant moves (nor does he observe the chance move) but he has the arbitrative power to select among the multiple equilibria of this game, and he prefers that 2 chooses h. Then we should expect that 1 will be persuaded by 2 to choose h. In the second game, the initial move is instead chosen by some player 3, whose payoffs are opposite to 1's, rather than by chance. Suppose further that 2 still has the same persuasive power to influence 1 in this second game, but that 3's choice is made before 2 can say anything. Then, although the relationship between players 1 and 2 in stage 2 is exactly the same in both games, and player 3 must in equilibrium be randomizing 50–50 like the chance move in the first game, we must conclude that player 2 will not be able to persuade player 1 to choose h for sure in the second game because 1 randomizes in the unique equilibrium. This suggests that some care is needed to define solutions to sequential principal–agent problems, where the principal will retain his persuasive power to influence equilibrium expectations in later stages of the game. Something like the *principal's quasiequilibrium* of Myerson (1982) may be needed to resolve this difficulty. We will return to this issue in Section 7.

The assumption that players can negotiate effectively also should apply to subcoalitions as well as to the grand coalition of all players. To see this, consider the two-player divide-the-dollars game with a dummy third player. We normally expect that the two nondummy players will coordinate on an allocation that divides all the money between themselves, because their subcoalition could negotiate effectively to block any allocation in which they give money to the dummy. However, the three-player majority game (where any allocation of the available money can be implemented if it is approved by a majority of the three players), or any other game with an empty core, shows that the ability of one subcoalition to negotiate effectively must be in some sense limited by the ability of other coalitions to negotiate effectively. The *Shapley value* and other characteristic function solution concepts are attempts to describe how the conflicting abilities of various subcoalitions of players to negotiate effectively among themselves should be reconciled.

3   The equity hypothesis

To begin an analysis of negotiated outcomes of games, we may use the following *equity hypothesis:* The reasonable outcomes of effective negotiations in which the players have equal opportunity to participate should be the same as the reasonable recommendations that would be made by an impartial arbitrator who has the same information as is common knowledge among the players during the negotiations. On the one hand, an impartial arbitrator should not steer the players to something that could be worse for some players than the outcome that they would have negotiated on their own, if this outcome is known. On the other hand, if it is obvious what an impartial arbitrator would have suggested, then the most persuasive argument in negotiations should be to settle on this equilibrium (see, e.g., Fisher and Ury 1981). Since we have not yet rigorously defined "symmetric effective negotiations" or "impartial arbitration," this equity hypothesis cannot be derived as a formal game-theoretic theorem. It is instead an assertion about two different intuitive concepts, both of which we want to formalize. The power of the equity hypothesis comes from the fact that it allows us to carry any restrictions that we can make on one concept over to the other.

For example, in the divide-the-dollars game (where two risk-neutral players can divide $100 if they can agree on its division, otherwise both get zero), we may predict the $50–$50 division as the outcome of a negotiated settlement because it is obviously the solution of an impartial arbitrator. More generally, the equity hypothesis suggests that the outcome of negotiations between players or symmetric negotiating ability should be an agreement that is in some sense *equitable* and *efficient*. That is, the equity hypothesis suggests an equivalence between the focal criteria (5) and (7) in Section 1.

Nash's (1950) axioms for two-person cooperative games may be viewed as normative restrictions on the way an ideal impartial arbitrator should behave. (The arbitrator's recommendations should be Pareto efficient and individually rational, should treat players symmetrically if their positions are symmetric in the feasible set and the disagreement outcome that would occur if all arbitration and negotiation failed, should depend only on the underlying decision-theoretic properties of the players' preferences, should not be based on any distinction among outcomes between which both players are indifferent, and should be independent of the elimination of options that would not be chosen with or without his arbitration.) Then the equity hypothesis translates these normative assumptions into a positive prediction that the outcome of negotiations between two players should maximize the product of their expected utility gains over the disagreement outcome.

On the other hand, we may have little intuition about how an impartial arbitrator should compromise between the conflicting interests of two different possible types of one player in a game of incomplete information. Thus, an analysis of the requirements for inscrutability in the case of negotiated settlements may help to determine what are reasonable arbitrated agreements for such a game.

4   Fundamental issues of cooperation under uncertainty

We now consider a series of basic propositions that should underlie any theory of cooperation under uncertainty.

(1) As developed by Harsanyi (1967–8; see also Mertens and Zamir 1985, Myerson 1985a), the Bayesian game model is the appropriate basic model for games in which the players have different information at the beginning of play, that is, games with *incomplete information*. To specify a Bayesian game, we first specify a set of players N. Then, for each player i in N, we must specify the set of i's possible actions C_i, and the set of i's possible types T_i. A *type* for i is any possible specification of all of i's private information relevant to the game. For each player i, we specify a utility function u_i that determines how i's payoff (measured in some von Neumann–Morgenstern utility scale) depends on the actions and types of all players. Finally, for each i, we specify a probability function p_i that determines the probabilities that i would assign to each possible combination of types for the other players, as a function of his own type. These structures of the Bayesian game model $(N, (C_i, T_i, u_i, p_i)_{i \in N})$ are supposed to describe all the information that is common knowledge among

the players at the beginning of the game. The private information of each player i is represented by this type, which is some element of the set T_i.

(2) In studying a Bayesian game, the appropriate object for welfare analysis by any outside arbitrator must be the mechanism (or decision rule) that determines the actions taken, rather than the actions themselves. Here, a mechanism is any rule for randomly determining the players' actions as a function of their types. That is, a mechanism is a function μ that specifies a probability distribution over the set of possible combinations of actions ($\times_{i \in N} C_i$) for every possible combination of types in $\times_{i \in N} T_i$. An outsider can hope to influence the process by which the players choose their actions as a function of their types but cannot influence their given types. Since the actual types are also unknown to any outsider, he can only judge the impact of the potential influence on the players by how he changes the mechanism by which they will choose their final actions, because the outsider generally cannot predict what those final actions actually will be without knowing their types.

(3) A mechanism is *incentive compatible* if it could be implemented by a central mediator who communicates directly and confidentially with each player in such a way that no player would have any incentive to lie to the mediator or disobey recommendations, when all other players are expected to be honest and obedient. When the basic Bayesian game is transformed by adding any kind of opportunities for communication among the players, any equilibrium of this transformed game must be equivalent to some incentive-compatible mechanism. (This is the *relevation principle.*) These incentive-compatible mechanisms can be formally characterized by a list of mathematical incentive constraints that assert that no player should expect to gain by dishonestly or disobediently manipulating the mechanism.

Thus, we should think of the set of incentive-compatible mechanisms as the set of feasible equilibria among which an arbitrator could choose. To see that choosing an incentive-compatible mechanism is the same as choosing among multiple equilibria, suppose that there are an infinite number of mediators, one for every incentive-compatible mechanism. Every mediator plans to receive a type report from every player and then return an action recommendation to every player, where the mediator's recommendation will be determined according to the mechanism the mediator represents. There are multiple equilibria of this game, which an arbitrator or negotiating players must choose among. Specifically, for any mediator, there is an equilibrium in which the players all send honest reports to him and obey his recommendations, and all players send meaningless type-independent reports to all other mediators, whose uninformative recommendations are then universally ignored.

(4) An incentive-compatible mechanism is *interim incentive efficient* (or simply *incentive efficient,* for short) in the sense of Holmström and Myerson (1983) if there does not exist any other incentive-compatible mechanism that gives higher expected utility to some types of some players and lower expected utility to none. Let $U_i(\mu \,|\, t_i)$ denote the expected utility for player i if his type is t_i and the players' actions are to be determined according to the mechanism μ. Then, μ is interim incentive efficient if and only if μ is an incentive-compatible mechanism and there does not exist any other incentive-compatible mechanism ν such that $U_i(\nu \,|\, t_i) \geq U_i(\mu \,|\, t_i)$ for every type t_i of every player i, with at least one strict inequality. Interim incentive efficiency is the basic welfare efficiency criterion that should be applied by any benevolent arbitrator. A mechanism is interim incentive efficient if and only if it is not common knowledge that some other feasible mechanism would be weakly preferred by every player, given his or her private information, and might be strictly preferred by some. That is, if a mechanism is not efficient in this sense, then there is a feasible change of mechanism that every player would approve, given current information, and which might be strictly preferable for some players.

(5) An incentive-efficient mechanism may generate outcomes that will not be Pareto efficient ex post, after all players' types are revealed, because the incentive constraints that bind in the mechanism selection problem will not be evident ex post. For example, an incentive-efficient mechanism may need to allow for a positive probability of a strike when the firm claims that its ability to increase wages is surprisingly low, in order to satisfy the incentive constraint that the firm should not expect to gain by underrepresenting its ability to pay. So incentive constraints can explain how regrettable outcomes may occur in a well-designed social system.

(6) Much economic analysis has been done under the assumption that the mechanism used in a cooperative game with incomplete information must be ex ante incentive efficient, in the sense that there is no other incentive-compatible mechanism that all players would have preferred (weakly, but with at least one strictly) before learning their types. This is a stronger criterion than interim incentive efficiency, but the argument for it does not seem compelling when we assume that each player already knows his own type at the time that any negotiation or arbitration begins, so that calculations of ex ante (pretype) expected utility are irrelevant to the player. (We are assuming that this game is not to be repeated, or, more generally, that any relevant repetitions of the existing situation are already included

in our definition of the game.) Thus, focusing on ex ante efficiency may lead to some systematic biases in the analysis of cooperative games. For example, it is easy to construct labor–management bargaining games in which costly underemployment (relative to the full information optimum) occurs with positive probability in all interim incentive-efficient mechanisms except those that are ex ante incentive efficient. (There are other examples, however, in which even ex ante incentive-efficient mechanisms have underemployment.)

(7) The equity hypothesis does not imply that arbitration and negotiation should be completely equivalent for cooperative games with incomplete information unless the players negotiate *inscrutably* (that is, without revealing anything about their private information during the negotiation process). Otherwise, the information that would become common knowledge during negotiations might be greater than the information that is common initially, which is all that an arbitrator could use in planning a mechanism. This issue is related to the distinction between efficiency and *durability* made by Holmström and Myerson (1983). However, Holmström and Myerson were considering a social choice environment in which the noncooperative actions available to the individual players were not specified, as Crawford (1985) has observed.

In general, to be able to negotiate inscrutably, a player must be able to phrase negotiating strategy in terms of type-contingent mechanisms, rather than just in terms of final combinations of actions. That is, if players can agree on mechanisms, then they can agree to share information without actually doing so during the negotiation process. Using this idea, Myerson (1983) has argued that there is no loss of generality in assuming that a principal with private information will choose an incentive-compatible mechanism inscrutably. The same inscrutability assumption is also used, but less convincingly, in the analysis of bargaining problems where two or more players can negotiate, in Myerson (1984a, b).

In any case, any definitive theory of negotiated settlements must ultimately specify a *reduced-form solution* that is a single incentive-compatible mechanism for the game in question. If the players do not negotiate inscrutably, then this reduced-form solution is the composition of a settlement function that maps type combinations into the agreements that may be reached at the end of the negotiations and an interpretive function that determines the ultimate combination of actions in $\times_{i \in N} C_i$ as a function of the players' types and the agreement reached.

(8) In general, there is an issue of *intertype* compromise as well as inter-

personal compromise that must be determined in any theory of cooperative games with incomplete information. For example, there may be two different interim incentive-efficient mechanisms that give the same expected payoffs to all types of player 2, but one may be better for type A of player 1 while the other is better for type B of player 1. If one of these is the (arbitrated, negotiated, or principal-selected) solution for the cooperative game, then some trade-off between payoffs to the two different potential types of player 1 must have somehow been made.

The most important basis for making interpersonal compromise is generally accepted to be the need to satisfy some kind of *equity* criterion (lest the subequitably treated players reject the agreement). The natural basis for determining intertype compromise (between two types of the same player) in negotiation is the player's need to satisfy some *inscrutability* condition, lest the other players infer something about type from negotiating strategy and use this information against that player. If type A of player 1 is not particularly concerned to conceal his type from player 2 (because A is the *good* type), then the inscrutable compromise will probably favor the preferences of type A. (If neither type of player 1 needs to conceal his information from player 2, then the situation described in the preceding paragraph probably would not arise.)

(9) To understand the issue of inscrutable intertype compromise, it is best to begin with the case of mechanism selection by a principal player, because this case is conceptually the simplest in the case of games with complete information. There is one important class of games in which we can define a clear resolution of the problem of compromise between the conflicting goals of the principal's types: These are the games in which the principal has a *strong solution,* in the sense of Myerson (1983). A strong solution for the principal is an incentive-compatible mechanism that has two properties: It would still be incentive compatible even if the principal's type were publicly revealed to all the other players, no matter what that type may be (so it is *safe* for the principal); and there is no other incentive-compatible mechanism that is weakly better for all of the principal's types and strictly better for some (so it is *undominated* for the principal). It can be shown that the strong solution must be essentially unique, if it exists. Because it is safe, the principal does not need to conceal his type when advocating a strong solution. On the other hand, it can be shown (using both properties of the strong solution) that any other mechanism would cease to be incentive compatible when the other players infer that the principal is in the set of types that prefer it over the strong solution.

Thus, although the strong solution is not necessarily the best incentive-compatible mechanism for any one type of the principal, it is the inscrutable compromise that all types must feel compelled to advocate.

For example, suppose that player 1, the principal, is selling a car that player 2 thinks may be worth either $1,000 or $2,000, depending on its quality (bad or good), which player 1 already knows. In either case, suppose that the car is worth $0 to player 1. Player 2 thinks that good or bad are equally likely, given current information, but can determine the quality with a costless inspection. Assume that 1 is risk averse, but 2 is risk neutral. The ex ante optimal mechanism for player 1 before learning the quality would have been to demand that player 2 pay $1,500 for the car without inspecting it, but it would be absurd for player 1 to try to negotiate such a deal when he already knows the quality. In technical terms, the constant $1,500 mechanism is not a strong solution, because player 2 would not want to accept the deal if he knew that player 1 had a bad car. The strong solution for player 1 is, of course, to demand $1,000 if bad and $2,000 if good and let player 2 check the quality of the car.

Any general theory of intertype compromise in negotiations should generalize the rule that a principal with private information advocates his strong solution, if one exists. Since the strong solution is not necessarily ex ante efficient, we must not assume that cooperative solutions should be ex ante efficient, just interim incentive efficient.

5   Neutral bargaining solutions for games with incomplete information

The derivation of Nash's (1950) bargaining solution for two-person games with complete information can be divided into two parts. First, the symmetry and efficiency axioms identify what the solutions must be for a class of relatively straightforward problems. Then these solutions are extended to all other problems by applying some independence axioms, which assert that certain (irrelevant) transformations of the problem should not change the solution. The derivation of *neutral bargaining solutions* by Myerson (1983, 1984a) for games with incomplete information proceeds analogously, beginning with the analysis of a class of straightforward games that have strong solutions [property (1) below], and then extending the analysis to other games by independence axioms [properties (2) and (3) below].

For two-person games with incomplete information, with a fixed disagreement point and actions that can be regulated, the neutral bargaining solution of Myerson (1984a) is defined as the smallest solution concept satisfying the following three properties: (1) If there is a strong solution for each player that leaves the other player at his disagreement payoff (so that it is obvious that each player would demand this strong solution if he were the principal) and if a 50-50 randomization between these two strong solutions is interim incentive efficient, then this 50-50 random dictatorship (being equitable and efficient) should be a bargaining solution. (2) If μ is an interim incentive-efficient mechanism for a game Γ and if, for each $\epsilon > 0$, there exists some game Γ' such that a bargaining solution for Γ' gives each type t_i of each player i a payoff not more than $U_i(\mu \mid t_i) + \epsilon$, and Γ' differs from Γ only in that Γ' allows the players more jointly feasible actions than Γ, then μ must be a bargaining solution for Γ. (3) The set of solutions is invariant under decision-theoretically irrelevant transformations of the utility and probability functions. General existence of these neutral bargaining solutions can be shown.

The neutral bargaining solutions can be characterized in terms of a concept called *virtual utility*. It is well known that the problem of satisfying economic constraints can be decentralized efficiently if the constrained quantities are multiplied by some (carefully chosen) shadow prices and then added into the individuals' payoff functions. This idea can also be applied to the problem of satisfying incentive constraints. The resulting transformation of individuals' payoff functions is called virtual utility by Myerson (1984a, 1985a). We may say that a type s_i *jeopardizes* another type t_i of player i if there is a positive shadow price assigned to the incentive constraint that type s_i of player i should not gain by pretending to be type t_i. Then, qualitatively, the virtual utility payoffs for type t_i of player i differ from the real payoffs in a way that exaggerates the difference from the (false) types that jeopardize t_i. An incentive-compatible mechanism μ is incentive efficient if and only if there exist virtual utility scales such that (i) only incentive constraints that bind in μ have positive shadow prices and (ii) the players' sum of virtual utility is always maximized ex post in μ. That is, any incentive-efficient mechanism is *virtually efficient* ex post, for appropriately chosen utility scales. If, in addition, each type of each player gets an expected virtual gain (over disagreement) that, in these virtual utility scales, is equal to the expected virtual gain of the other player, then this mechanism is a neutral bargaining solution. That is, neutral bargaining solutions are incentive-efficient mechanisms that are also *virtually equitable*.

The concept of (weighted) utility transfers has played a crucial role in the analysis of multiplayer cooperative games with complete information.

For games with incomplete information, however, transfers may be more complicated phenomena because they can serve a signaling role as well as a redistributive role. (I may give someone a gift to prove something about myself, as well as to repay a debt.) Myerson (1984b) has shown that, in a technical sense, the natural extension of the concept of *weighted utility transfers* to games with incomplete information is the concept of *state-dependent virtual utility transfers,* because these concepts both parametrically generate families of linear activities that can transform the efficient frontier into a hyperplane that supports any arbitrarily chosen incentive-efficient mechanism of the original game without transfers. Using this insight, a natural extension of the Shapley NTU value to multiplayer games with incomplete information has also been defined by Myerson (1984b) in terms of a coincidence of virtual efficiency and virtual equity, with respect to some virtual utility scales.

The *neutral optima* for a principal with private information are defined axiomatically to be a natural extension of the principal's strong solutions, and are shown to always exist by Myerson (1983). To get some intuition about these neutral optima, recall that strong solutions were required to be safe and undominated for the principal. Since strong solutions often do not exist, existence requires that we relax at least one of these requirements. In the definition of neutral optima, the safeness requirement is relaxed. That is, the principal's neutral optima are defined so that they are, in some sense, as close to "safe" as possible within the set of incentive-compatible mechanisms that are undominated for the principal. For example, the principal's neutral optimum is the mechanism with the least amount of pooling among the principal's undominated mechanisms in a trading game studied by Myerson (1985b) (the uniform additive bargaining-for-a-lemon game).

6   An example

Suppose that a monopolistic seller is facing a monopsonistic buyer of a unique indivisible object, and the following facts are common knowledge. The object may be worth $0 or $80 to the seller, and the buyer assigns subjective probabilities .75 and .25 to these events, respectively. The object may be worth $20 or $100 to the buyer, and the seller assigns subjective probabilities .25 and .75 to these events, respectively. Each individual knows his own value for the object.

An ex post efficient mechanism for this example would have the buyer promptly get the object except in the event that it is worth $80 to the seller and \$20 to the buyer, which happens (from our outsider's perspective) only with probability 0.0625. However, it can be shown that there is no incentive-compatible mechanism that is ex post efficient in this sense. That is, in any equilibrium of any trading game derived from this situation (by specifying in detail the rules by which terms of trade are proposed and ratified), there must be a positive probability that the seller keeps the object even though it is worth more to the buyer.

To understand this impossibility result, let us consider a class of trading mechanisms that treat the buyer and seller symmetrically. (If there were any ex post efficient incentive-compatible mechanism, there would be a symmetric one.) If the object is worth \$0 to the seller and \$100 to the buyer, then, for symmetry and ex post efficiency, let trade occur for sure at price \$50. If the object is worth \$80 to the seller and \$20 to the buyer, then let no trade occur. Now, let q denote the probability that trade occurs if the object is worth \$0 to the seller and \$20 to the buyer, and let x dollars denote the price of the object if trade occurs in this event. For symmetry, let q also be the probability that trade occurs if the object is worth \$80 to the seller and \$100 to the buyer, and let \$100$-x$ be the price if trade occurs in this event. To give each type of each trader an incentive to participate in the mechanism, we must have $x \le 20$ (otherwise, a low-type buyer would have negative expected gains from trade). To give a low-type seller an incentive to report his type honestly, we must have

$$.75(50) + .25xq \ge .75(100-x)q,$$

which implies that $q \le 37.5/(75-x)$. Thus, it is impossible to have $q = 1$, as ex post efficiency would require.

The mechanisms in this class that satisfy

$$q = 37.5/(75-x)$$

are all interim incentive efficient, so these are the natural mechanisms to consider in searching for an equitable arbitrated or negotiated solution to this trading problem. The *strong* types (that is, the seller's type with a reservation price of \$80 and the buyer's type with a reservation price of \$20) each prefer the mechanisms with lower x. The *weak* types (the seller's type with a reservation price of \$0 and the buyer's type with a reservation price of \$100) prefer the mechanism with higher x. Thus, the question of intertype compromise is essential to the analysis of this example.

In all of the symmetric incentive-efficient mechanisms described above, the weak type of trader is indifferent between honestly reporting type and claiming to be strong, given personal information. But for each of these mechanisms, a weak-type trader would strictly prefer to pretend to be strong if it is known that the other trader is weak. Thus, none of these mechanisms could be implemented by a process of unmediated bargaining in which the players, speaking one at a time and directly to each other, alternately announce offers until one accepts the other's latest offer. (Since the price in the accepted offer would have to depend on both players' types in any of these mechanisms, there would have to be some informative announcements before the end of bargaining. But, after the first such informative announcement, if it gave evidence of the announcer's weakness then the other trader could gain by always henceforth acting like a strong type.) Thus, as Farrell (1983) has observed, the use of a mediator may be essential to implement socially desirable mechanisms in a game. Confidential mediation is more than just a simplifying technical assumption; it is an important and practical way to let individuals reveal information or make concessions without reducing other individuals' incentives to also make concessions.

The ex ante criterion would suggest that the symmetric mechanism with the highest possible x, $x = 20$ (and so $q = .68$) would be desirable, since this maximizes the ex ante expected gains, before the traders learn their types. However, the traders already know their reservation prices, so this ex ante criterion is not relevant to them.

The symmetric mechanism with $x = 0$ and $q = .5$ is the neutral bargaining solution for this example. That is, the neutral bargaining solution resolves the intertype compromise question in favor of the strong types. This may seem reasonable in view of the fact that the problematic incentive constraints in this example are the constraints that a weak-type trader should not gain by pretending to be strong. That is, in negotiations, we might expect to see a weak ($0) type of seller pretending to be really the strong ($80) type, but we would not expect to see a strong type pretending to be weak. (Sellers may often overstate their reservation prices, but they usually do not understate them!) Thus it is reasonable that the traders should negotiate to the symmetric mechanism that is most preferred by the strong types. Since only the weak types feel the need to be inscrutable, the inscrutable compromise gets resolved completely in favor of the strong types. (If negative prices were allowed, the strong types would actually prefer to implement a symmetric mechanism with $x < 0$. But a strong trader would need to be inscrutable to negotiate for such strange mechanisms with negative x, since he would be offering negative gains to the other trader. Thus, the inscrutable compromise would still be at $x = 0$.)

All of the interim incentive-efficient symmetric mechanisms described above [with $q = 37.5/(75 - x)$] are optimal solutions to the mathematical problem of maximizing

$$\tfrac{11}{16}(U_s(\mu \mid 0) + U_b(\mu \mid 100)) + \tfrac{5}{15}(U_s(\mu \mid 80) + U_b(\mu \mid 20))$$

subject to the constraint that μ should be an incentive-compatible mechanism. [Here, $U_s(\mu \mid \theta)$ denotes the seller's expected utility from the mechanism μ if the seller's value for the object is θ dollars; similarly, $U_b(\mu \mid \theta)$ denotes the buyer's expected utility from μ if his value is θ dollars. Note that the objective function coefficients have been chosen so that the weights given to the strong types are slightly larger than the ex ante probabilities of these types.] In this optimization problem, the weak types jeopardize the strong types, and the shadow prices of these incentive constraints is $\tfrac{1}{16}$. With these coefficients and shadow prices, the virtual utility of each weak type is the same as actual utility, but the virtual utilities of the strong types exaggerate their difference from the weak types. Specifically, the strong type of the seller has a virtual value of $100 (greater than the actual value of $80) for the object, and the strong type of buyer has a virtual value of $0 (less than the actual value of $20) for the object. With these virtual values, there are no virtual gains from trade when one trader is weak and the other trader is strong, so the mechanisms that randomly determine whether trade occurs or not in such cases are virtually efficient ex post, as incentive efficiency requires. But only the symmetric incentive-efficient mechanism with $x = 0$ and $q = .5$ is virtually equitable, since all the others have the strong type of buyer paying more (and the strong type of seller getting less) than the virtual value when the trade occurs. So this mechanism satisfies the virtual equity conditions for a neutral bargaining solution.

Myerson (1985b) noted that neutral bargaining solutions tend to have the following property, called *arrogance of strength:* If two individuals have symmetric bargaining ability but one individual's type is surprisingly strong, then the outcome of the neutral bargaining solution tends to be similar to what would have been the outcome if this strong individual had been the principal, except that the probability of the disagreement outcome is larger. That is, we may predict that a low-probability strong type will try to dictate the optimal agreement and will either be successful in this arrogant Boulware strategy or else will fail and cause negotiations to break down. In this example, if the seller were the principal, he would (in either type) demand a price of $100, and the weak-type buyer would acquiesce to this price. The strong-type seller demands this same $100 price in the neutral bargaining solution, but the weak-type buyer acquiesces to it only with probability $\frac{1}{2}$. (In the other symmetric mechanisms, the behavior of the strong types goes from "arrogant" to "timid" as x increases from 0 to 20.)

Using risk neutrality, one can check that the neutral bargaining solution for this example is equivalent to a mechanism in which either the buyer or seller, each with probability $\frac{1}{2}$, gets to make a first-and-final price offer. Thus, the neutral bargaining solution for this example can be interpreted directly in terms of the random dictatorship axiom of Myerson (1984a).

In this example, we have remarked that there is no incentive-compatible trading mechanism that guarantees that trade will promptly occur when the object is worth more to the buyer, and that trade will never occur when the object is worth more to the seller. Thus, we must recommend mechanisms that allow a positive probability of no trade (or, in a dynamic model, a costly delay before trading) when one trader is strong and the other is weak, even though there actually is a range of mutually acceptable prices. Let us now consider what would happen if a mediator ignored this prescription and instead followed a policy of recommending trade at a mutually acceptable price whenever he can identify one. For example, a mediator might ask each trader to report his value for the object (insisting that the seller must report $0 or $80 and the buyer must report $20 or $100, since these ranges are common knowledge) and then recommend trade at a price that is halfway between the two reported values whenever the buyer's reported value is higher. For simplicity, let us suppose that this mediator also has the power to regulate the price, so that the mediator's price recommendations must be followed if trade occurs, although they cannot be forced to trade. Such a mediation plan induces a game that has three equilibria. In one equilibrium, the buyer always reports $20, even if weak, and the seller is honest, so that trade occurs at a price of $10 with probability 0.75. In another equilibrium, the seller always reports $80, even if weak, and the buyer is honest, so that occurs at a price of $90 with probability 0.75. In the third equilibrium, the strong type of each player is always honest, but the weak type randomizes between honestly reporting the value, with probability 20/75, and reporting the strong type's value, with probability 55/75. This third equilibrium treats the two traders symmetrically, unlike the other two equilibria, but the probability of trade in it is only .36. Thus, a mediation plan that fails to recognize binding incentive constraints can generate a communication equilibrium that is either very inequitable (like the first two equilibria) or very inefficient (like the third). As a matter of practical advice, it is better for a mediator to plan to pay the cost of incentive compatibility in a controlled incentive-efficient way than to try to avoid paying the costs of incentive compatibility at all.

7   Dynamic models of bargaining

The importance of ex post efficiency in economic analysis is derived not only from welfare considerations but from stability considerations. That is, one might wonder how the mechanisms discussed in the preceding section could actually be implemented if the seller can keep making offers to sell the object. After all, if the seller still has the object and knows that there is a positive probability that the buyer might be willing to pay more than the seller's reservation price, why should the seller not make another (slightly lower) offer to sell? It seems that it may make a difference whether this is a one-stage game or a multistage game in which the players can continue to propose potential terms of trade.

To analyze a simple dynamic bargaining game in continuous time, suppose that, in our example, the traders will trade as soon as one of them concedes weakness, at a price of x dollars if the seller concedes first and at a price of $100 - x$ dollars if the buyer concedes first (and at a price of $50 if they both concede simultaneously). Here, we let x be some given constant between 0 and 20. Suppose that the traders have the same discount rate δ. As long as the seller retains the object, he gets a constant stream of benefits, which, if extended forever, would have a present discounted value equal to the seller's value for the object. In this game, there is a symmetric equilibrium in which the strong types never concede, and the weak type of each player plans independently to concede somewhere between time 0 and time $(100 - 2x)(\ln(4))/(\delta x)$, using the cumulative distribution function

$$F(\tau) = \min\{1, \tfrac{4}{3}(1 - e^{-\tau\delta x/(100 - 2x)})\}$$

to determine time τ of concession. With this distribution, if one trader is weak and the other trader is strong, the expected time of concession by the weak trader is $(200 - 4x)/(3\delta x)$; letting $x = 10$ and $\delta = 0.10$ (when time is measured in years), this is 53.3 years! These long delays before trading greatly reduce the expected present discounted values of the gains for each type of trader. In fact, for each x, the symmetric equilibrium of this dynamic bargaining game is Pareto dominated (using the interim welfare criteria) by the corresponding symmetric mechanism (for the same

x) that was discussed in the preceding section. The problem is that having opportunities to trade later reduces the incentive for players to make concessions now.

In general, a player's inalienable right to take various actions in the future (i.e., to quit a job or to offer to sell something) generates strategic incentive constraints that reduce the set of incentive-compatible mechanisms relative to what it would have been if, at the beginning of the game, the player had the option to precommit to never take advantage of these opportunities. The basic principles for analyzing such dynamic incentive constraints in multistage games are discussed by Myerson (1986a). The key idea is that it suffices to consider centralized communication mechanisms in which, at every stage, each player confidentially reports new information to a central mediator, who in turn confidentially recommends the action each player should take at the current stage, such that all players have an incentive to be honest and obedient to the mediator. Furthermore, sequential rationality is actually easier to characterize in games with communication than in games without communication (as in Kreps and Wilson 1982), since Myerson (1986a) showed that a communication equilibrium is sequentially rational if and only if it avoids certain co-dominated actions. In a game where players move one at a time, these co-dominated actions can be identified simply by sequentially eliminating all dominated actions for all types of all players, beginning in the last stage and working backward.

Rubinstein (1982) and others have shown that many natural bargaining games have a unique perfect equilibrium. Most commonly, the games in which this occurs are games in which the players have no private information and never make simultaneous moves. In the above terminology, such results assert that the dynamic incentive constraints reduce the set of incentive-compatible mechanisms to a single point, which is certainly a very important result whenever it holds. However, games with incomplete information and games in which players can make simultaneous moves generally have large sets of equilibria, even when sequential rationality is required. (In our example, it was rather unnatural to suppose that the price x was exogenously given and constant over time. Once this assumption is dropped, the number of equilibria increases enormously.) Such multiplicity is actually good news to an arbitrator (or a principal, or a set of negotiating players) who can determine the equilibrium to be played, since more equilibria means a larger set to select from. Our problem is to predict how impartial arbitration or effective negotiation might select among these equilibria.

Multistage dynamics do more than just generate incentive constraints, however. They also generate new welfare criteria that may influence the cooperative determination of which equilibrium or incentive-compatible mechanism is to be implemented. For example, an equilibrium that gives high expected payoffs to all players, from their perspective at the beginning of the game, might actually give them all low payoffs after some event that has positive probability. [See Abreu, Pearce, and Stacchetti (1984) for some examples.] In such cases, even though the equilibrium is sequentially rational for each individual, we might suspect that the players would try to jointly renegotiate to some other equilibrium that seems better after this event, so that the initial equilibrium plan should not have been credible in the first place. Similarly, if there is one principal player who has a monopoly on the power to negotiate and can thus designate the equilibrium that everyone will play, he may find that exercise of this power at the first stage of the game is constrained by the other players' perception that he would reexercise this power at a later stage, after some event that makes his former selection seem less attractive than some other equilibrium. To understand such issues, we will need to develop a theory of *recursively negotiated* games in which (some or all of) the players at each stage can negotiate their current and future behavior, subject to the usual incentive constraints plus the constraints implied by renegotiation opportunities in later stages.

REFERENCES

Abreu, D., D. Pearce, and E. Stacchetti (1984), "Optimal cartel equilibria with imperfect monitoring," discussion paper, Harvard University.

Binmore, K. (1981), "Nash bargaining theory II," discussion paper, London School of Economics.

Crawford, V. P. (1985), "Efficient and durable decision rules: A reformulation," *Econometrica,* 53: 817-35.

Farrell, J. (1983), "Communication in games I: Mechanism design without a mediator," discussion paper, Massachusetts Institute of Technology.

Fisher, R. and W. Ury (1981), *Getting to yes,* Boston: Houghton Mifflin.

Harsanyi, J. C., (1967-8), "Games with incomplete information played by 'Bayesian' players," *Management Science,* 14: 159-82, 320-34, 486-502.

Harsanyi, J. C., (1975), "The tracing procedure: A Bayesian approach to defining a solution for *n*-person games," *International Journal of Game Theory,* 4: 61-94.

Holmström, B. and R. B. Myerson (1983), "Efficient and durable decision rules with incomplete information," *Econometrica,* 51: 1799-1819.

Kohlberg, E. and J. F. Mertens (1983), "On the strategic stability of equilibria," CORE Discussion Paper No. 8248, Université Catholique de Louvain.

24   **Roger B. Myerson**

Kreps, D. M. and R. Wilson (1982), "Sequential equilibria," *Econometrica*, 50: 863–94.
Luce, R. D. and H. Raiffa (1957), *Games and decisions*, New York: Wiley.
Mertens, J.-F. and S. Zamir (1985), "Formulation of Bayesian analysis for games with incomplete information," *International Journal of Game Theory*, 14: 1–29.
Myerson, R. B. (1982), "Optimal coordination mechanisms in generalized principal–agent problems," *Journal of Mathematical Economics*, 11: 67–81.
Myerson, R. B. (1983), "Mechanism design by an informed principal," *Econometrica*, 51: 1767–97.
Myerson, R. B. (1984a), "Two-person bargaining problems with incomplete information," *Econometrica*, 52: 461–87.
Myerson, R. B. (1984b), "Cooperative games with incomplete information," *International Journal of Game Theory*, 13: 69–96.
Myerson, R. B. (1985a), "Bayesian equilibrium and incentive compatibility: An introduction," in L. Hurwicz, D. Schmeidler, and H. Sonnenschein (Eds.), *Social Goals and Social Organization*, Cambridge: Cambridge University Press.
Myerson, R. B. (1985b), "Analysis of two-person bargaining games with incomplete information," in A. E. Roth (Ed.), *Game Theoretic Models of Bargaining*, Cambridge: Cambridge University Press.
Myerson, R. B. (1986a), "Multistage games with communication." *Econometrica*, 54: 323–358.
Myerson, R. B. (1986b), "An introduction to game theory," in S. Reiter (Ed.), *Studies in Mathematical Economics*, Washington, D.C.: Mathematical Association of America.
Nash, J. F. (1950), "The bargaining problem," *Econometrica*, 18: 155–62.
Nash, J. F. (1951), "Noncooperative games," *Annals of Mathematics*, 54: 289–95.
Nash, J. F. (1953), "Two-person cooperative games," *Econometrica*, 21: 128–40.
Rubinstein, A. (1982), "Perfect equilibrium in a bargaining model," *Econometrica*, 50: 97–109.
Selten, R. (1975), "Reexamination of the perfectness concept for equilibrium points in extensive games," *International Journal of Game Theory*, 4: 25–55.
Shelling, T. C. (1960), *The strategy of conflict*, Cambridge, Mass.: Harvard University Press.

CHAPTER 2

Repeated moral hazard with low discount rates

Roy Radner

1 Introduction

The owner of an enterprise wants to put it in the hands of a manager. In each of a number of successive periods (month, quarter, year) the profit of the enterprise will depend both on the actions of the manager and on the environment in which the enterprise is operating. The owner cannot directly monitor the manager's actions, nor can the owner costlessly observe all of the relevant aspects of the environment. The owner and the manager will have to agree on how the manager is to be compensated, and the owner wants to pick a compensation mechanism that will motivate the manager to provide a good return on the owner's investment, net of the payments to the manager.

This is the well-known *principal–agent* problem, with the additional feature that the relationship between the owner (principal) and the manager (agent) may last more than one decision period. Some other principal–agent relationships in economic life are client–lawyer, customer–supplier, regulator–public utility, and insurer–insured. The insurer–insured relationship gave rise to the term *moral hazard,* and the first formal economic analysis of moral hazard was probably given by K. J. Arrow.[1]

Early formal analyses of principal–agent relationships focused on "short-term" or "one-period" situations. The simplest of these can be modeled as a two-move game, in which (1) the principal chooses a compensation function (made known to the agent) and (2) the agent chooses the action. The outcome is then determined as a function of the agent's action and some exogenous stochastic event, and the principal compensates the agent as a function of that outcome, according to the compen-

I am grateful to Peter B. Linhart and Polly Roberts for comments on an earlier draft. The views expressed here are those of the author and not necessarily those of AT&T Bell Laboratories or of New York University.

sation function the principal previously announced in the first move. The resulting utility to the principal depends on the outcome and the compensation; for example, it might be the difference between the (monetary) outcome and (monetary) compensation paid to the agent. The resulting utility to the agent depends on his action and compensation; for example, if the agent's action is scaled according to "effort," his utility might be a decreasing function of effort and an increasing function of (monetary) compensation. The fact that compensation depends only on the outcome reflects the assumption that the principal can observe neither the agent's action nor the environmental event. In this formulation, the principal's *strategy* is the same as his *action,* but the agent's *strategy* is a *function (decision rule)* that determines the agent's action in response to the compensation function announced by the principal. (It is assumed here that the principal is committed to implementing the compensation function previously announced.) An *equilibrium* (Nash) is a pair of strategies for the respective players such that neither player can increase his expected utility by *unilaterally* changing his own strategy.

More complex models can be formulated to represent situations in which one or more of the following possibilities exist: (1) the principal may obtain some (incomplete or imperfect) information about the environment before choosing the compensation function; (2) the agent may do likewise before choosing his action; and (3) the principal may obtain some information about the agent's action and/or the environment before paying the compensation to the agent. In case (1), the principal's strategy will determine how his choice of compensation function depends on the information he received. In case (2), the agent's strategy will determine how his action depends on his own information as well as on the announced compensation function. In case (3), the compensation may be made to depend on the additional information available to the principal, as well as on the outcome (i.e., the compensation function may have more arguments). The results of this essay can be extended to such more complex models, but this will not be done explicitly here. (In fact, in many cases a suitable reinterpretation of the constituents of the "simple" model enables one to accommodate the "complexities" described above within its framework! For example, if the agent obtains information about the environment before choosing his action, we may reinterpret his "action" to be a *decision function* that determines his actual action as a function of his information.)

It is not necessary for this essay to give a detailed analysis of the basic model of the short-term (one-period) principal–agent game (for this, see Grossman and Hart 1983). The main point to make here is that in a large class of cases an equilibrium of the one-period game is inefficient, in the following sense. I shall say that one strategy-pair is *more efficient than* another strategy-pair if the first yields each player at least as much expected utility as the second, and yields at least one of the players strictly more. A strategy-pair is *efficient* if there is no other that is more efficient; otherwise it is *inefficient*.

Suppose that the agent is averse to risk, and that the principal is neutral toward risk. In this case, the inefficiency of equilibria of the one-period game stems from the conflict between reducing the agent's risk and increasing his incentive to perform well. An efficient strategy-pair must give the agent a nonrandom compensation (the principal must bear all the risk), but that implies that the compensation must be independent of the outcome. However, such a compensation function would not give the agent any incentive to work for a higher rather than a lower return.

In this chapter, I examine some ways that the two players can exploit a *long-term* principal–agent relationship to escape, at least partially, from the inefficiency of short-term equilibria. The long-term relationship will be modeled as a situation in which the one-period situation is repeated over and over again. These repetitions give the principal an opportunity to observe the results of the agent's actions over a number of periods, and to use some statistical test to infer whether or not the agent was choosing the appropriate action. The repetitions also provide the principal with opportunities to "punish" the agent for apparent departures from the appropriate action. Finally, the fact that the agent's compensation in any one period can be made to depend on the outcomes in a number of previous periods (e.g., on the average over a number of periods) provides the principal with an indirect means of *insuring* the agent, at least partially, against random fluctuations in the outcomes that are not due to fluctuations in the agent's actions. Thus, the repetitions provide an opportunity to reduce the agent's risk without reducing his incentive to perform well.

The same beneficial results could be obtained, of course, if the agent had some means of self-insurance, for example, through access to a capital market or because his wealth was substantial. However, in many interesting cases (such as the owner–manager relationship), the random fluctuations in outcome are too large compared to the agent's wealth or borrowing power to make such self-insurance practical. With such cases in mind, I shall confine my attention to *nonnegative* compensation functions.

The decision rule that the principal uses to adjust the agent's compensation in any one period in the light of previous observations constitutes the principal's *(many-period) strategy*. Likewise, the agent will have a (many-period) strategy for adjusting his actions in the light of the past history of the process. In principle, the players' strategy spaces are very large and contain very complex strategies. In Sections 3–6 I study the operating characteristics of some very simple strategies for the principal, under the assumption that the agent's strategy is an optimal response to the principal's strategy. In this part of the chapter, I also assume that the principal can *commit himself in advance* to a (many-period) strategy. I shall show how, with such simple strategies, the principal can induce the agent to behave in a way that yields both players discounted expected utilities that are close to one-period efficiency, provided that the players' discount rates (for future utility) are small, and the manager's potential tenure is long. An important step in the analysis is the derivation of a lower bound on the expected tenure of the manager, as a function of the manager's discount rate, his maximum potential tenure, and minimal information about his one-period utility function.

Here is an informal description of one class of such simple strategies for the principal, which I call "bankruptcy strategies": In this description, as in the remainder of the chapter, I shall use the language of the owner–manager story. The owner pays the manager a fixed compensation (wage) w per period until the end of the first period T in which the total of the gross returns in periods 1 through T fall below $T(r + w)$ by an amount at least s (where w, r, and s are parameters of the owner's strategy). At the end of such a period T, the manager is replaced and the owner engages another one under the same regime. This can be interpreted as requiring the manager to produce a "paper" gross return of $(r + w)$ each period (a net return of r), and also allowing any surplus to be added to a (paper) "cash reserve" and requiring any deficit to be subtracted. The manager starts with a positive "cash reserve" equal to s and is replaced by a new manager the first time the cash reserve falls to zero.

Since the cash reserve is only an accounting fiction, the bankruptcy strategy is really only a scoring formula for evaluating the manager's long-term performance, together with a criterion (based on the manager's score) for ending his tenure. The efficacy of another scoring rule is explored in Section 6 ("review strategies").

If precommitment by the owner to a many-period strategy is not feasible, the players must rely on strategy pairs that are "self-enforcing." For this analysis, the many-period situation is modeled as a many-period game, or *supergame,* and self-enforcing strategy pairs are modeled as Nash equilibria of the supergame (Section 7).

We shall see that there are many equilibria of the supergame, even if there is only one equilibrium of the one-period game. We shall also see that the set of supergame equilibria typically depends on the rates at which the players discount future expected one-period utilities. Finally, I shall show that if the players' discount rates are small, then there are supergame equilibria that yield the players discounted expected utilities close to one-period efficiency. These equilibria are constructed using strategies in which the manager's performance is reviewed periodically.

I am primarily interested in those supergame equilibria that can be sustained by relatively "simple" strategy pairs, or at least by strategy pairs in which the principal's strategy is simple. For this reason I have not here attempted to characterize those supergame equilibria that are exactly most efficient in the set of equilibria for any particular pair of player's discount rates.

The case of zero discount rates, with and without precommitment, is examined in Section 8. Further remarks and bibliographic notes are included in Section 9.

2   Repeated moral hazard

Let (X_t) be a sequence of independent and identically distributed random variables, representing the environment of the firm. In period t the manager chooses an action, A_t, and the resulting gross return to the firm is

$$G_t = \mathbf{G}(A_t, X_t). \tag{2.1}$$

The owner then pays the manager W_t, which leaves a net return of

$$R_t = G_t - W_t. \tag{2.2}$$

The manager's utility in period t is

$$U_t = \mathbf{U}(A_t, W_t), \tag{2.3}$$

indicating that the manager's utility depends on both the compensation and the action chosen. If the manager works for the firm during periods 1 through T (where T may be a random variable), then his resulting (normalized) discounted expected utility is[2]

$$v = E(1-\delta) \sum_1^T \delta^{t-1} U, \tag{2.4}$$

where δ is the manager's discount factor for future utility. This formula makes the implicit convention that the manager's expected utility after leaving the firm is zero, that is, zero is the origin from which the utility of working for the firm is measured.

The firm may have one or more managers in succession. In any case, the owner is interested in the (normalized) discounted expected present value of returns; the owner's discount factor need not be the same as the manager's. Thus the owner is assumed to be neutral toward risk.

The owner can observe the gross returns, G_t, but not the manager's actions, A_t, nor the environmental variables, X_t. The manager's compensation, W_t, is determined by a *compensation function, ω_t*, of the history of gross returns up through period t:

$$W_t = \omega_t(G_1, ..., G_t). \tag{2.5}$$

The *owner's strategy* is a sequence (ω_t) of such compensation functions.

The manager can observe the compensation functions, the gross returns, and of course his own actions, but not the environmental variables. The manager's action in period t, A_t, is determined by a *decision function, α_t*, as follows:

$$A_t = \alpha_t(\omega_1, ..., \omega_t, G_1, ..., G_{t-1}, A_1, ..., A_{t-1}). \tag{2.6}$$

The *manager's strategy* is a sequence (α_t) of such decision functions.

In a more general model, the manager and the owner might have more information than indicated here. However, moral hazard would be present as long as the owner's information about the environment and about the manager's actions was sufficiently incomplete so that the owner could not with certainty distinguish between bad luck and incorrect actions by the manager.

3   Control by "bankruptcy"

I first consider a strategy of the owner in which he pays the manager a fixed compensation per period, say w, as long as the manager's performance is "satisfactory" in a way that I shall define; thereafter, the manager is fired. Satisfactory performance is defined as maintaining a positive cumulative "score," where the score is determined recursively as follows:

$$S_0 = s,$$
$$S_t = S_{t-1} + G_t - r - w, \qquad t > 0. \tag{3.1}$$

The numbers s, r, and w are parameters of the owner's strategy, and are assumed to be positive.

This scoring rule can be interpreted in terms of a "cash reserve" and "bankruptcy," as noted in Section 1. Suppose that the manager is given an initial cash reserve equal to s. In each period the manager must pay the owner a fixed "return" equal to r, and the manager is paid a fixed "wage" equal to w. Any excess of the actual return over $(r+w)$ is added to the cash reserve, and any deficit is subtracted from it. The manager is declared "bankrupt" in the first period (if any) in which the cash reserve becomes zero or negative, and the manager is immediately fired. The cash reserve may be real or it may be an accounting fiction; I adopt the latter interpretation here.

I shall denote by T the first t such that S_t is zero or negative; note that T is a random variable. Let n be the maximum number of periods that the manager can work (n may be finite or infinite), and let $T(n)$ denote the minimum of T and n. If n is infinite, T may take the value infinity.

Suppose that the owner can commit in advance to a particular bankruptcy strategy, that is, to particular parameters s, r, and w. Suppose, too, that the manager chooses a strategy that is optimal for him given the owner's bankruptcy strategy. I shall examine the efficiency of such a pair of strategies, that is, how well the owner and manager do under these circumstances. More precisely, I shall give approximate lower bounds on the manager's expected discounted utility and the owner's expected discounted net return, when their discount factors are close to unity. I shall also examine how the performance depends on the parameters s, r, and w. I assume that each of the following is a finite set of integers:

1. The range of the function G.
2. The set of alternative actions in each period.
3. The parameters s, r, and w.

These assumptions imply, in particular, that the cash reserve, S_t, is a "controlled random walk" on the integers, with increments that are bounded uniformly in the manager's actions.

Until further notice, suppose that the manager's one-period compensation w is fixed. To simplify the notation, I shall suppress the reference to w as follows: Define

$$U_t = \mathbf{U}(A_t) = \mathbf{U}(A_t, w); \tag{3.2}$$

then the manager's expected discounted utility is

$$v = E(1-\delta) \sum_1^{T(n)} \delta^{t-1} U_t. \tag{3.3}$$

[If n is finite, then the normalization in (3.3) is not appropriate; the sum should be multiplied by $(1-\delta)/(1-\delta^n)$ instead of by $1-\delta$. This will be rectified at the end of Section 5, which is the first place that we compare the values of the manager's expected utility corresponding to different values of δ and n.]

Let $\hat{g}$ be some feasible expected gross return; think of $\hat{g}$ as the owner's "ideal" gross return. (Below, $\hat{g}$ will be the owner's gross return in an efficient one-period arrangement.)

Define $\hat{a}$ and $\hat{u}$ by

$$EG(\hat{a}, X) = \hat{g}, \tag{3.4}$$

$$\hat{u} = \mathbf{U}(\hat{a}). \tag{3.5}$$

The conflict of interest between the owner and the manager is captured in the assumption that there is another action by the manager that gives a higher immediate utility but yields a lower expected gross return. Define a^0, g^0, and u^0 by

$$\mathbf{U}(a^0) = \max_a \mathbf{U}(a) = u^0, \tag{3.6}$$

$$g^0 = EG(a^0, X). \tag{3.7}$$

Assume

$$g^0 < \hat{g}, \qquad u^0 > \hat{u} > 0. \tag{3.8}$$

The assumption that $\hat{u}$ is strictly positive states that the manager would prefer doing $\hat{a}$ to being fired.

4   The owner's return

Suppose that each successive manager uses the same strategy. This assumption is justified if successive managers are identical in their characteristics. (The results of this essay can, with some effort, be extended to cases in which successive managers have different characteristics.) The tenure of the mth manager will be called the mth *cycle*. Successive cycles constitute independent "experiments" under identical conditions. In any particular realization of the process, either (1) every cycle will have finite duration, and there will be an infinite number of cycles, or (2) some cycle will have infinite duration, and there will be only finitely many cycles.[3]

Let T_m denote the duration of the mth cycle, and let $M(t)$ denote the number of *completed* cycles through period t, that is,

$$M(t) = \max\{m \geq 0 : T_1 + \cdots + T_m \leq t\}.$$

The random variables T_m are independent and identically distributed, but they are "improper" in the sense that they may take on the value (positive) infinity. It is important to distinguish two cases:

Case 1: $\text{Prob}(T_m < \infty) = 1$. In this case there will be infinitely many cycles, with probability one.

Case 2: $\text{Prob}(T_m < \infty) < 1$. In this case there will be finitely many cycles, with probability one; this is because the probability that a cycle is infinite is positive and constant, and the cycles are independent. Of course, the total number of cycles will (typically) be a random variable.

In Case 1, each T_m is a proper random variable, although its expectation, ET_m, may be infinite. Let S'_m denote the cash reserve at the end of the mth cycle, that is,

$$S'_m = S_t \quad \text{if } t = T_1 + \cdots + T_m.$$

Note that the random variables S'_m are bounded because the function **G** is bounded. (The cash reserve is strictly positive in the next-to-last period of a cycle; hence it is bounded below in the last period of a cycle if the one-period returns are bounded below.)

    The owner's (net) return in period t is $R_t = G_t - w$. I shall suppose that the owner is interested in the expected present value of returns,

$$y(\gamma) = (1 - \gamma) E \sum_{t=1}^{\infty} \gamma^{t-1} R_t, \tag{4.1}$$

where γ, the owner's discount factor, is nonnegative and strictly less than unity ($0 \le \gamma < 1$). I shall be interested in obtaining a lower bound on $y(\gamma)$ when γ is close to unity.

Theorem 4.1. In Case 1,

$$\liminf_{\gamma \to 1} y(\gamma) \ge r - \frac{s - ES'_m}{ET_m},$$

where the right-hand side equals r if $ET_m = \infty$. In Case 2,

$$\liminf_{\gamma \to 1} y(\gamma) \ge r.$$

(Note that ET_m and ES'_m do not depend on m.)

    The proof of this theorem is given in the Appendix. However, a simple argument for Case 1 is sketched here in the special subcase in which ET_m is finite. Using a simple "recursion" formula familiar from Markov chain theory (or dynamic programming),

$$y(\gamma) = (1 - \gamma) E \sum_{t=1}^{T_1} \gamma^{t-1} R_t + (E\gamma^{T_1}) y(\gamma).$$

Solving this for $y(\gamma)$ gives

$$y(\gamma) = \frac{(1-\gamma)E\sum_1^{T_1}\gamma^{t-1}R_t}{1-E\gamma^{T_1}}. \tag{4.2}$$

Note that

$$\frac{1-E\gamma^{T_1}}{1-\gamma} = E\sum_1^{T_1}\gamma^{t-1},$$

so that (4.2) can be rewritten

$$y(\gamma) = \frac{E\sum_1^{T_1}\gamma^{t-1}R_t}{E\sum_1^{T_1}\gamma^{t-1}}. \tag{4.3}$$

Since R_t is bounded and $ET_1 < \infty$, it follows from Lebesgue's Theorem that

$$\lim_{\gamma\to 1} y(\gamma) = \frac{E\sum_1^{T_1}R_t}{ET_1}. \tag{4.4}$$

From (3.1) we have

$$S_1' = s + \sum_1^{T_1}R_t - T_1 r,$$

so that

$$E\sum_1^{T_1}R_t = (ET_1)r - s + ES_1'.$$

Substituting this in (4.4) gives

$$\lim_{\gamma\to 1} y(\gamma) = r - \frac{s-ES_1'}{ET_1}, \tag{4.5}$$

which is more precise than the conclusion of the theorem (but recall that $ET_1 < \infty$).

5   The efficiency of bankruptcy strategies

Theorem 4.1 tells us that if the owner's discount factor, γ, is close to unity, then an approximate lower bound on the owner's expected (normalized) present value of returns, $y(\gamma)$, depends on the expected number of periods that any one manager remains in office. More precisely,

$$\liminf_{\gamma\to 1} y(\gamma) \geq r - \frac{s-ES_m'}{ET_m}, \tag{5.1}$$

where we make the convention that the right-hand side of (5.1) is r if

$ET_m = \infty$ and/or $\text{Prob}(T_m = \infty) > 0$. Notice that S'_m is bounded, so that the right-hand side of (5.1) is close to r if ET_m is large.

In this section I derive a lower bound on ET_m when each manager follows an optimal strategy. This lower bound increases without limit as the manager's discount factor approaches unity and his potential tenure gets longer. This bound enables me to construct bankruptcy strategies that are close to one-period efficiency when the manager's discount factor is close to 1 and his potential tenure is long.

Let $T(n, \delta)$ denote the tenure of the (representative) manager if his maximum potential tenure is n, his discount factor is δ, and he follows an optimal policy, that is, a policy that maximizes (3.3) when the owner follows a bankruptcy strategy described in Section 3. A manager's optimal strategy will, of course, depend on the parameters s, r, and w of the bankruptcy policy.

Recall definitions and assumptions (3.4)–(3.8):

$$\hat{g} = E\mathbf{G}(\hat{a}, X) \tag{5.2}$$

$$\hat{u} = \mathbf{U}(\hat{a}), \tag{5.3}$$

$$u^0 = \max_a \mathbf{U}(a) = \mathbf{U}(a^0), \tag{5.4}$$

$$g^0 = E\mathbf{G}(a^0, X), \tag{5.5}$$

$$g^0 < \hat{g}, \qquad u^0 > \hat{u} > 0. \tag{5.6}$$

If $\hat{g} < r + w$, then the expected period-to-period change in the cash reserve might be negative whatever the manager does, and he would then go bankrupt eventually. Therefore, until further notice I shall assume that

$$\hat{g} > r + w. \tag{5.7}$$

The boundary case, $\hat{g} = r + w$, must be considered separately.

Theorem 5.1

$$ET(n, \delta) \geq \left(\frac{\hat{u}}{u_0}\right) E \sum_{1}^{\hat{T}(n)} \delta^{t-1} = \left(\frac{\hat{u}}{u_0}\right)\left(\frac{1 - E\delta^{\hat{T}(n)}}{1 - \delta}\right) \equiv h(n, \delta),$$

where $\hat{T}(n)$ is what the actual tenure of the manager would be if he had maximum potential tenure n and always used the action $\hat{a}$.

If the manager always used the action $\hat{a}$ (call this the *good-faith strategy*), then the cash reserve would be a random walk whose successive increments had expected value $\hat{g} - r - w$, which by (5.7) is strictly positive.

Hence, if the manager's potential tenure were infinite ($n = \infty$), there would be a positive probability, say $\hat{\pi}$, that he never goes bankrupt; that is

$$\hat{\pi} \equiv \text{Prob}(\hat{T} = \infty) > 0, \tag{5.8}$$

where $\hat{T} \equiv \hat{T}(\infty)$. Notice that

$$E\hat{T}(n) \geq n\hat{\pi}, \tag{5.9}$$

$$\lim_{\delta \to 1} E\delta^{\hat{T}} = 1 - \hat{\pi}. \tag{5.10}$$

Hence from Theorem 5.1 one can conclude:

Corollary

$$\lim_{\delta \to 1} h(n, \delta) = \left(\frac{\hat{u}}{u^0}\right) E\hat{T}(n) \geq \left(\frac{\hat{u}}{u^0}\right) n\hat{\pi}, \tag{5.11}$$

$$\lim_{n \to \infty} h(n, \delta) = \left(\frac{\hat{u}}{u_0}\right) E \sum_1^{\hat{T}} \delta^{t-1}, \tag{5.12}$$

$$\lim_{n \to \infty} \lim_{\delta \to 1} h(n, \delta) = \lim_{\delta \to 1} \lim_{n \to \infty} h(n, \delta) = \infty. \tag{5.13}$$

Proof of Theorem 5.1: Let v denote the manager's maximum expected discounted utility, as in (2.4). If the manager followed the good-faith strategy, his expected discounted utility would be

$$(1 - \delta) E \sum_1^{\hat{T}(n)} \delta^{t-1} \hat{u} = \hat{u}(1 - E\delta^{\hat{T}(n)}), \tag{5.14}$$

so that (5.14) is a lower bound on v. On the other hand, the manager cannot get more utility than u^0 in any single period, so that

$$v \leq (1 - \delta) E \sum_1^{T(n, \delta)} \delta^{t-1} u^0$$

$$\leq (1 - \delta) E \sum_1^{T(n, \delta)} u^0 = (1 - \delta) u^0 ET(n, \delta). \tag{5.15}$$

Putting (5.14) and (5.15) together, we get

$$\hat{u}(1 - E\delta^{\hat{T}(n)}) \leq u^0 ET(n, \delta),$$

from which we get the conclusion of the theorem. Note that in the second line of (5.15) I use the fact that $0 < \delta < 1$. ∎

I now show how the owner can get both players close to one-period efficiency in the many-period situation if the players' discount factors are close to 1 and the manager has a long potential tenure. Assume that the manager is averse to risk, that is, $U(a, w)$ is concave in w for each a. Recall that, in this case, efficiency in the one-period situation requires that the compensation to the manager be independent of the outcome. Thus let $(\hat{w}, \hat{a})$ be an efficient one-period compensation–action pair, and let

$$\hat{u} = U(\hat{a}, \hat{w}), \qquad \hat{g} = EG(\hat{a}, X), \qquad \hat{r} = \hat{g} - \hat{w}. \qquad (5.16)$$

Recall that, if the manager uses the good-faith strategy, then the cash reserve is a random walk. I make the further assumption that this random walk is aperiodic. By a well-known theorem about random walks, one can make $\hat{\pi}$ in (5.8) as close to 1 as one likes by taking the initial cash reserve, s, sufficiently large (see, e.g., Spitzer 1976, pp. 217–18). Suppose that the owner uses a bankruptcy strategy with $w = \hat{w}$, $r < \hat{r}$ but close to $\hat{r}$, and s large enough so that $\hat{\pi}$ is close to 1. By the corollary to Theorem 5.1, if n is large and δ is close to 1, then $ET(n, \delta)$ will be large. Hence, by Theorem 4.1, if γ is close to 1 then the owner's expected discounted return $y(\gamma)$ will be at least close to r, and hence close to $\hat{r}$.

Since we are going to compare the manager's expected normalized discounted utility for different values of n and δ, we must be careful about the normalization factor. The correct factor is $(1-\delta)/(1-\delta^n)$, so that the manager's expected utility is

$$v(n, \delta) = \left(\frac{1-\delta}{1-\delta^n}\right) E \sum_1^{T(n, \delta)} U_t. \qquad (5.17)$$

Corresponding to (5.14) we have the inequality

$$v(n, \delta) \geq \left(\frac{1-\delta}{1-\delta^n}\right) E \sum_1^{\hat{T}(n)} \delta^{t-1} \hat{u} = \frac{\hat{u}(1 - E\delta^{\hat{T}(n)})}{1-\delta^n}. \qquad (5.18)$$

One can show that (5.18) is jointly continuous in n and δ, and that its limit is $\hat{u}\hat{\pi}$. Hence if n is large and δ is close to 1 the manager's expected utility will be at least close to $\hat{u}\hat{\pi}$, and hence at least close to $\hat{u}$.

Note: One can make the preceding paragraph precise as follows: (1) specify $\epsilon > 0$; (2) choose r so that $\hat{r} - \epsilon \leq r < \hat{r}$; (3) choose s so that $\hat{\pi} \geq 1 - \epsilon$; (4) choose τ so that

$$\frac{s - ES'_m}{\tau} \leq \epsilon;$$

(5) choose δ close to 1 and n large enough so that

$$ET(n, \delta) \geq \tau, \qquad v(n, \delta) \geq (\hat{\pi} - \epsilon)\hat{u};$$

(6) choose γ close to 1 so that

$$y(\gamma) \ge r - \frac{s - ES'_n}{ET(n, \delta)} - \epsilon.$$

It then follows that

$$y(\gamma) \ge r - 2\epsilon \ge \hat{r} - 3\epsilon, \qquad v(n, \delta) \ge \hat{u}(1 - 2\epsilon).$$

6   Review strategies

In this section I shall discuss a family of *review strategies,* in which the manager's performance is reviewed periodically, and he is replaced if his cumulative performance since the last review is unsatisfactory in a sense to be defined.

A review strategy for the owner has three parameters ℓ, r, and s, where:

1. ℓ is the number of periods covered by each review, and
2.   the manager is replaced immediately after any review for which the total return during the ℓ periods preceding the review does not exceed $\ell r - s$.

Thus the first review occurs at the end of period ℓ, and the manager is replaced if

$$S_\ell = R_1 + \cdots + R_\ell \le \ell r - s; \tag{6.1}$$

otherwise the manager continues in office until the end of period 2ℓ, at which time he is replaced if

$$S_{2\ell} - S_\ell = R_{\ell+1} + \cdots + R_{2\ell} \le \ell r - s, \tag{6.2}$$

and so on. The manager's total tenure, say T, will be some random multiple of ℓ, that is,

$$T = N\ell. \tag{6.3}$$

I shall call the periods from $[(n-1)\ell + 1]$ to $n\ell$ the nth *review phase;* thus ℓ is the length of each review phase and N is the number of review phases in the manager's tenure.

I assume that the manager's normalized expected discounted utility is v as in (2.4), and that during his tenure the manager receives from the owner a fixed payment per period, as in Section 3. Consider a period t that is in the nth review phase, and take the "state of the system" at the end of period t to be the pair

$$(t - n\ell, S_t - S_{(n-1)\ell});$$

then with this state space the manager faces a standard finite-state dynamic programming problem. We may therefore, without loss of generality, suppose that the manager uses a strategy that is "stationary" in the sense that:

1. in each period, action depends only on the state of the system at the end of the previous period;
2. in periods $1, \ell+1, 2\ell+1$, and so on, action is the same and independent of the history of the process.

In other words, the beginning of each review phase is a point of renewal of the process.

I shall study the properties of the manager's optimal response to a review strategy, the resulting return to the owner, and the efficiency of review strategies in the context of the model of Sections 2 and 3 (but with a review strategy instead of a bankruptcy strategy). For the sake of brevity, I shall consider only the special case in which:

1. the manager's potential tenure is infinite;
2. the owner's objective function is his expected long-run average expected return. (As we have seen in Section 4, the owner's expected normalized discounted return will be close to the long-run average if the discount factor is close to 1.)

Let $T(\delta)$ denote the (representative) manager's actual tenure if the discount factor is δ and he or she uses an optimal policy. In every review phase but the last, the total return is at least $\ell r - s$, and in the last review phase the total return is at least $-\ell b$, where $-b$ is a lower bound on the return in any one period. Recall from (6.3) that the number of review phases is $T(\delta)/\ell$, and hence the total return during the manager's tenure is at least

$$\left(\frac{T(\delta)}{\ell} - 1\right)(\ell r - s) - \ell b = \frac{T(\delta)}{\ell}(\ell r - s) - (\ell r - s) - \ell b.$$

Therefore, by the renewal theorem, a lower bound on the owner's long-run average return is given by

$$y \equiv \lim_{m \to \infty} \frac{1}{m} \sum_{1}^{m} R_t \geq r - \frac{s}{\ell} - \frac{\ell r - s - \ell b}{ET(\delta)}. \tag{6.4}$$

An examination of the right-hand side of (6.4) shows that y will be close to r if the following are all small:

$$\frac{s}{\ell}, \frac{\ell}{ET(\delta)}, \frac{s}{ET(\delta)}. \tag{6.5}$$

I shall now show how to choose s and ℓ to accomplish this for δ sufficiently close to 1.

First, let $\hat{T}$ denote what the manager's tenure would be if he or she used the good-faith strategy (always used $\hat{a}$). The argument leading up to Theorem 5.1 is still valid in this situation, so we have

$$ET(\delta) > \left(\frac{\hat{u}}{u_0}\right)E\sum_1^{\hat{T}}\delta' = \left(\frac{\hat{u}}{u_0}\right)\left(\frac{1-E\delta^{\hat{T}}}{1-\delta}\right) \equiv h(\delta). \tag{6.6}$$

(However, the corollary to Theorem 5.1 is not applicable here.) Therefore, we need to study how $h(\delta)$ depends on δ and on the parameters ℓ and s of the review strategy. The parameter r will be fixed as

$$r = \hat{r} \equiv \hat{g} - \hat{w} = E\mathbf{G}(\hat{a}, X) - \hat{w} \tag{6.7}$$

[cf. equation (5.16)].

Let $\hat{\phi}$ denote the probability that the manager "fails" the first review if he uses the good-faith strategy. Note that $\hat{\phi}$ is strictly positive if s is not too large relative to ℓ and the variance of the one-period return is not zero, which I shall suppose to be the case. It follows that the number of review phases in the manager's tenure has a geometric distribution with mean $1/\hat{\phi}$, and so

$$E\hat{T} = \ell/\hat{\phi}. \tag{6.8}$$

From (6.6) and (6.8),

$$\lim_{\delta \to 1} h(\delta) = \left(\frac{\hat{u}}{u_0}\right)E\hat{T} = \left(\frac{\hat{u}}{u_0}\right)\left(\frac{\ell}{\hat{\phi}}\right). \tag{6.9}$$

By Chebyshev's Inequality,

$$\hat{\phi} \le \ell\hat{k}/s^2, \tag{6.10}$$

where

$$\hat{k} \equiv \operatorname{Var} \hat{R}_t, \qquad \hat{R}_t \equiv \mathbf{G}(\hat{a}, X_t) - w. \tag{6.11}$$

Hence

$$\lim_{\delta \to 1} h(\delta) \ge \left(\frac{\hat{u}}{u_0}\right)\left(\frac{s^2}{\hat{k}}\right). \tag{6.12}$$

Let β and ρ be given numbers such that

$$\beta > 0, \qquad \tfrac{1}{2} < \rho < 1, \tag{6.13}$$

and relate s to ℓ by

$$s = \beta\ell^\rho. \tag{6.14}$$

Putting together equations (6.4)–(6.14), we have the following theorem.

Theorem 6.1. For every $\epsilon > 0$ there exist ℓ_ϵ, s_ϵ, and δ_ϵ such that, for every δ satisfying $\delta_\epsilon < \delta < 1$,

$$y \geq \hat{r} - \epsilon, \tag{6.15}$$

where y is the manager's long-run average return when the manager, with discount factor δ, uses a strategy that is optimal against the owner's review strategy with "target return" $\hat{r}$, length of review phase ℓ_ϵ, and "margin for error" s_ϵ.

The rest of this section is devoted to the construction of review strategies that are approximately one-period efficient for small δ. [The construction is somewhat detailed, and the reader can skip to Section 7 without loss of continuity.]

For any given $\epsilon > 0$ we want δ_ϵ and ℓ_ϵ, with s given by (6.14) so that (6.15) holds and also

$$v(\delta_e) \geq \hat{u} - \epsilon, \tag{6.16}$$

where $v(\delta_\epsilon)$ is the manager's expected discounted utility when he optimizes against the review strategy determined by ℓ_ϵ.

If the manager uses the good-faith strategy, then his expected utility is

$$(1-\delta)E\sum_1^{\hat{T}} \delta^{t-1}\hat{u} = \hat{u}(1 - E\delta^{\hat{T}}).$$

Hence

$$v(\delta) \geq \hat{u}(1 - E\delta^{\hat{T}}). \tag{6.17}$$

Let M be the number of review phases (cycles) during the manager's tenure. As noted above, M has a geometric distribution with mean $1/\hat{\phi}$. Then

$$E\delta^{\hat{T}} = E\delta^{M\ell} = \sum_{m=1}^{\infty} (1-\hat{\phi})^{m-1}\hat{\phi}\delta^{m\ell}$$

$$= \hat{\phi}\delta^\ell \sum_{m=0}^{\infty} [(1-\hat{\phi})\delta^\ell]^m = \frac{\hat{\phi}\delta^\ell}{1-(1-\hat{\phi})\delta^\ell}. \tag{6.18}$$

From (6.17) we see that $v(\delta)$ will be close to $\hat{u}$ if $E\delta^{\hat{T}}$ is small, and from (6.18) this will be so if

$$\hat{\phi}\delta^\ell/(1-\delta^\ell) \tag{6.19}$$

is small. From (6.10) and (6.14),

$$\hat{\phi} \le C\ell^{-\alpha}, \qquad C \equiv \hat{k}/\beta^2, \qquad \alpha \equiv 2\rho - 1;$$

hence (6.19) will be small if

$$\ell^{-\alpha}\delta^{\ell}/(1-\delta^{\ell}) \tag{6.20}$$

is small.

On the other hand, by (6.4)–(6.6), (6.9), and (6.14), $y(\gamma)$ will be close to $\hat{r}$ if $\ell/h(\delta)$ is small, that is, if

$$\ell(1-\delta)/(1-E\delta^{\hat{T}}) \tag{6.21}$$

is small. Since we are also trying to make $E\delta^{\hat{T}}$ small, we see that we want to let δ approach 1 and ℓ increase without bound in such a way that, simultaneously,

$$\lim \ell(1-\delta) = 0, \tag{6.22}$$

$$\lim \frac{\ell^{-\alpha}\delta^{\ell}}{1-\delta^{\ell}} = 0. \tag{6.23}$$

I shall now show that this can be accomplished by taking

$$\delta = e^{-x}, \qquad \ell = x^{-\xi},$$

and letting x approach 0, where ξ is any number satisfying

$$\frac{1}{1+\alpha} < \xi < 1. \tag{6.24}$$

First note that

$$\lim_{x \to 0} \delta^{\ell} = \lim_{x \to 0} \exp(-x^{1-\xi}) = 1. \tag{6.25}$$

Second,

$$\ell(1-\delta) = \frac{1-e^{-x}}{x^{\xi}},$$

and by l'Hôpital's Rule, the limit of this (as x approaches 0) is easily seen to be 0, since $\xi < 1$. Finally, by (6.25), to demonstrate (6.23) it suffices to show that

$$\lim_{x \to 0} \frac{\ell^{-\alpha}}{1-\delta^{\ell}} = 0.$$

Again, this is accomplished with l'Hôpital's Rule:

$$\lim_{x \to 0} \frac{\ell^{-\alpha}}{1-\delta^{\ell}} = \lim_{x \to 0} \frac{x^{\alpha\xi}}{1-\exp(-x^{1-\xi})}$$

$$= \left(\frac{\alpha\xi}{1-\xi}\right) \frac{x^{\alpha\xi-1+\xi}}{\exp(-x^{1-\xi})} = 0,$$

since (6.24) implies that $\alpha\xi - 1 + \xi > 0$.

7   Self-enforcing agreements

Up to this point in the analysis of repeated moral hazard I have assumed that the owner (principal) could precommit to a particular strategy, even though the manager (agent) could not. In fact, such precommitments are the exception rather than the rule in owner–manager relations, although precommitment, in the form of contracts, can be found in other principal–agent relationships (e.g., customer–supplier and client–broker).

For the strategies that have been considered in previous sections, there are many situations in which the owner might be tempted to change strategy in mid-course. For example, in the case of the bankruptcy strategy, if the manager has accumulated an unusually large cash reserve, he can be expected to "coast" for many periods while the cash reserve falls to a lower level (but one that is still "safe" from the manager's point of view). Similarly, if the manager is near the end of the maximum potential tenure, and has a relatively safe cash reserve, he will have an incentive to coast. In both of these situations the owner would be tempted to replace the manager immediately with a new one. Analogous situations arise under the review strategies. The manager would be expected to move away from the actions that produce the highest returns if the reserve were sufficiently high or sufficiently low. In both cases the probability of passing review would be very little affected by the manager's choice of actions during the remainder of the review period, and so the manager would have an incentive to choose actions that gave him higher one-period utility.

On the other side of the balance, there may be costs to the owner of replacing a manager, costs that have not been taken into account in the models of the previous sections. First, the owner may find it more difficult to find replacements for the manager's position if the owner has departed in mid-course from a previously announced strategy, or in other words has "reneged" on a promise or understanding. Second, there may be replacement costs that are incurred whether or not the replacement conforms to the announced strategy, due to a breaking-in period for the new manager, replacements of subordinates, interruptions of established routines, and so on. These costs would give the owner an incentive to avoid replacement as a deterrent even in the announced strategy and to find some other means of inducing good behavior by the manager.

These considerations lead me to consider, in this section, a model in which the manager is *never* replaced, but the consequence of poor performance is a temporary reversion to a "noncooperative" or "adversarial" phase in which the manager receives a less satisfactory compensation than under the normal "cooperative" phase. To the extent that the noncooperative phases are also less favorable for the owner, the owner will be deterred from ending the cooperative phases prematurely. As we shall see, we can transform the bankruptcy and review strategies described above into *self-enforcing* agreements by prescribing the noncooperative phases to be Nash equilibria of the one-period game that are inferior to the cooperative phases (in expected value) for both the owner and the manager.

In the model of the present section, the owner may not replace the manager, and the manager has no incentive to quit. A more general model would explicitly incorporate the costs to the owner and manager of such actions, and the analysis would show how the structure of self-enforcing agreements (including the use of noncooperative phases) would depend on those costs and on the other parameters of the problem. I am not aware that any such general formal analysis has been done to date.

In this essay, the intuitive notion of a self-enforcing agreement will be formally modeled as a Nash equilibrium of a repeated game, or *supergame,* as it is often called. The strategies available in the supergame to the two players, the owner and the manager, were described in Section 2. The supergame utility for the manager is assumed to be the expected normalized sum of discounted one-period utilities, v, as defined in equations (2.1)–(2.4), and the supergame utility for the owner is the expected normalized sum of discounted returns, y, as defined in equation (4.1). Recall that in this formulation the owner is assumed to be neutral toward risk, although this assumption is not necessary for the analysis (see Section 9). Recall also that the discount factors of the two players need not be identical.

Let (ω^*, α^*) be a Nash equilibrium of the one-period game, that is to say, (1) for any compensation function ω announced by the owner, $\alpha^*(\omega)$ is the manager's optimal action,[4] and (2) ω^* is the compensation function that is optimal for the owner, given that the manager uses the strategy α^*. Let

$$a^* = \alpha^*(\omega^*)$$
$$G^* = \mathbf{G}(a^*, X), \qquad W^* = \omega^*(G^*), \tag{7.1}$$
$$u^* = E\mathbf{U}(a^*, W^*), \qquad r^* = E(G^* - W^*).$$

(Note that G^* and W^* are random variables.) Let $(\hat{a}, \hat{w})$ be an efficient action–compensation pair, with

$$\hat{G} = \mathbf{G}(\hat{a}, X),$$

$$\hat{u} = \mathbf{U}(\hat{a}, \hat{w}), \qquad \hat{r} = E\hat{G} - \hat{w}. \tag{7.2}$$

The parameters $\hat{a}$ and $\hat{w}$ correspond to the parameters $\hat{a}$ and w of Section 3; see (3.4) and (3.5). The manager is assumed to be averse to risk, that is, the function $\mathbf{U}$ is concave, so that in the efficient action–compensation pair the compensation, $\hat{w}$, must be independent of the realized outcome. Finally, assume that the efficient action–compensation pair is strictly better for both the owner and the manager than the one-period Nash equilibrium, that is,

$$\hat{r} > r^*, \qquad \hat{u} > u^*. \tag{7.3}$$

I shall show how to construct Nash equilibria of the supergame that are superior, from the point of view of both players, to the one-period Nash equilibrium, provided the players' discount factors are not too small. These supergame equilibria will be built up from the family of review strategies described in Section 6. I shall also state, but not prove, a theorem to the effect that if the players' discount factors are close to 1 then there are supergame equilibria (in review strategies) that are almost one-period efficient. The case in which the discount factors are *equal* to 1 will be treated in Section 8.

Supergame equilibria can also be constructed using other types of strategies, but space limitations do not permit their discussion here.

Although in the present section I assume that the owner cannot commit himself in advance to using a particular supergame strategy, I shall assume that he is committed in any single period to implementing the compensation function announced at the beginning of the period. This assumption is made to make the supergame an actual repetition of the one-period game, but it is possible to analyze – in the same spirit – alternative formulations without any precommitment whatsoever.

I now describe the review strategies that will be used to construct the Nash equilibria of the supergame. The strategies are organized into a sequence of "cycles," each cycle beginning with a *review phase,* and (depending on the outcome of the review) possibly by a *noncooperative phase.* The review phase is defined as in Section 6, including the criterion for passing or failing review. During the review phase the owner pays the manager a constant compensation of $\hat{w}$ per period, independent of the actual returns. If the manager passes the review, then a new review phase and a new cycle are started. If the manager fails the review, then the owner uses the compensation function ω^* for m periods, and then a new cycle is started; the number m is a parameter of the owner's review strategy, along with the other parameters, ℓ and s. These m periods will be called a *noncooperative phase*.

What are the characteristics of the manager's optimal response to the owner's review strategy? First, by suitably defining the "state of the system," we see that the manager faces a stationary dynamic programming problem. The state description includes (1) whether the process is in a review phase or a noncooperative phase, (2) the number of periods remaining in the current phase, (3) the history of actual gross returns G_t and both players' actions during the current cycle up to the current period, and (4) the owner's action in the current period.

Second, during each period of a noncooperative phase it is optimal for the manager to use the action a^*. In fact, I shall suppose that the manager uses the *one-period strategy* α^* in each period of a noncooperative phase; the reason for this will become apparent shortly. The use of α^* in any period will be called *myopic optimization*.

Third, the manager must have a strategy for the review phases. Such a strategy is a (finite) sequence of functions, $\alpha_1, \ldots, \alpha_\ell$; the function α_t determines the manager's action in the tth period of the current review phase as a function of the current state of the system. If the owner does indeed stick to his announced review strategy, then the functions $\alpha_1, \ldots, \alpha_\ell$ must be optimal for the manager in that situation. However, they must also describe what the manager would do if the owner departed from his announced strategy during a review phase, that is, if the owner failed to pay the fixed compensation $\hat{w}$. I shall suppose that in this case the manager will optimize myopically during the remaining periods of the current review phase and for m' additional periods; the number m' is another parameter of the strategies. Thereafter, the manager would behave as at the beginning of a new cycle.

Notice that the preceding specification of the manager's strategy describes what he would do in each period in each possible state of the system. This includes what the manager would do *even if the owner at some period failed to follow his announced review strategy*. Such a specification is needed to deter the owner from such behavior.

The owner, of course, cannot observe the manager's actions directly, but only the gross returns G_t and his own actions. Therefore, the owner cannot directly observe whether or not the manager is following announced strategy. This basic asymmetry of information is the source of the moral hazard in the supergame as well as in the one-period game.

Finally, for completeness, one should specify what each player would do if he did not follow his own strategy at some previous period. (This specification, which may appear arcane to many readers, will be used to show that the equilibrium satisfies a criterion like perfectness; this point will be discussed in Section 9.) If the principal does not pay the constant compensation $\hat{w}$ during some period in a review phase, then he will use the compensation function ω^* during the remaining periods of what would have been the review phase plus an additional m' periods. Otherwise, if either player has not followed his own strategy at some period, as described above, then he will nevertheless continue to follow it in subsequent periods.

To summarize, the owner's strategy is determined by the parameters ℓ, s, m, and m', and the manager's strategy is determined by the parameters ℓ, s, m, and m', and by the functions $\alpha_1, ..., \alpha_\ell$. (In principle, the parameters ℓ, s, m, and m' for the owner need not be the same as those for the manager, but in equilibrium they will be.) Furthermore, the functions $\alpha_1, ..., \alpha_\ell$, are chosen by the manager to be personally optimal given the parameters ℓ, s, and m. A strategy pair of the above form that constitutes a (Nash) equilibrium of the supergame will be called a *review strategy equilibrium*. In what follows I shall address the following questions:

1. Are there any review strategy equilibria?
2. Given the players' respective discount factors γ and δ, are there review strategy equilibria that yield the owner and manager supergame utilities greater than r^* and u^*, respectively?
3. If γ and δ are both "close" to 1, are there review strategy equilibria that yield the owner and the manager supergame utilities that are "close" to $\hat{r}$ and $\hat{u}$, respectively?

A "yes" answer to one of these questions implies, of course, a "yes" answer to the preceding one(s). Before turning to the answers, I want to display a particular "degenerate" equilibrium, namely: In each period the owner uses the compensation function ω^* and the manager optimizes myopically. One might call this the *stubborn equilibrium!* It is simply an infinite repetition of one-period equilibria, and yields the owner and manager supergame utilities r^* and u^*, respectively. Notice that the stubborn equilibrium exists for all pairs of discount factors. In a sense, it is a degenerate case of a review strategy equilibrium with $\ell = 0$.

I now turn to the answer to the above questions. For a given pair of discount factors, (γ, δ), let $W(\gamma, \delta)$ denote the set of supergame utility pairs (y, v) corresponding to review strategy equilibria (the owner gets y

and the manager gets v). In what follows, the discount factors are always strictly less than 1.

Theorem 7.1. Let (γ_n) and (δ_n) be any sequences of discount factors converging to 1; there is a corresponding sequence (y_n, v_n) of supergame utility pairs such that

1. for each n, (y_n, v_n) is in $W(\gamma_n, \delta_n)$;
2. (y_n) converges to $\hat{r}$ and (v_n) converges to $\hat{u}$.

Theorem 7.1 can be strengthened in an important way. Observe that, whereas the parameters (ℓ, s, m, m') completely determine the owner's review strategy, the manager's strategy requires the specification of the optimal functions $\alpha_1, \dots, \alpha_\ell$, and these in turn depend on the manager's discount factor δ. The statement of Theorem 7.1 leaves open the possibility that, to get within a given distance of $(\hat{r}, \hat{u})$, the parameters would have to depend on the discount factors even when they were close enough to 1. A stronger theorem states that this is not so.

Theorem 7.2. For every $\epsilon > 0$ (sufficiently small) there exist γ_ϵ, δ_ϵ, ℓ_ϵ, s_ϵ, m_ϵ, and m'_ϵ such that, for every (γ, δ) with $\gamma_\epsilon < \gamma < 1$ and $\delta_\epsilon < \delta < 1$, there is a review strategy equilibrium corresponding to $(\ell_\epsilon, s_\epsilon, m_\epsilon, m'_\epsilon)$ that yields the owner and manager supergame utilities at least $\hat{r} - \epsilon$ and $\hat{u} - \epsilon$, respectively.

The proofs of Theorems 7.1 and 7.2 are given elsewhere (see Section 9). A key part of the argument is contained in Section 6, but that argument must be modified to take account of the different regime, in which noncooperative phases with the same manager take the place of the replacements of the successive managers. It turns out that, as the length of the review phase ℓ is lengthened to adjust to the manager's discount factor, the lengths of the noncooperative phases, m and m', may be taken to be proportional to ℓ. In addition, the margin for error s may be related to ℓ as in (6.14).

8   The case of no discounting

In this section I consider the case in which neither the owner nor the representative manager discount the future, and the manager's potential tenure is infinite ($n = \infty$). Formally, this is represented by taking the owner's and manager's utilities to be, respectively,

$$Y \equiv \liminf_{t \to \infty} \frac{1}{t} \sum_{n=1}^{t} R_n, \qquad V \equiv \liminf_{t \to \infty} \frac{1}{t} \sum_{n=1}^{t} U_n. \tag{8.1}$$

Again, one wants to distinguish between two situations according to whether the owner can – or cannot – precommit himself to a particular strategy. I shall consider here the case of precommitment only for the bankruptcy strategies and the case of self-enforcing equilibria only for the review strategies. References to results for other cases are given in Section 9.

8.1   Bankruptcy strategies with precommitment by the owner

Suppose that the owner can precommit to a bankruptcy strategy, as in Sections 3–5, but the manager's objective function is (8.1). Specifically, consider the model of (5.2)–(5.6).

Theorem 8.1. For any $r < \hat{g} - w$, if the managers follow a policy that is optimal for them, then the owner's long-run average return[5] will be at least r, that is,

$$Y \geq r, \quad \text{almost surely.} \tag{8.2}$$

To prove the theorem, consider first the manager's problem. In order to get a positive long-run average utility v [see (8.1)], the manager must use a strategy for which the probability of never going bankrupt is positive. Let T be the length of the manager's tenure for a particular policy, and suppose to the contrary that (for a given s), $\text{Prob}(T < \infty) = 1$. Then for almost every realization of the process the manager's realized long-run average utility is

$$V = \lim_{n \to \infty} \frac{1}{n} \sum_{1}^{n} U_t = \lim_{n \to \infty} \frac{1}{n} \sum_{1}^{T} U_t = 0. \tag{8.3}$$

On the other hand, the manager can obtain a strictly positive $v = EV$ as follows. Let a be any action such that

$$EG(a, X) \equiv g > r - w \quad \text{and} \quad U(a) > 0; \tag{8.4}$$

for example, take $a = \hat{a}$. If the manager always uses the action a, then the cash reserve is a random walk whose increments have expected value $g - r - w > 0$. Hence, there is a positive probability, say $\pi(a, s)$, that $T = \infty$, given that the initial cash reserve is s. For such a policy, the manager's long-run average utility is either 0, if $T < \infty$, or $U(a)$, if $T = \infty$. Hence, the manager's expected long-run average utility is

$$v = \pi(a, s)\mathbf{U}(a) > 0. \tag{8.5}$$

Now consider the owner's long-run average return Y given that $T = \infty$ with positive probability. As before, let $M(t)$ be the number of completed cycles at date t, and let S'_m be the cash reserve at the end of cycle m (see Section 4). Since the cash reserve is positive except at the end of a cycle, one easily verifies (Section A in the Appendix) that

$$\sum_{n=1}^{t} R_n \geq tr - M(t)s + \sum_{m=1}^{M(t)} S'_m,$$

or equivalently,

$$\frac{1}{t} \sum_{n=1}^{t} R_n \geq r - \frac{M(t)s}{t} + \frac{1}{t} \sum_{m=1}^{M(t)} S'_m. \tag{8.6}$$

Since T is infinite with positive probability for each successive manager, the number of managers is finite (almost surely), and so

$$\lim_{t \to \infty} M(t) = M < \infty, \quad \text{almost surely}, \tag{8.7}$$

where M is, of course, a random variable. Hence, the limit of the right-hand side of (8.6) is r, as t increases without bound, which completes the proof of the theorem.

The argument leading to (8.5) can be extended to estimate a lower bound on the best the manager can do. It is well known from the theory of random walks that if $g - r - w > 0$, then for every $\epsilon > 0$ there is an initial cash reserve, say $s(\epsilon)$, such that $\pi[a, s(\epsilon)] \geq 1 - \epsilon$. Suppose the manager uses the following policy: He uses the action $\hat{a}$ until such time, if ever, that the cash reserve reaches (or exceeds) $s(\epsilon)$; after that action a is used. With this policy, the probability that the cash reserve reaches or exceeds $s(\epsilon)$ before reaching zero is at least $\hat{\pi}(s) \equiv \pi(\hat{a}, s)$, so that the manager's expected long-run average utility is at least

$$\hat{\pi}(s)(1 - \epsilon)\mathbf{U}(a).$$

Since this is true for each $\epsilon > 0$, it shows that

$$\sup v \geq \hat{\pi}(s) \sup\{\mathbf{U}(a): E\mathbf{G}(a, X) > r + w\}. \tag{8.8}$$

It is interesting that there may be no optimal policy that achieves the supremum of v over all policies. For example, suppose that $g^0 > r + w$, where (as in Section 3) a^0 maximizes $\mathbf{U}(a)$ and $g^0 = E\mathbf{G}(a^0, X)$. Then for any policy,

$$v \leq \mathbf{U}(a^0) \operatorname{Prob}(T = \infty \mid S_0 = s). \tag{8.9}$$

Suppose also that

$$\text{Prob}(T = \infty \mid S_0 = s) \le \hat{\pi}(s), \tag{8.10}$$

which would be true if, for example, the cash reserve could move up or down by only one unit in any one period. In this case, (8.9) and (8.10) imply that for any policy,

$$v \le \mathbf{U}(a^0) \hat{\pi}(s) \equiv \tilde{v}. \tag{8.11}$$

On the other hand, (8.8) implies that $\sup v \ge \tilde{v}$, so that

$$\sup v = \tilde{v}. \tag{8.12}$$

However, $\tilde{v}$ cannot be attained by any policy if $\mathbf{U}(a^0) > \mathbf{U}(\hat{a})$ and $g^0 < \hat{g}$. In order to achieve

$$\text{Prob}(T = \infty \mid S_0 = s) = \hat{\pi}(s)$$

exactly, the manager would have to use $\hat{a}$ all the time, but this policy yields only

$$v = \hat{\pi}(s) \mathbf{U}(\hat{a}),$$

which is less than $\hat{v}$.

8.2   *Self-enforcing equilibria with review strategies*

I shall now show, in the context of the model of Section 7, how to construct self-enforcing equilibria with review strategies in the case of no discounting. For this case one can obtain supergame equilibria that are *fully* one-period efficient. However, to accomplish this one must use review strategies in which review phases are longer and longer.

Before giving a precise statement of the theorem, I shall indicate why, with no discounting, review strategies with constant length cannot lead to full efficiency.

Consider again the model of Section 7. If the manager is to be deterred from departing from the (efficient) action $\hat{a}$, then the parameters ℓ and s must be chosen so that even if the manager uses $\hat{a}$ all the time, the probability $\hat{\phi}$ of failing any one review will be strictly positive. If this probability were the same for all review phases, then the long-run frequency of failure would be $\hat{\phi}$, and the manager's long-run average utility would be

$$(1 - \hat{\phi})\hat{u} + \hat{\phi}u^*,$$

which is strictly less than $\hat{u}$.

In order to overcome this problem, I shall make successive review phases longer. Let λ and ν be strictly positive numbers, and let ℓ_n, the length of the nth review phase, be

$$\ell_n = \lambda n^\nu. \tag{8.13}$$

As in Sections 6.3 and 7, we shall relate the other parameters of the review strategy to the lengths of the review phases. Let β, ρ, μ, and μ' be strictly positive numbers, and set

$$s_n = \beta \ell_n^\rho, \qquad m_n = \mu \ell_n, \qquad m_n' = \mu' \ell_n, \tag{8.14}$$

where these parameters of the review strategies correspond in the nth cycle to the parameters s, m, and m' in Section 7. I further require that

$$\tfrac{1}{2} < \rho < 1, \qquad \nu > 1/(2\rho - 1). \tag{8.15}$$

Finally, I make the following important modification of the manager's strategy during the review phases, namely,

$$A_t = \hat{a} \quad \text{during review phases.} \tag{8.16}$$

(In other words, the manager uses good-faith strategy during the review phases.)

With these modifications, one can now define, in the obvious way, a pair of supergame strategies corresponding to those of Section 7, but with successive cycles governed by parameters that change according to equations (8.13)–(8.14).

In order to prove the desired result, it appears that some additional restrictions on the functions U and G are needed, beyond those assumed in Sections 2 and 3. One sufficient condition is the following: There exists a strictly positive number K such that, for all actions a,

$$[U(a, \hat{w}) - \hat{u}] + K[EG(a, X_t) - \hat{w} - \hat{r}] \le 0. \tag{8.17}$$

This condition, which I shall call the condition of Positive Linear Support (or PLS), will be satisfied if, for example, both $U(a, \hat{w})$ and $EG(a, X)$, when considered as functions of a, are concave.

I am now in a position to state the main result for the case of no discounting.

Theorem 8.2. For any set of data specifying the model of Section 7, there exist μ and μ' sufficiently large so that the pair of review strategies determined by conditions (8.13)–(8.16) constitute an equilibrium of the supergame without discounting.

A proof of Theorem 8.2 is given in the Appendix. However, I do want to point out here an interesting property of this equilibrium, namely, that (amost surely) the manager will fail review only finitely many times. Thus, after some random but finite time there will be no more noncooperative phases, the manager will have a utility $\hat{u}$ in each period, and the owner will have an expected return of $\hat{r}$ in each period.

9 Further remarks and bibliographic notes

In this section I shall gather (1) further remarks on the material discussed thus far, including extensions of the results and open questions, (2) references to the literature on which the results reported here are based, and (3) other references that will enable the interested reader to explore the related literature. I shall make no attempt here to survey the already large literature on moral hazard, principal–agent theory, and repeated games; a few key references will have to suffice.

9.1 *Previous research on moral hazard and the principal–agent model*

In the field of economics, the first formal treatment of the principal–agent relationship and the phenomenon of moral hazard was probably given by Arrow (1963, 1965), although a paper by Simon (1951) was an early forerunner of the principal–agent literature. Inefficiencies in principal–agent relationships are usually categorized as resulting from moral hazard, misrepresentation, or adverse selection, or any combination of these three. In his doctoral dissertation, Groves (1969, 1973) analyzed a model of decentralized decision making with one principal and several interacting agents, and showed how, in particular cases and with risk-neutral agents, both truthful communication and efficient decision making could be induced by appropriate compensation mechanisms. Other early work on moral hazard was done by Ross (1973) and Mirrlees (1974, 1976), and a less formal treatment was suggested by Alchian and Demsetz (1972) in their discussion of the theory of the firm. For more recent contributions and references to the literature on moral hazard, see the following: Mayers and Smith (1981), Grossman and Hart (1983), Stiglitz (1983), Myerson (1983), and Radner (1985).

The first analyses of repeated moral hazard were by Radner (1981) and Rubinstein (1979). Radner (1981) showed that for sufficiently long but finite principal–agent supergames, with no discounting, one can sustain approximate efficiency by means of approximate equilibria. Rubinstein showed in an example how to sustain exact efficiency in an infinite supergame with no discounting.

For the case of discounting, the material of Section 7 on self-enforcing equilibria is based on Radner (1985), and the material of Sections 3-5 on models with precommitment by the owner is based in part on unpublished research by P. B. Linhart and myself. Not a lot is known about the detailed characteristics of equilibria (with or without precommitment) that are efficient (Pareto optimal) among the class of all equilibria with discounting. Such equilibria are sometimes called *second best*. Rogerson (1982, 1985) has shown that, in finitely repeated games with precommitment, second-best equilibria involve contracts in which the agent's compensation in any one period depends on outcomes in previous periods as well as in the current period.

9.2   *Continuity of the equilibrium correspondence*

The proof of Theorem 8.2 on self-enforcing equilibria with no discounting is based on the first, unpublished, version of Radner (1985), but has not been previously published. Putting together Theorems 7.1 and 8.2 one has a continuitylike result for the equilibrium correspondence (in the case of self-enforcing equilibria) as the players' discount factors approach 1, but it falls short of a demonstration that the correspondence is continuous at that point.

Extending the definition given in Section 7, define the *equilibrium correspondence W* as follows: For each γ and δ between 0 and 1 let $W(\gamma, \delta)$ denote the set of pairs (r, v) of normalized discounted expected utilities of the players, corresponding to equilibria of the supergame with respective players' discount factors γ and δ. Let $\hat{W}$ denote the set of efficient one-period expected utility pairs. The conclusion of Theorem 7.1 is: For every pair $(\hat{r}, \hat{v})$ in $\hat{W}$ that is superior to (r^*, v^*) (i.e., $\hat{r} > u^*$ and $\hat{v} > v^*$), and every neighborhood A of $(\hat{r}, \hat{v})$, there is a neighborhood B of $(1, 1)$ such that for every (γ, δ) in B the intersection of $W(\gamma, \delta)$ and A is not empty. From Theorem 8.2 we know that $(\hat{u}, \hat{v})$ is in $W(1, 1)$. This falls short of showing that the equilibrium correspondence is lower-hemi-continuous at $(1, 1)$. To show the latter, one would have to show that for every point (r, v) in $W(1, 1)$, every neighborhood A of that point, and every neighborhood B of $(1, 1)$, there are points (r', v') in A and (γ, δ) in B such that (r', v') is in $W(\gamma, \delta)$. A complete characterization of $W(1, 1)$ is not known to me; in particular, I do not know whether all of $\hat{W}$ is in $W(1, 1)$.

Although the continuitylike property of the repeated principal–agent game demonstrated here may seem intuitively plausible, it is not a general feature of repeated games. For example, in a "partnership game" two or more players share an outcome that depends jointly on the partners' actions and on a stochastic environment. The partners cannot fully monitor each others' actions or the environment. Each partner's utility depends directly on his own action and share of the (stochastic) outcome. In the one-period version of this game, the equilibrium is typically inefficient; in addition to the moral hazard problem that is present in the principal–agent game, there is a free-rider problem. In the repeated version of this game, with no discounting, one can construct supergame equilibria that are efficient, thus overcoming the moral hazard and free-rider problems (Radner 1986). On the other hand, for the case of discounting, one can give an example of a repeated partnership game in which the set of equilibrium expected utility vectors [corresponding to $W(\gamma, \delta)$ above] is bounded away from the set of one-period efficient one-period expected utility vectors (corresponding to $\hat{W}$ above), *uniformly in the players' discount factors* γ and δ, provided that these are strictly less than unity (Radner, Myerson, and Maskin 1986).

Thus, the inefficiency due to moral hazard alone (the principal–agent game) can be approximately remedied in the repeated game if the players discount the future very little, but the combination of moral hazard and free-riding leads to inefficiency that may be only partly remedied in the repeated games even if the players discount the future very little.

9.3 Credible equilibria

It is known that one must typically impose some further restriction on (self-enforcing) Nash equilibria of sequential games in order to assure that they will be "credible," that is, that any threats that are implicit in the players' strategies are credible. Space limitations allow me only a few remarks here for the already initiated reader. For recent discussions, see Kohlberg and Mertens (1982) and Kreps and Wilson (1982).

One such restriction is subgame perfectness. The criterion of subgame perfectness in the supergame has not been formally invoked here because, strictly speaking, there are typically no proper subgames after the principal's first move. This is implied by the fact that the principal can never observe the agent's actions directly, and if the probability of success is never 0 nor 1, then all finite sequences of consequences have positive probability. Nevertheless, both the agent and the principal can immediately detect any departure from a preannounced strategy of the principal. An alternative concept of "credible equilibrium" that seems useful in this situation, called *sequential equilibrium,* has been proposed by Kreps and Wilson (1982). In fact, one can show that the review strategy equilibria constructed in Sections 7 and 8.2 satisfy their definition.

9.4   Sequential games of moral hazard

It is likely that in most applications the appropriate model will not be a game that is repeated, strictly speaking. Rather, it will typically be the case that there is some "state variable" that changes endogenously from one period to the next, depending on past actions as well as exogenous events. An example of this is provided by Linhart, Radner, and Sinden (1983), who study a mechanism of direct price regulation of a public utility monopoly. In this case the actions of the manager (agent) affect changes in productivity, and the regulator (principal) controls the changes in prices of the firm's outputs. Thus, the state variable in any period is the vector describing the current productivity of the firm and the current prices. For a strategy by the regulator analogous to the bankruptcy strategy of Section 3, one can prove results corresponding to those of Sections 4 and 5, namely, for any rate, say r, of price decrease that is feasible *on the average* (i.e., in expected value), there is a strategy for the regulator that induces managerial behavior such that the actual realized long-run average rate of price decrease will be close to r if the managers' potential tenures are long and their discount factors are close to unity.

Appendix

A   *Proof of Theorem 4.1*

Define $T'(t)$ by $T'(t) = 0$ if $M(t) = 0$ and

$$T'(t) = T_1 + \cdots + T_{M(t)}, \quad \text{if } M(t) > 0.$$

Then one easily verifies that

$$\sum_1^t R_k = \begin{cases} tr - [M(t)+1]s + \sum_1^{M(t)} S'_m + S_t, & T'(t) < t, \quad (A.1) \\ tr - M(t)s + \sum_1^{M(t)} S'_m, & T'(t) = t, \quad (A.2) \end{cases}$$

Since $S'_m \leq 0$, and $S_t > 0$ for $T'(t) < t$, it follows that

$$\frac{1}{t} \sum_1^t R_k \geq r - \frac{M(t)s}{t} + \left(\frac{1}{t}\right)^{M(t)} \sum_1 S'_m. \tag{A.3}$$

Case 1. $\text{Prob}(T_m < \infty) = 1$. In this case, $M(t)$ increases without limit as t does. Therefore,

$$\lim_{t \to \infty} \frac{M(t)+1}{M(t)} = 1.$$

Observe that

$$\frac{T_1 + \cdots + T_{M(t)}}{M(t)} \leq \frac{t}{M(t)} \leq \left(\frac{T_1 + \cdots + T_{M(t)}}{M(t)+1}\right)\left(\frac{M(t)+1}{M(t)}\right).$$

By the strong law of large numbers,

$$\lim_{t \to \infty} \frac{T_1 + \cdots + T_{M(t)}}{M(t)} = \lim_{t \to \infty} \frac{T_1 + \cdots + T_{M(t)+1}}{M(t)+1} = ET_m,$$

$$\lim_{t \to \infty} \frac{S'_1 + \cdots + S'_{M(t)}}{M(t)} = ES'_m,$$

almost surely. Hence, from (A.3)

$$\liminf_{t \to \infty} \frac{1}{t} \sum_1^t R_k \geq r - \frac{s - ES'_m}{ET_m}. \tag{A.4}$$

By a refinement of Abel's Theorem,

$$\liminf_{\gamma \to 1}(1 - \gamma) \sum_1^\infty \gamma^{t-1} R_t \geq \liminf_{t \to \infty} \frac{1}{t} \sum_1^t R_k. \tag{A.5}$$

(This can be derived by adapting the proof of Theorem 55 of Hardy 1949, p. 108.) Combining this with (A.4) yields

$$\liminf_{\gamma \to 1}(1 - \gamma) \sum_1^\infty \gamma^{t-1} R_t \geq r - \frac{s - ES'_m}{ET_m}, \tag{A.6}$$

almost surely. The application of Fatou's Lemma now yields the conclusion of the theorem in Case 1. (Note that the above argument is valid even if $ET_m = +\infty$.)

Case 2. $\text{Prob}(T_m < \infty) < 1$. In this case there is a finite-valued random variable, say M, such that, almost surely,

$$\lim_{t \to \infty} M(t) = M, \qquad \lim_{t \to \infty} T'(t) = T_1 + \cdots + T_M.$$

From (A.1) it follows that

$$\liminf_{t \to \infty} \frac{1}{t} \sum_{1}^{t} R_k \geq r, \tag{A.7}$$

almost surely. Again, Fatou's Lemma leads to the conclusion of the theorem.

B   *Proof of Theorem 8.2*

I first show that, with the strategy pair described in Section 8.2, the manager's long-run average utility is equal to $\hat{u}$, and the owner's long-run average return is equal to $\hat{r}$. Let $\hat{\phi}_n$ denote the probability that the manager fails the nth review. By Chebyshev's Inequality and conditions (8.13)–(8.16),

$$\hat{\phi}_n \leq \frac{\hat{k}\ell_n}{s_n^2} = \frac{\hat{k}}{\beta^2 \ell_n^{2\rho-1}} = \frac{\hat{k}}{\beta^2 \lambda^{2\rho-1} n^{\nu(2\rho-1)}}, \tag{B.1}$$

where, as in (6.26),

$$\hat{k} = \operatorname{Var} \hat{R}_t = \operatorname{Var}[\mathbf{G}(\hat{a}, X_t) - \hat{w}].$$

By (8.15), $\nu(2\rho-1) > 1$, so that $\sum_{1}^{\infty} \hat{\phi}_n < \infty$. Hence, by the Borel–Cantelli Lemma, the agent will fail review at most finitely many times (almost surely), that is, there is some random time N such that $\operatorname{Prob}(N < \infty) = 1$ and, for all $t > N$,

$$A_t = \hat{a}, \qquad U_t = \hat{u}, \qquad ER_t = \hat{r}. \tag{B.2}$$

This implies that

$$v \equiv \lim_{t' \to \infty} \frac{1}{t'} \sum_{1}^{t'} U_t = \hat{u}, \tag{B.3}$$

and with the strong law of large numbers implies that

$$y = \lim_{t' \to \infty} \frac{1}{t'} \sum_{1}^{t'} R_t = \hat{r}. \tag{B.4}$$

Next I show that the manager's strategy is an optimal response to the owner's strategy. Suppose the manager uses another strategy. Recall that the returns are bounded, so that for some number b,

$$|R_t - \hat{r}| \leq b. \tag{B.5}$$

Also, as in Section 3, define

$$u_0 = \max_a \mathbf{U}(a, \hat{w}),$$

and recall that

$$u_0 \geq \hat{u} > u^*. \tag{B.6}$$

Let $\mathbf{C}^n$ denote the periods in the nth review phase, and let $F_n = 0$ or 1 according as the nth review phase does or does not end in a failure. By the condition of Positive Linear Support, (8.17), and the fact that the beginning of every cycle is a renewal point of the process,

$$E \sum_{\substack{\text{cycle} \\ n}} U_t \leq E \sum_{\mathbf{C}^n} [\hat{u} - K(R_t - \hat{r})] + E F_n m_n u^*. \tag{B.7}$$

If the manager passes the nth review, then

$$\sum_{\mathbf{C}^n} (R_t - \hat{r}) \geq -s_n,$$

whereas if the manager fails one can only be sure that

$$\sum_{\mathbf{C}^n} (R_t - \hat{r}) \geq -\ell_n b.$$

Hence,

$$\sum_{\mathbf{C}^n} (R_t - \hat{r}) \geq -(1 - F_n)s_n - F_n \ell_n b, \tag{B.8}$$

and so, by (B.7),

$$E \sum_{\substack{\text{cycle} \\ n}} (U_t - \hat{u}) \leq E\{Ks_n + F_n[-Ks_n + K\ell_n b + m_n(\hat{u} - u^*)]\}. \tag{B.9}$$

Examining the right-hand side of (B.9), we see that $-Ks_n \leq 0$ and that

$$K\ell_n b - m_n(\hat{u} - u^*) \leq 0,$$

if

$$\mu = \frac{m_n}{\ell_n} \geq \frac{Kb}{\hat{u} - u^*}. \tag{B.10}$$

Hence, with the additional specification of (B.10),

$$E \sum_{\substack{\text{cycle} \\ n}} (U_t - \hat{u}) \leq Ks_n. \tag{B.11}$$

Fix T, and let N denote the number of cycles completed through period T, and let T' denote the last period in cycle N. By (B.11) and (B.6),

$$E\frac{1}{T}\sum_1^T (U_t - \hat{u}) \le E\frac{1}{T}\left[K\sum_1^N s_n + (T-T')(u_0 - \hat{u})\right]. \quad (B.12)$$

Recall the specification of ℓ_n and s_n in (8.13)–(8.15):

$$\ell_n = \lambda n^\nu, \qquad s_n = \beta \ell_n^\rho = \beta \lambda^\rho n^{\rho\nu},$$
$$\tfrac{1}{2} < \rho < 1, \qquad \nu > 1/(2\rho - 1). \quad (B.13)$$

On the right-hand side of (B.12), we first turn our attention to

$$\sum_1^N s_n = \beta \lambda^\rho \sum_1^N n^{\rho\nu}. \quad (B.14)$$

The following inequalities will be useful:

$$\frac{N^{x+1}}{x+1} \le \sum_1^N n^x \le \frac{(N+1)^{x+1}}{x+1}, \quad (B.15)$$

where x is any positive number; these follow from the inequalities

$$\int_1^{N+1} (n-1)^x \, dn \le \sum_1^N n^x \le \int_0^{N+1} n^x \, dn.$$

Applying the second inequality in (B.15) to (B.14), one gets

$$\sum_1^N s_n \le \frac{\beta \lambda^\rho (N+1)^{\rho\nu+1}}{\rho\nu+1}. \quad (B.16)$$

Next, note that

$$(T-T') \le \ell_{N+1} + m_{N+1} = (1+\mu)\ell_{N+1} \le (1+\mu)\lambda(N+1)^\nu. \quad (B.17)$$

Third, using (B.13) and the first inequality in (B.15),

$$T \ge \sum_1^N \ell_n = \lambda \sum_1^N n^\nu \ge \frac{\lambda N^{\nu+1}}{\nu+1},$$

which implies

$$N \le \left[\left(\frac{\nu+1}{\lambda}\right)T\right]^{1/(\nu+1)}. \quad (B.18)$$

Combining (B.16)–(B.18), we have, for suitable constants c_1 and c_2,

$$\frac{1}{T}\sum_1^N s_n \le c_1 T^{-(1-\rho)\nu/(\nu+1)}, \qquad \frac{1}{T}(T-T') \le c_2 T^{-1/(\nu+1)}. \quad (B.19)$$

Note that the bounds in (B.19) are not stochastic, These bounds, with (B.12), imply

$$E \frac{1}{T} \sum_{1}^{T} (U_t - \hat{u}) \le K c_1 T^{-(1-\rho)\nu/(\nu+1)} + (u_0 - \hat{u}) c_2 T^{-1/(\nu+1)},$$

$$\liminf_{T \to \infty} \frac{1}{T} \sum_{1}^{T} (U_t - \hat{u}) \le 0, \tag{B.20}$$

$$\liminf_{T \to \infty} \frac{1}{T} \sum_{1}^{T} U_t \le \hat{u}.$$

Hence, no other strategy can yield the manager a long-run average expected utility greater than $\hat{u}$.

Finally, it remains to show that the owner's strategy is an optimal response to the manager's strategy. Consider any other strategy by the owner. During any period in a review phase, the owner's expected return is

$$E(R_t \mid H_{t-1}) = \hat{r},$$

where H_{t-1} is the history of the process up through period $t-1$. If during a review phase the owner fails to pay the manager the compensation $\hat{w}$, the owner will trigger a noncooperative phase. (Noncooperative phases are also triggered when the manager fails to pass review.) In any period in a noncooperative phase, the compensation function ω^* is a best response to the manager's (myopic) decision rule α^*, and hence in such a period

$$E(R_t \mid H_{t-1}) \le r^* < \hat{r}.$$

Hence, for *all* periods t,

$$E(R_t \mid H_{t-1}) \le \hat{r},$$

and so for each T,

$$E \sum_{1}^{T} R_t \le T\hat{r},$$

and

$$\limsup_{T \to \infty} \frac{1}{T} \sum_{1}^{T} R_t \le \hat{r},$$

which proves that no other strategy can yield the owner a long-run average return greater than $\hat{r}$.

NOTES

1 See Arrow (1963, 1965). See also the bibliographic notes in Section 9, where the references to the relevant literature are gathered.

2 The discounted utility is normalized in the sense that if the utility in each period is u, and the number of periods is infinite, then the normalized utility will also equal u. This normalization facilitates the comparison of situations with different discount rates. For further comments on this point, see the end of Section 5.

3 If a manager's maximum tenure is finite, then of course every cycle will have finite duration.

4 The initiated will recognize that I am requiring the equilibrium to be subgame perfect. See Section 9.3.

5 Unless otherwise specified, "return" will mean "net return."

REFERENCES

Alchian, A. A. and H. Demsetz (1972), "Production, information costs, and economic organization," *American Economic Review, 62*: 777–95.

Arrow, K. J. (1963), "Uncertainty and the welfare economics of medical care," *American Economic Review, 53*: 941–73.

Arrow, K. J. (1965), *Aspects of the theory of risk-bearing*. Helsinki: Yrjö Jahnssonin Säätiö, Lecture 3.

Grossman, S. J. and O. D. Hart (1983), "An analysis of the principal–agent problem," *Econometrica, 51*: 7–45.

Groves, T. F. (1969), "The allocation of resources under uncertainty: The informational and incentive roles of prices and demands in a team," NSF Technical Report No. 1, Center for Research in Management Science, University of California, Berkeley (unpublished).

Groves, T. F. (1973), "Incentives in teams," *Econometrica, 41*: 617–31.

Hardy, G. H. (1949), *Divergent series*. Oxford: Clarendon Press.

Kohlberg, E. and J. F. Mertens (1982), "On the strategic stability of equilibria," CORE Discussion Paper 8248, Université Catholique de Louvain, Louvain-la-Neuve, November (unpublished).

Kreps, D. M. and R. B. Wilson (1982), "Sequential equilibria," *Econometrica, 50*: 863–94.

Linhart, P. B., R. Radner, and F. W. Sinden (1983), "A sequential principal–agent approach to regulation," Bell Laboratories Discussion Paper (unpublished).

Mayers, A. B. and C. W. Smith (1981), "Contractual provisions, organizational structure, and conflict control in insurance markets," *Journal of Business, 54*: 407–34.

Mirrlees, J. (1974), "Notes on welfare economics, information, and uncertainty," in Balch et al. (Eds.), *Essays on economic behavior under uncertainty*, Amsterdam: North-Holland.

Mirrlees, J. (1976), "The optimal structure of incentives and authority within an organization," *Bell Journal of Economics, 7*: 1-5-31.

Myerson, R. (1983), "Mechanism design by an informed principal," *Econometrica, 52*: 461–87.

Radner, R. (1981), "Monitoring cooperative agreements in a repeated principal-agent relationship," *Econometrica, 49*: 1127–48.

Radner, R. (1985), "Repeated principal–agent games with discounting," *Econometrica*, 53: 1173-98.

Radner, R. (1986), "Optimal equilibria in some repeated partnership games with imperfect information and no discounting," *Review of Economic Studies*, 53: 43-57.

Radner, R., R. Myerson, and E. Maskin (1986), "An example of a repeated partnership game with discounting and with uniformly inefficient equilibria," *Review of Economic Studies*, 53: 59-69.

Rogerson, W. P. (1982), "The structure of wage contracts in repeated agency models," IMSSS Technical Report N. 288, Stanford University, Stanford, Calif. (unpublished).

Rogerson, W. P. (1985), "Repeated moral hazard," *Econometrica*, 53: 69-76.

Ross, S. (1973), "The economic theory of agency: The principal's problem," *American Economic Review*, 63: 134-9.

Rubinstein, A. (1979), "Offenses that may have been committed by accident – an optimal policy of retribution," in S. J. Brams et al. (Eds.), *Applied game theory*, Wurzburg: Physica-Verlag.

Simon, H. A. (1951), "A formal theory of the employment relationship," *Econometrica*, 19: 293-305.

Spitzer, F. (1976), *Principles of random walk*, 2nd ed., New York: Springer-Verlag.

Stiglitz, J. E. (1983), "Risk, incentives, and the pure theory of moral hazard," *The Geneva Papers on Risk and Insurance*, 8: 4-33.

CHAPTER 3

Existence, regularity, and constrained suboptimality of competitive allocations when the asset market is incomplete

John D. Geanakoplos and Heraklis M. Polemarchakis

In 1951, Kenneth Arrow and Gerard Debreu independently established what is still today probably the central argument of economic theory: They proved that any competitive equilibrium of an "Arrow–Debreu" economy is Pareto optimal. In 1954, they jointly discovered a subclass of economies, now referred to as convex Arrow–Debreu economies, for which competitive equilibria always exist. Debreu (1970) introduced the techniques of differential topology into economics and proved that the competitive equilibria of smooth, convex Arrow–Debreu economies are generically locally unique. In this chapter we extend the study of the existence, optimality, and local uniqueness of competitive equilibria to a wider class of economies: The class of economies, suggested by Arrow in 1953, in which the asset market is possibly incomplete. We show that when assets pay off in some *numéraire* commodity, equilibria exist and are typically locally unique, even when the asset market is incomplete. However, when the asset market is incomplete, competitive equilibrium allocations are typically Pareto suboptimal in a strong sense: The market does not make efficient use of the existing assets.

The old proof of Pareto optimality (see, e.g., Lange 1942) essentially assumed differentiable utilities and strictly positive competitive equilibrium allocations. One considered the problem of how to divide the aggregate endowment to maximize the utility of one individual subject to the constraint that no other individual suffer a loss in utility. It was pointed out that the first-order necessary conditions for a strictly positive allocation, x, to be a local maximum to this problem are satisfied if the allocation is a competitive equilibrium. Moreover, it is now commonly known that in a concave programming problem the first-order necessary conditions are also sufficient for global optimality. Thus, if we add the hypoth-

This work was supported in part by National Science Foundation grant SES 84-11149.

65

esis that all the utilities are concave and apply this argument for x in turn to each individual, this old approach yields that competitive equilibria are Pareto optimal.

The new argument for Pareto optimality introduced by Arrow (1951) and Debreu (1951) does not require the differentiability of utilities, or even utility representations at all, nor does it require convexity of preferences or strict positivity of the equilibrium allocation. It depends on the fact that in a competitive equilibrium all potential allocations can be unambiguously valued at the equilibrium prices. If an alternative allocation makes an individual better off without harming anyone else, then the bundle allocated to this individual must cost strictly more than the endowment, while the bundle allocated to any other individual must cost at least as much as the endowment (given local nonsatiation). But this contradicts the feasibility of the alternative allocation. This new argument for Pareto optimality is analytically simple and requires a minimum of assumptions; it suffices, roughly speaking, that the preferences of individuals not display local satiation. What is demanding is the appropriate interpretation of the notion of a commodity or a market: As argued in Debreu (1959), it is required that commodities be differentiated, not only by qualitative, but by temporal and contingent characteristics as well, and that there be at the initial period, with all individuals present, a single market for the exchange of all commodities so specified. If the market in contingent commodities is thus complete, individuals optimize under one budget constraint and one price system. Economic activity past the initial contracting period is limited to the execution of contracts; further trading in subsequent periods is not permitted, nor is it necessary.

It was Arrow's (1953) contribution to suggest an alternative to a complete market in contingent commodities: a complete asset market. If, for each time period and realization of uncertainty, a pure security exists that yields one unit of "revenue" or of a *numéraire* commodity at that date-event pair and zero otherwise, any allocation obtained as a competitive equilibrium with a complete market in contingent commodities at the initial period can be alternatively obtained as a competitive equilibrium with a complete market in pure securities in the initial period, and subsequent spot markets.

In Arrow's formulation, and in the more general model of Radner (1968) in which there may not be a complete system of assets, markets in commodities and assets are active at distinct periods and under alternative realizations of uncertainty. In such a framework of sequential exchange, if the asset market is indeed incomplete, individuals face a nontrivial multiplicity of budget constraints and price systems, and the Arrow–Debreu argument for the Pareto optimality of competitive equilibrium fails. Indeed, so does the Arrow–Debreu proof of the existence of equilibrium, as Radner (1972) showed in a general model, where assets are thought of as claims on a vector of commodities indexed by states. Hart (1975) gave an explicit example in such a general framework of an economy with incomplete markets that has no competitive equilibrium.

In this chapter we consider economies in which the assets are real; but they yield payoffs denominated in a single *numéraire* commodity – such as gold. (Others [Cass (1984), Duffie (1985), Geanakoplos and Mas-Collel (1985) and Werner (1985)] have considered the case of financial securities where asset yields are in terms of units of account.) Individuals can buy or sell short any amount of each of the *numéraire* assets, in some limited collection. After the state of nature is revealed, they trade in the spot market with income derived from the sale of their initial endowments, plus the deliveries of the *numéraire* good they receive or make as a result of their portfolio holdings. Individuals are assumed, in equilibrium, to have perfect conditional foresight: They may not agree on the probability of the states, but they all understand what spot prices will prevail conditional on the state. In addition we postulate that in equilibrium all the asset and spot markets clear; in particular, there is no bankruptcy.

Let us consider a concrete example with three states of nature $s = 0, 1, 2$, $L + 1$ commodities and only two assets $a = 0, 1$ with *numéraire* payoffs in the three states given by the matrix

$$R = \begin{bmatrix} 1 & 0 \\ 0 & 1 \\ 0 & 1 \end{bmatrix}.$$

We can think of state 0 as period 0 and $s = 1, 2$ as states 1 and 2 in period 1. The above asset structure allows individuals to save from period 0 to period 1, by holding a negative amount of asset 0 and a positive amount of asset 1, but not to insure between consumption in states 1 and 2. One can see at once that a competitive equilibrium for such an economy is not likely to be Pareto optimal. The question we address in Section 7 is to what extent the market uses efficiently the limited assets that do exist.

Before our analysis of the constrained optimality question, we prove in Section 2 that competitive equilibria always exist as long as preferences are monotonic for the *numéraire* good in each state, and arbitrage *is* possible when assets are free. The first difficulty to overcome in the proof is that since individuals are allowed to sell short assets, there is no a priori lower bound that can be assumed for asset demands. As Hart (1975) showed, this is fatal for existence when asset payoffs are in multiple commodities or when asset payoffs depend more generally on prices (Hart 1974; see, however, Cass 1984, Duffie 1985, and Werner 1985 for the financial asset case). Second, since pure insurance involves assets that pay positive and negative amounts, some equilibrium asset prices may be negative; since asset demand is not continuous at prices equal to zero, we must carefully choose the space of asset prices on which to apply a fixed point argument.

In Section 3 we show that under smoothness conditions, demand is differentiable, and in Section 6 we use the same transversality techniques introduced first by Debreu (1972), which we explain in Section 5, to prove that equilibria are generically locally unique. This is in contrast to the study of Geanakoplos and Mas-Colell (1985), which shows that there is an essential real indeterminacy when assets pay off in units of account.

The question of what is the appropriate definition of constrained optimality when the asset market is incomplete has been vexing at least since Hart (1975) gave an example of an incomplete markets economy, which has two competitive equilibria that are Pareto comparable or, alternatively, in which a further reduction in the set of assets traded leads to a Pareto improvement at equilibrium. Newbery and Stiglitz (1979) provided a second example and intuition. Grossman (1977) gave a definition of constrained optimality under which the first two theorems of welfare analysis still apply, but, as Hart has remarked, it seems absurd to say that the economy is using its markets efficiently at one equilibrium when there is another equilibrium in which everyone is better off. A satisfactory definition of constrained optimality that recognizes that the underlying reasons for the incompleteness of markets may also limit a central planner has only recently been given by Stiglitz (1982) and Newbery and Stiglitz (1982). These latter studies, and also Greenwald and Stiglitz (1984), suggest that constrained suboptimality is a general phenomenon. They do not, however, develop the formal arguments and analytical apparatus needed to prove that claim.

We say that the asset allocation at a competitive equilibrium is *constrained suboptimal* if a reallocation of assets alone can lead to a Pareto improvement when prices and allocations in the commodity spot markets adjust to maintain equilibrium.[1]

We show in Section 7 that, when the asset market is incomplete, the portfolio allocation at a competitive equilibrium is generically constrained suboptimal; this is true even if the portfolio reallocations are required to satisfy every agent's budget constraint at the original equilibrium prices. In the context of our earlier example, this means that if only the individuals could have been induced to save different amounts, they could all have been made better off. The intuition for this result is as follows: An asset reallocation in any economy has two effects on an individual's utility – a direct effect from the income transfer and an indirect effect due to the relative price change in the commodity spot markets. When markets are complete, the income reallocation caused by the price change can be decomposed into a combination of assets that have already been priced by the market. When the asset market is incomplete, it is generically the case that the price changes will cause an income redistribution that the market itself could not directly implement. In essence, the central planner has access to a wider class of assets than those directly traded. In Section 7.2 we discuss some special, nongeneric cases where competitive equilibria nevertheless can be constrained optimal.

Our method of proof is reminiscent of the old necessary conditions for local optimality, dressed up in modern matrix notation. We consider the matrix of utility effects caused by the various portfolio reallocations, and we prove that if the asset market is incomplete, for a generic economy, this matrix has full row rank. It follows immediately that there is a portfolio reallocation that makes everyone better off.

1   The economy

Transactions occur in real securities called assets before the state of nature is known, and then subsequently in commodities, after the state of nature is known. States of nature are $s \in S = \{0, 1, ..., S\}$.[2]

Commodities are $\ell \in L = \{0, 1, ..., L\}$. Commodity ℓ in state s is denoted $\ell(s)$. A consumption plan is a vector $x = (..., x(s), ...) \in E_+^{(S+1)(L+1)}$. At state s, commodity $0(s)$ is the designated *numéraire* commodity.

Individuals, $h \in H = \{0, 1, ..., H\}$ have preferences over consumption plans represented by utility functions $W^h: E_+^{(S+1)(L+1)} \rightarrow E$.[3,4] For some problems we shall assume that W^h is representable as a von Neumann–Morgenstern expected utility, $W^h = \Sigma_{s \in S} \pi^h(s) U^h(s)$. Individuals have endowments $e^h \in E_+^{(S+1)(L+1)}$.

Assets $a \in A = \{0, 1, ..., A\}$ yield returns, denominated in the *numéraire*.

The return of asset a in state s is $r_a(s)$, which may be negative or positive; the vector of asset returns at s is $r(s) = (\ldots, r_a(s), \ldots)$; the matrix of asset returns or asset return structure is $R = \{r_a(s)\}_{s \in S}^{a \in A}$, an $(S+1) \times (A+1)$ matrix. A portfolio is $y \in E^{A+1}$; again, the sign of y_a may be positive or negative – there are no restrictions on short sales. The asset market is called complete if and only if R also has full row rank; equivalently, if and only if any distribution of revenue across states can be attained by a suitable choice of a portfolio. If $S > A$, the asset market is necessarily incomplete.

We allow free disposal of commodities, and hence we only need to consider nonnegative commodity prices: $p = (\ldots, p(s), \ldots) \in E_+^{(S+1)(L+1)}$. Asset prices are $q \in E^{A+1}$; they may be positive or negative.

Given prices $(q, p) \in E^{A+1} \times E_+^{(S+1)(L+1)}$, the budget set of individual h is defined as $B^h(q, p) = \{(y, x) \in E^{A+1} \times E_+^{(S+1)(L+1)} \mid q \cdot y = 0$ and $p(s) \cdot (x(s) - e^h(s)) \le p_0(s)(r(s) \cdot y)$, for all $s \in S\}$.

A commodity allocation is $\mathbf{x} = (x^h : h \in H)$ such that

$$\sum_{h \in H} (x^h - e^h) \le 0.$$

A portfolio or asset allocation is $\mathbf{y} = (y^h : h \in H)$ such that

$$\sum_{h \in H} y^h = 0.$$

An allocation is a pair $(\mathbf{y}, \mathbf{x})$.

A competitive equilibrium for the economy with real, *numéraire* assets is a 4-tuple of asset prices, commodity prices, an asset allocation and a commodity allocation, $(q, p, \mathbf{y}, \mathbf{x})$ which satisfies

$$\sum_{h \in H} (x^h - e^h) = 0 \quad \text{if } p_\ell(s) > 0 \text{ for all } s \in S, \ \ell \in L;$$
$$(y_h, x_h) \text{ is maximal in } B^h(q, p) \quad \text{for all } h \in H.$$

For a given asset allocation $\mathbf{y}$ a spot market competitive equilibrium is a pair $(p, \mathbf{x})$ which satisfies

$$\sum_{h=0}^{H} (x^h - e^h) = 0 \quad \text{if } p_\ell(s) > 0 \text{ for all } s \in S, \ \ell \in L;$$
$$x^h \text{ is maximal in } B^h(p; y^h) \quad \text{for all } h \in H.$$

The budget set $B^h(p; y^h)$ is defined by

$$B^h(p; y^h) = \{x \in E_+^{(S+1)(L+1)} \mid p(s) \cdot (x(s) - e^h(s)) \le p_0(s)(r(s) \cdot y^h)$$
$$\text{for all } s \in S\}.$$

That is, a spot market equilibrium allows individuals to optimize in their choice of consumption bundles but not in their portfolio choice.

A commodity allocation $\mathbf{x}$ is suboptimal if there exists an alternative commodity allocation $\mathbf{x}'$ such that

$$W^h(x'^h) \geq W^h(x^h) \quad \text{for all } h \in H, \text{ with some strict inequality.}$$

An allocation $(\mathbf{y}, \mathbf{x})$ is constrained suboptimal if there exists an alternative commodity allocation $\mathbf{x}$ such that

$$W^h(x''^h) \geq W^h(x^h) \quad \text{for all } h \in H, \text{ with some strict inequality;}$$

there exists a commodity price vector p and a portfolio allocation $\mathbf{y}''$ such that $(p, \mathbf{x}'')$ is a spot market competitive equilibrium for the portfolio allocation $\mathbf{y}''$.

Constrained suboptimality is a stronger notion; it recognizes the constraints imposed by the asset structure, which suboptimality does not. Note that by the second welfare theorem the two notions coincide if the asset market is complete.

This appears to be the most natural, fully tractable model with real assets.[5] Radner (1968, 1972) gave a general formulation in which it is impossible to prove in general the existence of a full equilibrium. Hart (1975), for example, showed that, if assets pay off in multiple commodities, then it is possible to construct an economy with no competitive equilibria. In the next section we show that under mild conditions competitive equilibria with real *numéraire* assets always exist. One might think of our formulation as an abstraction of the theory of general equilibrium with possibly incomplete markets under the "gold standard." Geanakoplos and Mas-Colell (1985) show how the "gold standard equilibria" can be used to understand the set of "financial equilibria" when "money" is not tied to any standard. There, these equilibria are more precisely called financial securities competitive equilibria.

As early as 1953 Arrow defined a financial securities competitive equilibrium for the special financial security structure $\tilde{R}$ equal to the identity. In a general financial securities equilibrium, there is a given securities structure $\tilde{R}$, where $\tilde{r}_b(s)$ gives the payoff of financial security (bond) b in state s in units of account. The budget set $\tilde{B}^h(q, p)$ is now defined as $\tilde{B}^h(q, p) = \{(y, x) \in E^{A+1} \times E_+^{(L+1)(S+1)} \mid q \cdot y = 0 \text{ and } p(s) \cdot (x(s) - e^h(s)) \leq r(s) \cdot y \text{ for all } s \in S\}$, and (q, p) is allowed to vary over $E^{A+1} \times E_+^{(L+1)(S+1)}$. Arrow showed that, when $\tilde{R} = I$ (the case of a complete set of "Arrow securities"), an allocation is part of a financial securities competitive equilibrium if and only if it is an Arrow–Debreu equilibrium allocation. The object of study of Geanakoplos and Mas-Colell (1985) is the set of financial securities equilibrium allocations for general $\bar{R}$, when the rank $\bar{R} < (S+1)$.

We return to equilibria in which the asset payoffs $r_a(s)$ are in units of the *numéraire* good $0(s)$, $a \in A$, and $s \in S$. When R has full row rank and the asset market is thus complete, the set of equilibrium allocations is identical to the set of Arrow–Debreu equilibrium allocations. At first this might seem surprising, since, for example, an asset a with payoff $r_a(0) = -r_a(1) = 1$ appears to fix the rate of exchange between commodity 0 in state 0 and commodity 0 in state 1. But this is misleading, for the rate of exchange also depends on the asset prices q and the asset return structure. To see this, let $(\bar{p}, \mathbf{x})$ be an Arrow–Debreu equilibrium with $\bar{p} \gg 0$. One can define the vector $v \gg 0$ by $v(s) = \bar{p}_0(s)$, $s \in S$, and q to be $q = R'v$. Then $(q, \bar{p}, \mathbf{y}, \mathbf{x})$ is a competitive equilibrium with real *numéraire* assets for some $\mathbf{y}$. The argument in the reverse direction requires Farkas' lemma and is given in the next section.

Although we have indexed the spot commodity markets by referring to different states of nature, these could be reinterpreted, given the proper asset structure R, as time and state indexed; the same analysis thus covers a broad range of problems. One case of central importance occurs when state 0 is interpreted to be period 0 and state s, for $s = 1,, ..., S$, is interpreted to be period 1 in state s. If asset 0 is given by $r_0(0) = 1$, $r_0(s) = 0$ for $s = 1, ..., S$, and all other assets pay $r_a(0) = 0$ for $a = 1, ..., A$, then we can interpret our model as one in which individuals decide at the same time on consumption in period 0 and their holdings of risky assets before knowing the state that will be revealed in period 1.

Another interesting special case occurs when the set of date–event consumption nodes can be represented as a tree [see Debreu (1959)]. Consumers are supposed to know where in the tree they are when they act, but not which of the successor nodes will occur. Utilities are given by $W^h(x) = \sum_{s \in S} \pi^h(s) U^h(x(s); s)$, and agents update by Bayes' law. Suppose also that at every date–event node s consumers can trade all future commodities contingent on which successor node s' will occur. This is a situation of complete markets in the sense of Debreu. It can be represented in our model by an asset structure R that associates to every node s in the tree an asset $a(s)$ such that $r_{a(s)}(s) = 1 = -r_{a(s)}(P(s))$, where $P(s)$ is the predecessor of s, and $r_{a(s)}(s') = 0$ for $s' \notin \{s, P(s)\}$.

With these introductory remarks out of the way, we now state our assumptions:

(A1) W^h is continuous and quasiconcave on $E_+^{(S+1)(L+1)}$; the range of W^h can be extended to $E \cup \{-\infty\}$.

(A2) $e^h \gg 0$.

(A3) W^h is monotonic in commodity $0(s)$ for each $s \in S$: Let $\tilde{x}$ be any consumption plan that is nonnegative in every coordinate, and strictly positive at $0(s)$ for some $s \in S$. Then for all $x \in E_+^{(S+1)(L+1)}$, $W^h(x + \tilde{x}) > W^h(x)$.

(A4) When securities are free, there is arbitrage: There is $\bar{y} \in E^{A+1}$ with $R\bar{y} > 0$.

(D1) R has full column rank.

(D2) W^h is twice continuously differentiable, $DW^h \gg 0$, and $D^2 W^h$ is negative definite on $E_{++}^{(S+1)(L+1)}$.

(D3) The closure of the indifference curves of W^h do not intersect the boundary of $E_+^{(L+1)(S+1)}$.

(S) The asset market is incomplete: $A < S$.

(CS) Every set of $A+1$ rows of R are linearly independent, and there is a portfolio y with $r(s) \cdot y \neq 0$ for all $s \in S$.

Under assumptions A1–A4 we shall show in the next section that competitive equilibria exist. Note that under the von Neumann–Morgenstern hypothesis, $W^h(x) = \sum_{s \in S} \pi^h(s) U^h(x(s), s)$, A3 implies $\pi^h(s) > 0$ for all $s \in S$. Under the additional hypotheses D1–D3, excess demand for assets and commodities is differentiable over the domain of "nonarbitrage" prices, which we shall specify. Assumptions A1–A4 and D1–D3 also suffice to guarantee regularity of the equilibrium set. Finally, we show in the last section that asset market equilibria are generically Pareto suboptimal when $A < S$ and even generically constrained suboptimal when CS holds.

2 Existence of competitive equilibria

The proof of the existence of an asset market competitive equilibrium turns out not to be much more complicated than the standard existence proof for Arrow–Debreu equilibria pioneered by Arrow–Debreu (1954), and refined by Debreu (1959). When the consumption sets are bounded, the demand correspondences of the individuals are upper hemi-continuous. The only difficulty is finding the appropriate convex, compact price space on whose boundary aggregate excess demand is properly behaved. Here it turns out to be the set of nonarbitrage prices.

The recent work of Werner (1985) and Cass (1984) shows that the difficulties with existence in the Radner–Hart models are absent in models of financial securities competitive equilibria. Here we show that the same is true for real *numéraire* assets, a convenient middle ground between the purely nominal securities in the latter models and complicated vector-commodity assets in the former models. Of course, an equilibrium with real *numéraire* return structure R is also a financial market equilibrium with return structure $\tilde{R} = R$. Our equilibrium existence proof thus implies the existence of financial equilibria. The importance of the distinction between financial securities and real *numéraire* assets is discussed in Geanakoplos and Mas-Colell (1985). There are some other, minor differences between Werner's existence result and ours. He specializes to the case where financial security 0 pays off only in state 0 and other financial securities pay nothing in state 0. We have a more general asset structure. In the Werner model, financial securities pay out nonnegative amounts in every state. Strictly speaking, insurance is a transfer of wealth from one state to another, and that is why we have not restricted asset payoffs to be nonnegative. In practice what is typically called insurance is a transfer of wealth from the current period to some subset of future periods. It may thus be achieved by a combination of selling (going short) in the 0th Werner financial security, and buying another financial security with the appropriate nonnegative payoffs. Our more general asset structure introduces complications which we return to when we discuss A4 before the proof of Lemma 2.

Lemma 1. Consider the truncated individual demand correspondence

$$d^h(q,p;K) = \{(\hat{y},\hat{x}) \in \arg\max_{(y,x)\in K}[W(x) \mid q\cdot y = 0 \text{ and } p(s)\cdot(x(s)-e^h(s))$$
$$= p_0(s)(r(s)\cdot y) \text{ for all } s \in S]\},$$

where $K \subseteq E^{A+1} \times E^{(S+1)(L+1)}$ is a closed rectangle with center at the origin. Under A1–A3, $d^h(p,q;K)$ is nonempty, compact, convex valued, and upper hemi-continuous at each $(q,p) \in E^{A+1} \times E_+^{(S+1)(L+1)}$ with $q \neq 0$ and $p(s) \neq 0$ for all $s \in S$.

Proof: By continuity and compactness $d^h(q,p;K)$ is nonempty; by concavity and convexity, it is convex valued.

Let $(q_n,p_n)_n (q,p)$ and $(y_n,x_n)_n (y,x)$ where $(y_n,x_n) \in d^h(q_n,p_n;K)$. Suppose that $(\hat{y},\hat{x}) \in \{(y',x') \in K \mid q\cdot y' = 0 \text{ and } p(s)\cdot(x'(s)-e^h(s)) = p_0(s)(r(s)\cdot y')\}$ and $W^h(\hat{x}) > W^h(x)$. We shall derive a contradiction. Take $\lambda < 1$ but sufficiently large so that $W^h(\lambda\hat{x}) > W^h(x)$; by continuity, it also follows that for n large $W^h(\lambda\hat{x}) > W^h(x_n)$. Define

$$\hat{y}_n = \arg\min_{y'} \{\|\hat{y} - y'\| \mid q_n \cdot y' = 0\}.$$

Note that for $q \neq 0$, $\hat{y}_{nn} \hat{y}$. Now consider that

$$p(s) \cdot (\lambda \hat{x}(s) - e^h(s)) - p_0(s)(r(s) \cdot \lambda \hat{y}_n) < 0$$

for all s, for n large, since $p(s) \cdot e^h(s) > 0$ for all s and $\lambda < 1$. But this is a contradiction, for $(\lambda y_n, \lambda x)$ is preferred to (y_n, x_n) for n large.

Q.E.D.

Let $d(q, p; K) = \sum_{h=0}^{H} d^h(q, p; K)$ be the aggregate truncated demand correspondence. Recall that the sum of upper hemi-continuous, nonempty, compact, convex-valued correspondences is upper hemi-continuous, and nonempty, compact, convex valued.

If $(y^h, x^h) \in d^h(q, p; K)$, then $q \cdot y^h = 0$ and $p(s) \cdot (x^h(s) - e^h(s)) = p_0(s)(r(s) \cdot y^h)$, for all $s \in S$. Hence if $(y, x) \in d(q, p; K)$, then $q \cdot y = 0$ and $p(s) \cdot (x(s) - \sum_{h=0}^{H} e^h(s)) = p_0(s)(r(s) \cdot y)$. This is the modified Walras law that holds for economies with possibly incomplete asset markets.

We must look for the appropriate price space – one that is convex and has an appropriate boundary – to apply a fixed point argument.

Commodity prices pose no problem. Since a separate budget constraint must be satisfied at every state s, we may restrict our attention to

$$p = (\ldots, p(s), \ldots) \in \Delta^{L(S+1)} = \underset{s \in S}{\times} \Delta^L,$$

where

$$\Delta^L = \left\{ p(s) \in E_+^{L+1} \mid \sum_{\ell \in L} p_\ell(s) = 1 \right\}.$$

Since we have allowed securities to pay off negative amounts in some states, the equilibrium asset prices q may well have to have some negative components. On the other hand, since demand is not upper hemi-continuous at $q = 0$, it is not immediately obvious what price domain to limit attention.

Assumption A4 allows us to describe a convex, compact set of potential equilibrium asset prices, which we call nonarbitrage prices. The assumption is trivially satisfied when assets pay off in nonnegative amounts, or when the asset market is complete. If there are no assets, or only one asset, then in equilibrium there can be no trade in assets. Thus, both the no-asset and one-asset cases are isomorphic to models with one asset that pays a strictly positive amount in every state, and there A4 applies. It is perhaps curious that we need to assume the possibility of arbitrage in order to find an equilibrium without arbitrage, but the idea is clear: To apply a standard fixed point argument, we must eliminate 0 as a potential equilibrium.

We say that the asset prices $q \in E^{A+1}$ do not permit *arbitrage* if and only if there is no $y \in E^{A+1}$ with $q \cdot y \le 0$ and $Ry > 0$.

Lemma 2. Suppose A4 and D1 hold. Let

$$\bar{C} = \{q \in E^{A+1} \mid q = R'v, v \in E_+^{(S+1)}\}.$$

Then $\bar{C}$ is a closed, convex cone. Furthermore, $q \in \text{int } \bar{C}$ if and only if q does not permit arbitrage. In particular, if $\hat{q} \in \bar{C}/\text{int } \bar{C}$, then there is $\hat{y}$ with $\hat{q} \cdot \hat{y} = 0$ and $R\hat{y} > 0$. Finally, there is $\hat{q} \in E^{A+1}/\bar{C}$.

Proof: $\bar{C}$ is by construction a finite cone. All finite cones are convex and closed. Note that int $\bar{C} \ne \phi$, for if $v \gg 0$, then $q = R'v \in \text{int } \bar{C}$, since R has linearly independent columns. Suppose $q \in \text{int } \bar{C}$. Let $Ry > 0$. Since $q \in \text{int } \bar{C}$, $q - \epsilon y \in \text{int } \bar{C}$ for small enough positive ϵ; that is, $R'v = q - \epsilon y$ for some $v \ge 0$. Now suppose that $q \cdot y \le 0$. Then $v'Ry = (q \cdot y) - \epsilon(y \cdot y) < 0$. But then, if $\bar{v}_s = v_s + \delta$ for very small δ, $s \in S$, $\bar{v} \gg 0$ and still $\bar{v}'Ry < 0$, contradicting $Ry > 0$. Thus if $q \in \text{int } \bar{C}$, and $Ry > 0$, then $q \cdot y > 0$. So int $\bar{C}$ consists only of no arbitrage prices.

Recall now that by hypothesis there is some $\bar{y}$ with $R\bar{y} > 0$. Hence it follows from the above that $0 \notin \text{int } \bar{C}$, and hence that $\bar{C} \ne E^{A+1}$.

Take $\hat{q} \in E^{A+1}$, $\hat{q} \notin \text{int } \bar{C}$. Since int $\bar{C}$ is convex, we can find a nontrivial hyperplane ($\hat{y} \ne 0$) $H_{\hat{y}} = \{q \in E^{A+1} \mid q \cdot \hat{y} = \hat{q} \cdot \hat{y}\}$ through $\hat{q}$ with $q \cdot \hat{y} \ge \hat{q} \cdot \hat{y}$ for all $q \in \bar{C}$. Since $0 \in \bar{C}$, $\hat{q} \cdot \hat{y} \le 0$ and $q \cdot \hat{y} \ge 0$ for all $q \in \bar{C}$. Since $\hat{y} \ne 0$ and R has independent columns, this means $R\hat{y} > 0$. So we conclude that if $\hat{q} \notin \text{int } \bar{C}$, then there is a $\hat{y}$ that gives rise to arbitrage at prices $\hat{q}$. Note that if $\hat{q} \in \bar{C}/\text{int } \bar{C}$, then in the above demonstration we must have an arbitrage portfolio with $\hat{q} \cdot \hat{y} = 0$.   Q.E.D.

For $q = R'v \in \bar{C}$, various interpretations of the vector v are possible. Since its components are all nonnegative, one can think of v as a measure on S. With this measure, the price of each asset is the expectation of its future payments. In the language of finance, the asset prices q display the martingale property.

Given any finite cone $\bar{C} \subsetneq E^{A+1}$ as above, there is a hyperplane H (of dimension A) in E^{A+1} such that $0 \ne q \in \bar{C}$ if and only if there is some $\lambda > 0$ with $\lambda q \in H \cap \bar{C}$, provided that $\bar{C}$ contains no full line segment (otherwise take H to be half the unit sphere).

Let $Q = H \cap \bar{C}$ be the set of normalized security prices. Q^0, the interior of Q relative to H, is the set of *normalized nonarbitrage security prices*. Q is closed, bounded, and convex (acyclic absolute neighborhood retract if H is a half-sphere).

We are now ready to state and prove our main proposition in this section.

Proposition 1 (Existence). If A1–A4 are satisfied, a competitive equilibrium for the economy with real *numéraire* assets exists.

Proof: Without loss of generality, we may assume that D1 is satisfied, since, once we have priced a maximal set of linearly independent assets, the prices of the remaining assets are determined by arbitrage.

Consider a rectangle K with center at the origin in $E^{A+1} \times E^{(S+1)(L+1)}$ so large that it contains $(0, 2\Sigma_{h=0}^{H} e^h)$. Let Q be as above. Consider the correspondence $\Phi^K: Q \times \Delta^{L(S+1)} \times K \to Q \times \Delta^{L(S+1)} \times K$ defined componentwise as follows: Let $\Phi_3^K(q, p, (y, z)) = d(q, p; K) - (0, \Sigma_{h \in H} e^h)$ be the aggregate truncated excess demand correspondence. By Lemma 2 this correspondence is upper hemi-continuous and nonempty, compact, convex valued.

Define $\Phi_1(q, p, (y, z)) = \{\hat{q} \in \arg\max_{\bar{q} \in Q} \bar{q} \cdot y\}$ and similarly let $\Phi_2 = (\dots, \Phi_2(s), \dots)$, $s = 0, 1, \dots, S$, where

$$\Phi_2(q, p, (y, z))(s) = \{\hat{p}(s) \in \Delta^L \mid \hat{p}(s) \in \arg\max_{\bar{p} \in \Delta^L} \bar{p} \cdot z(s)\}.$$

Since Q and the Δ^L are compact and convex, it is trivial to verify that Φ_1 and Φ_2 are upper hemi-continuous and nonempty, compact, convex valued (acyclic if H is the half-sphere).

By Kakutani's (Eilenberg–Montgomery's 1946) fixed point theorem, there must be some point

$$(q^*, p^*, y^*, z^*) \in \Phi^K(q^*, p^*, y^*, z^*).$$

Note first that $Ry^* \leq 0$, for if $r(s) \cdot y^* > 0$ for some s, then

$$q^* + (0, \dots, 1, \dots, 0)'R \equiv q$$

satisfies $q \cdot y^* > 0$ and $\lambda q \in Q$ for some $\lambda > 0$, contradicting the maximality of $q^* \cdot y^* = 0$. By Walras' law it now follows that $p^*(s) \cdot z^*(s) \leq 0$ for all $s \in S$, and hence that $z_\ell^*(s) \leq 0$ for all $s \in S$ and $\ell \in L$ (otherwise there would be $p \in \Delta^L$ with $p \cdot z^*(s) > 0 \geq p^*(s) \cdot z^*(s)$). But since $x^h \geq 0$, it follows from $z^* \leq 0$ that $\|x^h\| \leq \|\Sigma_{h' \in H} e^{h'}\|$ for all h.

Now let K_n be a sequence of successively larger rectangles. For each n there must be a fixed point $[q_n^*, p_n^*, y_n^* = \Sigma_{h \in H} y_n^{*h}, z_n^* = \Sigma_{h \in H} (x_n^{*h} - e^h)]$

for Φ^{K_n}. From the above compactness of the $\|x_n^{*h}\|$ it follows that by passing to convergent subsequences we must have $q_{nn}^* q^*$, $p_{nn}^* p^*$, and for all h, $x_{nn}^{*h} x^{*h}$. Suppose that $p_0^*(s) > 0$ for all $s \in S$. Then

$$r(s) \cdot y = \frac{1}{p_0^*(s)} [p^*(s)(x^{*h}(s) - e^h(s))] \quad \text{for all } s \in S$$

has a unique solution $y^{*h} = \lim_{n \to \infty} y_n^{*h}$. It is immediate that

$$(q^*, p^*, \mathbf{y}^* = (\ldots, y^{*h}, \ldots), x^* = (\ldots, x^{*h}, \ldots))$$

is an asset equilibrium. For large n, (y^{*h}, x^{*h}) is interior to K_n, and hence by continuity and convexity of W^h, (y^{*h}, x^{*h}) is maximal in $B^h({}^*q, {}^*p)$. By continuity, if $y^* \equiv \sum_{h \in H} y^{*h}$ then $q^* \cdot y^* = 0$ and from the first paragraph, $(Ry^*) \le 0$. But then $y^* = 0$, for by hypothesis R has independent columns, and if $Ry^* < 0$, then $R(-y^*) > 0$, and consumer h could better choose $y^h = y^{*h} + (-y^*)$, contradicting the maximality of (y^{*h}, x^{*h}) in $B^h(q^*, p^*)$. Finally, if $y^* = 0$, then by Walras' law $p^*(s)z^*(s) = 0$, and since $z^*(s) \le 0$ it must be that $z_\ell^*(s) = 0$ if $p_\ell^*(s) > 0$.

It only remains to check that it is impossible that $\lim_{n \to \infty} p_0^*(s)_n = p_0^*(s) = 0$ for some $s \in S$. Suppose $p_0^*(s) = 0$. Let $u_0(s)$ be the unit vector in $E^{(S+1)(L+1)}$ in the $0(s)$ direction. For any consumer h, let $k = \min_{\ell \in L} e_\ell^h(s)$; by monotonicity, $W^h(x^{*h} + ku_0(s)) > W^h(x^{*h})$, and by continuity of W^h, since $(p_0^*(s)_n)_n 0$ and $x_{nn}^{*h} x^{*h}$, $W^h((1 - (p_0^*(s))_n)x^{*h} + ku_0(s)) > W^h(x_n^{*h})$ for large enough n. But if $p_0^*(s)_n < 1$, then

$$[(1 - (p_0^*(s))_n)y^{*h}, (1 - (p_0^*(s))_n)x_n^{*h} + ku_0(s)] \in B^h(q_n^*, p_n^*) \cap K_n,$$

contradicting the fact that $(y_n^{*h}, x_n^{*h}) \in d^h(q_n^*, p_n^*; K_n)$.   Q.E.D.

3   Continuous differentiability of demand

We have shown in the last section that the interior of $\bar{C}$ is the set of non-arbitrage asset prices, an open set in E^{A+1}. If $q \in \text{int } \bar{C}$, then there is no $y \ne 0$ with $q \cdot y = 0$ and $Ry \ge 0$, if R has independent columns. Let $(q, p) \in \text{int } \bar{C} \times E_{++}^{(S+1)(L+1)}$. It follows that the demand $d^h(q, p)$ is nonempty: With positive prices p there is only a compact set of y which satisfy $q \cdot y = 0$ and leave consumer h with nonnegative wealth in every state.

We shall now show that if A1–A4 and D1–D3 are satisfied, the individual demand $d^h(q, p)$ is a continuously differentiable function on

$$\text{int } \bar{C} \times E_{++}^{(S+1)(L+1)}.$$

Clearly $d^h(q, p)$ is a singleton and lies in $E^{A+1} \times E_{++}^{(S+1)(L+1)}$.

Without loss of generality, $p_0(s) = 1$, $s \in S$. The necessary and sufficient first-order conditions for an interior optimum are

$$\left. \begin{array}{l} D_{x(s)} W^h - \lambda(s) p(s) = 0, \\ p(s) = (x(s) - e^h(s)) - r(s) \cdot y = 0, \end{array} \right\} \quad \text{for all } s \in S,$$

$$\lambda' R - \mu q = 0, \qquad q \cdot y = 0,$$

for $\lambda = (\dots, \lambda(s), \dots) \in E_{++}^{S+1}$ and $\mu \in E$. Totally differentiating the first-order conditions, we obtain the matrix of coefficients

$$A = \begin{bmatrix} D^2 W & P & 0 & 0 \\ P' & 0 & R & 0 \\ 0 & R' & 0 & q \\ 0 & 0 & q' & 0 \end{bmatrix}.$$

From the implicit function theorem, continuous differentiability obtains if $|A| \neq 0$. Suppose that for some $\hat{z} = (\hat{x}, \hat{\lambda}, \hat{y}, \hat{\mu})$, $A\hat{z} = 0$ and so $(\hat{z})' A(\hat{z}) = 0$. Multiplying out one finds that from the negative definiteness of $D^2 W^h$, $\hat{x} = 0$. Since $p(s) \neq 0$ for all $s \in S$ and $q \neq 0$, it follows that $\hat{\lambda}(s) = 0$ for all $s \in S$ and $\hat{\mu} = 0$. Finally, since R has full colinear rank, $\hat{y} = 0$ as well. Hence $\hat{z} = 0$, which completes the argument.

The aggregate demand function $d(q, p) = (y(q, p), x(q, p))$ and the aggregate excess demand function

$$f(q, p) = (y(q, p), x(q, p)) - (0, \Sigma_{h \in H} e^h)$$

are similarly well defined and continuously differentiable on $E^{A+1} \times E_{++}^{(S+1)L}$.

4 The space of economies

Rather than concentrating on an arbitrary fixed economy, we now consider a broader class of economies, within which we shall establish properties of "typical" economies. Consider an open set $I \subset E_{++}^{(S+1)(L+1)(H+1)}$ of possible endowments for each of the $H + 1$ agents. Assume that I is bounded and that the closure if I, $\bar{I}$, does not intersect any boundary: That is, assume all possible endowments are bounded away from zero for every commodity.

We have already described our hypothesis on W^h. What is important is that on some large but bounded rectangle containing the largest possible aggregate endowment from I, the W^h are twice continuously differentiable and strictly concave in the interior, and satisfy the previously discussed boundary condition. Note that adding to such a W^h a sufficiently small multiple ϵf of any smooth function f (f must be smooth on the boundary as well) will produce another utility $V \equiv W^h + \epsilon f$ also satisfying the same assumptions. We shall take our space of utilities W to be a finite dimensional manifold of utility functions as above that is sufficiently rich in perturbations. Explicitly, if $W \in W$ and ϵf is quadratic and separable between states, then for all sufficiently small ϵ, $V = W + \epsilon f \in W$. Note that if W^h is of the form $W^h = \sum_{S=0}^{S} \pi^h(s) U^h(s)$ then so is $W + \epsilon f$.

In the remainder of the chapter we shall argue that certain properties hold for "nearly all" choices of economies $(\mathbf{e}, \mathbf{W}) \in \mathbf{E} = I \times W^{H+1}$. In Section 5 we describe the mathematical technique of transversality we shall use in Sections 6 and 7.

5   Transversality

The crucial mathematical idea we use to establish our generic results is the so-called transversality theory. Debreu (1970) was the first to apply these ideas to the study of economics.

Suppose that M and N are smooth m- and n-dimensional manifolds, respectively, lying in some finite dimensional Euclidean space. Let $f: M \to N$ be a smooth map.[6] Let 0 be a point in N. We say that f is *transverse to* 0, and we write $f \pitchfork 0$, if for all $x \in M$ with $f(x) = 0$, $Df \mid_x$ has full rank n. Note that if $m < n$, then it is impossible that $Df \mid_x$ has rank n; in that case $f \pitchfork 0$ if and only if $f^{-1}(0)$ is empty.

If $f \pitchfork 0$, then $f^{-1}(0)$ is either an $m - n$-dimensional manifold, or else empty. In particular, if $m = n$, and $f^{-1}(0)$ is not empty, then $f^{-1}(0)$ is a zero-dimensional manifold, and thus is a discrete set of points. If $K \subset M$ is any compact set, then $f^{-1}(0) \cap K$ consists of at most a finite number of points.

Consider now a third manifold L, of dimension ℓ, and a smooth function $f: L \times M \to N$. Suppose that $f \pitchfork 0$. We know from the preceding discussion that $f^{-1}(0) \subset L \times M$ is an $(\ell + m - n)$-dimensional manifold, or else empty. Let x be any fixed element of L, and consider the smooth function $f_x: M \to N$ given by $f_x(y) \equiv f(x, y)$ for all $y \in M$. A natural question arises: Is it likely that f_x is transverse to 0? Likely can be taken in two senses. With any manifold there is a natural definition of measure zero or null set. So we might say that likely means for all $x \in L$ except those x in some null set. Recall that any set whose complement is null must be dense. Alternatively, we might take likely to mean for all x in some open and dense set.

Transversality theorem. Let L, M, and N be manifolds of dimension ℓ, m, and n, respectively. Let $f \pitchfork 0$, for a point $0 \in N$. Then except for a null set of $x \in L$, $f_x \pitchfork 0$. Moreover, for any compact set $K \subset M$, the set of x in L for which $f_x \pitchfork 0$, when f_x is restricted to K, is open in L. In particular, if $f^{-1}(0) \subset L \times K$, for some compact $K \subset M$, then the set of x in L such that $f_x \pitchfork 0$ is open, dense, and its complement is null.

We call any open, dense set with null complement a *generic* set. The two cases of most importance to us will be when $m = n$, or when $m < n$. Suppose $m = n$, and $f \pitchfork 0$, and $f^{-1}(0) \subset L \times K$ for some compact K. We can conclude that for a generic set $D \subset L$, if $x \in D$, then $f_x \pitchfork 0$ and $f_x^{-1}(0)$ is a finite set. If $m < n$ and $f \pitchfork 0$, then for a generic set $D \subset L$, if $x \in D$, then $f_x^{-1}(0) = \varnothing$.

Let us see how the transversality theorem can be used to show that an $n \times n$ matrix is generically invertible. This shall be the basis of our proof in Section 7. The set $R^{n \times n}$ of matrices is certainly a manifold. Let e_{ij} be the matrix that is 0 everywhere except at the (i, j)th element, which is 1. The matrices e_{ij} form a basis for the manifold of $n \times n$ matrices. Consider also the compact $(n-1)$-dimensional manifold

$$S^{n-1} = \{z_1, \ldots, z_n \mid \Sigma_{i=1}^n z_i^2 = 1\}.$$

Let $f : R^{n \times n} \times S^{n-1} \to R^n$ be defined by $f(A, z) = zA$. Note that f is smooth. Moreover, A is invertible if and only if $f_A^{-1}(0)$ is empty. Suppose that we could show $f \pitchfork 0$. Then by the transversality theorem we could conclude that for a generic matrix A, $f_A \pitchfork 0$. But f_A maps an $(n-1)$ manifold into a n manifold; hence, as we have said, it can be transverse to 0 only if $f_A^{-1}(0)$ is empty, that is, only if A is invertible.

Thus, to conclude the proof that a generic matrix is invertible, it suffices to show that $f \pitchfork 0$. Let e_j be the jth unit vector in R^n. We must show that if $\bar{z}'\bar{A} = 0$, then for any direction e_j we can find some directional derivative of f, evaluated at $(\bar{A}, \bar{z})$, that gives a multiple λe_j of e_j, $\lambda \neq 0$. Note that

$$\left. \frac{\partial f}{\partial e_{ij}} \right|_{\bar{A}, \bar{z}} = \bar{z}_i e_j.$$

Since there must be at least one element $\bar{z}_i$ of $\bar{z} \in S^{n-1}$ that is nonzero, we conclude that indeed $\bar{D}f|_{\bar{A}, \bar{z}}$ has full rank, and hence that $f \pitchfork 0$.

In fact our proof can be slightly modified to produce a stronger result. Suppose that we replace the set of all matrices with a smaller manifold L

that has the property that for any $A \in L$, small symmetric perturbations of A are also in L. In other words, assume that we can have derivatives with respect to $e_{ij} + e_{ji}$. Then once again consider $f: L \times S^{n-1} \to R^n$, $f(A, z) = zA$. Let $\bar{z}'\bar{A} = 0$. Let e_j be given. If $\bar{z}_j \neq 0$, then

$$\frac{\partial f}{\partial(e_{jj} + e_{jj})}\bigg|_{\bar{A}, \bar{z}} = 2\bar{z}_j e_j$$

gives a nonzero multiple of e_j. If $\bar{z}_j = 0$, take some i with $\bar{z}_i \neq 0$. Then

$$\frac{\partial f}{\partial(e_{ij} + e_{ji})}\bigg|_{\bar{A}, \bar{z}} = \bar{z}_i e_j + \bar{z}_j e_i = \bar{z}_i e_j,$$

which is again a nonzero multiple of e_j.

One final fact that we use is that if D' is generic in D, which is generic in E, then D' is generic in E.

6   Regularity

In this section we prove the following two propositions:

Proposition 2 (Regularity). If A1–A4 and D1–D3 are satisfied, then for any choice of utilities $\mathbf{W} \in W^{H+1}$, there is a generic set $I(\mathbf{W})$ of endowments in I such that for every economy $(\mathbf{e}, \mathbf{W})$, with $\mathbf{e} \in I(\mathbf{W})$, the set of competitive equilibria[7] is a continuously differentiable function of the endowment allocation $\mathbf{e}$.

Proposition 3 (Strong regularity). If A1–A4 and D1–D3 are satisfied, there is a generic set of economies $D \subset E$ on which

the set of competitive equilibria is finite, and is a continuously differentiable function of the endowment and utility assignment $(\mathbf{e}, \mathbf{W})$;

the spot market competitive equilibrium corresponding to any competitive equilibrium portfolio allocation is, locally, a continuously differentiable function of the portfolio allocation $\mathbf{y}$.

Proof of generic regularity: Without loss of generality we may assume that asset 0 satisfies $r(s) \geq 0$ for all $s = 0, \ldots, S$. In other words, if $\bar{y}' = (1, 0, \ldots, 0)$, $R\bar{y} > 0$. It follows that for $q \in \text{int } \bar{C}$, $q_0 \neq 0$, and hence we can normalize asset prices by setting $q_0 = 1$. Similarly, we take commodity

$0(s)$ to be the *numéraire* in each state s. The price domain is thus $M = E^A \times E_{++}^{(S+1)L}$. This is an open set, and hence a manifold, of dimension $A + (S+1)L$. The excess demand function for assets and commodities other than the *numéraire* $a = 0$ and $0(s)$, $s \in S$, we denote by

$$f = (y, z): \mathbf{E} \times M \to E^A \times E^{(S+1)L};$$

no confusion should arise. Let us now fix the utility allocation $\mathbf{W}$. On account of Walras' law if all but the *numéraire* markets clear then they do too, so $f_{\mathbf{W}}^{-1}(0)$ is the graph of the equilibrium correspondence. Let us check that $f_{\mathbf{W}} \pitchfork 0$. Given an element $(\bar{e}, \bar{q}, \bar{p}) \in f_{\mathbf{W}}^{-1}(0)$ and any spot commodity $j(s)$, we can look at the change in excess demand when agent 0's endowment of good $j(s)$ is increased by 1 and the endowment of good $0(s)$ is decreased by $p_j(s)$. Evidently, demand stays the same, but now supply in the $j(s)$ market has increased by 1, so there is a net effect of $(0, \ldots, -1, \ldots, 0)$ on excess demand. Similarly, for any asset $a = 1, \ldots, A$, we can increase agent 0's endowment of good 0 in state s by $r_a(s) - q_a r_0(s)$, for each $s = 0, \ldots, S$. Clearly, the effect on agent 0's demand will be a decrease in asset a by 1, an increase in asset 0 by q_a, and nothing else. Thus, by varying over assets $a = 1, \ldots, A$, and commodities s and $s(j)$ ($s = 0, \ldots, S$, $j = 1, \ldots, L$), we can show $f_{\mathbf{W}} \pitchfork 0$. Notice that we have shown that $D_{e^0} f_{\mathbf{W}}$ has full rank, not using prices, or endowments for agents $1, \ldots, H$ at all.

It is also easy to see, given that I is contained in some compact set, and hence has compact closure, that $f_{\mathbf{W}}^{-1}(0) \subset I \times K$ for some compact set K. Hence we can apply the full transversality theorem, deducing that for any utility allocation $\mathbf{W}$ and a generic endowment $\mathbf{e} \in I(\mathbf{W})$, $f_{(\mathbf{e}, \mathbf{W})} \pitchfork 0$.

$$\text{Q.E.D.}$$

Proof of generic strong regularity: The proof of generic strong regularity is almost as simple. Let $N = \mathbf{E} \times M$ and let $f: N \to E^A \times E^{(S+1)L}$ be the non-*numéraire* excess demand function, this time with utilities free to vary as well.

Consider for each $h \in H$ the function $\hat{z}^h: E^{A+1} \times E_{++}^{(S+1)L} \to E^{(S+1)L}$ given by $\hat{z}^h(y^h, p)$, the excess demand by agent h for commodities $\ell(s)$, $s \in S$, $\ell = 1, \ldots, L$, given that the agent's portfolio is fixed at y^h. Let

$$\hat{z}: E^{(H+1)(A+1)} \times E_{++}^{(S+1)L} \to E^{(S+1)L}$$

be given by $\hat{z}(\mathbf{y}, p) = \hat{z}(y^0, \ldots, y^H, p) = \sum_{h \in H} \hat{z}^h(y^h, p)$. We must show that for a generic economy (W, e) in $\mathbf{E} = W^{H+1} \times I$, if $\mathbf{y}$ is an equilibrium portfolio allocation and if p is the corresponding vector of commodity prices, then $D_p \hat{z}(\mathbf{y}, p)$ is invertible.

The essential idea of the proof is borrowed from demand theory. We know that for any consumer, say $h = 0$, if we perturb the second derivatives $D^2 W^h$, without disturbing the first derivatives DW^h at the point of demand x^h, given prices p and income specified by y^h, then the demand $\hat{z}^h(y^h, p)$ will be unaffected at the old (y^h, p), but the derivative $D_p \hat{z}^h$ can be altered by any symmetric matrix K. [Recall the Slutsky equations with a single budget constraint: $D_p z = K - vz'$, where K is symmetric and negative definite, but otherwise K and v can be chosen arbitrarily by varying $\cdot D^2 W$, leaving p and z' fixed – see Geanakoplos and Polemarchakis (1980).]

Consider now the function

$$G: N \times S^{(S+1)L-1} \to E^A \times E^{(S+1)L} \times E^{(S+1)L}$$

given by $G(\eta, r) = (f(\eta), r'D_p \hat{z})$ where $\eta = (e, W, q, p)$ and where $\hat{z} = \hat{z}(e, W, y(\eta), p)$ and $D_p \hat{z}$ is the Jacobian with respect to the last argument, holding y fixed. The vector r is any element of the sphere $S^{(S+1)L-1}$ of dimension $(S+1)L-1$.

From the foregoing proof that $f \pitchfork 0$ and from the remarks on the generic invertibility of matrices admitting symmetric perturbations given in Section 5, together with our observation that by varying the utility W^0 of agent 0 in the right way, it is possible to perturb $D_p \hat{z}$ without changing f, it follows that $G \pitchfork 0$. Hence, by the transversality theorem, for a generic choice $(e, W) \in E$, $G_{(e, W)} \pitchfork 0$. But then since the domain of $G_{(e, W)}$ has dimension one less than the range, $G_{(e, W)}^{-1}(0) = \phi$. Thus for a generic $(e, W) \in E$, (e, W) is a regular economy and at each equilibrium $r'D_p \hat{z} = 0$ has no solution, that is, $D_p \hat{z}$ is invertible and (e, W) is strongly regular.

Q.E.D.

7   Suboptimality

Let us suppose that there are at least two assets. We can imagine $2H$ independent allocations of the assets. Let $a^{h'}$ be the amount of asset a that individual 0 gives individual h', $a = 0, ..., A$, $h' = 1, ..., H$. If $a^{h'}$ is small enough, then by our strong regularity theorem, after the transfer is made, it is possible to calculate the unique small change in the spot market allocation and prices that will clear those markets. Thus, it is possible to calculate the effect on the final utility levels of all the individuals resulting from such a reallocation of assets between two of them. One can imagine the $(H+1) \times [H \times (A+1)]$ matrix expressing the derivatives of W^h with respect to $a^{h'}$:

$$
\begin{array}{c}
\quad\quad \cdots \;\; 0^1 \;\; 1^1 \;\; 1^2 \;\; \cdots \;\; 1^H \;\; \cdots \\
\begin{array}{c} W^0 \\ W^1 \\ \vdots \\ W^H \end{array}
\left[\quad\quad A = \{ a_h^{h'} \}_{h \in H}^{h' \in H/\{0\}} \quad\quad\quad\quad \right]
\end{array}
$$

Notice in the diagram we have listed explicitly only $H+1$ of the possible columns. Clearly there are many more.

The remarkable property is this: To prove generic constrained suboptimality, it suffices to show that the matrix A has full row rank! For then in particular there is an infinitesimal change $da^{h'}$ in the various $a^{h'}$ that increases each W^h. This matrix formulation of suboptimality was first articulated by Smale (1974).

Let us consider more carefully whether we should expect this matrix to have full rank or not. Note first that A is the sum of two matrices, $A = T + P$, where T is the direct transfer effect on utilities and P is the effect on utilities caused by the price redistribution. Let us concentrate first on T:

$$
T = \begin{array}{c}
\quad\quad\quad 0^1 \quad\; 1^1 \quad\; 1^2 \quad\; 1^3 \quad\; 1^H \\
\begin{array}{c} W^0 \\ W^1 \\ W^2 \\ W^3 \\ \vdots \\ W^H \end{array}
\left[\begin{array}{ccccc}
-q_0 & -q_1 & -q_1 & -q_1 & -q_1 \\
q_0 & q_1 & 0 & 0 & 0 \\
0 & 0 & q_1 & 0 & 0 \\
0 & 0 & 0 & q_1 & 0 \\
\vdots & \vdots & \vdots & \vdots & \vdots \\
0 & 0 & 0 & 0 & q_1
\end{array} \right]
\end{array}
$$

We have normalized the utilities by the appropriate marginal utility of income. One sees at once that the matrix T does not have full row rank: Indeed, letting u be the vector in E^{H+1} consisting of all 1's, $u'T = 0$. The redistribution of assets alone, without any further change in the spot markets, will not cause a Pareto improvement. On the other hand, looking at the columns $1^1, \ldots, 1^H$ (assuming $q_1 \neq 0$), it is clear that the rank of T is already H.

7.1 Suboptimality

Proposition 4 (Suboptimality). If the asset market is incomplete (S), and if A1–A4 and D1–D3 are satisfied, then for any economy $(e, \mathbf{W}) \in D$, a generic set, all competitive equilibria are suboptimal.

Proof: Consider another asset α not in the span of R, and now replace column 0^1 in T with α^1, getting the matrix $\hat{T}$. We can easily show that for a generic economy, at each equilibrium the corresponding $\hat{T}$ has full row rank. In fact, by inspection of $\hat{T}$ it is obvious that if the sum of elements in the column α^1 is not equal to zero, then $\hat{T}$ has full row rank.

Let $G: N \to E^A \times E^{(S+1)L} \times E$ be given by $G(\eta) = (f(\eta), \Sigma_{h \in H} \alpha_h^1)$, where α_h^1 is the hth element in the column α^1 evaluated at assignment of goods given by $f(\eta)$, where $\eta = (\mathbf{e}, \mathbf{W}, q, p)$. We shall show now that it is always possible to find a linear perturbation of individual 0's utility W^0 that will leave f and α_h^1, $h = 1, ..., H$, unaffected, but will change α_0^1. Since we have already shown that $f \pitchfork 0$, this will imply that $G \pitchfork 0$, and that $G^{-1}(0) = \phi$; hence $\Sigma_{h \in H} a_h' \neq 0$ whenever $f(\eta) = 0$.

Perturb W^0 by the linear function $x \to \Delta \cdot x$ given as follows. Since the asset α payoff is not in the span of R, we can find $\Delta_0 = (\Delta_0(s); s \in S)$ such that $\Delta_0' R = 0$ and yet $\Delta_0 \cdot \alpha \neq 0$. That is, if we perturb the $0(s)$th marginal utilities of W^0 by $\Delta_0(s)$, $s \in S$, then the marginal utilities to agent 0 of assets $a = 0, 1, ..., A$ are all unchanged, while that of the hypothetical asset does change. Hence α_0^1 must be different. On the other hand, if we let $\Delta_\ell(s) = p_\ell(s) \Delta_0(s)$, $s \in S$, $\ell = 1, ..., L$, then individual 0's demand for commodities and existing assets (given that α is unavailable) is left unaltered.

Q.E.D.

7.2   Constrained suboptimality

To prove the generic constrained suboptimality of competitive equilibrium allocations when the asset market is incomplete is of course much more difficult than proving Pareto suboptimality, because it must be done with the existing assets. For ease of notation, and not because it makes the proof easier, we shall assume W^h is separable:

$$W^h(x) = \sum_{s \in S} \pi^h(s) U^h(x(s); s).$$

A central role in our analysis is played by the vector of marginal utilities of the *numéraire* good over the different states of nature:

$$\nabla^h = (..., \nabla^h(s), ...), \quad \text{where } \nabla^h(s) = \frac{\partial U^h(x(s); s)}{\partial x_0(s)} \bigg/ \mu^h \text{ for } s = 0, 1, ..., S.$$

Recall that at an equilibrium $(q, p, \mathbf{y}, \mathbf{x})$, we must have $R\nabla^h = q$ for all $h \in H$. We have already seen that when asset markets are incomplete, then generically the vectors ∇^h are not equal.

Consider a strongly regular economy $(\mathbf{W}, \mathbf{e})$ and one of its competitive equilibria, $(q, p, \mathbf{y}, \mathbf{x})$. Recall that by definition the associated excess demand function, with the portfolios y^h held fixed, for the $(S+1)L$ non-*numéraire* commodities given by $\hat{z}(\mathbf{y}, p)$ has $D_p\hat{z}$ invertible. We can thus calculate the change in equilibrium spot prices when $\mathbf{y}$ is perturbed from the implicit function theorem:

(i) $dp = -(D_p\hat{z})^{-1}(D_\mathbf{y}\hat{z})\,d\mathbf{y}.$

This expression can be made more explicit after we introduce some notation. Let $V^h \in E^{(S+1)L}$ be the vector of income effects. We can think of V^h as a $(S+1)$ list of L-vectors, where the L-vector $V^h(s)$ gives the additional consumption that would occur in the L goods, $\ell(s) = 1(s), ..., L(s)$ given an extra unit of state s income. Notice that the separability hypothesis allows us to assume that an extra dollar in state s has no effect on consumption in state $s' \neq s$. Define a *list* α as an ordered collection of $(S+1)$ $i \times j$ matrices. Suppose β is a list of $(S+1)$ $j \times k$ matrices. Then we shall write $\alpha \times \beta$ to mean the list of $(S+1)$ $i \times k$ matrices obtained by the componentwise product of α and β.

Let us return to our expression for dp. Recall that $a^{h'}$ is the gift of one unit of asset a by agent 0 to agent h'. Let R_a be the ath column of R. Think of R_a as a list of 1×1 matrices; then for column $a^{h'}$,

(ii) $dp_{a^{h'}} = -(D_p\hat{z})^{-1}(V^{h'} - V^0) \times R_a da^{h'}.$

Let $\hat{z}^h$ be the $(S+1)L$ vector of excess demands of agent h. We can think of $\hat{z}^h$ as an $(S+1)$ list of $1 \times L$ matrices. We can now write the expression for the change in utility dW^h given a change in the portfolio allocation $d\mathbf{y}$ (using the envelope theorem):

(iii) $dW^h = \nabla^h \cdot R\,dy^h - \nabla^h \cdot (\hat{z}^h \times D_\mathbf{y} p).$

From this expression it is easy to derive the matrices $A = T + P$. To calculate $\partial W^h/\partial a^{h'}$, for $h' \neq 0$, set $dy_a^{h'} = 1 = -dy_a^0$ and $dy_{a'}^{h''} = 0$ for all other h'' and a'.

The first term in (iii), $\nabla^h \cdot R\,dy^h$ is the direct effect of the transfer of assets dy^h, assuming all prices remain constant. It can equivalently be written $q \cdot dy^h$. The second term is the effect on utility produced by the change in relative prices p stemming from the portfolio change $d\mathbf{y}$.

We must now show that for a generic economy, there is no vector $r \in S^H$, the H-dimensional sphere, with $r'A = 0$. By combining expressions (i), (ii), and (iii) we see that there are a number of special cases where $r' = (1, 1, ..., 1)$ solves $r'A = 0$, and hence allows for constrained optimality. [Most of these cases have been pointed out by Stiglitz (1982).]

7.2.1 Some nongeneric examples where constrained optimality is possible.

First, suppose that markets are complete, so $A = S$. From Arrow's (1953) analysis, we know that we must be at a full Pareto optimum. We can see that locally, in our analysis, by checking that if R is square, then $R'\nabla^h = q$ has a unique solution ∇^h, so all the ∇^h are the same, and we must be at a full local Pareto optimum. Of course, any Pareto optimum must be a constrained optimum. Indeed, taking $r = (1, \ldots, 1)$ allows $r'A = 0$. For the first term of (iii), corresponding to the T matrix, we already saw that $(1, \ldots, 1)T = 0$, no matter what the ∇^h, since $\Sigma_{h \in H} dy^h = 0$ and $R'\nabla^h = q$ for all h. As for the second term, when all the ∇^h are identical, we obtain $\Sigma_{h \in H} \nabla^h \cdot (\hat{z}^h \times dp) = \nabla^h \cdot (\Sigma_{h \in H} \hat{z}^h \times dp) = \nabla^h \cdot 0 \cdot dp = 0$, since in equilibrium $\Sigma_{h \in H} \hat{z}^h = 0$.

There are other cases when we do not have full optimality, and yet we may have constrained optimality. Suppose that $A < S$, and that the ∇^h are not colinear at some equilibrium. If at the equilibrium there is no trade, $\hat{z}^h = 0$ for all h, then the second expression disappears, and again we must have $(1, \ldots, 1)A = (1, \ldots, 1)T = 0$.

Alternatively, if $V^{h'} = V^0$ for all h', then we see from (ii) that once again the second term in (iii) disappears. Relative spot prices will not readjust when income is redistributed among the agents. The standard examples of equality among income effects occur when they are all equal to zero. For example, if there is only one good, good 0, in each state, then of course nothing is ever spent on goods $1, \ldots, L$. This is the case studied by Diamond (1967), for which he proved constrained optimality. Another example is where $W^h = \Sigma_{s \in S} \pi^h(s) U^h(x(s); s)$ and each $U^h(s)$ can be written $U^h(x_0(s), x_1(s), \ldots, x_L(s)) = x_0(s) + \hat{U}^h(x_1(s), \ldots, x_L(s); s)$, that is, the case of constant marginal utility of "money" (the *numéraire* good).

A final case to consider is where all individuals h have identical and homothetic von Neumann–Morgenstern utilities, $W^h = \Sigma_{s \in S} \pi^h(s) U(s)$.

In the next section we show that all of the above cases are fortuitous accidents. If we are allowed to perturb the endowments, typically there will be trade in equilibrium. If we are allowed quadratic perturbations of the utilities, then typically the income effect terms V^h will be distinct.

Before moving to the formal proof, let us note that if the portfolio reallocation dy were required to satisfy the budget constraint $q \cdot dy^h = 0$ for all h, then the direct effect would entirely disappear. The second term would be slightly altered, giving

(iv) $\qquad \dfrac{\partial W^h}{\partial a^{h'}} = \nabla^h \cdot \left\{ \hat{z}^h \times \left[-(D_p \hat{z})^{-1} (V^{h'} - V^0) \times \left(R_a - \dfrac{q_a}{q_0} R_0 \right) \right] \right\}.$

The same special cases of constrained optimality apply here as well.

7.2.2 Proof of constrained suboptimality

Proposition 5 (Constrained suboptimality). Suppose $0 < 2L \leq H < SL$. If the asset market is incomplete, S, and if A1–A4, D1–D3, and CS are satisfied, then for any economy $(\mathbf{e}, \mathbf{W}) \in D$, a generic set, all competitive equilibria are constrained suboptimal as long as there are at least two assets, $(A+1) \geq 2$. If $(A+1) \geq 3$, this remains true even if the reallocation of assets must satisfy the asset budget constraint for each individual at the equilibrium asset prices.

Remark: An upper bound on H is necessary if Pareto improvement is to take place through reallocations that satisfy the original budget constraint. From (iv) we know that we can write

$$D_y W^h = (\nabla^h \times \hat{z}^h) \cdot D_y p,$$

and there cannot be more than $(S+1)L$ linearly independent vectors $(\nabla^h \times \hat{z}^h)$.

Proof of constrained suboptimality: Suppose that $0 < 2L \leq H < SL$ and that D is a generic set of economies such that all economies in D are regular and strongly regular, and each of their equilibria satisfy:

(1) For the $H+1$ different portfolio reallocations $d\mathbf{y}$ given by $d0^1, d1^1, ..., d1^H$, the $(S+1)L$-dimensional vectors $D_y p \, d0^1, ..., D_y p \, d1^H$ are linearly independent, even if attention is restricted to any SL of their coordinates (by ignoring an arbitrary state).

(2) Given any vector $r \in S^H$, it is possible in at least S of the $S+1$ states s to arbitrarily perturb $\sum_{h \in H} r^h V^h(s) \hat{z}^h(s)$ by perturbing the economy $(\mathbf{e}, \mathbf{W})$ in D without changing aggregate excess demand, or the derivative of aggregate excess demand $D_p \hat{z}$ or the income effect terms V^h for any $h \in H$, all evaluated at the given equilibrium $(q, p, \mathbf{y}, \mathbf{x})$ for $(\mathbf{e}, \mathbf{W})$.

Notice that condition (1) is at least possible if $H+1 \leq SL$, and condition (2) is possible if $H > L$. Notice that (2) implies that it is possible to alter the weighted sum $\sum_{r \in H} r^h \nabla^h(s) z^h(s)$ without altering the sum $\sum_{h \in H} z^h(s)$ of excess demands. We shall show that in fact there is a generic D where both (1) and (2) hold. Clearly (2) could not hold for $r = (1, ..., 1)$ if all the ∇^h were identical under all perturbations of (W, e).

Given (1) and (2), let $N = D \times E^A \times E_{++}^{(S+1)L}$ and consider the map F: $N \times S^H \to E^A \times E^{(S+1)L} \times E^{H+1}$ given by $F(\eta, r) = (f(\eta), r'A)$, where η is an economy and equilibrium, f is the non-*numéraire* excess demand function, $r \in S^H$, and A is the matrix $T + P$ of utility effects of the $H+1$ portfolio reallocations described in the last section. Since we have already shown that $f \pitchfork 0$, it suffices to show that by perturbations in D that leave f unaffected, we can make the function $\mu(\eta, r) = r'A$ transverse to 0. We know from the last section that for each column $a^{h'}$ of A, we can write the corresponding entry of $r'P = r'(A - T)$ as:

$$\mu(\eta, r) = \left(\sum_{h \in H} (r^h \nabla^h \times \hat{z}^h) \right) \cdot (D_y p \, da^{h'}).$$

From hypothesis (2) we know that for SL coordinates we can perturb the vector $\gamma = (\sum_{h \in H} r^h \nabla^h \times \hat{z}^h)$ arbitrarily, and from hypothesis (1) the vectors $dp_{a^{h'}} = (D_y p \, da^{h'})$ are linearly independent even when restricted to those SL coordinates. Hence for each column of the P matrix there is a perturbation of the economy $(\mathbf{e}, \mathbf{W})$ that changes γ in a way which has nonzero dot product with $dp_{a^{h'}}$, and zero with all the other H vectors of price changes. At the same time this perturbation leaves the aggregate excess demands, hence f unchanged, and also the derivatives $D_p \hat{z}$. But recall that each column $dp_{a^h} = (D_y p) \, da^{h'} = -(D_p \hat{z})^{-1}(V^{h'} - V^0) \times R_a da^{h'}$, and by hypothesis (2) none of this is changed by the perturbation, nor is $r'T$.

Thus, we have shown that by perturbing $(\mathbf{e}, \mathbf{W})$ we can change any element of $r'A$, without changing the others, and without changing f. This implies that $F \pitchfork 0$. But then for a generic set of economies $D' \subset D \subset E$, if $(W, e) \in D'$, then $F_{(\mathbf{e}, \mathbf{w})} \pitchfork 0$. But the domain of $F_{(\mathbf{e}, \mathbf{w})}$ has one less dimension than the range, hence $F_{(W, e)}^{-1}(0) = \varnothing$. Thus, for a generic $(\mathbf{e}, \mathbf{W})$ in D, if $f(\mathbf{e}, \mathbf{W}, q, p) = 0$, then $r'A$ has no solution. In other words, for a generic $(\mathbf{e}, \mathbf{W}) \in E$, all its equilibria are constrained suboptimal. Thus to verify our proof, we need only check that there is a generic set D of strongly regular economies that satisfy conditions (1) and (2).

Before proceeding to this part of the proof, notice that we have made no use of the direct utility effects of the transfer. Exactly the same theorem would hold if in addition we required that $q \cdot dy^h = 0$ for all $h \in H$. (We would then need to require at least three assets.)

Let us begin by reviewing what can be changed by perturbations of the utilities. Note that [as shown, for example, in Geanakoplos and Polemarchakis (1980)] the Jacobian (with portfolios held fixed) of non-*numéraire* excess demand $\hat{z}^h(p)$ at a point p in state s may be written

$$\lambda^h(s) K^h(s) - V^h(s) z^h(s)',$$

where K is symmetric and negative definite, but otherwise $K^h(s)$ and $V^h(s)$ can be perturbed arbitrarily by altering the second derivatives $D^2U^h(s)$ at $x^h(s) = e^h(s) + z^h(s)$ without changing the demand at p. To verify that (1) generically holds, we must show that $(V^1 - V^0) \times R_0$ and $(V^{h'} - V^0) \times R_1$ for $h' \in H/\{0\}$ are linearly independent when restricted to any SL coordinates at every equilibrium of a generic economy. Note first that, on account of CS, perhaps by relabeling assets, we may assume that $r_1(s) \neq 0$ for all $s \in S$. We also know from CS that there is another asset, say 0, such that restricted to any S states R_0 and R_1 are linearly independent. To verify condition (1) then it suffices to use our standard transversality argument. Take $F = (f, g)$, where f is excess demand and $g = 0$ only if (1) is not met. Then, since we can perturb the V^h, and hence g, without disturbing f, generically $F^{-1}(0) = \varnothing$. We have given this argument too many times to repeat it again formally here.

As for condition (2), note again that if $H \geq L$, it can be shown in the usual manner that for any set of $L + 1$ distinct individuals, $h_0, \ldots, h_L$, the differences $V^{h_0}(s) - V^{h_1}(s), \ldots, V^{h_0}(s) - V^{h_L}(s)$ are all linearly independent for all s at any equilibrium of a generically chosen economy. In particular, it follows that any vector $\Delta \in E^L$ may be written as a linear combination of these L differences. From now on D shall denote the open, dense, full-measured (i.e., generic) set of economies that are regular, strongly regular, to which condition (1) applies, and for which at any equilibrium, and state s, and collection of $L + 1$ individuals, $\{V^{h'} - V^{h_0}\}$ span E^L.

We now want to show that we can perturb a weighted sum of individual excess demands without disturbing the aggregate excess demand (unweighted sum) or its derivatives. It is not difficult to increase individual 0's excess demand and decrease some other individual's by the same amount, thus changing the weighted but not the unweighted sum. This, however, is not enough because from the Slutsky equation we know that such a change would affect the derivatives of the excess demand. Our method consists of choosing changes in the excess demands that produce symmetric changes in the Jacobian of the excess demand, which can then be undone by simultaneously perturbing the utilities.

Consider now an arbitrary perturbation Δ of the endowment of agent h_0's non-*numéraire* L commodities in state s at some equilibrium (q, p) of an economy in D. Perturb the endowment $e_0^h(s)$ by just the right amount $\Delta_0(s)$ to keep h's income constant at the equilibrium spot prices $p(s)$, $\Delta_0(s) + (s) \cdot \Delta = 0$. Choose another consumer $h' \neq h_0$ and perturb the h' endowment $(e_0^{h'}(s), e^{h'}(s))$ by $-(\Delta_0(s), \Delta)$. Then aggregate demand is unchanged though individual h_0's excess demand has changed by $-\Delta$. But we can do even better than that, since the perturbation to h_0 and h' alone may change $D_p z$. Let us write $\Delta = \sum_{i=1}^{L} \Delta^i$, where each Δ^i is a scalar multiple of $V^{h_i}(s) - V^{h_0}(s)$ for the $L+1$ distinct individuals $h_0, h_1, \ldots, h_L$. If we altered the endowments of agents h_i, $i = 1, \ldots, L$, by $-(\Delta_0^i(s), \Delta^i)$, where $\Delta_0^i(s) = -p(s) \cdot \Delta^i$, then once again agent h_0's excess demand in state s has been changed arbitrarily by $-\Delta$, without changing aggregate excess demand. Furthermore, from the Slutsky decomposition

$$D_{p(s)} \hat{z}^h(s) = \lambda^h(s) K^h(s) - V^h(s) z^h(s)',$$

we see that the derivative of aggregate excess demand has been altered by $\sum_{i=1}^{L} (V^{h_i}(s) - V^{h_0}(s))(\Delta^i)'$, which is symmetric. Hence by simultaneously perturbing some agent's K matrix, we can also maintain the derivative $D_{p(s)} \hat{z}(s)$ of aggregate excess demand in state s.

Suppose finally that the numbers m_s^h are given, and that we are interested not in $\Delta + \sum_{i=1}^{L} (-\Delta^i)$, but in $\beta = m^{h_0}(s)\Delta + \sum_{i=1}^{L} m^{h_i}(s)(-\Delta^i)$. When, by choosing Δ arbitrarily and then constructing Δ^i as above, can we be sure to obtain any vector β? Clearly, if all the m^{h_i} are the same for $i = 1, \ldots, L$, it is impossible to achieve any β other than 0, since by construction $\Delta - \sum_{i=1}^{L} \Delta^i = 0$. On the other hand, we now show that if $m^{h_i}(s) \neq m^{h_0}(s) \neq 0$, then it is possible. Let B be the $L \times L$ matrix whose ith column is $V^{h_i} - V^{h_0}$, and let m be the $L \times L$ diagonal matrix with ith diagonal element equal to $m^{h_i}(s)$. Then we must solve $\beta = [m^{h_0}(s)I - BmB^{-1}]\Delta$. Clearly, this has a solution for all β if and only if the matrix BmB^{-1} does not have an eigenvalue equal to $m^{h_0}(s) \neq 0$, that is, if and only if $m^{h_i}(s) \neq m^{h_0}(s) \neq 0$ for all $i = 1, \ldots, L$.

In summary, we have shown so far that given $L+1$ numbers

$$m^{h_0}(s), \ldots, m^{h_L}(s),$$

if $m^{h_0}(s) \neq 0$ and $m^{h_0}(s) \neq m^{h_i}(s)$, $i = 1, \ldots, L$, it follows that by perturbations of the economy $(\mathbf{e}, \mathbf{W})$ in D it is possible to perturb

$$\sum_{i=0}^{L} m^{h_i}(s) \hat{z}^{h_i}(s)$$

at a given equilibrium arbitrarily, without affecting aggregate excess demand, in any state, or the derivative of excess demand, or the income efffect terms V^h of any individual h at the given equilibrium.

We are interested finally in the case where $m^h(s) = r^h \nabla^h(s)$, where $r \in S^H$ can be arbitrary. Suppose that $\nabla^h(s)/\nabla^h(s') \neq \nabla^{h'}(s)/\nabla^{h'}(s')$ for any pairs $h \neq h'$, $s \neq s'$ and that $\nabla^h(s) \neq 0$ for all h, s. We will show that in at least all but one of the states there are individuals $h_0, h_1, \ldots, h_L$ such that $0 \neq r^{h_0}\nabla^{h_0}(s) \neq r^{h_i}\nabla^{h_i}(s)$ for $i = 1, \ldots, L$. To see this, take h_0 so that $r^{h_0} \neq 0$ (there must be one since $r \in S^H$). Take any s; by hypothesis

$$m^{h_0} = r^{h_0} \nabla^{h_0}(s) \neq 0,$$

since ∇^{h_0} has no zero elements. Suppose it is impossible to find L other agents with $r^h \nabla^h(s) \neq m^{h_0}(s)$. Then if $H \geq 2L$, it must be that for at least L of them, $m^h(s) = m^{h_0}(s)$. But then by the hypothesis on the $\nabla^h(s)$, $0 \neq m^{h_0}(s) \neq m^{h'}(s')$ for all other states s', for all of these individuals.

Thus, to conclude the proof we need only check that for a generic set of economies in D, at each equilibrium $\nabla^h(s)/\nabla^h(s') \neq \nabla^{h'}(s)/\nabla^{h'}(s')$, if $h \neq h'$ and $s \neq s'$. If asset markets are incomplete by 2, $(A \leq S-2)$, then there is some $\nabla \in E^{S+1}$ with $\nabla(s) \neq 0 = \nabla(s')$ such that $\nabla'R = 0$. By adding ∇ to ∇^h but not to $\nabla^{h'}$, we can change $\nabla^h(s)/\nabla^h(s')$ but not excess demand or $\nabla^{h'}(s)/\nabla^{h'}(s')$. A familiar transversality argument will then show that for a generic economy in D, all its equilibria satisfy the above gradient conditions.

If $A = S-1$, then there is a unique ∇ with $\nabla R = 0$, and it may happen that $\nabla^h(s)/\nabla^h(s') = \nabla(s)/\nabla(s')$, so we must give a slightly longer argument. Perturb all the ∇^h by adding ϵ in the sth position. Add $\epsilon r(s)$, the sth row of R, to q. Then still $R'\nabla^h = q$ for all h. Change each y_0^h by dy^h to maintain, at the new prices q, $q \cdot y^h = 0$. Change each consumer's 0th endowment in every state by $de_0^h(s) = r_0(s) dy^h$. This does not change aggregate excess demand $(\Sigma_{h \in H} dy^h = 0 = \Sigma_{h \in H} e_0^h(s))$, but it does change all the $\nabla^h(s)/\nabla^h(s')$. Thus, generically, we cannot have $\nabla^h(s)/\nabla^h(s') = \nabla(s)/\nabla(s')$ in equilibrium. But now perturb ∇^h by adding ∇, without changing $\nabla^{h'}$.   Q.E.D.

8   Conclusion

The normative appeal of competitive equilibrium rests nowadays on its Pareto optimality. Yet, the analysis of this chapter shows, as Stiglitz has suggested, that when the asset market is incomplete the existing opportunities for trade are typically not efficiently used in a competitive equilibrium. To be sure, there are exceptions: If all consumers have identical income effects or if there is no trade, incomplete markets' competitive equilibria can be constrained Pareto optimal. But we believe that for general economies the notion of the efficiency of the market must be reexamined. Kenneth Arrow, among others, has for a long time asserted that markets are incomplete and therefore to move toward Pareto optimality might require active (government) intervention in the economic arena. The preceding analysis strengthens that assertion by showing that even if the government is limited to the same assets as the market, it can still typically effect Pareto improvements.

When markets are incomplete, knowledge of demand functions is not sufficient information to recover preferences. (Think, for example, of the case of two states of nature and no assets; in that case it is impossible to deduce the relative importance to a consumer of consumption in the two states from a knowledge of the demand functions.) Whether it is generically possible to effect a Pareto-improving portfolio reallocation when knowledge of investors' preferences is limited to market demand functions is an open question.

To be sure, in order to effect a Pareto-improving reallocation of assets, the government must be able to forecast all the resulting adjustments in spot market prices and their effects on individual's utilities. This is an enormous information burden, which it may be argued the government cannot carry. But such an argument against market intervention, based on the presumed ignorance of the government, is radically different from the standard argument for Pareto optimality that does not rely on any lack of information.

NOTES

1 We show in Section 6 that, generically, in a neighborhood of a competitive equilibrium, the equilibrium prices and allocations in the commodity spot markets are uniquely determined by the asset allocation.
2 We use the same symbol to denote a set and also its last element – no confusion should arise.
3 E denotes the real numbers, E_+ the nonnegative reals, and E_{++} the positive reals. Similarly, we use E^k, E^k_+, and E^k_{++}.
4 Given two vectors y and z, we write $y \geq z$; $y > z$; $y \gg z$ to mean $y_i \geq z_i$ for all i; $y_i \geq z_i$ for all i and $y \neq z$; and finally $y_i > z_i$ for all i, respectively.
5 It suffices, more generally, that for each state there be an a priori specified bundle of commodities in which the returns of all assets are denominated.
6 For the transversality theorem that follows, smooth can be taken to mean $\max[1, m-n]$ times continuously differentiable.
7 A set is a differentiable function if all its elements are differentiable functions.

REFERENCES

Arrow, K. J. (1951), "An extension of the basic theorems of classical welfare economics," in J. Neyman (Ed.), *Proceedings of the second Berkeley symposium on mathematical statistics and probability,* Berkeley and Los Angeles: University of California Press, pp. 507–32.
Arrow, K. J. (1953), "Le rôle des valeurs boursières pour la répartition la meilleure des risques," *Econometrica,* Colloques Internationaux du C.N.R.S., 11, 41–7.
Arrow, K. J. and G. Debreu, (1954), "Existence of equilibrium for a competitive economy," *Econometrica,* 22: 265–90.

Balasko, Y. (1975), "Some results on uniqueness and on stability of equilibrium in general equilibrium theory," *Journal of Mathematical Economics,* 2: 95–118.

Cass, D. (1984), "Competitive equilibrium with incomplete financial markets," Working Paper No. 84–09, C.A.R.E.S.S., University of Pennsylvania.

Debreu, G. (1951), "The coefficient of resource utilization," *Econometrica,* 19: 273–92.

Debreu, G. (1959), *Theory of value,* New Haven: Yale University Press.

Debreu, G. (1970), "Economies with finite set of equilibria," *Econometrica,* 38: 387–92.

Debreu, G. (1972), "Smooth preferences," *Econometrica,* 40: 603–15.

Diamond, P. (1967), "The role of the stock market in a general equilibrium model with technological uncertainty," *American Economic Review,* 57: 759–76.

Dubey, P. (1978), "Finiteness and inefficiency of Nash equilibria," Discussion Paper No. 508R, Cowles Foundation, Yale University.

Duffie, D. (1985), "Stochastic equilibria with incomplete financial markets," mimeo, Graduate School of Business, Stanford University.

Eilenberg, S. and D. Montgomery (1946), "Fixed point theorems for multi-valued transformations," *American Journal of Mathematics,* 68: 214–22.

Geanakoplos, J. and A. Mas-Colell (1985), "Real indeterminacy with financial assets," mimeo.

Geanakoplos, J. and H. Polemarchakis (1980), "On the disaggregation of excess demand functions," *Econometrica,* 48: 315–31.

Greenwald, B. and J. Stiglitz (1984), "Pecuniary and market mediated externalities," Working Paper No. 1304, N.B.E.R.

Grossman, S. J. (1977), "A characterization of the optimality of equilibrium with incomplete markets," *Journal of Economic Theory,* 15: 1–15.

Hart, O. D. (1974), "On the existence of equilibrium in securities models," *Journal of Economic Theory,* 19: 293–311.

Hart, O. D. (1975), "On the optimality of equilibrium when the market structure is incomplete," *Journal of Economic Theory,* 11: 418–43.

Lange, O. (1942), "The foundations of welfare analysis," *Econometrica,* 10: 215–28.

Newbery, D. M. G. and J. E. Stiglitz (1979), "Pareto inferior trade and optimal trade policy," Discussion Paper No. 23, Department of Economics, Cambridge University.

Newbery, D. M. G. and J. E. Stiglitz (1982), "The choice of technique and the optimality of equilibrium with rational expectations," *Journal of Political Economy,* 90: 223–46.

Radner, R. (1968), "Competitive equilibrium under uncertainty," *Econometrica,* 36: 31–58.

Radner, R. (1972), "Existence of equilibrium of plan, prices and price expectations," *Econometrica,* 40: 289–303.

Smale, S. (1974), "Global analysis and economics III: Pareto optima and price equilibria," *Journal of Mathematical Economics,* 1: 107–18.

Stiglitz, J. E. (1982), "The inefficiency of stock market equilibrium," *Review of Economic Studies,* 49: 241–61.

Werner, Jan (1985), "Equilibrium in economies with incomplete financial markets," *Journal of Economic Theory,* 36: 110–19.

CHAPTER 4

Asset pricing theories

Michael Rothschild

1   The asset pricing problem

A central problem of the analysis of private economies is determining the prices of commodities that are risky. Almost all work on this problem takes as its starting point the extension of general equilibrium theory to uncertainty, which is due to Arrow (1963–4) and Debreu (1959). However, the Arrow–Debreu model, even when modified to take account of imperfect and heterogeneous information, can do little more than state conditions for the existence of equilibrium and the compatibility of equilibrium with various measures of efficiency. Not surprisingly, it is difficult to think of any empirical work that tests or otherwise exposes this model to data. In sharp contrast, modern theories of asset pricing offer very sharp predictions about relative asset prices; these theories have spawned hundreds of empirical papers that purport to confirm or reject various aspects of the theory. In this chapter, I will offer a critical perspective on two leading theories of asset pricing: the capital asset pricing model [henceforth CAPM, which is due to Treynor (1961), Sharpe (1964), Lintner (1965), and Mossin (1966)] and the arbitrage pricing theory (APT), which is due to Steven Ross (1976). I shall largely focus on the theoretical properties of the models. Indeed, one major purpose is to demonstrate a simple analytical structure that makes developing and comparing the two theories straightforward. Since this is an empirical subject, much of what follows is directed toward empirical work.

The plan of this essay is as follows: In the remainder of this section I set out the asset pricing problem and establish some notation. The next

I am grateful to Gary Chamberlain, Bernd Luedecke, and James Stock for helpful conversations and to the National Science Foundation for research support. A preliminary version of this contribution was presented as an invited address at the August 1984 meeting of the Econometric Society in Sydney, Australia.

section discusses the unusually rich data that can be used to examine asset pricing in the United States. I argue that for a theory to use this data effectively, it must be capable of making predictions when analysts have less complete information than the agents whose actions determine prices. The third section sets out a mathematical framework within which asset pricing theories can be developed. In the fourth and fifth sections the CAPM and the APT are developed and assayed. Much is made of the fact that the APT (but not the CAPM) is well suited for situations in which the analyst has less good information than the agents whose actions determine asset prices.

1.1   *The context*

The question this theory attempts to answer may be stated simply: Given a bunch of random variables, what determines their prices? In the simplest case, and the only one discussed here, the random variables are being traded this period for money and yield random payoffs next period. [1] A natural choice of units for this problem would be expected value. We could specify z_i as the amount of asset i needed to provide an expected next period payoff of 1. The literature generally chooses a different normalization. Following it we specify that x_i is an asset that can be bought for one dollar. This specification is strange to an equilibrium theorist for it assumes that prices have been determined already. In most of economics, one starts out with preferences, technology, and supply and asks whether or not equilibrium, and thus equilibrium prices, can exist. In asset pricing theory, for the most part, one starts with a set of equilibrium prices and asks what conditions they must satisfy. Let $E(x_i) = \mu_i$ be the mean return on asset i. If there is a riskless asset, of which more later, and it has a rate of return of ρ (that is, for one dollar, one can purchase enough of the riskless asset to ensure a return of ρ dollars next period), then the risk premium for asset i is $\mu_i - \rho$. The aim of asset pricing theories is to explain why different assets have different risk premia.

1.2   *Notation*

At this point, it is appropriate to introduce some notation and assumptions. There is a large number of assets, potentially a countable infinity. As mentioned, x_i is the return from a one-dollar investment in asset i. We assume that means and variances are uniformly bounded and denoted by

$$\mu_i = E(x_i), \qquad \sigma_{ii} = V(x_i), \qquad \sigma_{ij} = \text{cov}(x_i, x_j). \qquad (1)$$

We suppose that the assets are arranged in order and we shall often have occasion to refer to the vector of the means of the first N assets, which we denote μ_N. The corresponding variance–covariance matrix is Σ_N. We assume that Σ_N is nonsingular for all N. The matrix of second moments is

$$\Gamma_N = \Sigma_N + \mu_N \mu_N'. \tag{2}$$

Throughout this essay we will be concerned with linear combinations of assets, which we will call portfolios. In parts of the sequel, particularly those dealing with conditional inference, it will be useful to maintain the pedantic distinction between a portfolio that is a random variable and the distribution of that random variable. That is, included in the definition of the random variable x_i are the events in which they give payoffs of various amounts. The probability of these events cannot be specified without specifying a probability distribution. This distinction is important because, when we deal with conditional inference, we shall be concerned with the relationship of different probability assessments of the same events. Thus, if $p = \Sigma_i \alpha_i x_i$ and $q = \Sigma_i \gamma_i x_i$ are portfolios *and* if we specify first and second moments of returns as in (1) and (2), we can write $\operatorname{cov}(p, q) = \alpha' \Sigma \gamma$ and $E(pq) = \alpha' \Gamma \gamma$.

1.3   *Internal theories*

Given that the problem is to explain mean returns or risk premia, we can distinguish between two kinds of theories. *Internal* theories explain expected returns in terms of the characteristics of the probability distribution of returns on all assets. For the most part, internal theories are second-moment theories. That is, they seek to explain means in terms of variances and covariances. The CAPM is a theory of this sort. Its pricing equation is

$$\mu_i = \rho + \beta_i(\mu_M - \rho), \tag{3}$$

where p_M is the market portfolio (normalized to cost one dollar), $\beta_i = \operatorname{cov}(x_i, p_M)/V(p_M)$, and μ_M and $V(p_M)$ are the mean and variance of p_M.

1.4   *External theories*

In contrast, *external* theories use information beyond the distribution of returns to explain asset prices. A good example of such a theory is the paper by Chen, Roll, and Ross (1983), which uses macroeconomic variables to explain asset prices. Of course, internal and external theories are not exclusive alternatives. One of the virtues of a tight internal theory is that it specifies the way in which external forces influence asset prices.

If a macroeconomic variable is to influence the structure of asset prices, and if the CAPM holds, then equation (3) states how that variable will affect asset prices.

2   Empirical setting

The goal of asset pricing theory is to explain expected returns, μ_N, possibly using the second moments of returns, Σ_N. Both μ_N and Σ_N are expectations. They cannot be directly observed. For testing and verification, empirical counterparts of μ_N and Σ_N are required. In the United States, rich data on *actual* returns are available, which can be used to estimate expected returns. Despite the quality and volume of data, the estimates are not very precise. However, for empirical work, actual return data seem more promising than any alternative.[2] It is worth spending some time describing the characteristics of returns data. The theories we will discuss must be evaluated, at least in part, in terms of their ability to use, and be validated by, this data.

2.1   *The CRSP data*

The Center for Research on Security Prices (CRSP) of the University of Chicago has on tape the daily returns from holding any stock listed on the New York or American Stock Exchanges for 1962–83. Monthly returns are available for stocks traded on the New York Stock Exchange for 1925–83.

Two characteristics of these data are noteworthy. First, a large number of assets is included. There are over 4,000 assets in the daily returns file and almost 3,000 assets in the monthly return file. These data are appropriate for theories that assume a large number of assets.

Second, it is not *comprehensive*. Even though the CRSP files have information on a huge number of assets, many investors hold assets in their portfolios that are not included in the CRSP data. Although CRSP does collect data on the returns from U.S. government bonds that could be used together with the stock returns, comparable data for many marketed assets do not exist. Commodities, foreign exchange, options, futures contracts, corporate bonds, and debt and equity traded outside the United States are examples. Furthermore, many important assets are not traded on organized exchanges. The classic examples are human capital[3] and real estate. A theory that requires for its predictions of risk premia data on the returns from all assets an investor might hold cannot be rejected using the CRSP data alone. Given this, it is not clear in what sense the CRSP data can verify such a theory. The CAPM is a theory of this sort.

2.2 Estimating μ_N and Σ_N using the CRSP data

The most straightforward way to estimate expected returns using CRSP data is to form the sample mean. That is, given observations on the random returns on N assets for T periods, calculate

$$\hat{\mu}_N = \sum_{t=1}^{T} \tilde{x}_{Nt}. \tag{4}$$

This procedure is justified by some assumption like

$$\tilde{x}_{Nt} = \mu_N + \tilde{\omega}_{Nt}, \tag{5}$$

where the $\tilde{\omega}_{Nt}$ are independent, identically distributed random variables.

There are at least two problems with this approach. First, the assumption that the $\tilde{x}_t$ have a distribution that is constant over time seems contradicted by the data. Stock returns behave differently in different periods. For example, Luedecke (1984) reports that during the period 1971–4 the daily mean return on 392 stocks was -0.00015%, whereas during the period 1975–8 the mean return on the same 392 stocks was 0.0009%. The first figure corresponds to an annual loss of about 5%, the second to an annual gain of about 30%. It is hard to believe that investors expected the same returns in 1973 as they did in 1977. Most investigators who use the CRSP daily data split the approximately twenty years of data into a number of subperiods each no longer than six years in length.

Second, actual returns are quite volatile. As a result, it is hard to estimate μ_N in (5) precisely using a short time series. The many observations CRSP daily data files contain do not alleviate this problem. The accuracy of the estimate of the mean is determined by the length of time the process is observed and not by the frequency of the observations. Most models of stock returns suppose that the returns process is some kind of (possibly geometric) Brownian motion. Suppose that z_t evolves according to $dz = \alpha \, dt + \sigma \, dW$, where W is a Weiner process. Consider trying to estimate the parameter α from observations of the process over the interval $[0, T]$. The accuracy of the estimate of α is a function of T and is independent of how often z_t is observed. Suppose that we have observations of z_t at $t = 0, 1/n, 2/n, \ldots, Tn/n$. Then $y_t = z_t - z_{t-1}$ is a normal random variable with mean α/n and variance σ^2/n. The sample information may as well be considered as consisting of the observations y_t, $t = 1, \ldots, nT$.

A sufficient statistic for the mean is then $\Sigma_t y_t = x_T - x_0$. Thus the accuracy of the estimate of the mean can depend only on T and not on n.

In contrast, more frequent observations do permit more accurate estimates of the variance term σ^2. The variance of most estimates of σ^2 are of order $1/nT$; frequent observations of the x_t process let one see how much it fluctuates.

Both of these results carry over to the multivariate case. Accuracy of estimates of the mean vector μ are not improved by more frequent sampling. Accuracy of estimates of the variance–covariance matrix Σ is of the order of $1/nT$; the variance of each of the terms of Σ is of order $1/nT$ (Anderson 1958, p. 161).

2.3   Conditional and unconditional expectations

When combined with the fact that it is hard to estimate expected returns over intervals sufficiently short to make the assumption of constancy plausible, the possibility that the distribution of asset returns is not constant over time suggests an alternative model. Suppose that instead of (5) we assume that there is a state variable s such that (x_{Nt}, s_t) is jointly distributed. Conditional on s, x_{Nt} is independent of t. That is, the distribution of $(x_{Nt} \mid \tilde{s}_t = s)$ is independent of t. Suppose also that s_t has a stationary distribution.

This specification invites many interpretations. For example, different values of s could represent different information available to different traders; alternatively, s could be an index representing general economic conditions in different time periods. In either case, investors use information about the conditional distribution of returns, $(x_{Nt} \mid s)$, when making investment decisions. Insofar as their choices depend on the first two moments of returns, the portfolios they choose to hold will be functions of $\mu_{Ns} = E(x_N \mid \tilde{s} = s)$ and

$$\Sigma_{Ns} = E[(x_N - \mu_{Ns})(x_N - \mu_{Ns})' \mid \tilde{s} = s].$$

If the variable s is unobservable, the analyst cannot hope to estimate μ_{Ns} or Σ_{Ns}. However, if s has a stationary distribution, he can estimate unconditional first and second moments. Let $\Gamma_{Ns} = \Sigma_{Ns} + \mu_{Ns}\mu'_{Ns}$. Then the analyst can estimate $\mu_N = E(\mu_{Ns})$, $\Sigma_N = E(\Sigma_{Ns}) + V(\mu_{Ns})$, and $\Gamma_N = E(\Gamma_{Ns})$ using (4) to estimate μ_N and an analogous procedure for Σ_N and Γ_N. Suppose for simplicity that there are a finite number (S) of states and that the stationary or ergodic distribution of s is given by $\pi_s = \Pr\{s_t = s\}$. Then unconditional means and covariances are $\mu_N = \Sigma_s \pi_s \mu_{Ns}$, and

$$\Sigma_N = \Sigma_s \pi_s \Sigma_{Ns} + \Sigma_s \pi_s (\mu_{Ns} - \mu_N)(\mu_{Ns} - \mu_N)'.$$

Both μ_N and Σ_N can be estimated from data on actual returns. With this specification, it is legitimate to use the entire times series of observations to estimate expected returns. However, the mere fact that unconditional expectations can be estimated does not mean that they are of any interest. For them to be useful, it is necessary to have a theory that makes predictions about unconditional expectations. As we will see, the CAPM does not do this.

2.4 Summary

The data most likely to be used for testing asset pricing theories is very rich. However, it is not perfect. In particular, it is not comprehensive, and it is unlikely that the asset pricing process is stationary over time periods short enough to estimate expected reurns with much accuracy. It may be possible to estimate unconditional expectations accurately.

3 Mathematical setting

We will be considering many assets;[4] we need a mathematical structure that allows us to let $N \to \infty$. Let $F_N = [x_1, \ldots, x_N]$, the linear subspace consisting of all linear combinations[5] of (portfolios formed from) the assets $x_1, \ldots, x_N$. Now let $F = \bigcup_{N=1}^{\infty} F_N$, the space of all portfolios. Unfortunately F is not large enough for our purposes. Some of the arguments in asset pricing theory involve diversification; they require that we be able to make sense out of things like the limit of the sequence of portfolios $\{p_N\}$, where

$$p_N = \sum_{i=1}^{N} \frac{1}{N} x_i. \tag{6}$$

Each p_N costs a dollar; if asset returns are uncorrelated, then in the limit p_N converges to a riskless asset. We need a mathematical structure that gives meaning to $\lim_{N \to \infty} p_N$. For this, two things are needed: a space of investments that includes things not in F and a way of measuring distance between portfolios that allows us to give meaning to the convergence of portfolios like those defined in (6). Then we can frame a theory that deals with portfolios and the limits of portfolios. One way to do this is to suppose that asset returns are defined on some underlying probability space. Let $L_2(P)$ be the set of all random variables with finite variances defined on that space. We measure the length of a portfolio (or its distance from another portfolio) as $\|p\|$ where $\|p\| = E(p^2)^{1/2}$. Associated with this mean square norm is an inner product denoted (p, q) and defined as $(p, q) = E(pq)$. Note that $\|p\|^2 = (p, p)$. If

$$p = \sum_{i=1}^{N} \alpha_i x_i \quad \text{and} \quad q = \sum_{i=1}^{N} \gamma_i x_i,$$

then $\|p\|^2 = \alpha' \Gamma_N \alpha$ and $(p, q) = \alpha' \Gamma_N \gamma$. Analysis now takes place in $\bar{F}$, the closure of F. Things in $\bar{F}$ but not in F are *limit portfolios;* in the sequel, we use the term portfolio to refer to all objects in $\bar{F}$ whether or not they belong to some F_N; $\bar{F}$ is a Hilbert space.

If p and q are portfolios and if $(p, q) = 0$, then we say that p is orthogonal to q and write $p \perp q$. If L is a linear subspace, then $L^{\perp} = \{p \mid p \perp q$ for all $q \in L\}$ is its orthogonal complement. Many of the arguments we use are based on the projection theorem, which states that if L is a closed subspace in $\bar{F}$, then every $p \in \bar{F}$ has a unique decomposition as $p = p_1 + p_2$, where $p_1 \in L$ and $p_2 \in L^{\perp}$. Note that p_1 is the point in L closest to p; p_1 is the *projection* of p onto L; the distance from p to L is $\|p_2\|$. In the sequel, we will let $\|p - L\|$ denote the distance from p to the subspace L. Thus, $\|p - [b_1, \ldots, b_N]\|$ is this distance from p to the space spanned by the vectors $b_1, \ldots, b_N$.

3.1   *The mean and cost functionals*

Our analysis of asset pricing models will use some linear functionals[6] defined on the space of portfolios. These are the mean functional and the cost functional. If $p = \sum_{i=1}^{N} \alpha_i x_i$, then its expected value is $E(p) = \sum_{i=1}^{N} \alpha_i \mu_i$. It is easy to calculate

$$E(p) = (m_N, p) \quad \text{for any } p \in F_N, \tag{7}$$

where the portfolio m_N is given by $m_N = \Gamma_N^{-1} \mu_N' x_N$. The cost of any portfolio, $C(p) = \sum_i \alpha_i$, is also a linear functional. Again it is easy to calculate that $C(p) = (c_N, p)$ for any $p \in F_N$ where $c_N = \Gamma_N^{-1} e_N' x_N$ and $e_N = (1, \ldots, 1)'$ is a vector of N ones.

When (7) holds, we say that m_N *represents* the linear functional $E(\cdot)$. A linear functional $L(\cdot)$ is *continuous* if $\|p_n\| \to 0$ implies $L(p_n) \to 0$. A basic mathematical result, the Reisz representation theorem, states that if L is a continuous linear functional on a Hilbert space H, then there is an element q in H that represents L in the sense that $L(p) = (p, h)$ for all $p \in L$. It is easy to see from its definition that the mean functional is continuous on $\bar{F}$. Since $\|p\| = E(p)^2 + V(p)$ if $\|p_n\| \to 0$, $E(p_n) \to 0$. Thus, there is an $m \in \bar{F}$ such that $E(p) = (m, p)$ for all $p \in \bar{F}$. Furthermore, if m_N represents $E(\cdot)$ on F_N, then $m_N \to m$.

Arbitrage and the continuity of the cost functional. Without further assumptions, the cost functional is not continuous. However, if we assume that the set of portfolios does not permit arbitrage opportunities, then it is easy to show that the cost functional must be continuous. Let $\{p_N\}$ be a sequence of finite portfolios. Then we say the market permits no arbitrage opportunities if the following two conditions hold:

$$\text{if } V(p_N) \to 0 \text{ and } C(p_N) \to 0, \text{ then } E(p_N) \to 0; \tag{A.i}$$

$$\text{if } V(p_N) \to 0, \ C(p_N) \to 1, \text{ and } E(p_N) \to \eta, \text{ then } \eta > 0. \tag{A.ii}$$

Condition (A.i) simply states that it is not possible to make an investment that is costless, riskless, and yields a positive return. Ross (1976) has shown that if (A.i) fails, many (but not all) risk-averse investors will want to take infinitely large positions. This is, of course, incompatible with equilibrium. A similar argument justifies (A.ii). Suppose that (A.ii) does not hold; that is, suppose that the market allows investors to trade a portfolio that, approximately, costs a dollar and has a riskless, nonpositive return. Then investors face no budget constraints; by selling this portfolio short, they can generate arbitrarily large amounts of cash while incurring no future obligations. This too is incompatible with equilibrium.

It is straightforward to show (see Chamberlain and Rothschild 1983) that (A.ii) implies that the cost functional is continuous. Thus, there is a portfolio c that represents $C(\cdot)$ in the sense that

$$C(p) = (c, p) \quad \text{for all } p \in \bar{F}. \tag{8}$$

Furthermore, if c_N represents $C(\cdot)$ on F_N, then $c_N \to c$.

One important implication of these conditions concerns the trade-off between risk and return that the market permits. Define

$$\delta = \sup |E(p)|/V^{1/2}(p) \quad \text{subject to } p \in \bar{F}, \ C(p) = 0, \text{ and } p \neq 0. \tag{9}$$

If a market does not permit arbitrage, it permits only limited trade-offs between mean and variance. In particular, Luedecke (1984) has shown the following proposition.

Proposition 1. (A.i) implies δ is finite.

Proof: Suppose not. Then there is a sequence of portfolios $\{p_N\}$ such that $C(p_N) = 0$ and $\delta_N = E(p_N)/V(p_N)^{1/2}\uparrow\infty$. Let $q_N = p_N/\delta_N(V(p_N)^{1/2})$. Then $E(q_N) = 1$ and $V(q_N) = (\delta_N)^{-2} \to 0$. This violates (A.i). ∎

3.2   *Riskless assets*

We assume the Σ_N are nonsingular. Thus, if $p = \Sigma_{i=1}^{N} \alpha_i x_i = \alpha' x_N$ is a portfolio in F_N, $V(p) = \alpha' \Sigma_N \alpha > 0$ if $\alpha \neq 0$. If p is a portfolio in $\bar{F}$, this conclusion need not hold. If there is a sequence of portfolios $\{p_N\}$ such that $p_N \to p$, $V(p_N) \to 0$, and $C(p_N) \to 1$, then we say that p is a *riskless asset*. If there is a riskless asset, the market permits investors to diversify away all risk. Chamberlain and Rothschild give necessary and sufficient conditions on the sequence Σ_N for there to be a riskless asset.

4   The capital asset pricing model

The CAPM is an asset pricing model that captures the notion that an asset's risk premium is determined by its nondiversifiable risk. In the CAPM, an asset's nondiversifiable risk is measured by its covariance with the market and is called beta. We will define beta precisely below. The CAPM rests on the premise that all investors choose mean–variance efficient portfolios. That is, faced with the problem of selecting portfolios from $\bar{F}$, all investors will choose portfolios that are, for some parameters γ and η, solutions to

choose p to minimize $V(p)$ subject to $C(p) = \gamma$ and $E(p) = \eta$.   (Q)

It follows from the definition of the mean square norm $\|\ \|$ and the portfolios c and m, which represent the cost and mean functionals, that problem (Q) is equivalent to

$$\min\|p\| \text{ subject to } (c, p) = \gamma \text{ and } (m, p) = m.   \text{(P)}$$

Since the assumption that investors choose mean–variance efficient portfolios drives the CAPM, it is natural to ask what justifies it. The answer is: very strong assumptions. Together, two conditions are sufficient. Whereas if either of these conditions is not true, an investor could still choose a mean–variance efficient portfolio, he is extremely unlikely to do so. The first condition is that assets in $\bar{F}$ are comprehensive, that they comprise the entire universe from which investors choose investments. We have already indicated that this is unlikely to be true if $\bar{F}$ is portfolios formed from assets for which returns data is available. The second condition is that investors evaluate risky returns from investments in terms of their first two moments. This requires either quadratic utility functions or very special assumptions about the process generating returns. As $N \to \infty$, a kind of conditional normality is required. For finite N, the weaker but still strong assumption of spherical symmetry is required (Chamberlain 1983a).

4.1 *The market portfolio belongs to* $[m, c]$

We now derive the basic CAPM pricing equation. Let $[m, c]$ denote the space spanned by m and c. Note that if m and c are collinear ($m = \lambda c$), all portfolios of a given cost will have a mean entirely determined by that cost. Problem (P) will not have a solution for arbitrary γ and η; the market does not exhibit a well-defined trade-off between mean and variance. For this reason, we assume dimension $[m, c] = 2$. The following proposition is basic to the CAPM.

Proposition 2. Any solution to (P) belongs to $[m, c]$.

Proof: Suppose a portfolio p solves (P) but that p does not belong to $[m, c]$. Let q be the projection of p onto $[m, c]$. Then one can show that $E(q) = E(p)$ and $C(q) = C(p)$. However, since $\|p\|^2 = \|p - q\|^2 + \|q\|^2$ and $p - q \neq 0$, $\|p\| > \|q\|$. Thus, $V(p) > V(q)$ and p cannot be a solution to (P). ∎

Define the market portfolio, denoted p_M, as the portfolio (normalized to have unit cost) formed by summing the investments of all investors. Since every investor chooses mean–variance efficient portfolios (portfolios that belong to $[m, c]$), p_M is a linear combination of portfolios that belong to $[m, c]$. Thus, for some coefficients α and γ,

$$p_M = \alpha m + \gamma c. \tag{10}$$

4.2 *The CAPM pricing equation*

We will now show that the CAPM pricing equation is a consequence of equation (10). If p is any portfolio, define $\beta_p = \text{cov}(p, p_M)/V(p_M)$. The CAPM pricing equation states that there exist constants a and b such that, for any portfolio q,

$$E(q) = aC(q) + b\beta_q. \tag{11}$$

This is not the usual form of the CAPM. However, (11) can be written

$$E(q) - aC(q) = b\beta_q,$$

which states that an asset's risk premium is proportional to its beta.

Proposition 3. If $p_M \in [m, c]$ and there exist two unit cost portfolios p and q such that $\beta_p \neq \beta_q$, then (11) holds.

This is simple arithmetic; (10) implies

$$(p_M, q) = \text{cov}(p_M, q) + E(p_M)E(q) = \alpha(m, q) + \gamma C(q),$$

or

$$\text{cov}(p_M, q) = E(q)(\alpha - E(p_M)) + \gamma C(q).$$

Thus

$$\beta_q = (E(q)(\alpha - E(p_M)) + \gamma C(q))/V(p_M). \tag{12}$$

Now if $\alpha = E(p_M)$, (12) implies $\beta_q = \gamma C(q)/V(p_M)$ so all unit cost portfolios have the same beta; thus we can assume $\alpha \neq E(p_M)$ and divide to get (11) with $a = -\gamma/(\alpha - E(p_M))$ and $b = V(p_M)/(\alpha - E(p_M))$. ∎

We now prove a converse of Proposition 3.

Proposition 4. Equation (11) implies p_M belongs to $[m, c]$.

Proof: Let q be a portfolio that is orthogonal to $[m, c]$. It will suffice to show that q is orthogonal to p_M. Since q is orthogonal to $[m, c]$, $E(q) = (q, m) = 0$ and $C(q) = (c, q) = 0$. Thus (11) implies $\beta_q = 0$. However, $(q, p_M) = E(q)E(p_M) + \beta_q = 0$. ∎

The coefficients a and b in the CAPM pricing equation (11) have interesting interpretations. Suppose there is a riskless asset. Let q be this riskless asset in (11) and conclude that $a = \rho$, the rate of return on the riskless asset. Now let q be p_M and conclude that $b = E(p_M) - \rho$. Thus we may write (11) as

$$E(q) = \rho C(q) + \beta_q(E(p_M) - \rho). \tag{13}$$

If there is no riskless asset, (13) still holds when ρ is interpreted as the rate of return on a "zero beta" portfolio, that is, a portfolio that is uncorrelated with the market.

The development did not use the technology of Section 3. All that was required was the existence of portfolios m and c, which represented the mean and cost functionals. As we noted, such portfolios always exist on finite asset markets. On a market with infinitely many assets, assumptions are required [(A.ii) will do] to ensure that a portfolio that represents the cost function [satisfies (8)] exists.

4.3   The CAPM in a conditional setting

The CAPM does not easily accommodate the conditional model of returns described above.[7] To see this, suppose that there are a finite number N of assets and, for concreteness, consider the version of the model in which at time t all investors' expectations are determined by the state variable $\tilde{s}_t$. In this section, we will omit the subscript N. To compensate for this notational laxity, we will be especially pedantic about the distinction between portfolios (which are random variables) and their probability distributions. Portfolios are simply linear combinations of the assets, $x_1, \ldots, x_N$. As such, they are independent of beliefs. The distribution of these random variables is determined by beliefs. For example, the vector $e = (1, \ldots, 1)$ gives the cost of all assets under any set of beliefs. If beliefs about second moments of returns are represented by Γ_s, then the portfolio c_s represents the cost functional under these beliefs where $c_s = \gamma_s' x$ and $\gamma_s = \Gamma_s^{-1} e$. Similarly, the vector μ_s is the vector of mean returns under beliefs s, the portfolio m_s represents the mean functional under these beliefs, and $m_s = \alpha_s' x$ where the portfolio weights α_s are given by $\alpha_s = \Gamma_s^{-1} \mu_s$.

If the CAPM holds conditionally, then for each s there exist constants a_s and b_s, such that if p is a portfolio of unit cost,

$$E(p \mid s) = a_s + b_s (\text{cov}(p_M, p) \mid s). \tag{14}$$

Does this imply that the CAPM equation (11) holds? Clearly not in general. Suppose that $b_s = b$ for all s, then taking expectations in (14) and letting $a = E(a_s)$, we see that

$$E(p) = a + b E(\text{cov}(p_M, p) \mid s).$$

But

$$\text{cov}(p_M, p) = E(\text{cov}(p_M, p) \mid s) + \text{cov}[E(p_M \mid s), E(p \mid s)].$$

Thus, we see that (11) holds only if

$$\text{cov}[(E(p_M \mid s), E(p \mid s))] = 0. \tag{15}$$

If, as will generally be the case, b_s is not a constant but a random variable that fluctuates with s, things are worse. Now we require also that

$$\text{cov}[b_s, \text{cov}((p, p_M) \mid s)] = 0. \tag{16}$$

Neither (15) nor (16) seems plausible. The CAPM requires that each equation hold for *every* p. Thus (15) requires that the expected market return be uncorrelated with the expected return on every portfolio. This seems unlikely. We conclude that even if the CAPM holds for conditional data, the unconditional data available to the analyst will not be consistent with the CAPM pricing equation.

The preceding discussion of the relationship between the conditional CAPM and unconditional CAPM concentrated on the validity of the CAPM pricing equation (32). A slightly different argument, with the same negative conclusion, focuses on the question of whether or not the fact that the market portfolio is mean–variance efficient in every state implies that the unconditional market portfolio is mean–variance efficient. Intuition suggests that if the market portfolio is mean–variance efficient in every state, then it must be unconditionally mean–variance efficient. Intuition is wrong. For a simple counterexample, consider the two hedge portfolios with the following state-dependent means and variances:

$$E(p \mid 1) = V(p \mid 1) = 1, \qquad E(p \mid 2) = V(p \mid 2) = 2,$$

and

$$E(q \mid 1) = E(q \mid 2) = 1, \qquad V(q \mid 1) = V(q \mid 2) = 1.1.$$

For hedge portfolios mean–variance efficiency is determined by the ratio of mean to variance. Thus, in each state, p is mean–variance efficient relative to q. However, if states are equally likely, $E(p) = 1.5$ and $V(p) = 1.5 + 0.25$, so that $E(p)/V(p) = 1.5/1.75 < E(q)/V(q) = 1/1.1$. Unconditionally, q is mean–variance efficient relative to p. If $E(p)$ did not vary with s, then conditional mean–variance efficiency would imply unconditional mean–variance efficiency. Similarly, inspection of (15) reveals that the CAPM will hold and the market portfolio will be mean–variance efficient if the conditional mean of the market portfolio is the same in every state. This is a stringent requirement.

Up to this point I have ignored the problem that the market portfolio may change as the state s changes. As the proportion of different assets in the market portfolio is determined by supply and demand conditions, which vary from period to period, the composition of the market portfolio will change as the state changes. Here it is not entirely clear what the statement that the market portfolio is mean–variance efficient means.

One possible interpretation is that the average or expected market portfolio is (unconditionally) mean–variance efficient. This is unlikely to be the case. We can write the market portfolio as $p_{Ms} = \delta_s' x$ where the portfolio weights δ_s are given by

$$\delta_s = f_s \alpha_s + g_s \gamma_s. \tag{17}$$

In (17), f_s and g_s are numbers and α_s and γ_s are vectors of portfolio weights that represent the conditional mean and cost functionals. These weights are random variables with long-run average or ergodic values given by

$$\delta = \Sigma_s \pi_s \delta_s = \Sigma_s \pi_s (f_s \alpha_s + g_s \gamma_s). \tag{18}$$

We can then identify the long-run ergodic market portfolio p_M as the portfolio with these weights. One possible version of an unconditional CAPM would be the requirement that this portfolio be mean–variance efficient, that is,

$$p_M \in [m, c]. \tag{19}$$

We now show that the conditional CAPM [equation (17)] does not imply this version of the unconditional CAPM. Note that (19) defines δ as a linear function of $f = (f_1, \ldots, f_S)$ and $g = (g_1, \ldots, g_S)$. Thus we may write (18) as

$$\delta = L \begin{pmatrix} f \\ g \end{pmatrix} \tag{20}$$

where L is an $N \times 2S$ matrix with typical entry

$$L_{ns} = \begin{cases} \alpha_{ns} \pi_s & \text{for } s \le S, \\ \gamma_{ns-S} \pi_{s-S} & \text{for } s > S. \end{cases}$$

Theory in no way restricts the vectors f and g in (20). Thus, (17) can hold only if rank L is 2 or less. But theory also provides no reason to expect that L is so restricted. Suppose, for example, that all states are equally likely so that $\pi_s = S^{-1}$ for all s. Then for L to be of rank 2, it is necessary that dimension $[\Gamma_1^{-1} e, \ldots, \Gamma_s^{-1} e] \le 2$. I see no reason to expect this to happen.

A similar argument holds if s is interpreted as the information of different investors. Under the assumptions of the CAPM, each investor chooses a portfolio that is, according to his beliefs, mean–variance efficient. That is, his portfolio is in $[m_s, c_s]$ if his beliefs are indexed by s. However one specifies unconditional information, the mean–variance efficient set relative to this information is a two-dimensional subspace of portfolios. The market portfolio is a particular portfolio whose composition is determined by the interaction of supply and demand. Whatever assumptions are made about supply, the market portfolio is unlikely to belong to a particular two-dimensional subspace. If assets (random variables) are made available to the economy by a constant returns-to-scale technology, then this technology determines asset prices, while the distribution of tastes, wealth, and information determines the quantities of assets held. That aggregate demand (the market portfolio in this case) should belong to a particular two-dimensional subspace is an event of probability zero.

If assets are in fixed supply – as in Admati's (1985) model of a noisy rational expectations equilibrium – the same conclusion emerges. For the remainder of this section only, let x be a vector of assets whose returns are specified in *physical* units. As before, μ and Σ are the mean vector and covariance matrix of x. Then $q = \alpha'x$ is a portfolio. In Admati's model, different agents have different information about the distribution of returns. Also, aggregate supply Z is a random variable. Admati studies how the market clearing price P is determined by information agents have about x and aggregate supply Z.

The market portfolio is $p_M = Z'x$. It is easy to see that, in general, p_M will not be mean–variance efficient relative to unconditional information (however this unconditional information is specified).

If prices are P and the unconditional probability distribution of x has mean μ_I and covariance matrix Σ_I, then a necessary (but not sufficient) condition for a portfolio $q = \alpha'x$ to be mean–variance efficient is

$$\alpha \in [\Sigma_I^{-1}P, \Sigma_I^{-1}\mu_I].$$

(This is straightforward. For q to be mean–variance efficient, it is necessary that $q \in [m^*, c^*]$ where m^* and c^* are the portfolios that represent the mean and cost functions relative to the covariance inner product on the space of portfolios of risky assets. Clearly $m^* = (\Sigma_I^{-1}\mu)'x$ and $c^* = (\Sigma_I^{-1}P)'x$.)

To show that Z is not mean–variance efficient, it will suffice to demonstrate that $Z \notin [\Sigma_I^{-1}P, \Sigma_I^{-1}\mu_I]$, where P is the random price vector, μ_I is the (possibly random) mean and Σ_I the covariance of x. This is straightforward for any reasonable specification for the distribution of x.

First, suppose that the relevant distribution is the unconditional distribution of x; that is, $\mu_I = \mu$ and $\Sigma_I = \Sigma$. Then, as Admati shows, in equilibrium, $P = A_0 + A_1x - A_2Z$, and we ask whether

$$Z \in [\Sigma^{-1}(A_0 + A_1x - A_2Z), \Sigma^{-1}x].$$

Since Z and x are independent, the probability of this happening is zero.

The probability that Z is a scalar multiple of $\Sigma^{-1}x$ is zero. For fixed Z, the vector $\Sigma^{-1}(A_0 + A_1 x - A_2 Z)$ is a normal random vector with a co-variance matrix of full rank; the probability that it belongs to any plane, in particular the one generated by $\Sigma^{-1}\mu$ and Z, is zero.

Now suppose mean–variance efficiency is measured relative to the information in prices; then $\mu_I = B_0 + B_2 P$. The necessary condition for mean-variance efficiency is

$$Z \in [\Sigma_I^{-1}(A_0 + A_1 x - A_2 Z), \Sigma_I^{-1}(B_0 + B_2(A_0 + A_1 x - A_2 Z))].$$

For fixed Z, the right-hand side of this equation is a plane of the form $[T_1 + Q_1 x, T_2 + Q_2 x]$ where the T_i are vectors and the Q_i are matrices. The probability that *any* nonzero vector belongs to this subspace is zero.

4.4   Intertemporal asset pricing models

The discussion of the last section is well summarized by Admati's (1985, p. 641) remark that the CAPM does not hold in a conditional model because the law of iterated expectations does not hold for second moments. There are asset pricing models that can, under certain conditions, justify something like the CAPM pricing equation. These are intertemporal models whose theoretical starting point is an equation involving only first moments. As a consequence, the law of iterated expectations may be applied; the models hold for unconditional as well as conditional data. Consider a consumer's intertemporal allocation problem. In each period, the consumer must decide what to consume, what to save, and, if he saves, what assets to invest in. If there is a single consumption good, then at t, the optimal decision must satisfy

$$E[\delta U'(y_{t+1})x_{it} \mid I_t] = U'(y_t), \tag{21}$$

where y_t is consumption at date t, I_t is the information the consumer has, and x_{it} is the return on asset i in period t. With assumptions on the form of the utility function (constant relative risk aversion is helpful), the nature of economic institutions (complete markets and Pareto optimality make aggregation easier), and the nature of the stochastic process driving asset returns (normality – sometimes justified by an appeal to continuous time – is helpful), equation (21) can be manipulated to yield an asset pricing model. The particular model produced depends on the assumptions employed. Possibilities include intertemporal versions of the CAPM, the consumption beta model of Breeden (1979) in which assets' risk premia are determined by their covariance with (the rate of growth of) aggregate

consumption and various hybrids (e.g., Brown and Gibbons 1985). All
these models take equation (21) as a starting point. Note that the law of
iterated expectations implies that equation (21) holds for unconditional
as well as conditional data; that is, since (21) holds for all I_t, we may integrate to obtain $E[\delta U'(y_{t+1})x_{it}] = U'(y_t)$. Thus, if a model is derived from
(21), it should hold for unconditional as well as conditional data.

Much recent literature derives and estimates pricing models based on
equation (21). I shall not review the literature here. The interested reader
is referred to Brock (1982), Grossman and Shiller (1982), and Grossman,
Melino, and Shiller (1985).

I find the assumptions required to derive a useful asset pricing model
from a consumer's intertemporal optimization problem quite implausible;
however, the adequacy of these models is an empirical question that will
(possibly) be narrowed by empirical research now being done.

4.5   Tests of the CAPM

Many researchers have tested the predictions of the CAPM. Some view
the results of these tests as evidence for and others as evidence against the
CAPM. Which view one takes depends in part on how one views the relationship between theory and data in economics. Pragmatists argue that
the best that theory can do is suggest variables that might belong in regression equations. The theory behind the CAPM suggests that beta belongs in regression equations. Evidence shows that beta does help to explain risk premia. Thus, the evidence tends to support CAPM. Supporters
of the CAPM often suggest that an additional reason for believing in the
CAPM is that it's the only game in town. Although hardly perfect, it is,
they assert, the best model we now have for explaining risk premia.

Those who believe that the data does not support the theory behind
the CAPM make three major points. The first is that a theory's prediction about what is not in a regression equation are no less important than
its suggestions of what should be in a regression equation. In this light,
CAPM is a very strong theory. Nothing but beta should explain risk premia. In theory, R^2 in regressions of risk premia on beta should be unity.
The only explanation for worse results is measurement error; the ability
of other variables to explain risk premia can only be accounted for in this
way.

Despite the fact that the CAPM has no room for other variables, the
evidence is that other variables explain a significant part of risk premia.
The most frequently cited variables are firm size [see Schwert (1983) for a

judicious survey of this work] and an asset's own variance [see Roll and Ross (1980) and Chen (1983) for references]. Whereas some have argued that measurement error is partly responsible for the ability of these variables to explain risk premia, no one has suggested that measurement error is the whole story. The ability of these theoretically extraneous variables to explain risk premia remains a mysterious anomaly to supporters of the CAPM – it is damning evidence against the theory to its detractors.

A second and related argument against the CAPM is that beta does not explain risk very well. Schwert (1983, p. 4) notes: "Statistical evidence supporting the positive relation between risk (beta) and expected return is surprisingly weak... The association between firm size and average stock returns is about as strong as the association between risk and average returns." The argument that the CAPM is the only game in town is not persuasive if it's not a very good game.

A final argument, due to Roll (1977), is that the CAPM has not been, and probably cannot be, tested. Since the CAPM is logically equivalent to the statement that the market portfolio is mean–variance efficient, it cannot be tested unless the market portfolio is specified and observed. The typical test of the CAPM uses some sort of index of returns on common stocks (the Standard and Poor 500 or a value-weighted portfolio of the stocks traded on the New York Stock Exchange) as the market portfolio. These indices are not the market portfolio. All one can conclude from such a test is that the particular proxy for the market portfolio is, or is not, mean–variance efficient. One cannot conclude that the CAPM is, or is not, valid. This criticism must be somewhat muted by Stambaugh's (1982) work. Stambaugh constructed monthly series of values and returns on real estate, consumer durables, and various kinds of bonds – the assets that together with equities comprise most of nonhuman wealth. From this data, he constructed a number of different "market" portfolios. Then he conducted sophisticated tests of the CAPM in order to see whether the inferences one would draw about the validity of the CAPM depended crucially on the composition of the market portfolio. He found that they did not. (He also found that the question: "Does the data support the CAPM?" did not seem to have a clear-cut yes or no answer; however, the ambiguity had little to do with the composition of the market portfolio.)

5 The arbitrage pricing theory

The arbitrage pricing theory rests on three assumptions. The first is that the market should not permit arbitrage opportunities; in our terms, (A) holds.

The second assumption is that the market has a factor structure; the third is that there are a large number of assets. The basic result of the APT, which is known as Ross' theorem, is that under these assumptions many risks (all those not correlated with factors) can be almost completely diversified away. The implications of the APT for asset pricing are familiar from the CAPM: In equilibrium, the market rewards only undiversifiable risk. The two theories define undiversifiable risk differently. In the APT, undiversifiable risk is factor risk; in the CAPM, it is correlation with the market. The APT is a useful theory if, and only if, factors and factor risk can be easily identified. [For an alternative discussion of some of these issues, see Ingersoll (1984).]

5.1   *Factor structure and Ross' theorem*

Ross originally developed the APT for an asset market with an *exact K factor structure*. There is an exact K factor structure if asset returns may be described as

$$x_i = \mu_i + \sum_{k=1}^{K} \beta_{ik} f_k + \theta_i, \tag{22}$$

where the f_k and the θ_i are all uncorrelated and $V(f_k) = 1$. This specification implies that

$$\Sigma_N = B_N B_N' + D_N,$$

where B_N is an $N \times K$ matrix whose ith row is $(\beta_{i1}, \ldots, \beta_{iK})$ and D_N is a diagonal matrix. The β_{ik} are called factor loadings. Equation (22) states that the divergence of asset i from its expected value can be partitioned into factor risk $\Sigma_k \beta_{ik} f_k$ and idiosyncratic risk θ_i. The key insight of the APT is that on a large asset market it ought to be possible to diversify away all idiosyncratic risk. The market will not reward people for holding the risk represented by θ_i. If this were strictly true, then there would exist numbers τ_k (which could be described as factor risk premia) such that

$$\mu_i - \rho = \sum_{k=1}^{K} \beta_{ik} \tau_k, \quad \text{for all } i. \tag{23}$$

If (23) holds, then the mean vector μ_N is a linear combination of a vector of 1's and the factor loadings, the columns of B_N. That is, (23) implies

$$\mu_N \in [e_N, B_N]. \tag{24}$$

Approximate factor structure. Except for some special cases, (24) is not exactly correct. However, for large N, a weaker result holds. We will prove this in the context of an *approximate factor structure* – a concept we now define. The requirement (of an exact factor structure) that the idiosyncratic disturbances be uncorrelated is unnecessarily restrictive both for theoretical and empirical purposes. Given a symmetric matrix C, let $g_i(C)$ denote the ith largest eigenvalue of C. The nested sequence of variance–covariance matrices $\{\Sigma_N\}$ has an approximate K factor structure if there is a sequence $\{(\beta_{i1}, ..., \beta_{iK})\}_{i=1}^{\infty}$ such that for all N,

$$\Sigma_N = B_N B_N' + R_N, \tag{25}$$

where $(\beta_{i1}, ..., \beta_{iK})$ is the ith row of the $N \times K$ matrix B_N and R_N is a sequence of positive semidefinite matrices with

$$\bar{\lambda} \equiv \sup_N g_1(R_N) < \infty. \tag{26}$$

Note that Σ_N can have approximate K factor structure if (22) holds even if idiosyncratic disturbances are correlated. What is required is that the θ_i should be uncorrelated with the factors and that the eigenvalues of the variance–covariance matrix of the $\theta_1, ..., \theta_N$ should be uniformly bounded. Chamberlain and Rothschild (1983) characterized approximate factor structures. Given a nested sequence of positive definite matrices $\{\Sigma_N\}$, define $\lambda_{jN} = g_j(\Sigma_N)$ and $\lambda_K = \sup_N \lambda_{KN}$.

Theorem 1. Suppose $\lambda_\infty = \inf_N \lambda_{NN} > 0$. Then $\{\Sigma_N\}$ has an approximate K factor structure if and only if $\lambda_{K+1} < \infty$.

Proof: One implication is easy. Suppose there is an approximate factor structure. Then

$$g_{K+1}(\Sigma_N) \leq g_{K+1}(B_N B_N') + g_1(R_N) = g_1(R_N) \leq \bar{\lambda} < \infty.$$

The proof that if λ_{K+1} is finite, then there is an approximate factor structure is in Chamberlain and Rothschild (1983).

Chamberlain and Rothschild also showed that if there is an approximate factor structure, it is unique in the following sense: If there is a nested sequence of $N \times K$ matrices C_N such that $\Sigma_N = C_N C_N' + S_N$ where $g_1(S_N)$ is uniformly bounded, then $C_N C_N' = B_N B_N'$.

If there is an approximate K factor structure, then it is a reasonable hypothesis that for $k = 1, ..., K$ the λ_{kN} should grow linearly. Since

$$g_K(B_N B_N') + g_1(R_N) \geq g_K(\Sigma_N) \geq g_K(B_N B_N'),$$

λ_{kN} grows at the same rate as $g_k(B_N B_N') = g_k(B_N' B_N)$. Suppose that factor loadings for different assets are independent, identically distributed random vectors with a positive definite second-moment matrix Ω. Then

$B'_N B_N/N$ converges almost surely to Ω; the eigenvalues of $B'_N B_N$ will converge to N times the eigenvalue of Ω; they will grow linearly.

We now prove that if the market does not permit arbitrage opportunities, then (24) is approximately true.

Ross' Theorem. If (A) holds and if there is an approximate K factor structure, then there exist numbers $\tau_0, \tau_1, \ldots, \tau_K$ such that

$$\sum_{i=1}^{\infty} (\mu_i - \tau_0 - \tau_1 \beta_{i1} - \cdots - \tau_K \beta_{iK})^2 < \infty. \tag{27}$$

This is an approximate result. Risk premia are not exactly linear functions of factor loadings. They are, however, close; (27) cannot hold unless the average pricing error is small. Ross' theorem is an immediate consequence of Theorem 2, which is somewhat more useful for empirical work. Suppose there are N assets with mean vector μ and variance-covariance matrix Σ. Let p be a portfolio and define δ as in (9). Suppose that Σ can be decomposed as $\Sigma = BB' + R$ where B is $N \times K$ and R is nonnegative definite. For vectors p in R^N, let $\|p\|_2$ denote the standard Euclidean norm. Let γ be the (Euclidean) distance of the mean vector m from the space spanned by the columns of B and a vector of 1's; then, in an obvious notation, $\gamma = \|\mu - [e, B]\|_2$. If the entries of B are interpreted as factor loadings, γ^2 is a measure of the amount by which pricing differs from exact arbitrage pricing.

Theorem 2. $\gamma^2 \leq g_1(R)\delta^2$.

The proof given here is essentially due to Huberman (1982).

Proof: For this proof, we use the symbol $\perp$ to denote orthogonality in the Euclidean norm. Let $\mu = y + z$ where $y \in [e, B]$ and $z \perp [e, B]$. Then $\gamma^2 = z'z$. Consider $p = z'x$. Since $z \perp e$, $C(p) = 0$. Thus $\delta \geq E(p)/V(p)^{1/2}$, and it will suffice to show that

$$E(p)^2/V(p)^2 \geq \gamma^2 g_1(R)$$

or

$$g_1(R) \geq V(p)\gamma^2/E(p)^2.$$

However,

$$E(p) = z'\mu = z'z = \gamma^2,$$

so what must be demonstrated is that

$$g_1(R) \geq \frac{V(p)}{z'z}.$$

Since

$$V(p) = z'\Sigma z = z'BB'z + z'Rz = z'Rz,$$

what is required is that

$$g_1(R) \geq \frac{z'Rz}{z'z},$$

which follows from the definition of $g_1(R)$ as the largest eigenvalue of R. ∎

Note that in extending this theorem to prove Ross' theorem, what is required is that δ be bounded. As we observed above, this is a consequence of assumption (A.i).

5.2 Diversifiable risk

It remains to show that risk premia are rewards for holding undiversifiable risk.

Well-diversified portfolios. We begin by noting that the norm $\|\cdot\|_2$ introduced in the last section can be applied to portfolios and is a measure of diversification. If $p \in F_N$ and $p = \Sigma_i \gamma_i x_i$, then $\|p\|_2 = [\Sigma_i \gamma_i^2]^{1/2}$. Chamberlain (1983b) shows that $\|p\|_2$ can be extended from F to the limit portfolios in $\bar{F}$ in such a way that if $\{p_N\} \to p$, then $\|p_N\|_2 \to \|p\|_2$. If $\|p\|_2 = 0$, then we will say that p is a *well-diversified* portfolio. This terminology is justified by the fact that if p is well diversified, then it contains only factor risk and no idiosyncratic risk. If p is well diversified, there is a sequence of finite portfolios $p_N = \gamma_N' x_N$ such that $p_N \to p$ and $\|p_N\|_2 = \gamma_N' \gamma_N \to 0$. Then

$$V(p_N) = \gamma_N' \Sigma_N \gamma_N = \gamma_N' B_N' B_N \gamma_N + \gamma_N' R_N \gamma_N.$$

Since $\gamma_N' R_N \gamma_N \leq g_1(R_N) \gamma_N' \gamma_N$,

$$V(p) = \lim_{N \to \infty} V(P_N) = \lim_{N \to \infty} \gamma_N' B_N' B_N \gamma_N.$$

It is also easy to show that if there is a riskless asset and if $\lambda_\infty > 0$, then the riskless asset must be well diversified. For a finite portfolio p,

$$V(p) = \gamma' \Sigma_N \gamma \geq \|p\|_2 \lambda_\infty.$$

The last inequality follows from the characterization of the smallest eigenvalue of a symmetric matrix Z as the solution to the problem: Find a nonzero vector α to minimize $\alpha'Q\alpha/\alpha'\alpha$.

Chamberlain shows that the space $\bar{F}$ of all portfolios can be partitioned into the space of well-diversified portfolios D and a space of portfolios J that are uncorrelated with the well-diversified portfolios, in the sense that every portfolio can be decomposed uniquely into a portfolio in D and a portfolio in J; $p = p_D + p_J$ where p_D is uncorrelated with p_J.

If there is an approximate K factor structure and if $\lambda_{KN} \to \infty$, then D is a finite-dimensional vector space. If there is a riskless asset, then D is of dimension $K+1$ and consists of the riskless asset and portfolios, which are related to the eigenvalues corresponding to the K largest eigenvectors of the variance–covariance matrix Σ_N in the following sense. Let t_{jN} be the eigenvector of Σ_N corresponding to λ_{jN} normalized so that $\|t_{jN}\|_2 = 1$. Let $q_{jN} = \lambda_{jN}^{-1/2} t_{jN}$. Now consider the portfolios $p_{jN} = q'_{jN} x_{jN}$. It is easy to see that

$$\text{cov}(p_{jN}, p_{kN}) = \begin{cases} 1 & \text{if } k = j, \\ 0 & \text{if } k \neq j. \end{cases}$$

Furthermore, $\|p_{jN}\|_2^2 = 1/\lambda_{jN}$. Thus if for $j \le K$, p_{jN} converges, it must converge to a well-diversified portfolio; Chamberlain and Rothschild (1983) showed that the p_{jN} converge. These limit portfolios form a set of K-uncorrelated portfolios that, together with the riskless asset, span the set D. If there is no riskless asset, then D consists of the K-limit portfolios $p_j = \lim_{N \to \infty} p_{jN}$ for $j = 1, \ldots, K$.

If there is an approximate K factor structure so that (25) and (26) hold, then a way to find it is to use the eigenvectors corresponding to the K largest eigenvalues of Σ_N. Consider the matrix B_{NM} whose jth column consists of the first N elements of q_{jM}. Then $\lim_{M \to \infty} B_{NM} B'_{NM} = B_N B'_N$.

Risk premia as rewards for holding factor risk. The sharpest result relating risk premia to factor loadings is due to Chamberlain (1983b). We will give his result when there is a riskless asset with rate of return ρ; an analogous result holds if there is not a riskless asset. Suppose there is an approximate K factor structure. Then D, the space of well-diversified portfolios, is of dimension $K+1$ and we may choose as a basis for D the riskless asset s and K portfolios $f_1, \ldots, f_K$, which are uncorrelated and have unit variance. These portfolios are factors. For each asset i define $\beta_{ik} = \text{cov}(x_i, \beta_k)$. Now let

$$\gamma(\tau) = \sum_{i=1}^{\infty} (\mu_i - \tau_0 - \tau_1 \beta_{i1} - \cdots - \tau_K \beta_{iK})^2, \tag{28}$$

where $\tau = (\tau_0, \tau_1, \ldots, \tau_K)$. Chamberlain showed that $\gamma(\tau) < \infty$ if and only if

$$\tau_0 = \rho, \quad \tau_k = E(f_k) - \rho C(f_k) \quad \text{for } k = 1, \ldots, K.$$

In this equation the coefficients τ_k are factor risk premia.[8]

5.3   Bounds

If $\gamma(\tau) = 0$, then factor pricing is exact; an asset's price is determined entirely by its factor loadings. Clearly it is important to know when factor pricing is exact and, more generally, to get an estimate of the amount by which it fails to be exact. We discuss this topic now. Suppose there is an approximate K factor structure. Let $\gamma_N = \|\mu_N - [e_N, B_N]\|_2^2$. Luedecke's dissertation (1984) contains a version of Theorem 2, which is useful for empirical work. Let T_{NK} be an $N \times K$ matrix whose columns are the eigenvectors corresponding to the K largest eigenvalues of Σ_N. Define

$$\delta_N = \sup |E(p)| / V^{1/2}(p) \quad \text{subject to } p \in F_N, \; C(p) = 0.$$

Then

$$\|\mu_N - [e, T_{NK}]\|_2^2 \leq \lambda_{K+1,N} \delta_N^2. \tag{29}$$

Chamberlain (1983b) obtained bounds of a different sort. He showed that if there is a riskless asset with rate of return ρ, then

$$\lambda_\infty^2 \rho^2 \|c\|_2^2 \leq \gamma(\tau) \leq \lambda_{K+1} \rho^2 \|c\|_2^2, \tag{30}$$

where c is the portfolio that represents the cost functional and $\gamma(\tau)$ is given by (28). It is an implication of (30) that factor pricing is exact if and only if c is well diversified. An analogous result holds if there is no risky asset. These bounds are especially interesting because they provide sharp upper and lower bounds on the accuracy of the APT.

Connor (1984) has developed an interesting set of conditions for factor prices to be exact. The setting is an exchange economy in which the participants exchange assets (random variables with given distributions). Let x be these assets. Connor's model is a general equilibrium model so the x's are specified in physical units. Suppose the x's have an approximate K factor structure and that idiosyncratic risk is mean independent of factor risk. That is, when disturbances are written as in (22), $E(\theta \mid f) = 0$. Let y be the vector of per capita endowments of assets in this economy. Connor shows that if y is well diversified, then in competitive equilibrium asset prices for this economy are consistent with exact factor pricing; a set of asset prices in which factor pricing is not exact cannot be a competitive equilibrium.[9] We may phrase this result somewhat loosely as stating that if the economy is large, in the sense that there are many investors and many assets, then factor pricing should be close to exact. In two similar papers, Dybvig (1983) and Grinblatt and Titman (1983) have shown how close to exact factor pricing must be. Both papers assume a strict factor structure in which factors and idiosyncratic noise are independent. The argument can be easily extended to deal with an approximate factor structure, but the independence assumption seems crucial. Dybvig's bounds are so sharp (his rough estimates suggest that no asset's risk premium should deviate from its factor price – $\Sigma_k \tau_k \beta_{ik}$ – by no more than 0.04 percent) that his work turns the APT into a theory like the CAPM in the sense that it provides a complete explanation of risk premia. However, this does not imply that the R^2 in regression tests of the APT must be high. Measurement error (in estimating expected returns and factors) is a serious problem in empirical work.

5.4   *The APT in a conditional setting*

Unlike the CAPM, the arbitrage pricing theory works well in a conditional setting. Our conditional model assumes that market participants have information s and make investment decisions on the basis of conditional distributions of asset returns. The analyst cannot observe s and can only estimate aspects of the unconditional or stationary distributions of asset returns. Suppose that the unconditional returns have an approximate K factor structure and that none of the conditional distributions (as described by μ_s and Σ_s) permit arbitrage. About the best result one could hope for is the following result due to Stambaugh (1983):

Theorem 3. Suppose unconditional returns have an approximate K factor structure and that conditional distributions do not permit arbitrage. Then

$$\|\bar{\mu} - [e_N, \bar{B}_N]\|_2 \quad \text{is uniformly bounded.}$$

Proof: It will suffice to show that assumption (A.i) holds for the unconditional data. Suppose that (A.i) does not hold for the conditional data. Then there is a sequence of portfolios $\{p_N\}$ such that $V(p_N) \to 0$. Also, $C(p_N) \to 0$ whereas $E(p_N)$ remains, at least on a subsequence, bounded away from 0. Let $q_N = p_N / E(p_N)$. Then

$$V(q_N) \to 0, \quad C(q_N) \to 0, \quad \text{and} \quad E(q_N) = 1.$$

The variance decomposition formula, $V(x) = E[V(x)|\tilde{s}] + V[E(x|\tilde{s})]$, implies that $V(q_{Ns}) \to 0$ and $E(q_{Ns}) \to 0$ for all s. Note that the cost of the portfolio q_N is independent of s. Thus the cost of q_N converges to zero, whereas for those whose beliefs are given by s,

$$V(q_N|s) \to 0 \quad \text{and} \quad E(q_N|s) \to 1.$$

Thus (A.i) is violated conditionally. ∎

Although this is a satisfying result, one would like to know more about the relationship between conditional and unconditional inferences in the context of the APT. There should be a sense in which unconditional arbitrage pricing is less exact than conditional arbitrage pricing. In particular, it would be interesting to compare how the bounds discussed above behave in conditional and unconditional settings.

5.5   Empirical tests of the APT

Tests of the arbitrage pricing theory have tended to focus on three questions: First, can factors be identified and used to explain risk premia? Second, are the explanations of risk premia sharp and are there a usefully small number of factors? Third, does the APT explain or resolve the anomalies that investigators of the CAPM have discovered? That is, after one has done the best job possible explaining risk premia in terms of factor loadings, do such anomalous variables as firm size and own variance still contribute to an explanation of risk premia?

Empirical work has not yet conclusively answered these three questions.[10] My reading of the current fragmentary state of the evidence is that the answers are "Yes" to the first question and "Partially" to the second and third questions.

The evidence on the first question is clearest. Several investigators have found factors and used them to explain risk premia. A common finding is that factors explain risk premia better than beta.[11] Representative studies are Roll and Ross (1980), Brown and Weinstein (1983), Chen (1983), and Luedecke (1984).

The evidence on the quality of the explanations of risk premia is more ambiguous. Several issues are involved. First is the question of how tight the explanations of risk premia should be in terms of the theoretical bounds discussed above. Equations (29) and (30) show how much of the variance in risk premia must be explained by factor loadings. If δ or $\|c\|_2$ is small, then R^2 in regressions of risk premia on factor loadings must be high.

Luedecke's attempts to estimate these quantities using CRSP data produced disappointingly large results.[12] Second is the question of how many factors there are. The APT is a useful theory only if a small number of factors explain risk premia well. Theorem 1 states a criterion for determining the number of factors in terms of the behavior of the eigenvalues of Σ_N. If there are K factors, K eigenvalues of Σ_N will grow without bound and all the others will remain bounded. Since one cannot determine in a finite sample whether an increasing sequence is bounded, this result is of somewhat limited value. Nonetheless, it suggests that it might be a good idea to construct sequences of variance–covariance matrices and look at the behavior of λ_{kN} as N grows. Both Luedecke (1984) and Trzcinka (1984) have done this. Their results are disappointing. They found that the first eigenvalue was much larger than the others and that it seemed to grow linearly. However, other eigenvalues are also growing. It is impossible to tell from their data whether there are two, seven, or fifteen factors. The hypothesis that there is just one factor does not seem attractive because Luedecke found that in regressions with risk premia as dependent variables the factors corresponding to eigenvalues other than the largest eigenvalue are often significant.

This evidence shows that it is not true that a few factors must explain risk premia well. It does not suggest that they cannot.[13] Even though there are a large number of factors in the sense of Theorem 1, it may well be that only a few factors are priced: Risk premia may be well explained by a small number of factors. Luedecke's results in this respect are quite encouraging. Using the daily returns for 392 securities over the period July 1962 to December 1981, he obtains an R^2 of 43.8 in a regression that explains risk premia with a constant and four factors; with one R^2 it is 23.7; with 10 factors it is 50.7. For cross-sectional regressions, these are very good results. In light of the discussion of conditional and unconditional versions of the APT, it is important to note that Luedecke's results are best when he uses all the data; results for separate subperiods do not make much sense. Using all of the data is justified by Theorem 3 above.

The third question research on the APT has focused on is whether or not factors provide explanations for such anomalies as the own variance effect and the firm size effect. Here again the results are mixed. Most researchers have found that factors (and not very many of them) make the own variance effect disappear. The evidence on the size effect is less clear. Chen (1983) and Chan, Chen, and Hsieu (1983) find that firm size does not explain risk premia in a factor model. Others, in particular Luedecke

(1984), have not found this. However, Luedecke notes that the firm size effect he finds is of no economic significance. Investors could not earn significantly higher returns by investing in the stocks of small firms.

NOTES

1 I deal exclusively with one-period models in this essay.
2 Not all researchers have restricted themselves to actual returns data. Cragg and Malkiel (1982) attempted to collect data on expectations that was sufficiently rich it could be used to examine the determination of assets' prices. They collected nine years of forecasts (by financial institutions) of growth and earnings for 260 of the companies whose stocks are traded on the New York Stock Exchange. Although rich, this data is quite meager compared to the CRSP data on actual returns (described in the next section). The Cragg and Malkiel data is annual whereas the CRSP data is daily or monthly. Cragg and Malkiel cover less than a tenth of the number of firms included in the CRSP files. Furthermore, it is not clear that the financial institutions that provided the raw data to Cragg and Malkiel would be willing to do so again. One of Cragg and Malkiel's findings was that analysts' forecasts did not contain much information. Although expectations data is unlikely to be used in preference to data on actual returns, it does reveal some interesting things. Cragg and Malkiel convincingly demonstrated that expectations are not homogeneous. Indeed, they found that one of the best measures of risk for the stock of a firm was the extent to which forecasts of the firm's growth differed.
3 The current U.S. administration is working hard to improve the market for human capital. However, one doubts that CRSP will soon have good data on the return to human capital. It is unfortunate that the period when data on the return to liquid human capital were relatively good (Fogel and Engerman 1974) was a period when asset markets were relatively undeveloped.
4 This section is taken from Chamberlain and Rothschild (1983). Many details are omitted.
5 In this essay, linear combinations are always finite linear combinations.
6 A linear functional is a real-valued linear mapping.
7 For an alternative discussion of the relation between conditional and unconditional mean–variance efficiency, see Hansen and Richard (1984).
8 The result that the τ_k are factor risk premia does not depend on factor pricing being exact. See Admati and Pfleiderer (1985) for a simpler proof; see also Ingersoll (1984) for an interpretation of this result.
9 Connor's definition of well diversified is different from Chamberlain's. However, in the context of an appropriate K factor structure, they are equivalent. Connor does not note, but it is easy to prove, that an approximate K factor structure implies that his condition (5), necessary and sufficient for exact factor pricing, holds.
10 The last revision of this essay that the indulgent editors would allow me was finished before I had a chance to read Lehman and Modest's massive and

careful study of the empirical properties of the APT. Although their results complement, qualify, and enrich the brief characterization given here, they do not contradict it. I commend their 1985 papers to anyone interested in the empirical status of the APT.

11   Confusion abounds about the relationship of the CAPM and the APT. Conversations with colleagues suggest that many economists believe that if the CAPM holds, then there must be a one-factor structure with that factor being the market portfolio. This is not true. Suppose that returns on a sequence of assets are normally distributed. The first N assets have variance–covariance matrix Σ_N. Because returns have a normal distribution, all risk-averse investors will choose mean–variance efficient portfolios. The CAPM will hold. However, whether or not there is a factor structure (exact or approximate) depends on the properties of the sequence $\{\Sigma_N\}$, which is in no way restricted. There could be a one-factor structure, a K factor structure, or no factor structure at all. What is true is that if factor pricing is exact – in the sense that (24) holds – and if asset pricing is consistent with the CAPM, then the market portfolio must be a linear combination of the factors. Thus, with exact factor pricing and a one-factor structure, if the CAPM holds, the market portfolio and the single factor are identical. Despite the lack of a necessary relationship, empirical work has found that factors and the market portfolio are closely related. In many studies, the largest or more important factor is closely correlated with the market portfolio. See, for example, Luedecke (1984).

12   It should be emphasized that Luedecke's attempts to estimate $\|c\|_2$ were quite casual.

13   This is somewhat too strong. In (30), Chamberlain shows that $\|c\|_2$ provides an upper bound on the quality of explanations of risk premia in terms of factor loadings. A conclusive finding that $\|c\|_2$ were large would preclude a tight explanation of risk premia by factor loadings.

REFERENCES

Admati, A. R. (1985), "A noisy rational expectations equilibrium for multi-asset securities markets," *Econometrica,* 53: 629–48.

Admati, A. R. and P. Pfleider (1985), "Interpreting the factor risk premia in the arbitrage pricing theory," *Journal of Economic Theory,* 35: 191–97.

Anderson, T. W. (1958), *An introduction to multivariate statistical analysis,* New York: Wiley.

Arrow, K. J. (1963–4), "The role of securities in the optimal allocation of risk-bearing," *Review of Economic Studies,* 31: 91–6.

Breeden, D. T. (1979), "An intertemporal asset pricing model with stochastic consumption and investment opportunities," *Journal of Financial Economics,* 7: 265–96.

Brock. W. A. (1982), "Asset pricing production economy," in John J. McCall (Ed.), *The economics of uncertainty and information,* Chicago: University of Chicago Press.

Brown, D. P. and M. R. Gibbons (1985), "A simple econometric approach for utility-based asset pricing models," *Journal of Finance,* 40: 359–81.

Brown, S. J. and M. I. Weinstein (1983), "A new approach to testing asset pricing models: The bilinear paradigm," *Journal of Finance,* 38: 711–44.

Chamberlain, G. (1983a), "A characterization of the distributions that imply mean–variance utility functions," *Journal of Economic Theory,* 28: 183–92.

Chamberlain, G. (1983b), "Funds, factors and diversification in arbitrage pricing models," *Econometrica,* 51: 1305–24.

Chamberlain, G. and M. Rothschild (1983), "Arbitrage, factor structure, and mean–variance analysis on large asset markets," *Econometrica,* 51: 1281–1304.

Chan, K. C., Nai-Fu Chen, and D. Hsieu (1983), "An explanatory investigation of the firm size effect," Working Paper No. 99, Center for Research in Security Prices, Graduate School of Business, University of Chicago.

Chen, Nai-Fu (1983), "Some empirical tests of the arbitrage pricing theory," *Journal of Finance,* 38: 1393–1414.

Chen, Nai-Fu, R. Roll, and S. A. Ross (1983), "Economic forces and the stock market: Testing the APT and alternative asset pricing theories," Working Paper No. 119, Center for Research in Security Prices, Graduate School of Business, University of Chicago.

Connor, G. (1984), "A unified beta pricing theory," *Journal of Economic Theory,* 34: 13–31.

Cragg, J. and B. Malkiel (1982), *Expectations and the structure of share prices,* Chicago: University of Chicago Press.

Debreu, G. (1959), *The theory of value,* New York: Wiley.

Dybvig, P. H. (1983), "An explicit bound on an individual asset's deviations from APT pricing in a finite economy," *Journal of Financial Economics,* 12: 483–96.

Fogel, R. W. and S. L. Engerman (1974), *Time on the cross,* Boston: Little Brown.

Grinblatt, M. and S. Titman (1983), "Factor pricing in a finite economy," *Journal of Financial Economics,* 12: 497–507.

Grossman, S. J. and R. J. Shiller (1982), "Consumption correlatedness and risk measurement in economies with non-traded assets and heterogenous information," *Journal of Financial Economics,* 10: 195–210.

Grossman, S. J., A. Melino, and R. J. Shiller (1985), "Estimating the continuous time consumption based asset pricing model," unpublished paper.

Hansen, L. P. and S. F. Richard (1984), "A general approach for deducing testable restrictions implied by asset pricing models," mimeo.

Huberman, G. (1982), "A simple approach to arbitrage pricing theory," *Journal of Economic Theory,* 28: 183–92.

Ingersoll, J. E. (1984), "Some results in the theory of arbitrage pricing," *Journal of Finance,* 38: 711–44.

Jensen, M. C. (1972), "Capital markets: Theory and evidence," *Bell Journal of Economics and Management Science,* 3: 357–98.

Lehman, B. N. and D. M. Modest (1985a), "The empirical foundation of the arbitrage pricing theory I: The empirical tests," Columbia University Department of Economics Discussion Paper.

Lehman, B. N. and D. M. Modest (1985b), "The empirical foundation of the arbitrage pricing theory II: The optimal construction of basis portfolios," Columbia University Department of Economics Discussion Paper.

Lehman, B. N. and D. M. Modest (1985c), "The empirical foundation of the arbitrage pricing theory III: A comparison of benchmarks and benchmark comparisons," Columbia University Department of Economics Discussion Paper.

Lintner, J. (1965), "The valuation of risky assets and the selection of risky investments in stock portfolios and capital budgets," *Review of Economics and Statistics,* 47: 13–37.

Luedecke, B. P. (1984), "An empirical investigation into arbitrage and approximate K-factor structure on large asset markets," unpublished doctoral dissertation, University of Wisconsin.

Mossin, J. (1966), "Equilibrium in a capital asset market," *Econometrica,* 34: 768–83.

Roll, R. (1977), "A critique of the asset pricing theory's tests," *Journal of Financial Economics,* 4: 129–76.

Roll, R. and S. A. Ross (1980), "An empirical investigation of the arbitrage pricing theory," *Journal of Finance,* 35: 1073–1103.

Ross, S. A. (1976), "The arbitrage theory of capital asset pricing," *Journal of Economic Theory,* 13: 341–60.

Schwert, G. W. (1983), "Size and stock returns, and other empirical regularities," *Journal of Financial Economics,* 12: 3–12.

Sharpe, W. F. (1964), "Capital asset prices: A theory of market equilibrium under conditions of risk," *Journal of Finance,* 19: 425–42.

Stambaugh, R. F. (1982), "On the exclusion of asset from tests of the two-parameter model: A sensitivity analysis," *Journal of Financial Economics,* 10: 237–68.

Stambaugh, R. F. (1982), "Arbitrage pricing with information," *Journal of Financial Economics,* 12: 357–69.

Treynor, J. L. (1961), "Towards a theory of market value of risky assets," unpublished paper.

Trzcinka, C. (1984), "On the number of factors in the arbitrage pricing model," University of Buffalo.

CHAPTER 5

Independence versus dominance in personal probability axioms

Thomas Marschak

1   Introduction

Why dig once again in a field as thoroughly ploughed as expected utility? Only because a mass of experimental work, and some recent theory as well, has pushed the *practitioner* of expected utility – and the teacher of future practitioners – into an uncomfortable corner. By the practitioner I mean the consultant or "decision analyst," hired as a professional guide through a tangled thicket by a decider faced with complex choices under uncertainty. Such a practitioner's main tool was and remains the original expected utility rule in its personal probability form. Up to now this rule stands alone in its simplifying power. It lets the practitioner break up the client's (the decider's) complex task of ranking alternative acts into manageable pieces. It permits the practitioner to elicit the client's beliefs and attitudes by asking small questions, to piece the responses together into a ranking of the contemplated complex acts, and to argue that the ranking is inescapable if the client wants to be consistent with personal attitudes and beliefs, consistent with a few basic axioms (constraints on the final ranking), and consistent with the rules of logic.

Yet the experiments of more than two decades have shown that competent persons cheerfully violate one or more of the classic axioms.[1] This has called forth some new theory, notably Machina's elegant "generalized" expected utility theory (Machina 1982), wherein both obeyers and violators of certain classic axioms exhibit the same kind of consistency: Both rank acts – specifically they rank probability distributions on a wealth interval – according to a smooth functional defined on such distributions. From the practitioner's viewpoint, however, there are two difficulties with the new theory: Probabilities are treated as "objective" (given to the decider without ambiguity) and the practitioner has no guidelines as to their elicitation; and there appears to be no general way of building up the required functional from answers to simple questions.

Decision analysis is, of course, vulnerable in a number of respects, quite aside from violations of the classic axioms themselves. The client may be uncomfortable even with the small questions and may give them contradictory answers.[2] Hence the procedure is best used when combined with appropriate "sensitivity analyses," which reveal the robustness of the final ranking when attitudes and beliefs are perturbed. Possibly, indeed, its most appealing form will eventually turn out to be one that yields conclusions like this: "If your beliefs belong to this family and your attitudes (utilities) to that family, then your ranking of the contemplated acts must be the following; if, on the other hand,. . . ." When taking such a form, and when judiciously applied to situations not outlandishly alien to the client's previous experience, decision analysis is unlikely to have a serious challenger when it comes to reducing complex choices to small questions.

Where, then, does the practitioner stand? The practitioner's possible responses to the experimental evidence include two extremes. One is to say that the experimental evidence is fatally damaging and to close up shop forever. The other is to say that any experimental evidence is totally irrelevant to prescriptive theory and to continue as if nothing had happened. The first response is abject surrender. The second, on the other hand, is insensitive, unrealistic, and self-defeating. The client is intelligent and, if not explicitly told the axioms on which the practitioner's advice rests, can surely smoke them out so as to ponder their acceptability. Having done so, the client may reject one or more of them and so may reject the analyst's ranking.

We take the view here that the practitioner's proper response lies between the two extremes. The honest, effective practitioner ought to attempt nothing less than teaching the client the elements of the prescriptive theory before proceeding to apply it, that is, to present the axioms one by one and then to sketch the argument that shows that the axioms imply the expected utility rule. If one or more of the axioms have been violated by competent persons in laboratory settings, then the client should be told so and should be invited to test his or her own compliance. If the client feels he or she is a confirmed violator, then analyst and client part company. That may strike some as a romantic picture of client and analyst, a world in which clients (deciders) are mathematicians, as inaccessible as a world in which philosophers are kings. Savage's advice that his book be read "sitting bolt upright in a hard chair" was, after all, addressed to mathematical statisticians and not to businessmen.

Nevertheless, it is toward such a relation between client and analyst that the experimental evidence has, I believe, pushed us. What remains quite undeveloped is the theory and practice of honest, effective, and realistically brief decision analysis *pedagogy*, wherein the smallest possible burden is placed on experimentally vulnerable axioms.[3]

We are concerned here with one step toward such a pedagogy, specifically with axiom systems that place a minimal burden on what is probably the most experimentally vulnerable of the classic personal probability axioms – the "independence" axiom. We shall present a system in which this burden is "small" (in a sense to be made precise) and shall compare it with (1) the Pratt–Raiffa–Schlaifer (PRS) axiom system (Pratt, Raiffa, and Schlaifer 1964) wherein the burden is a bit "larger," and (2) Marschak and Radner's (MR) finite version (Marschak and Radner 1972, Chapter 1) of the original Savage system (Savage 1954) wherein the burden is as "large" as it can be. The system to be presented, as well as the PRS system, do rely heavily on "dominance," or rather on its generalization, to be called "admissibility." We argue, however, that (in the absence of other evidence), dominance (and admissibility) appears to be a less vulnerable requirement than independence.

All three axiom systems are, of course, very close to each other; indeed to the newcomer (the client, for example) the differences may seem trivial. But it is precisely to such "trivial" differences that experimental work has sensitized us. Small differences in the way questions are asked (*framing*) may yield large differences in response. We may expect, analogously, that small differences between axiom systems yield large differences in pedagogical effectiveness – in a client's understanding and acceptance of the axiom system after honest instruction of the sort just sketched. The new system to be presented below would probably be viewed by many as more "complicated" than, say, the MR system, and the argument yielding the main expected utility theorem is doubtless more cumbersome. It may well be that extra complexity is the price one pays for suppressing the independence requirement.

To introduce the ideas, consider first two purely verbal axioms in which basic terms are not rigorously defined. One axiom (dominance) says, "If one act never has a worse result than another and sometimes a better result, then I prefer it." A second axiom (independence) says, "How I feel about one act versus another has nothing to do with the way they perform when both yield exactly the same result." I have presented these two informal statements to some thirty classes (advanced undergraduate and MBA students) at the start of their study of expected utility; they numbered about 600 students. They were asked to write responses to three questions: (1) Do either of these statements imply the other? (2) Do you personally agree with the first statement? (3) Do you personally agree with the second statement? About 80 percent of all students answered "no" to the first question. About 87 percent answered "yes" to the second. About 59 percent answered "yes" to the third. A series of classrooms, spanning a number of years, is far removed from a proper laboratory. Nevertheless, the experience would make me bet heavily that in the proper experimental setting a similar pattern would emerge. Dominance is a simple and persuasive norm; one need only think of the violator as a player of Russian roulette. I would judge (on the basis of considerably more sketchy classroom experience) that the bulk of those who accept dominance would also accept its generalization to admissibility. Admissibility, informally put, adds a second sentence to the dominance statement: "If one of two acts never has a worse result than the other and if I prefer the first act to the second, then the first must sometimes have a better result than the second."

Independence, on the other hand, has (I suggest) less of an immediate intuitive pull. To understand it requires more thought than dominance and, once understood, many may hesitate to accept it or may reject it. The experimental evidence indeed suggests that independence – when framed in concrete terms – is easily rejected.

Consider the classic Ellsberg experiment. The subject is asked to imagine an urn with ninety balls, thirty of them Red and sixty of them Green or Yellow, with the Green/Yellow split completely unknown. A pair of acts a and b are proposed in which \$100 and \$0 are the consequences:

	R	G	Y
a	100	0	0
b	0	100	0
$\hat{a}$	100	0	100
$\hat{b}$	0	100	100

The frequently observed Ellsberg violator prefers a to b; when pressed for articulation, the violator may say something about dislike of ambiguity. Asked next about $\hat{a}$ versus $\hat{b}$, the subject now prefers $\hat{b}$ and may again allude to a dislike of ambiguity. The subject has violated independence.

Now one *can* attempt to talk such a subject out of the violation by saying the following:

> You have accepted dominance and its generalization to admissibility. Note that I could *restate* acts $a, b, \hat{a}, \hat{b}$ in the following way. Under act a, if Yellow occurs, you get zero, But if Yellow does not occur, then you get a piece of paper (call it coupon α) which yields 100 for Red and zero for Green. Under act b, if Yellow occurs, you get zero and if Yellow does not occur you get another piece of paper (call it coupon β) which yields zero for Red and 100 for Green. Similarly, under $\hat{a}$, you get 100 if Yellow occurs and coupon α if it doesn't. Under $\hat{b}$, you get 100 if Yellow occurs and coupon β if it doesn't. If you accept admissibility, then your preference of a over b must mean that you like coupon α better than coupon β. But similarly your preference of $\hat{b}$ over $\hat{a}$ must mean that you like coupon β better than coupon α. You are not being consistent with your professed desire to obey admissibility.

Appealing again to nonrigorous classroom experience, I suggest that for a majority of Ellsberg violators this line of dissuasion does not work. Only around 40 percent of the student violators I observed announced a change of view in response to the statement. Many who resisted dissuasion commented that the introduction of the coupon changed the original story; it was not what they had in mind when they contemplated $a, b, \hat{a}, \hat{b}$, and it was *also* not what they had in mind when they accepted admissibility. Admissibility, in the context of the four acts, has to do with dollars as results and *not* with coupons as results.[4]

A central aim in what follows is precisely to clarify what kind of independence is implied by various kinds of admissibility. If an admissibility axiom explicitly included objects like coupon α and coupon β – *subacts* as we shall call them – then the dissuasive argument would be valid and the acceptor of admissibility could not engaged in such a violation of independence. *Elementary* admissibility (as we shall call it) deals only with the set of results used to define the acts being ordered (with dollars in the Ellsberg example). Elementary admissibility does not imply independence. Generalized admissibility, however, deals with subacts. It says that the subacts in a certain class can be ranked and that if the first of two acts is never worse than the second with regard to their subacts then the first act is preferred if and only if one subact is better for the first act then for the second. Such generalized admissibility *does* imply independence with respect to certain sets of act quadruples $(a, b, \hat{a}, \hat{b})$. The richer the set of rankable subacts, the larger the class of act quadruples exhibiting independence.

We continue to suppose that admissibility – even in a generalized form – is an appealing property unlikely to be widely rejected. Independence, however, is not innocuous, and we want each individual axiom to imply independence for as few act quadruples as possible. Accordingly, we shall be interested in axiom systems whose *precalibration* axioms imply independence for small sets of act quadruples because those axioms imply generalized admissibility only for small classes of subacts. Precalibration axioms are those that do *not* serve to introduce probabilities and utilities. They will be easily identifiable in the three axiom systems to be considered here. The *entire package* of axioms in a system implies the expected utility rule, and that in turn implies independence for all quadruples $(a, b, \hat{a}, \hat{b})$ in which (as in the Ellsberg example) $\hat{a}, \hat{b}$ are obtained from a, b by replacing one "column of common consequences" with another.[5] But the whole experimental effort – or at least that part of it specifically dealing with personal-probability axioms – has turned on the acceptability of key *individual* axioms, not the acceptability of the whole package. A subject who has no problem with any separate axiom but then notices that the entire package prevents engaging in behavior the subject finds natural (e.g., the Ellsberg violation) is in a very different position from a subject who finds one or two crucial axioms (e.g., the precalibration axioms) objectionable *in themselves*. The former subject has indeed learned something new about his or her behavior – namely, that it is inconsistent with principles to which the subject subscribes. The subject may seriously wish to reexamine his or her behavior.

The setting of the axiom system in Section 2 is quite similar to that of the PRS system. We are dealing with what Fishburn (1970, Chapter 13) calls "extraneous probabilities." There is a finite set E of "real-world" states e, and in addition there are sets X and Y of "benchmark outcomes." In the PRS case, X and Y are each the unit interval, $X \times Y$ is the unit square, a benchmark outcome is a point in the unit square, and a benchmark event (to which real-world events will be compared) is a rectangle in the unit square. Although the structure of several proofs is essentially to be found in the PRS paper (the proof of the basic probability properties; the final proof of the expected utility rule), the system of Section 2 has the following novelties:

(1) The benchmark outcomes are elements of a set $X \times Y$ that is infinite but denumerable. This somewhat softens an uncomfortable anomaly in the PRS system, namely, that the decider contemplates a finite set of real-world states but is asked to imagine a set of benchmark outcomes that is not only infinite but nondenumerable.

(2) In the PRS system there is a (finite) set C of consequences, and the acts to be ranked are functions from $E \times X \times Y$ to C. In Section 2, on the other hand, there is a (finite) set C of basic consequences and a set T of

tickets; a ticket is a function from $E \times X \times Y$ to C, but it is a function taking at most two values. An act is a function from $E \times X \times Y$ to T; the symbol A denotes the set of acts.

(3) We study an ordering defined not for all act pairs in $A \times A$ but only for a subset $\mathcal{Q}$ of such pairs.

(4) Calibration of beliefs and attitudes is optional. Only for the events in some set Ω of the subsets of E is there a personal probability; Ω, moreover, is not required to be a sigma field. Utilities are defined only for some subset Λ of the basic consequences in C. But since $\mathcal{Q}$ is specified *independently* of Ω and Λ, it need not be true that the ordering to be studied covers *all* acts that partition E into events that belong to Ω and yield tickets whose consequences belong to Λ. Thus the "optional" complication is not a completely trivial one.

(5) Section 2 adds a new axiom (Axiom 3) dealing with the equivalence of an act yielding *bets* – a bet is a ticket whose consequences are either W (the best consequence in C) or L (the worst) – with an appropriately constructed act yielding not bets but rather single-valued tickets, some of which have only W as a consequence and others only L. This axiom appears to be totally innocuous in itself, though its vulnerability is quite untested.

By permitting the ordering to be confined to an arbitrary subset of $A \times A$, and letting probabilities and utilities be optional, we permit another possible escape route for violators of the conventional axioms. The violator is free to take the position that even full acceptance of *all* the Section 2 axioms does not preclude the violator's behavior (e.g., in the Ellsberg example, it does not preclude "a is preferred to b and $\hat{b}$ is preferred to $\hat{a}$"). That is to say, the "violating" behavior does not in fact violate the expected utility ranking implied by the Section 2 axioms, because the probabilities and utilities needed to obtain that ranking are simply missing. Of course, the price to be paid for this flexibility is that the final expected utility theorem (Theorem 3 below) is a conditional one: Only if the required probabilities and utilities are available can two given acts be ranked according to expected utility. The decision analyst needs to obtain at least those probabilities and utilities if the expected utility rule is to be applied. The expected utility theorem of Section 2 becomes the normal one when $\mathcal{Q}$ is $A \times A$, Ω is the set of all subsets of E, and Λ is C itself.

In Section 3 we develop the tools needed to talk about (generalized) admissibility and independence for *any* ordering, and to compare any two orderings with regard to the "scope" of admissibility and of independence they exhibit.

Since we want to talk about (generalized) admissibility and independence for orderings on the ticket-yielding acts studied in Section 2, as well as for orderings on more conventionally defined acts (without tickets), the discussion of Section 3 requires a general setting, accommodating acts of both kinds. Accordingly the basic concepts are now "states" and "results," and an act is a function from states to results. The possible acts comprise the set A. A *subact* is a function from some subset of the states to the set of results. For a given subset of states, a *subact ordering* ranks all the subacts that can be defined for that subset. For an ℓ-fold *partitioning* of the set of states, we may speak of *subact ℓ-tuples*. But such a subact ℓ-tuple is, in fact, an act in A, since, as we pass over all the sets of the partitioning, we specify a result for every state. Given an ℓ-fold partitioning of the states, we can also speak of an *ℓ-tuple of subact orderings,* where each ordering of that ℓ-tuple ranks all the subacts defined for one of the partitioning's ℓ sets. Then, given an ℓ-fold partitioning of the states, given an ordering $\leq_A$ on the acts in A, and given a subset Δ of A, we say that a given ℓ-tuple of subact orderings *agrees with $\leq_A$ on Δ* if the following holds for any two subact ℓ-tuples a and b, where a and b (which are also acts) lie in Δ: if a is not worse than b with regard to any of its subacts (preference being indicated by the given ℓ-tuple of subact orderings), and if a is better than b with regard to one of its subacts, then $b <_A a$; if $b <_A a$ and a is not worse than b with regard to any of its subacts, then a is better than b with regard to at least one of its subacts.

The "agrees with $\leq$ on Δ" concept permits us to study the "scope" of (generalized) admissibility for a given ordering $\leq_A$. For a set Σ of partitionings of the states and a function ψ from Σ to the subsets of A, we say that $\leq_A$ is *admissible with respect to (Σ, ψ)* if and only if for every partitioning in Σ – say an ℓ-fold partitioning σ – there exists an ℓ-tuple of subact orderings that agrees with $\leq_A$ on the set $\psi(\sigma)$. If, in particular, Σ is the set of all possible partitionings, if ψ assigns to any partitioning the entire set A, and if the ordering $\leq_A$ is admissible with respect to that particular pair (Σ, ψ), then $\leq_A$ exhibits the widest possible (generalized) admissibility.

In a similar spirit, we define the statement "$\leq_A$ is independent with respect to (Σ, ψ)." Again, if we have found the pairs (Σ, ψ) with respect to which the ordering $\leq_A$ is independent, then we have found – in a precise sense – the scope of the independence property for that ordering. We are able, then, to make comparisons between two orderings with regard to the scope of both admissibility and independence.

In Section 3.1 we develop the concepts just sketched. In Section 3.2 we illustrate the concepts with regard to three *types* of orderings: an ordering that obeys the PRS precalibration axioms (suitably restated), an ordering that obeys the precalibration axioms of Section 2, and an ordering that obeys the MR precalibration axioms. In Section 3.3 we prove that admissibility with respect to a pair (Σ, ψ) implies independence with respect to that pair provided the pair obeys a certain simple condition (Theorem 4); and that under two further conditions the converse holds (Theorem 5). The conditions required in Theorems 4 and 5 are met for certain pairs (Σ, ψ) in each of the three illustrative orderings; but they are not met for *any* ordering if Σ contains only the "elementary" partitioning, each of whose sets is a singleton. In Section 3.4 we apply Theorem 4 to the three orderings and find that the independence property holds as widely as possible in the (precalibration) MR ordering, less widely in the PRS ordering, and less widely still in the ordering of Section 2. Here the term *less widely* is given two alternative precise meanings. It remains open whether independence can hold still less widely for still other precalibration axioms (still other axioms which, together with calibration, imply the expected utility rule). In any case there *are* axiom systems less vulnerable with regard to the scope of independence implied by their precalibration elements than the Savage system in its finite (MR) form. The PRS system and that of Section 2 are examples. As we shall note below, moreoever, the Ellsberg (and the Allais) violation – totally excluded by the MR precalibration axioms – *is* consistent with the precalibration axioms of the other two systems.

2   An axiom system wherein the independence required by the precalibration axioms is narrow in scope and probability and utility are optional

2.1   *Notation and preliminary definitions*

We are given the following sets:

1. E, a finite set of *real-world states e*.

2. For any integer $n \geq 1$, two n-element sets, $X^n \equiv \{x_1^n, \ldots, x_n^n\}$ and $Y^n \equiv \{y_1^n, \ldots, y_n^n\}$ of *benchmark outcomes*. The symbols x^n, y^n will denote, respectively, the typical element of each set. Thus, x^n can take the values $x_1^n, \ldots, x_n^n$ and y^n can take the values $y_1^n, \ldots, y_n^n$. The symbols X, Y denote infinite Cartesian products, namely, $X^1 \times X^2 \times \cdots$ and $Y^1 \times Y^2 \times \cdots$, respectively. The symbols x, y denote $(x^1, x^2, \ldots)$ and $(y^1, y^2, \ldots)$, respec-

tively. Thus $x \in X$ and $y \in Y$. The symbol S will sometimes be used to denote the set $E \times X \times Y$; the symbol s will sometimes be used to denote a typical element (e, x, y) of S. The typical element $s = (e, x, y)$ will sometimes be called a *state*.

If $E_0, X_0, X_0^i, Y_0, Y_0^i, S_0$ are, respectively, subsets of E, X, X^i, Y, Y^i, S, then the symbols $\bar{E}_0, \bar{X}_0, \bar{X}_0^i, \bar{Y}_0, \bar{Y}_0^i, \bar{S}_0$ will denote, respectively, the complementary sets $E \setminus E_0$, $X \setminus X_0$, $X^i \setminus X_0^i$, $Y \setminus Y_0$, $Y^i \setminus Y_0^i$, and $S \setminus S_0$.

3. A set C of *basic consequences,* with typical element c. The elements of C include a basic consequence called W ("win") and a basic consequence called L ("lose").

Definition 1. A function t from $E \times X \times Y$ to C, which is *at most two-valued,* is called a *ticket;* it takes the value $t(e, x, y) \in C$ for (e, x, y) in $E \times X \times Y$ and the set $\{t(e, x, y): (e, x, y) \in E \times X \times Y\}$ has one or two elements.

A *constant-valued* ticket t, that is, a ticket for which the set has just one element, is called a *sure ticket*. For c in C, the symbol t_c denotes the sure ticket defined by $t_c(e, x, y) = c$ for all (e, x, y) in $E \times X \times Y$.

The symbol T denotes the set of all tickets. The symbol $\bar{T}$ denotes the set of all sure tickets.

From here on, the phrase "all (e, x, y)" will be understood to mean "all (e, x, y) in $E \times X \times Y$."

Definition 2. A function a from $E \times X \times Y$ to T is called an *act;* its value for (e, x, y) is denoted $a(e, x, y)$. An act is *simple* if and only if it yields only sure tickets, that is, if and only if

$$a(e, x, y) \in \bar{T}, \quad \text{for all } (e, x, y).$$

An act is *compound* if it is not simple. If for some c in C the simple act a satisfies

$$a(e, x, y) = t_c, \quad \text{for all } (e, x, y),$$

then a is called a *sure act* and is denoted a_c. The set of all acts is denoted A; the set of all simple acts is denoted $\bar{A}$.

Interpretation: For a given state $(\bar{e}, \bar{x}, \bar{y})$ the act a yields a ticket in T, namely, the ticket $a(\bar{e}, \bar{x}, \bar{y})$, which we may, if we wish, denote by $t^{a\bar{e}\bar{x}\bar{y}}$. The ticket $t^{a\bar{e}\bar{x}\bar{y}}$, like any ticket, specifies a basic consequence (one of a set of at most two basic consequences) for *every* state (e, x, y). But since the state $(\bar{e}, \bar{x}, \bar{y})$ has already occurred when the holder of the ticket $t^{a\bar{e}\bar{x}\bar{y}}$

acquires that ticket, the holder in fact experiences only *one* basic consequence, namely, the basic consequence $t^{a\bar{e}\bar{x}\bar{y}}(\bar{e}, \bar{x}, \bar{y})$.

We are interested in a decider's ordering on the act pairs contained in some subset $\mathcal{Q}$ of $A \times A$, the set of *all* act pairs. We denote the ordering by $\leq$. For (a', a'') in $\mathcal{Q}$, either $a' \leq a''$ or $a'' \leq a'$.

Definition 3. For (a', a'') in $\mathcal{Q}$,

> $a' \sim a''$ means $a' \leq a''$ and $a'' \leq a'$;
> $a' < a''$ means $a' \leq a''$ and not $a' \sim a''$;
> $a' > a''$ means $a'' < a'$.

We sometimes use the terms "is indifferent to" or "is equivalent to" instead of the symbol $\sim$.

2.2 The axioms

We now impose conditions (axioms) on the set $\mathcal{Q}$ and the ordering $\leq$, pausing from time to time to interpret the conditions, to make remarks, to introduce further definitions, and to establish intermediate results. We shall often write $a \leq b$ (or $a < b$ or $a \sim b$), where (a, b) is some pair of acts in $\mathcal{Q}$, without troubling to add the statement $(a, b) \in \mathcal{Q}$. In such cases the missing statement will be seen to follow in an obvious way from the assumption being made.

Axiom 1

(i) (Reflexivity). For all (a', a'') in $\mathcal{Q}$, $a' \sim a''$.

(ii) (Transitivity). If (a', a''), (a'', a'''), (a', a''') are in $\mathcal{Q}$ and if $a' \leq a''$ and $a'' \leq a'''$, then $a' \leq a'''$.

(iii) (All sure-act pairs are ordered.) The set $\mathcal{Q}$ includes the set $\{(a_{c'}, a_{c''}): c', c'' \in C\}$.

(iv) [There is a best sure act (yielding the "win ticket" t_W) and a worst sure act (yielding the "lose ticket" t_L).] For any basic consequence c in C, with $c \neq L$, $c \neq W$, we have $a_L \leq a_c$ and $a_c \leq a_W$. Also $a_L < a_W$.

Remark 1: In the usual way, (ii) has the following implication for (a', a''), (a'', a'''), and (a', a''') all in $\mathcal{Q}$:

> if $a' \leq a''$ and $a'' < a'''$, then $a' < a'''$;
> if $a' < a''$ and $a'' \leq a'''$, then $a' < a'''$;
> if $a' \sim a''$ and $a'' \sim a'''$, then $a' \sim a'''$.

Definition 4. Two tickets t', t'' in T are said to be *comparable for* $\mathcal{Q}, \leq$ if and only if $(a^{t'}, a^{t''}) \in \mathcal{Q}$, where for any t in T we define the (simple) act a^t by

$$a^t(e, x, y) = t_{t(e, x, y)} \in \bar{T}.$$

(Recall that the symbol t_c denotes the sure ticket associated with the basic consequence c). If t', t'' are comparable tickets, then we write:

$$t' \lesssim_T t'' \quad \text{if and only if } a^{t'} \lesssim a^{t''};$$
$$t' \sim_T t'' \quad \text{if and only if } a^{t'} \sim a^{t''};$$
$$t' <_T t'' \quad \text{if and only if } a^{t'} < a^{t''}.$$

Interpretation: With any ticket t we can associate the simple act a^t which yields, for any state (e, x, y), the sure ticket corresponding to the basic consequence $t(e, x, y)$. Two tickets can be ordered if the simple acts associated with them can be ordered.

Remark 2: It follows from (iii) of Axiom 1 and from Definition 4 that the sure tickets t_W, t_L are comparable for $\mathcal{Q}, \leq$. It follows from (iv) of Axiom 1 and Definition 4 that $t_L < t_W$.

Remark 3: Suppose that the acts a', a'' with $(a', a'') \in \mathcal{Q}$ are of the form

$$a'(s) = \begin{cases} t_W & \text{if } s \in S', \\ t_L & \text{otherwise,} \end{cases} \qquad a''(s) = \begin{cases} t_W & \text{if } s \in S'', \\ t_L & \text{otherwise,} \end{cases}$$

where $S' \subseteq S$, $S'' \subseteq S$. (We shall shortly be calling these acts an *act-bet on S'* and an *act-bet on S''*.) Then the tickets t', t'' defined by

$$t'(s) = \begin{cases} W & \text{if } s \in S', \\ L & \text{otherwise,} \end{cases} \qquad t''(s) = \begin{cases} W & \text{if } s \in S'', \\ L & \text{otherwise,} \end{cases}$$

are, according to Definition 4, comparable for $\mathcal{Q}, \leq$. (We shall be calling t', t'' a *ticket-bet on S'* and a *ticket-bet on S''*.)

Axiom 2 (Elementary admissibility). Suppose that a', a'' satisfy

   (i) $(a', a'') \in \mathcal{Q}$;
   (ii) for every (e, x, y), the tickets $a'(e, x, y)$ and $a''(e, x, y)$ are comparable;
   (iii) for all (e, x, y), $a'(e, x, y) \lesssim_T a''(e, x, y)$;
   (iv) for some (e, x, y), $a'(e, x, y) <_T a'(e, x, y)$.

                          (2.1)

Then we have

(v) $a' < a''$.

In addition,

(vi) If (i), (ii), (iii), and (v) hold, then so does (iv).

Remark 4: Axiom 2 implies that $a' \lesssim a''$ if $a'(e, x, y) \lesssim_T a''(e, x, y)$ for all (e, x, y). Axiom 2 also implies "elementary substitutability," that is, it implies that if a', a'' satisfy (i) to (iii) with $\sim_T$ replacing $\lesssim_T$, then $a' \sim a''$. Moreover, (vi) is implied by elementary substitutability and the statement that (2.1) implies (v). That is to say, an axiom equivalent to Axiom 2 consists of elementary substitutability plus the statement that (2.1) implies (v).

Definition 5. If $S_0 \subset S$, then the (simple) act a in A is called an *act-bet on S*, and is denoted $\beta(S_0)$ if and only if

$$a(s) = \begin{cases} t_W & \text{if } s \in S_0, \\ t_L & \text{otherwise.} \end{cases}$$

On the other hand, the ticket t in T is called a *ticket-bet on S_0*, and is denoted $\beta^T(S_0)$, if and only if:

$$t(s) = \begin{cases} W & \text{if } s \in S_0, \\ L & \text{otherwise.} \end{cases}$$

For $S_0 = E_0 \times X \times Y$ and $E_0 \subseteq E$, we define

$$\gamma(E_0) \equiv \beta(S_0), \qquad \gamma^T(E_0) \equiv \beta^T(S_0).$$

For $S_0 = E \times X^1 \times \cdots \times X^{i-1} \times X_0^i \times X^{i+1} \times \cdots \times Y$ and $X_0^i \subseteq X^i$, we define

$$\gamma(X_0^i) \equiv \beta(S_0), \qquad \gamma^T(X_0^i) \equiv \beta^T(S_0).$$

For $S_0 = E \times X \times Y^1 \times \cdots \times Y^{i-1} \times Y_0^i \times Y^{i+1} \times \cdots$ and $Y_0^i \subseteq Y^i$, we define

$$\gamma(Y_0^i) \equiv \beta(S_0), \qquad \gamma^T(Y_0^i) \equiv \beta^T(S_0).$$

For $S_0 = E \times X^1 \times \cdots \times X^{i-1} \times X_0^i \times X^{i+1} \times \cdots \times Y^1 \times \cdots \times Y^{j-1} \times Y_0^j \times Y^{j+1} \times \cdots$ and $X_0^i \subseteq X^i$, $Y_0^j \subseteq Y^j$, we define

$$\gamma(X_0^i, Y_0^j) = \beta(S_0), \qquad \gamma^T(X_0^i, Y_0^j) \equiv \beta^T(S_0).$$

Axiom 3. Certain compound acts can be modified to obtain equivalent acts that are simple or are "closer" to being simple; certain simple acts can be modified to obtain equivalent compound acts.

First part: Suppose the acts $a, \tilde{a}$ satisfy, for some $E_0 \subset E$, $x^* \in X$

(i) $a(e, x^*, y) = \begin{cases} t_W & \text{if } e \in E_0, \\ t_L & \text{if } e \in \bar{E}_0, \end{cases}$

where (to recall) $\bar{E}_0$ denotes $E \setminus E_0$;

(ii) $a(e, x^*, y) = \gamma^T(E_0)$, all e in E, all y in Y;

(iii) $a(e, x, y) = \tilde{a}(e, x, y)$, all (e, x, y) in $E \times (X \setminus \{x^*\}) \times Y$.

Then

$$(a, \tilde{a}) \in \mathcal{Q} \quad \text{and} \quad a \sim \tilde{a}.$$

Second part: Suppose $a, \tilde{a}$ satisfy, for some $E_0 \subset E$, $y^* \in Y$

(i) $a(e, x, y^*) = \begin{cases} t_W & \text{if } e \in E_0, \\ t_L & \text{if } e \in \bar{E}_0; \end{cases}$

(ii) $a(e, x, y^*) = \gamma^T(E_0)$, all e in E, all x in X;

(iii) $a(e, x, y) = \tilde{a}(e, x, y)$, all (e, x, y) in $E \times X \times (Y \setminus \{y^*\})$.

Then

$$(a, \tilde{a}) \in \mathcal{Q} \quad \text{and} \quad a \sim \tilde{a}.$$

Third part: Suppose $a, \tilde{a}$ satisfy, for some e^* in E, $X_0^i \subseteq X^i$, i a positive integer,

(i) $a(e^*, x, y) = \begin{cases} t_W & \text{if } x^i \in X_0^i, \\ t_L & \text{if } x^i \in \bar{X}_0^i; \end{cases}$

(ii) $\tilde{a}(e^*, x, y) = \gamma^T(X_0^i)$, all x in X, all y in Y;

(iii) $a(e, x, y) = \tilde{a}(e, x, y)$, all (e, x, y) in $(E \setminus \{e^*\}) \times X \times Y$.

Then

$$(a, \tilde{a}) \in \mathcal{Q} \quad \text{and} \quad a \sim \tilde{a}.$$

Fourth part: Suppose $a, \tilde{a}$ satisfy, for some e^* in E, $Y_0^i \subseteq Y^i$, i a positive integer,

(i) $a(e^*, x, y) = \begin{cases} t_W & \text{if } y^i \in Y_0^i, \\ t_L & \text{if } y^i \in \bar{Y}_0^i; \end{cases}$

(ii) $\tilde{a}(e^*, x, y) = \gamma^T(Y_0^i)$, all x in X, all y in Y;

(iii) $a(e, x, y) = \tilde{a}(e, x, y)$, all (e, x, y) in $(E \setminus \{e^*\}) \times X \times Y$.

Then

$$(a, \tilde{a}) \in \mathcal{Q} \quad \text{and} \quad a \sim \tilde{a}.$$

Fifth part: Suppose $a, \tilde{a}$ satisfy, for some x^* in X, $Y_0^i \subseteq Y^i$, i a positive integer,

(i) $a(e, x^*, y) = \begin{cases} t_W & \text{if } y^i \in Y_0^i, \\ t_L & \text{if } y^i \in \bar{Y}_0^i; \end{cases}$

(ii) $\tilde{a}(e, x^*, y) = \gamma^T(Y_0^i)$, all e in E, all y in Y;

(iii) $a(e, x, y) = \tilde{a}(e, x, y)$, all (e, x, y) in $E \times (X \setminus \{x^*\}) \times Y$.

Then

$$(a, \tilde{a}) \in \mathcal{Q} \quad \text{and} \quad a \sim \tilde{a}.$$

Sixth part: Suppose $a, \tilde{a}$ satisfy, for some y^* in Y, $X_0^i \subseteq X^i$, i a positive integer,

(i) $a(e, x, y^*) = \begin{cases} t_W & \text{if } x^i \in X_0^i, \\ t_L & \text{if } x^i \in \bar{X}_0^i; \end{cases}$

(ii) $\tilde{a}(e, x, y^*) = \gamma^T(X_0^i)$, all e in E, all x in X;

(iii) $a(e, x, y) = \tilde{a}(e, x, y)$, all (e, x, y) in $E \times X \times (Y \setminus \{y^*\})$.

Then

$$(a, \tilde{a}) \in \mathcal{Q} \quad \text{and} \quad a \sim \tilde{a}.$$

Interpretation: The statement of the axiom is cumbersome (a compact version is elusive and in any case the above six-part version makes subsequent reference easier). But the idea is simple. Consider the first part. The act $\tilde{a}$ is a compound act yielding a ticket-bet on E_0 if $x = x^*$. The act a modifies $\tilde{a}$ so as to bring it "closer" to a simple act: Under a, the decider receives, if $x = x^*$, not a proper ticket-bet (yielding W for some states and L for others) but rather the sure ticket t_W or the sure ticket t_L. The act a would, in fact, be a simple act if $a(e, x, y)$ were also a sure ticket for all $x \neq x^*$. Alternatively, the act $\tilde{a}$ may be viewed as modifying act a (which might be simple) so that it becomes a compound act with respect to the states in $E_0 \times \{x^*\} \times Y$ (i.e., for those states it now yields a proper ticket-bet rather than a sure ticket).

The interpretation of the remaining five parts of the axiom is analogous.

Axiom 4 (Benchmark outcomes and the ordering of benchmark act-bets)

(i) For any integer $i > 0$, any integer g in $[1, i]$, and any two g-tuples $(\ell_1, \ldots, \ell_g)$, $(m_1, \ldots, m_g)$, each composed of distinct integers selected from $[1, g]$, we have

$$[\gamma(\{x_{\ell_1}^i, x_{\ell_2}^i, \ldots, x_{\ell_g}^i\}), \gamma(\{x_{m_1}^i, x_{m_2}^i, \ldots, x_{m_g}^i\})] \in \mathcal{Q},$$

and these two act-bets are indifferent;

$$[\gamma(\{y_{\ell_1}^i, y_{\ell_2}^i, \ldots, y_{\ell_g}^i\}), \gamma(\{y_{m_1}^i, y_{m_2}^i, \ldots, y_{m_g}^i\})] \in \mathcal{Q},$$

and these two act-bets are indifferent.

(ii)   For any positive integers i, k we have

$$[\gamma(\{x_1^i\}), \gamma(\{x_1^{ik}, x_2^{ik}, \ldots, x_i^{ik}\})] \in \mathcal{Q},$$

and these two act-bets are indifferent;

$$[\gamma(\{y_1^i\}), \gamma(\{y_1^{ik}, y_2^{ik}, \ldots, y_k^{ik}\})] \in \mathcal{Q},$$

and these two act-bets are indifferent.

(iii)   (Bets on "double" benchmark events): Given positive integers i, j, r, s, r', s' with $r, r' \in [0, i]$ and $s, s' \in [0, j]$; given an r-tuple and an r'-tuple of distinct integers selected from $[0, i]$, say $(\ell_1, \ldots, \ell_r)$, $(\ell_1', \ldots, \ell_r')$; and given an s-tuple and an s'-tuple of distinct integers selected from $[0, j]$, say $(m_1, \ldots, m_s)$, $(m_1', \ldots, m_{s'}')$; we then have

$$[\gamma(\{x_{\ell_1}^i, x_{\ell_2}^i, \ldots, x_{\ell_r}^i\}, \{y_{m_2}^j, y_{m_2}^j, \ldots, y_{m_s}^j\}),$$
$$\gamma(\{x_{\ell_1}^i, x_{\ell_2}^i, \ldots, x_{\ell_{r'}}^i\}, \{y_{m_1'}^j, y_{m_2'}^j, \ldots, y_{m_{s'}'}^j\})] \in \mathcal{Q},$$

and if $r = r'$ and $s = s'$, the two act-bets in this pair are indifferent.

(iv)   (A bet on a double benchmark event is indifferent to a bet on an appropriate single benchmark event.) Given positive integers i, j, m, n, with $m \leq i$, $n \leq j$, we have

$$[\gamma(\{x_1^i, \ldots, x_m^i\}, \{y_1^j, \ldots, y_n^j\}), \gamma(\{x_1^{ij}, \ldots, x_{mn}^{ij}\})] \in \mathcal{Q},$$

and these two act-bets are indifferent.

Interpretation: There are two families of benchmark devices, the X family and the Y family. For any integer i, there is an "ith X device" and an "ith Y device." Each of these has i possible outcomes. Part (i) says that a bet on the event composed of any g of these i outcomes (g might equal one) and a bet on the event composed of any other g of these i outcomes can be ordered and are indifferent to each other. Part (ii) says [in conjunction with Part (i)] that a bet on any one of the ith X device's outcomes can be ordered with respect to a bet on the event composed of any k of the (ik)th X device's outcomes, and these two bets are indifferent to each other; and similarly for the Y devices. Part (iii) concerns "double outcomes," that is, a pair composed of two outcomes, one from an X device and one from a Y device. It says that a bet on the event composed of any rs double outcomes of an X device and a Y device (r outcomes from the former and s from the latter) can be ordered with respect to the event composed of $r's'$ such double outcomes and that the two bets are indifferent if $r = r'$, $s = s'$. Part (iv) says that a bet on the event composed of the double outcomes corresponding to the first m outcomes of the ith X device and the first n outcomes of the jth Y device can be ordered with respect to a bet on the event composed of the first mn outcomes of the (ij)th X device, and that the two bets are indifferent. In view of (i), (iii), and (iv), that statement holds also when "any m," "any n," and "any mn" replace "the first m," "the first n," and "the first mn."

Remark 5: With each of the benchmark act-bets, say $\gamma(S_0)$, described in (i)–(iv) (where $S_0 \subset S$ is a benchmark event), we can associate a ticket-bet $\gamma^T(S_0)$, following Definition 5. (Recall that an act-bet yields the ticket t_W or the ticket t_L; a ticket-bet yields W itself or L itself.) Each of (i)–(iv) imposes the condition that a certain *pair* of act-bets lies in $\mathcal{C}$. It then follows from Remark 3 that the corresponding pair of ticket-bets is comparable for $\mathcal{C}$, $\leq$.

We now have an intermediate result.

Lemma 1. Let $m, n, k', k'', \bar{k}', \bar{k}''$ be positive integers with $k' \leq m$, $k'' \leq n$, $\bar{k}' \leq m$, $\bar{k}'' \leq n$. Let $(\ell'_1, \ldots, \ell'_{k'})$, $(\bar{\ell}'_1, \ldots, \bar{\ell}'_{\bar{k}'})$ be, respectively, a k'-tuple and a $\bar{k}'$-tuple of distinct integers selected from $[1, m]$. Similarly let $(\ell''_1, \ldots, \ell''_{k''})$, $(\bar{\ell}''_1, \ldots, \bar{\ell}''_{\bar{k}''})$ be, respectively, a k''-tuple and a $\bar{k}''$-tuple of distinct integers selected from $[1, n]$. Then if $(\mathcal{C}, \leq)$ satisfies Axioms 1–4, we have

$$[\gamma(\{x^m_{\ell'_1}, \ldots, x^m_{\ell'_{k'}}\}, \{y^n_{\ell''_1}, \ldots, y^n_{\ell''_{k''}}\}), \gamma(\{x^m_{\bar{\ell}'_1}, \ldots, x^m_{\bar{\ell}'_{\bar{k}'}}\}, \{y^n_{\bar{\ell}''_1}, \ldots, y^n_{\bar{\ell}''_{\bar{k}''}}\})] \in \mathcal{C}; \tag{2.2}$$

and in addition we have that the first of these act-bets is indifferent to the second if and only if

$$k'k'' = \bar{k}'\bar{k}''. \tag{2.3}$$

Proof: Statement (2.2) is given directly in (iii) of Axiom 4. By (iii) and (iv) of Axiom 4, moreover,

$$\gamma(\{x^m_{\ell'_1}, \ldots, x^m_{\ell'_{k'}}\}, \{y^n_{\ell''_1}, \ldots, y^n_{\ell''_{k''}}\}) \sim \gamma(\{x^m_1, \ldots, x^m_{k'}\}, \{y^n_1, \ldots, y^n_{k''}\})$$
$$\sim \gamma(\{x^{mn}_1, \ldots, x^{mn}_{k'k''}\})$$

and

$$\gamma(\{x^m_{\bar{\ell}'_1}, \ldots, x^m_{\bar{\ell}'_{\bar{k}'}}\}, \{y^n_{\bar{\ell}''_1}, \ldots, y^n_{\bar{\ell}''_{\bar{k}''}}\}) \sim \gamma(\{x^m_1, \ldots, x^m_{\bar{k}'}\}, \{y^n_1, \ldots, y^n_{\bar{k}''}\})$$
$$\sim \gamma(\{x^{mn}_1, \ldots, x^{mn}_{\bar{k}'\bar{k}''}\}).$$

In view of (ii) of Axiom 1 (transitivity), therefore, it is enough to show that (2.3) holds if and only if

$$\gamma(\{x_1^{mn}, \ldots, x_{k'k''}^{mn}\}) \sim \gamma(\{x_1^{mn}, \ldots, x_{\bar{k}'\bar{k}''}^{mn}\}). \tag{2.4}$$

As stated in Remark 2, the sure tickets t_W, t_L are comparable for $\mathcal{Q}, \leq$ and, moreover, $t_L \leq_T t_W$. Now suppose that (2.3) holds. Then using the elementary substitutability implied by Axiom 2 (see Remark 4), we immediately have (2.4). Suppose, on the other hand, that (2.4) holds. It follows from (ii) of Axiom 2 that if $kk' > \bar{k}'\bar{k}''$ or $kk' < \bar{k}'\bar{k}''$ then (2.4) could not hold. Hence (2.3) must hold. That completes the proof.   ∎

Definition 6 (Personal probability). Let Ω be that set of subsets of E such that for all sets $E_0 \in \Omega$ there exist positive integers m, n for which

$$n \geq m > 0, \qquad [\gamma(E_0), \gamma(\{x_1^n, \ldots, x_m^n\})] \in \mathcal{Q},$$

and

$$\gamma(E_0) \sim \gamma(\{x_1^n, \ldots, x_m^n\}).$$

For $E_0 \in \Omega$, we define

$$P(E_0) \equiv \frac{m}{n}.$$

$P(E_0)$ is called the *(personal) probability* of E_0.

Remark 6: It follows from (ii) of Axiom 4 that if $E_0 \in \Omega$ and $P(E_0) = m/n$, then $\gamma(E_0) \sim \gamma(\{y_1^n, \ldots, y_m^n\})$. Further, Axioms 1–4 imply that if $E_0 \in \Omega$, then the number $P(E_0)$ is unique.

Proof: Suppose $\gamma(E_0) \sim \gamma(\{x_1^n, \ldots, x_m^n\})$ and also $\gamma(E_0) \sim \gamma(\{x_1^{n'}, \ldots, x_{m'}^{n'}\}$. Then by (iii) of Axiom 4 and (ii) of Axiom 1 (transitivity) we also have

$$\gamma(E_0) \sim \gamma(\{x_1^{nn'}, \ldots, x_{mn'}^{nn'}\}) \quad \text{and} \quad \gamma(E_0) \sim \gamma(\{x_1^{nn'}, \ldots, x_{m'n}^{nn'}\}).$$

By transitivity,

$$\gamma(\{x_1^{nn'}, \ldots, x_{mn'}^{nn'}\}) \sim \gamma(\{x_1^{nn'}, \ldots, x_{m'n}^{nn'}\}).$$

By Remark 2 (on the comparability of the tickets t_W, t_L) and by Axiom 2, it then follows that

$$\frac{m}{n} = \frac{m'}{n'}.   ∎$$

Remark 7: Note that we do not require that Ω be a sigma field. The decider may simply decline to assign a probability to $E \cup F$, even though one is assigned to E and to F.

We now have two theorems concerning the "optional" personal probabilities just defined.

Theorem 1. If $E \in \Omega$, then $P(E) = 1$.

Proof: It follows from Definition 4 (bets) that the act-bet $\gamma(E)$ is identical to, and hence [by (i) of Axiom 1] indifferent to, the act-bet $\gamma(\{x_1^m, ..., x_m^m\})$ for any $m > 0$. Hence $P(E) = m/m = 1$.

Theorem 2. If Ω contains E_1, E_2 and $E_1 \cup E_2$, if E_1 and E_2 are disjoint, and if $(\mathcal{Q}, \leq)$ obeys Axioms 1–4, then

$$P(E_1 \cup E_2) = P(E_1) + P(E_2).$$

Proof: We can choose integers $n, \bar{m}_1, \bar{\bar{m}}_2, m_{12}$ so that

$$P(E_1) = \frac{m_1}{n}, \quad P(E_2) = \frac{m_2}{n}, \quad P(E_1 \cup E_2) = \frac{m_{12}}{n}.$$

Let $X_0^2 = \{x_1^2\}$ and hence $\bar{X}_0^2 = \{x_2^2\}$. Consider the simple act a_1 defined by

$$a_1(e, x, y) = \begin{cases} t_W & \text{if } y^n \in \{y_1^n, ..., y_{m_{12}}^n\}, \ x^2 \in X_0^2 \\ t_L & \text{if } y^n \in \{y_{m_{12}+1}^n, ..., y_n^n\}, \ x^2 \in X_0^2, \\ t_L & \text{if } x^2 \in \bar{X}_0^2. \end{cases}$$

Consider the compound[6] act

$$\tilde{a}_1(e, x, y) = \begin{cases} \gamma^T(\{y_1^n, ..., y_{m_{12}}^n\}) & \text{if } x^2 \in X_0^2, \\ a_1(e, x, y) & \text{otherwise}. \end{cases}$$

By the fourth part of Axiom 3, we have

$$a_1 \sim \tilde{a}_1. \tag{2.5}$$

But by the definition of P and Remark 5, the ticket-bets $\gamma^T(\{y_1^n, ..., y_{m_{12}}^n\})$, $\gamma^T(E_1 \cup E_2)$ are comparable for $(\mathcal{Q}, \leq)$ and

$$\gamma^T(\{y_1^n, ..., y_{m_{12}}^n\}) \sim_T \gamma^T(E_1 \cup E_2). \tag{2.6}$$

Now consider the compound act $\tilde{a}_2$ defined by

$$\tilde{a}_2(e, x, y) = \begin{cases} \gamma^T(E_1 \cup E_2) & \text{if } x^2 \in X_0^2, \\ \tilde{a}_1(e, x, y) & \text{otherwise}. \end{cases}$$

In view of (2.5), (2.6), and Axiom 2 (specifically its elementary substitutability implication), we have

$$\tilde{a}_1 \sim \tilde{a}_2. \tag{2.7}$$

In view of the definitions of $\tilde{a}_1$ and a_1, we can also write

$$\tilde{a}_2(e, x, y) = \begin{cases} \gamma^T(E_1 \cup E_2) & \text{if } x^2 \in X_0^2, \\ t_L & \text{otherwise.} \end{cases}$$

Consider the simple act defined by

$$a_2(e, x, y) = \begin{cases} t_W & \text{if } e \in E_1 \cup E_2, \ x_2 \in X_0^2, \\ t_L & \text{if } e \notin E_1 \cup E_2, \ x_2 \in X_0^2, \\ t_L & \text{otherwise.} \end{cases} \tag{2.8}$$

We have, by the first part of Axiom 3,

$$\tilde{a}_2 \sim a_2. \tag{2.9}$$

Next note that we can also write, in view of (2.8),

$$a_2(e, x, y) = \begin{cases} t_W & \text{if } e \in E_1, \ x_2 \in X_0^2, \\ t_W & \text{if } e \in E_2, \ x_2 \in X_0^2, \\ t_L & \text{if } e \in E_1, \ x_2 \in \bar{X}_0^2, \\ t_L & \text{otherwise.} \end{cases}$$

Consider the compound act $\tilde{a}_3$ defined by

$$\tilde{a}_3(e, x, y) = \begin{cases} \gamma^T(X_0^2) & \text{if } e \in E_1, \\ \gamma^T(X_0^2) & \text{if } e \in E_2, \\ t_L & \text{otherwise.} \end{cases}$$

By *two* applications of the third part of Axiom 3, we have

$$a_2 \sim \tilde{a}_3. \tag{2.10}$$

Consider next another compound act, namely, $\tilde{a}_4$, defined by

$$\tilde{a}_4(e, x, y) = \begin{cases} \gamma^T(X_0^2) & \text{if } e \in E_1, \\ \gamma^T(\bar{X}_0^2) & \text{if } e \in E_2, \\ t_L & \text{otherwise.} \end{cases}$$

The act $\tilde{a}_4$ is well defined, since E_1 and E_2 are disjoint. By (i) of Axiom 4 and by Remark 5, the tickets $\gamma^T(X_0^2)$, $\gamma^T(\bar{X}_0^2)$ are comparable for $\mathcal{C}$, $\leq$ and $\gamma^T(X_0^2) \sim_T \gamma^T(\bar{X}_0^2)$.

Hence, by Axiom 2 (its elementary substitutability implication again) we have

$$\tilde{a}_3 \sim \tilde{a}_4. \tag{2.11}$$

Consider next the simple act a_4 defined by

$$a_4(e,x,y) = \begin{cases} t_W & \text{if } e \in E_1, \ x^2 \in X_0^2, \\ t_L & \text{if } e \in E_1, \ x^2 \in \bar{X}_0^2, \\ t_W & \text{if } e \in E_2, \ x^2 \in \bar{X}_0^2, \\ t_L & \text{if } e \in E_2, \ x^2 \in X_0^2, \\ t_L & \text{otherwise.} \end{cases}$$

By two applications of the first part of Axiom 3, we have

$$\tilde{a}_4 \sim a_4. \tag{2.12}$$

But we can also write, in view of the preceding definition of a_4,

$$a_4(e,x,y) = \begin{cases} t_W & \text{if } e \in E_1, \ x^2 \in X_0^2, \\ t_L & \text{if } e \in \bar{E}_1, \ x^2 \in X_0^2, \\ t_W & \text{if } e \in E_2, \ x^2 \in \bar{X}_0^2, \\ t_L & \text{if } e \in \bar{E}_2, \ x^2 \in \bar{X}_0^2. \end{cases}$$

Consider the compound act a_5 defined by

$$a_5(e,x,y) = \begin{cases} \gamma^T(E_1) & \text{if } x^2 \in X_0^2, \\ \gamma^T(E_2) & \text{if } x^2 \in \bar{X}_0^2. \end{cases}$$

By two applications of the first part of Axiom 3 we have

$$a_4 \sim a_5. \tag{2.13}$$

Now consider another compound act, namely, $\tilde{a}_6$, defined by

$$\tilde{a}_6(e,x,y) = \begin{cases} \gamma^T(\{y_1^n, \ldots, y_{m_1}^n\}) & \text{if } x^2 \in X_0^2, \\ \gamma^T(\{y_1^n, \ldots, y_{m_2}^n\}) & \text{if } x^2 \in \bar{X}_0^2. \end{cases}$$

Using the definition of P and Remark 5, we have that the ticket $\gamma^T(E_1)$ and $\gamma^T(\{y_1^n, \ldots, y_{m_1}^n\})$ are comparable for $\mathcal{C}, \geq$; $\gamma^T(E_2)$ and $\gamma^T(\{y_1^n, \ldots, y_{m_2}^n\})$ are comparable as well; and

$$\gamma^T(E_1) \sim_T \gamma^T(\{y_1^n, \ldots, y_{m_1}^n\}), \qquad \gamma^T(E_2) \sim_T \gamma^T(\{y_1^n, \ldots, y_{m_2}^n\}).$$

Hence, by Axiom 2 (more precisely, by elementary substitutability),

$$a_5 \sim \tilde{a}_6. \tag{2.14}$$

Finally, consider the simple act a_6 defined by

$$a_6(e,x,y) = \begin{cases} t_W & \text{if } y^n \in \{y_1^n, \ldots, y_{m_1}^n\}, \ x^2 \in X_0^2, \\ t_L & \text{if } y^n \in \{y_{m_1+1}^n, \ldots, y_n^n\}, \ x^2 \in X_0^2, \\ t_W & \text{if } y^n \in \{y_1^n, \ldots, y_{m_2}^n\}, \ x^2 \in \bar{X}_0^2, \\ t_L & \text{if } y^n \in \{y_{m_2+1}^n, \ldots, y_n^n\}, \ x^2 \in \bar{X}_0^2. \end{cases}$$

By two applications of the sixth part of Axiom 3, we obtain

$$\tilde{a}_6 \sim a_6. \tag{2.15}$$

From (2.7), (2.9)–(2.15), and Axiom 1 (transitivity) we have

$$a_1 \sim a_6. \tag{2.16}$$

For every value of $[e, (x^1, x^3, x^4, \ldots), (y^1, \ldots, y^{n-1}, y^{n+1}, \ldots)]$, the act a_1 yields the ticket t_W for m_{12} of the $2n$ double benchmark outcomes in set $X^2 \times Y^n$ and yields the ticket t_L for the other double benchmark outcomes in that set.

On the other hand, for every value of

$$[e, (x^1, x^3, x^4, \ldots), (y^1, \ldots, y^{n-1}, y^{n+1}, \ldots)],$$

the act a_6 yields the ticket t_W for $m_1 + m_2$ of the same set of $2n$ double benchmark outcomes, whereas it yields t_L for the rest of them. Hence, by Lemma 1, we have, in view of (2.16),

$$m_1 + m_2 = m_{12},$$

and therefore

$$P(E) + P(F) = P(E \cup F).$$

That completes the proof.   ∎

Definition 7 (Utility). Let $\Lambda \subset C$ be the set of all basic consequences c such that for some nonnegative integers m_c, n_c we have $m_c \leq n_c$ and

$$[a_c, \gamma(\{x_1^{n_c}, \ldots, x_{m_c}^{n_c}\})] \in \mathcal{Q}, \qquad a_c \sim \gamma(\{x_1^{n_c}, \ldots, x_{m_c}^{n_c}\}).$$

We let $u(c)$ denote m_c/n_c and we call $u(c)$ the *utility of c*.

Remark 8: For any $c \in \Lambda$, the number m_c/n_c is unique if $(\mathcal{Q}, \leq)$ obeys Axioms 1–4. The proof is analogous to the proof of uniqueness of probability in Remark 6.

2.3   *The expected utility theorem*

We now have that version of the expected utility theorem that is appropriate to our axioms.

Theorem 3. Let the simple acts a, b satisfy

$a(e, x, y) = t_{c_i}$ if $e \in E_i$, $i = 1, \ldots, k$;

$E_1 \cap E_2 \cap \cdots \cap E_k$ is empty;

$E_1 \cup E_2 \cup \cdots \cup E_k = E$;

$E_i \in \Omega$, $i = 1, \ldots, k$;

$\bigcup_{r=1}^{j} E_r \in \Omega$, $j = 2, \ldots, k$;

$c_i \in \Lambda$, $i = 1, \ldots, k$;

and

$b(e, x, y) = t_{d_i}$ if $e \in F_i$, $i = 1, \ldots, \ell$;

$F_1 \cap F_2 \cap \cdots \cap F_\ell$ is empty;

$F_1 \cup F_2 \cup \cdots \cup F_\ell = E$;

$F_i \in \Omega$, $i = 1, \ldots, \ell$;

$\bigcup_{r=1}^{j} F_r \in \Omega$, $j = 2, \ldots, \ell$;

$d_i \in \Lambda$, $i = 1, \ldots, \ell$.

Let $\mathfrak{a}, \leq$ satisfy Axioms 1–4. Then $a \leq b$ if and only if

$$\sum_{i=1}^{k} u_i(c_i) P(E_i) \leq \sum_{i=1}^{\ell} u_i(d_i) P(F_i).$$

The proof of Theorem 3 is given in the appendix.

2.4 *Extensions*

Analogously to what is done in the PRS article (in its Section 7), we can give a behavioral definition of conditional probability. To do so we introduce a "status quo" consequence c_0.

We then say that for $E_0 \subseteq E$, $E_1 \subseteq E$, the conditional probability of E_0 given E_1 [written $P(E_0/E_1)$] equals m/n if and only if the act $\gamma(\{x_1^n, \ldots, x_m^n\})$ is indifferent to the act that yields the ticket-bet $\gamma^T(E_0)$ when $e \in E_0$ and yields the ticket t_{c_0} otherwise. We can then prove that (under Axioms 1–4) if $E_1 \in \Omega$, $P(E_1) \neq 0$, $E_0 \cap E_1 \in \Omega$, and $E_1 \in \Omega$, then

$$P\left(\frac{E_0}{E_1}\right) = \frac{P(E_0 \cap E_1)}{P(E_1)}.$$

Next, given a partitioning $\{E_1, \ldots, E_\ell\}$ of E, consider the possible rules for choosing an act in A in response to ℓ possible *signals:* the signal "e is in E_1," the signal "e is in E_2,"..., the signal "e is in E_ℓ." Such a response rule may itself be viewed as an act. We can show (under Axioms 1–4) that if the appropriate probabilities and utilities exist, then the first of two rules is preferred to the second if and only if for each signal the first rule yields a not lower conditional expected utility and for some signal the first yields a higher conditional expected utility.

3   Admissibility versus independence: a general treatment

3.1   *Preliminaries*

We are given S, a finite set of *states* with typical element s, and R, a set of *results*. Then A, with typical element a, is the set of *acts;* the act is a function from S to R and it takes the value $a(s)$ [yields the result $a(s)$ for the state s]. We are also given $\leqq_A$, a reflexive transitive ordering on the pairs in $A \times A$. The meaning of the associated symbols $\sim_A$, $<_A$, $>_A$ is that given in Definition 3 above.

We shall be considering, for any set $\Gamma \subseteq S$, the set A_Γ of *subacts* with typical element denoted a_Γ (or possibly $\hat{a}_\Gamma$, b_Γ, $\hat{b}_\Gamma$). A subact a_Γ in A_Γ is a function from Γ to R. If $\{S_1, \ldots, S_\ell\}$ is a partitioning of S, and if $a_{S_1}, \ldots, a_{S_\ell}$ are, respectively, subacts in $A_{S_1}, \ldots, A_{S_\ell}$, then the symbol $\{a_{S_1}, a_{S_2}, \ldots, a_{S_\ell}\}$ will denote an act in A, namely that act a satisfying

$$a(s) = a_{S_i}(s) \quad \text{if } s \in S_i, \; i = 1, \ldots, \ell.$$

Finally, we shall be considering a certain set Σ of partitionings of S; the symbol σ will denote the typical element of Σ. If $\sigma = \{S_1, \ldots, S_\ell\}$, then it will sometimes be convenient to use the symbol a^σ to denote the act $\{a_{S_1}, \ldots, a_{S_\ell}\}$ when the identity of the subacts (i.e., the functions) $a_{S_1}, \ldots, a_{S_\ell}$ is clear.

Given a set $\Gamma \subseteq S$, the symbol $\leqq_\Gamma$ will denote a reflexive transitive ordering on the pairs in $A_\Gamma \times A_\Gamma$, called a *subact ordering*. Thus, we shall write, for example, $a_\Gamma \leqq_\Gamma b_\Gamma$, where a_Γ, b_Γ are subacts in A_Γ. In the usual way, $a_\Gamma \sim_\Gamma b_\Gamma$ means "$(a_\Gamma \leqq_\Gamma b_\Gamma)$ and not $(b_\Gamma \leqq_\Gamma a_\Gamma)$," while $a_\Gamma <_\Gamma b_\Gamma$ (also written $b_\Gamma >_\Gamma a_\Gamma$) means "$(a_\Gamma \leqq_\Gamma b_\Gamma)$ and not $(a_\Gamma \sim_\Gamma b_\Gamma)$." A set $\{\leqq_{S_1}, \ldots, \leqq_{S_\ell}\}$, where $\{S_1, \ldots, S_\ell\}$ is a partitioning of S, will be called a *subact-ordering set*.

Definition 8. If $\sigma = \{S_1, \ldots, S_\ell\}$ is a partitioning of S and if Δ is a subset of A, then we shall say that the subact-ordering set $\{\leqq_{S_1}, \ldots, \leqq_{S_\ell}\}$ *agrees with $\leqq_A$ on Δ* if and only if

(i) $\{a_{S_1}, \ldots, a_{S_\ell}\}, \{b_{S_1}, \ldots, b_{S_\ell}\} \in \Delta$,

(ii) $a_{S_i} \leqq_{S_i} b_{S_i}, \; i = 1, \ldots, \ell$, and

(iii)   for some $i \in \{1, \ldots, \ell\}$, $a_{S_i} <_{S_i} b_{S_i}$

imply

(iv) $\{a_{S_1}, \ldots, a_{S_\ell}\} <_A \{b_{S_1}, \ldots, b_{S_\ell}\}$;

and in addition (i), (ii), and (iv) imply (iii).

Remark 9: The following is a consequence of Definition 8: If $\{\lesssim_{S_1}, \ldots, \lesssim_{S_\ell}\}$ agrees with $\lesssim_A$ on Δ, and if $\{a_{S_1}, \ldots, a_{S_\ell}\}, \{b_{S_1}, \ldots, b_{S_\ell}\} \in \Delta$, then

$$a \lesssim_A b \quad \text{if } a_{S_i} \lesssim_{S_i} b_{S_i}, \ i = 1, \ldots, \ell,$$

$$a \sim_A b \quad \text{if } a_{S_i} \sim_{S_i} b_{S_i}, \ i = 1, \ldots, \ell.$$

Definition 9 (Admissibility). If Σ is a set of partitionings of S, and ψ is a function from Σ to the set of subsets of A, then we shall say that the ordering $\lesssim_A$ is *admissible with respect to* (Σ, ψ) *or has the admissibility property with respect to* (Σ, ψ), if and only if

$$\sigma = \{S_1, \ldots, S_\ell\} \in \Sigma$$

implies that there exists a subact-ordering set $\{\lesssim_{S_1}, \ldots, \lesssim_{S_\ell}\}$ that agrees with $\lesssim_A$ on the set $\psi(\sigma)$.

Definition 10 (Independence). If Σ is a set of partitionings of S and ψ is a function from Σ to the set of subsets of A, then we shall say that the ordering $\lesssim$ is *independent with respect to* (Σ, ψ), *or has the independence property with respect to* (Σ, ψ), if and only if the following holds: Whenever a partitioning $\sigma = \{S_1, \ldots, S_\ell\}$ and four acts $a^\sigma, b^\sigma, \hat{a}^\sigma, \hat{b}^\sigma$ satisfy:

(i) $\sigma \in \Sigma;\ a^\sigma, b^\sigma, \hat{a}^\sigma, \hat{b}^\sigma \in \psi(\sigma);$

(ii) for some $i \in \{1, \ldots, \ell\}$,

$$a^\sigma(s) = b^\sigma(s), \quad \hat{a}^\sigma(s) = \hat{b}^\sigma(s), \quad \text{all } s \in S_i,$$
$$a^\sigma(s) = \hat{a}^\sigma(s), \quad b^\sigma(s) = \hat{b}^\sigma(s), \quad \text{all } s \notin S_i;$$

(iii) $a^\sigma \lesssim_A b^\sigma.$

Then also

(iv) $\hat{a}^\sigma \lesssim_A \hat{b}^\sigma.$

Whenever (i) and (ii) are true and in addition

(iii)′ $a^\sigma <_A b^\sigma,$

then also

(iv)′ $\hat{a}^\sigma <_A \hat{b}^\sigma.$

We shall need to consider three conditions on the partitioning set Σ and the function ψ (a function from Σ to the set of subsets of A).

Definition 11. We shall call a partitioning $\{T_1, \ldots, T_k\}$ of S a *coarsening* of a partitioning $\sigma = \{S_1, \ldots, S_\ell\}$ if and only if $k < \ell$ and for $i \in \{1, \ldots, k\}$, T_i is the union of sets in σ. The pair (Σ, ρ) will be said to *satisfy condition F* if and only if for any partitioning $\sigma = \{S_1, \ldots, S_\ell\}$ in Σ and any coarsening of σ, say σ^*, we have $\sigma^* \in \Sigma$, and

$$a^{\sigma^*} \in \psi(\sigma^*) \quad \text{if } a^\sigma \in \psi(\sigma).$$

Definition 12. The pair (Σ, ψ) will be said to *satisfy condition G* if and only if, for any partitioning $\sigma = \{S_1, \ldots, S_\ell\}$ in Σ, for any acts $a^* = \{a^*_{S_1}, \ldots, a^*_{S_\ell}\}$, $a^{**} = \{a^{**}_{S_1}, \ldots, a^{**}_{S_\ell}\}$ in $\psi(\sigma)$, and for any $i \in \{1, \ldots, \ell\}$, there exist acts $\hat{a}^*, \hat{a}^{**}$ in $\psi(\sigma)$ such that

$$\hat{a}^*(s) = a^*_{S_i}(s), \quad \hat{a}^{**}(s) = a^{**}_{S_i}(s), \quad \text{all } s \in S_i;$$
$$\hat{a}^*(s) = \hat{a}^{**}(s), \quad \text{all } s \in \bar{S}_i.$$

(As usual, the symbol $\bar{S}_i$ denotes the complement of S_i.)

Definition 13. The pair (Σ, ψ) will be said to satisfy *condition H* if and only if, for any $\sigma = \{S_1, \ldots, S_\ell\}$ in Σ, if

$$\{a_{S_1}, \ldots, a_{S_\ell}\}, \{b_{S_1}, \ldots, b_{S_\ell}\} \in \psi(\sigma),$$

then also

$$\{g_{S_1}, \ldots, g_{S_\ell}\} \in \psi(\sigma),$$

where

$$g_{S_i} \in \{a_{S_i}, b_{S_i}\}, \quad i = 1, \ldots, \ell.$$

Remark 10: It is clear that if Σ is the set of all partitionings of S and if, for every σ in Σ the set $\psi(\sigma)$ is the set of all acts, then the pair (Σ, ψ) satisfies F, G, and H.

Remark 11: If Σ contains only σ^*, the "elementary" partition each of whose sets is a singleton, and if $\psi(\sigma^*)$ is the set of all acts, then admissibility with respect to Σ, ψ becomes the "elementary admissibility" referred to in Section 1 above. In this case, moreover, Σ *fails to obey condition F*. Hence, for this case one *cannot* apply Theorem 4 below [which says that admissibility with respect to (Σ, ψ) implies independence with respect to (Σ, ψ) provided condition F holds].

3.2   *Three illustrations of the preceding concepts*

(a) An ordering satisfying the PRS precalibration axioms. For ease of comparison among our three illustrations, we replace the sets X, Y of

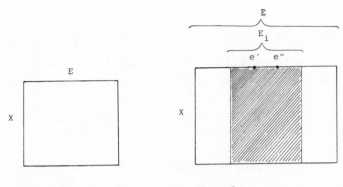

Figure 1.   Figure 2.

PRS (each is the unit interval) by the denumerable sets X, Y defined in Section 2 above.

In the PRS axiom system (with X, Y thus reinterpreted) we have

$$S = E \times X \times Y,$$

where E, X, Y are defined as in Section 2 above. The typical element of S is a triple (e, x, y). We have also $R = C$.

The central admissibility statement in the PRS system is PRS Axiom 4. To visualize this axiom in its original form (with X and Y being the unit interval), consider an act a that assigns a consequence in C to every point of the box in Figure 1. The act a is independent of the value taken by y. Consider, in particular, a "column" of such an act, portrayed by the shaded area in Figure 2. Such a column is associated with a set $E_i \subseteq E$. It consists of pairs (e, x) such that $a(e', x, y) = a(e'', x, y) = d_i(x)$ for all e', e'' in E_i and all x, y in $X \times Y$, where d_i is some function from X to C. (If E_i were a singleton, then the "column" would be portrayed as a vertical line.) Thus, given the act a, the column defines a subact $a_{E_i \times X \times Y}$ satisfying

$$a_{E_i \times X \times Y}(e, x, y) = d_i(x), \quad \text{all } e \in E_i, \text{ all } x \in X, \text{ all } y \in Y. \quad (3.1)$$

Now the PRS Axiom 4 can be interpreted in the following way. We first define a subact ordering, $\preceq_{E_i \times X \times Y}$, on pairs of subacts of the sort just described, say on the pair $\bar{a}_{E_i \times X \times Y}, \bar{\bar{a}}_{E_i \times X \times Y}$, defined by E_i and (respectively) by the functions $\bar{d}_i, \bar{\bar{d}}_i$ (from X to C). To do that, we associate with the two subacts the *acts* $\bar{a}, \bar{\bar{a}}$, where each act simply *repeats the column*, that is

$$\bar{a}(e, x, y) = \bar{d}_i(x), \quad \text{all } (e, x, y),$$
$$\bar{\bar{a}}(e, x, y) = \bar{\bar{d}}_i(x), \quad \text{all } (e, x, y).$$

Then we say that

$$\bar{a}_{E_i \times X \times Y} \lesssim_{E_i \times X \times Y} \bar{\bar{a}}_{E_i \times X \times Y} \quad \text{if and only if} \quad \bar{a} \lesssim_A \bar{\bar{a}},$$

where $\lesssim_A$ is a given ordering on $A \times A$. Then PRS Axiom 4 – a condition on the ordering $\lesssim_A$ – says, in a slightly modified form, that for any partitioning $\{E_1, \ldots, E_\ell\}$ of E the subact-ordering set $\{\lesssim_{E_1 \times X \times Y}, \ldots, \lesssim_{E_\ell \times X \times Y}\}$ so defined agrees with $\lesssim_A$ on the set of all acts $\{a_{E_1 \times X \times Y}, \ldots, a_{E_\ell \times X \times Y}\}$ such that for $i \in \{1, \ldots, \ell\}$ (3.1) is satisfied for some function d_i from X to C.

The axiom makes completely analogous statements with respect to partitionings $\{E_1, \ldots, E_\ell\}$ of E with subacts depending only on y; with respect to partitionings $\{X_1, \ldots, X_\ell\}$ of X with subacts depending only on e or only on y; and with respect to partitionings $\{Y_1, \ldots, Y_\ell\}$ of Y with subacts depending only on x or only on e. (Thus, in the Figures 1 and 2 one can label the horizontal side of the rectangle with any one of E, X, Y and can label the vertical side with any other out of E, X, Y.)

Clearly the axiom remains well defined if we give X and Y the denumerable interpretation of Section 2 rather than the PRS unit interval interpretation. We shall call the modified PRS Axiom 4 together with transitivity the *PRS precalibration axioms*. To obtain the expected utility rule, one only has to add an axiom guaranteeing the existence of probabilities and an axiom guaranteeing the existence of utilities, where the utility of a consequence c is, in the usual way, the probability of win (the best consequence in C) in a win/lose act indifferent to the act yielding c always (lose is the worst consequence in C).

We now wish to find a pair (Σ, ψ) such that an ordering $\lesssim_A$ satisfying the (modified) PRS Axiom 4 is admissible with respect to (Σ, ψ). The preceding discussion shows that this is the case if Σ and ψ are as follows:

$$\Sigma = \Sigma^E \cup \Sigma^X \cup \Sigma^Y.$$

A partitioning $\sigma = \{S_1, \ldots, S_\ell\}$ belongs to Σ^E if and only if

$$S_i = E_i \times X \times Y, \quad i \in \{1, \ldots, \ell\},$$

where $\{E_1, \ldots, E_\ell\}$ is any partitioning of E. Similarly, $\sigma \in \Sigma^X$ if and only if

$$S_i = E \times X_i \times Y, \quad i \in \{1, \ldots, \ell\},$$

where $\{X_1, \ldots, X_\ell\}$ is any partitioning of X; and $\sigma \in \Sigma^Y$ if and only if

$$S_i = E \times X \times Y_i, \quad i \in \{1, \ldots, \ell\}.$$

where $\{Y_1, \ldots, Y_\ell\}$ is any partitioning of Y.

For $\sigma = \{E_1 \times X \times Y, ..., E_\ell \times X \times Y\} \in \Sigma^E$, the set $\psi(\sigma) \subset A$ is defined by:

$a \in \psi(\sigma)$ if and only if, for every $i \in \{1, ..., \ell\}$, $a(e', x, y) = a(e'', x, y)$ for all e', e'' in E_i, all (x, y) in $X \times Y$.

Similarly, for $\sigma = \{E \times X_1 \times Y, ..., E \times X_\ell \times Y\} \in \Sigma^X$,

$a \in \psi(\sigma)$ if and only if, for every $i \in \{1, ..., \ell\}$, $a(e, x', y) = a(e, x'', y)$ for all x', x'' in X_i, all (e, y) in $E \times Y$;

and for $\sigma = \{E \times X \times Y_1, ..., E \times X \times Y_\ell\} \in \Sigma^Y$,

$a \in \psi(\sigma)$ if and only if, for every $i \in \{1, ..., \ell\}$, $a(e, x, y') = a(e, x, y'')$ for all y', y'' in Y_i, all (e, x) in $E \times X$.

The pair (Σ, ψ) meets condition F since a coarsening of any partitioning σ in Σ^E or Σ^X or Σ^Y yields another partitioning that again lies, respectively, in Σ^E or Σ^X or Σ^Y. At the same time, if a^σ is an act in $\psi(\sigma)$, then that act also qualifies as a member of $\psi(\bar{\sigma})$, where $\bar{\sigma}$ coarsens σ: for σ in Σ^E, say, the only requirement for membership in the act set $\psi(\sigma)$ is that the act not distinguish between two elements e', e'' of a given set in the original partitioning of E; but a fortiori such an act does not distinguish between two elements of a set in a coarser partitioning of E, and hence the act also qualifies for membership in $\psi(\bar{\sigma})$.

To see that the pair (Σ, ψ) meets condition G, consider

$$\sigma = \{E_1 \times X \times Y, ..., E_\ell \times X \times Y\} \in \Sigma^E,$$

and consider

$$a^* = \{a^*_{E_1 \times X \times Y}, ..., a^*_{E_\ell \times X \times Y}\}, \qquad a^{**} = \{a^{**}_{E_1 \times X \times Y}, ..., a^{**}_{E_\ell \times X \times Y}\}$$

in $\psi(\sigma)$. For i in $\{1, ..., \ell\}$, define acts $\hat{a}^*, \hat{a}^{**}$ by

$$\hat{a}^*(e, x, y) = a^*(e, x, y), \quad \hat{a}^{**}(e, x, y) = a^{**}(e, x, y), \quad e \in E_i,$$
$$\hat{a}^*(e, x, y) = \hat{a}^{**}(e, x, y) = r, \quad e \notin E_i,$$

where r is an arbitrary element of R ($= C$). Then it follows from the definition of ψ that $\hat{a}, \hat{a}^{**} \in \psi(\sigma)$. A similar argument holds when $\sigma \in \Sigma^X$ and when $\sigma \in \Sigma^Y$.

To see that (Σ, ψ) meets condition H, consider

$$\sigma = \{E_1 \times X \times Y, ..., E_\ell \times X \times Y\}$$

in Σ^E. Suppose the acts $\{a_{E_1 \times X \times Y}, ..., a_{E_\ell \times X \times Y}\}$, $\{b_{E_1 \times X \times Y}, ..., b_{E_\ell \times X \times Y}\}$ are in $\psi(\sigma)$. Consider, for example, the act $\{g_{E_1 \times X \times Y}, ..., g_{E_\ell \times X \times Y}\} = \{a_{E_1 \times X \times Y}, a_{E_2 \times X \times Y}, a_{E_3 \times X \times Y}, b_{E_4 \times X \times Y}, ..., b_{E_\ell \times X \times Y}\}$. Clearly, this act also meets the requirements for membership in $\psi(\sigma)$ since for $i \in \{1, \ldots, \ell\}$ we have

$$g_i(e', x, y) = g_i(e'', x, y) \quad \begin{cases} \text{all } e', e'' \text{ in } E_i, \\ \text{all } x, y \text{ in } X \times Y. \end{cases}$$

A similar argument holds when $\sigma \in \Sigma^X$ and when $\sigma \in \Sigma^Y$.

(b) An ordering satisfying the precalibration axioms (Axioms 1–3) of the axiom system of Section 2 when all act pairs can be ordered. We again have

$$S = E \times X \times Y.$$

But now,

$$R = T;$$

(a "result" is now a ticket t, where t is a function from S to the basic consequence set C). The set A is, as before, the set of functions from S to R. We shall assume, in the terminology of Section 2, that

$$\begin{aligned} &\mathcal{Q} = A \times A \text{ and } \leq_A \text{ is an ordering on } \mathcal{Q} \\ &\text{satisfying Axioms 1–3 of Section 2.} \end{aligned} \tag{3.2}$$

We shall argue that if (3.2) holds, then $\leq_A$ is admissible with respect to (Σ, ψ) where Σ is defined precisely as in (a) above, but for each $\sigma \in \Sigma$ the set $\psi(\sigma)$ is now *smaller* than in (a). To be precise, the function ψ is now defined as

$$\begin{aligned} &a \in \psi(\sigma) \text{ if and only if } a \text{ satisfies the requirement} \\ &\text{for membership in } \psi(\sigma) \text{ as stated in (a) above,} \\ &\text{and in addition for all } (e, x, y), \, a(e, x, y) \text{ equals} \\ &t_W \text{ or } t_L. \end{aligned} \tag{3.3}$$

To see that $\leq_A$ is admissible with respect to (Σ, ψ) as thus defined, consider first a partitioning $\sigma \in \Sigma^E$, that is,

$$\sigma = \{E_1 \times X \times Y, \ldots, E_\ell \times X \times Y\}.$$

Consider two acts

$$a = \{a_{E_1 \times X \times Y}, \ldots, a_{E_\ell \times X \times Y}\} \quad \text{and} \quad b = \{b_{E_1 \times X \times Y}, \ldots, b_{E_\ell \times X \times Y}\}$$

lying in the newly defined set $\psi(\sigma)$. For $i \in \{1, \ldots, \ell\}$ consider two subacts $a_{E_i \times X \times Y}, b_{E_i \times X \times Y}$. Each of these functions has the two-element set $\{t_W, t_L\}$ as its range and, since ψ obeys the conditions given in (a) above, the function $a_{E_i \times X \times Y}$ takes a constant value over all e in E_i, say the value $t^a \in \{t_W, t_L\}$. Similarly, $b_{E_i \times X \times Y}$ takes, say, the constant value $t^b \in \{t_W, t_L\}$ over all e in E_i. Now define the subact ordering $\leqslant_{E_i \times X \times Y}$ by

$$a_{E_i \times X \times Y} \leqslant_{E_i \times X \times Y} b_{E_i \times X \times Y} \quad \text{if and only if } t^a \leqslant_T t^b,$$

where $\leqslant_T$ denotes the ordering of comparable ticket pairs defined in Section 2 (Remark 2 showed that t^a, t^b are comparable). In an exactly similar manner, define the subact orderings $\leqslant_{E \times X_i \times Y}$ and $\leqslant_{E \times X \times Y_i}$ for partitionings $\{X_1, ..., X_\ell\}$ of X and $\{Y_1, ..., Y_\ell\}$ of Y. We have then defined a subact ordering for all subact pairs in $A_{S_i} \times A_{S_i}$ such that every subact in the pair takes values in $\{t_W, t_L\}$ and such that S_i is a set in some partitioning σ belonging to $\Sigma = \Sigma^E \times \Sigma^X \times \Sigma^Y$.

It is straightforward to show that for a partitioning $\sigma = \{S_1, ..., S_\ell\}$ in Σ, the subact-ordering set $\{\leqslant_{S_1}, ..., \leqslant_{S_\ell}\}$, as just defined, indeed agrees with $\leqslant_A$ on the set $\psi(\sigma)$ defined in (3.3). It is straightforward as well to show that (Σ, ψ) [with ψ defined in (3.3)] obey conditions F, G, and H.

Note that as long as the set C of (a) contains more than two elements, the set $\psi(\sigma)$ of (3.3) is indeed smaller than the set $\psi(\sigma)$ of (a).

(c) An ordering satisfying the precalibration axioms of the MR system.
One can interpret the MR finite version of the Savage axiom system in the same setting as that of (a) above, that is, once again let

$$S = E \times X \times Y, \qquad R = C.$$

Let s denote the typical element of S. Then if the ordering $\leqslant_A$ on $A \times A$ obeys the MR "independence condition 1" ("conditional preferences in one event are independent of consequences in other events"), one has an ordering of subact pairs a_{S_i}, b_{S_i} where S_i is *any* subset of S. Such an ordering, say $\leqslant_{S_i}$, is defined by

$$a_{S_i} \leqslant_{S_i} b_{S_i} \quad \text{if and only if } \alpha^{S_i} \leqslant_A \beta^{S_i},$$

where $\alpha^{S_i}, \beta^{S_i}$ are acts in A satisfying

$$\alpha^{S_i}(s) = \begin{cases} a_{S_i}(s) & \text{if } s \in S_i, \\ r_{S_i} & \text{otherwise,} \end{cases} \qquad \beta^{S_i}(s) = \begin{cases} b_{S_i}(s) & \text{if } s \in S_i, \\ r_{S_i} & \text{otherwise.} \end{cases}$$

and r_{S_i} is an arbitrary element of C.

The independence condition guarantees that this subact ordering remains unchanged as we vary r_{S_i}, so that the subact ordering is well defined. Moreover the independence condition, together with the transitivity of $\leqslant_A$, implies ("Sure thing theorem for conditional preferences") that for any partitioning $\{S_1, ..., S_\ell\}$ of S, the subact-ordering set $\{\leq_{S_1}, ..., \leq_{S_\ell}\}$ agrees with $\leq_A$ on the set of *all* acts $\{a_{S_1}, ..., a_{S_\ell}\}$. Thus $\leq_A$ is admissible with respect to (Σ, ψ), where Σ is now the set of *all* partitionings of S, and for any $\sigma \in \Sigma$, the set $\psi(\sigma)$ is the entire set A itself.

The independence condition and transitivity are the precalibration axioms of the MR system. An ordering satisfying these axioms obeys conditions F, G, and H in a trivial way (Remark 10).

3.3   Two theorems

We now show first that admissibility with respect to (Σ, ψ) implies independence with respect to (Σ, ψ) provided that condition F holds, and, second, that independence implies admissibility provided that conditions F, G, and H all hold. The latter theorem, Theorem 5, is simply a generalization of the "Sure-thing theorem for conditional preferences" in Marschak and Radner (1972, p. 18), which is, in turn, a finite version of Theorem 2 of Savage's Chapter 2 (1954, p. 24). Our Theorem 5 generalizes the MR theorem so as to allow for restrictions on (Σ, ψ). If Σ is the set of all partitionings of S and if, for any σ in Σ, the set $\psi(\sigma)$ is the set of all acts a^σ, then Theorem 5 and its proof reduce to the MR theorem and its proof. (See Remark 9 in this connection.) The role of condition H is to preserve the central device in the MR proof, namely, the construction of acts that "lie between" the two acts being compared.

Theorem 4. Suppose Σ is a set of partitionings of S and ψ is a function from Σ to the set of subsets of A. Suppose (Σ, ψ) obeys condition F. Suppose $\leq_A$ is a reflexive transitive ordering on $A \times A$ that is admissible with respect to (Σ, ψ). Then $\leq_A$ is also independent with respect to (Σ, ψ).

Proof: Let $\sigma = \{S_1, ..., S_\ell\} \in \Sigma$ and let $a = \{a_{S_1}, ..., a_{S_\ell}\}$, $b = \{b_{S_1}, ..., b_{S_\ell}\}$, $\hat{a} = \{\hat{a}_{S_1}, ..., \hat{a}_{S_\ell}\}$, $\hat{b} = \{\hat{b}_{S_1}, ..., \hat{b}_{S_\ell}\}$ be acts in $\psi(\sigma)$. Let $\bar{S}_1$ denote $S_2 \cup S_3 \cup \cdots \cup S_\ell$ and let the subacts $a_{\bar{S}_1}, \hat{a}_{\bar{S}_1}, b_{\bar{S}_1}, \hat{b}_{\bar{S}_1}$ satisfy

$$a_{\bar{S}_1} = \{a_{S_2}, ..., a_{S_\ell}\}, \qquad \hat{a}_{\bar{S}_1} = \{\hat{a}_{S_2}, ..., \hat{a}_{S_\ell}\},$$

$$b_{\bar{S}_1} = \{b_{S_2}, ..., b_{S_\ell}\}, \qquad \hat{b}_{\bar{S}_1} = \{\hat{b}_{S_2}, ..., \hat{b}_{S_\ell}\}.$$

Suppose, without loss of generality, that

(i) $a_{S_1}(s) = b_{S_1}(s)$, $\hat{a}_{S_1}(s) = \hat{b}_{S_1}(s)$, all s in S_1;

(ii) $a_{\bar{S}_1}(s) = \hat{a}_{\bar{S}_1}(s)$, $b_{\bar{S}_1}(s) = \hat{b}_{\bar{S}_1}(s)$, all s in $\bar{S}_1$;

(iii) $a <_A b$.

We then have to show that (under the hypothesis of the theorem)

(iv) $\hat{a} <_A \hat{b}$,

while if (iii) is replaced by

(iii)' $a \sim_A b$,

we then have

(iv)' $\hat{a} \sim_A \hat{b}$.

Suppose first that (i), (ii), and (iii) hold but (iv) is false, that is,

$$\hat{a} \gtrsim_A \hat{b}. \tag{3.4}$$

Since (Σ, ψ) satisfies condition F, the partition $\{S_1, \bar{S}_1\}$ lies in Σ and the acts $a, b, \hat{a}, \hat{b}$ lie in $\psi(\{S_1, \bar{S}_1\})$. Moreover, since $\lesssim_A$ is admissible with respect to Σ, ψ, there exists a subact-ordering pair $(\lesssim_{S_1}, \lesssim_{\bar{S}_1})$ that agrees with $\lesssim_A$ on $\psi(\{S_1, \bar{S}_1\})$. Suppose that [in addition to (3.4)]

$$\hat{a}_{\bar{S}_1} \lesssim_{\bar{S}_1} \hat{b}_{\bar{S}_1}. \tag{3.5}$$

Since [by (i)] $\hat{a}_{S_1} = \hat{b}_{S_1}$ and since $\lesssim_{S_1}$ is reflexive, we have

$$\hat{a}_{S_1} \sim_{S_1} \hat{b}_{S_1}. \tag{3.6}$$

But (3.5), (3.6), and the fact that $(\lesssim_{S_1}, \lesssim_{\bar{S}_1})$ agrees with $\lesssim_A$ on $\psi(\{S_1, \bar{S}_1\})$ imply that

$$\hat{a} \lesssim_A \hat{b},$$

which contradicts (3.4). So (3.5) cannot hold, that is, we must have

$$\hat{a}_{\bar{S}_1} >_{\bar{S}_1} \hat{b}_{\bar{S}_1}, \tag{3.7}$$

and so, since (ii) implies that $\hat{a}_{\bar{S}_1} = a_{\bar{S}_1}$, $\hat{b}_{\bar{S}_1} = b_{\bar{S}_1}$, we also have

$$a_{\bar{S}_1} >_{\bar{S}_1} b_{\bar{S}_1}. \tag{3.8}$$

Since $a_{S_1} = b_{S_1}$ [by (i)] we have

$$a_{S_1} \sim_{S_1} b_{S_1}. \tag{3.9}$$

But (3.8), (3.9), and the fact that $(\lesssim_{S_1}, \lesssim_{\bar{S}_1})$ agrees with $\lesssim_A$ on $\psi(\{S_1, \bar{S}_1\})$ imply that

$$a >_A b,$$

which contradicts (iii). So (3.4) must be false, that is, (iv) must hold.

A symmetrical argument shows that if (i), (ii), and $\hat{a} <_A \hat{b}$ hold, then we have $a <_A b$.

Now, to complete the proof, suppose (iii)′ holds. Then we cannot have $\hat{a} <_A \hat{b}$ since, by the symmetrical argument just alluded to, that implies $a <_A b$, which contradicts (iii)′. Similarly, $\hat{a} >_A \hat{b}$ is ruled out (by the symmetrical argument with a and b interchanged). Hence we must have $\tilde{a} \sim_A \tilde{b}$. That completes the proof. ■

Theorem 5. Let (Σ, ψ) obey conditions F, G, and H. Suppose that $\leq_A$ is a reflexive transitive ordering on $A \times A$ that is independent with respect to (Σ, ψ). Then $\leq_A$ is also admissible with respect to (Σ, ψ).

Proof: Let $\sigma = \{S_1, ..., S_\ell\}$ be in Σ. We have to find a subact-ordering set $\{\leq_{S_1}, ..., \leq_{S_\ell}\}$ that agrees with $\leq_A$ on $\psi(\sigma)$, that is, a subact-ordering set such that for any two acts $a^\sigma = \{a_{S_1}, ..., a_{S_\ell}\}$, $b^\sigma = \{b_{S_1}, ..., b_{S_\ell}\}$ in $\psi(\sigma)$, if

   (i)   for all $i \in \{1, ..., \ell\}$, $a_{S_i} \leq_{S_i} b_{S_i}$,

and

   (ii)   for some $i \in \{1, ..., \ell\}$, $a_{S_i} <_{S_i} b_{S_i}$,

then

   (iii) $a <_A b$;

while (i) plus (iii) implies (ii). To show this, it is sufficient to show "substitutability," that is, to show that (i) plus "$a_{S_i} \sim_{S_i} b_{S_i}$, $i = 1, ..., \ell$" imply $a \sim b$, or, to put it more compactly,

   (iv) $a_{S_i} \sim_{S_i} b_{S_i}$, $i = 1, ..., \ell$, implies $a \sim b$.

To define the required subact-ordering set, we first define, for any S_i, $i \in \{1, ..., \ell\}$ and any function d from $\bar{S}_i$ to R, the subact ordering $\leq_{S_i, d}$ on $\tilde{A}_{S_i} \times \tilde{A}_{S_i}$, where $\tilde{A}_{S_i}$ denotes the set $\{\bar{a}_{S_i} \in A_{S_i}:$ there exists an act $a \in \psi(\sigma)$ with $a = \{a_{S_1}, ..., a_{S_{i-1}}, \bar{a}_{S_i}, a_{S_{i+1}}, ..., a_{S_\ell}\}\}$. We have for $a^*_{S_i}, a^{**}_{S_i} \in \tilde{A}_{S_i}$,

$a^*_{S_i} \leq_{S_i, d} a^{**}_{S_i}$ if and only if $a^{*d} \leq_A a^{**d}$, and $a^*_{S_i} <_{S_i, d} a^{**}_{S_i}$
if and only if $a^{*d} <_A a^{**d}$, where a^{*d}, a^{**d} are the acts
in A defined by: $a^{*d}(s) = a^*_{S_i}(s)$, $a^{**d}(s) = a^{**}_{S_i}(s)$, all
$s \in S_i$; $a^{*d}(s) = a^{**d}(s) = d(s)$, all $s \in \bar{S}_i$.   (3.10)

It is easily checked that the membership of $\sigma = \{S_1, ..., S_\ell\}$ in Σ and the independence of $\leq_A$ with respect to (Σ, ψ) implies that

if d_1, d_2 are two functions from S_i to R and if $a^*_{S_i}, a^{**}_{S_i} \in \tilde{A}_{S_i}$,
then $a^*_{S_i}, a^{**}_{S_i}$ are ordered in the same way by $\leq_{S_i, d_1}$ and
$\leq_{S_i, d_2}$, i.e., $a^*_{S_i} \leq_{S_i, d_1} a^{**}_{S_i}$ if and only if $a^*_{S_i} \leq_{S_i, d_2} a^{**}_{S_i}$
and $a^*_{S_i} <_{S_i, d_1} a^{**}_{S_i}$ if and only if $a^*_{S_i} <_{S_i, d_2} a^{**}_{S_i}$.   (3.11)

Now since $\sigma = \{S_1, \ldots, S_\ell\} \in \Sigma$ and since (Σ, ψ) satisfies condition G, there exists for any $a_{S_i}^*, a_{S_i}^{**}$ in $\tilde{A}_{S_i}$ a pair of acts a^{*d_1}, a^{**d_1}, which are in $\psi(\sigma)$ and satisfy the equalities in (3.10). If $\psi(\sigma)$ also contains another such pair, say a^{*d_2}, a^{**d_2}, then, in view of (3.11), both pairs define the same subact ordering, namely, $\lesssim_{S_1, d_i}$ or equivalently $\lesssim_{S_1, d_2}$.

Thus we are entitled to conclude that the subact ordering $\lesssim_{S_i, d}$ of (3.10) is uniquely defined for any pair of subacts in $\tilde{A}_{S_i} \times \tilde{A}_{S_i}$. Henceforth the symbol $\lesssim_{S_i}$ refers to this ordering. Returning now to (i) and (ii) (which are now well defined) we observe first that condition H [assumed to be satisfied by (Σ, ψ)] implies [since $a^\sigma, b^\sigma \in \psi(\sigma)$] that

$$\{a_{S_1}, \ldots, a_{S_{i-1}}, b_{S_i}, b_{S_{i+1}}, \ldots, b_{S_\ell}\} \in \psi(\sigma), \quad i = 1, \ldots, \ell. \tag{3.12}$$

By the above definition of $\lesssim_{S_i}$, by (3.12) and the fact that $\{b_{S_1}, \ldots, b_{S_\ell}\}$ also lies in $\psi(\sigma)$, and by the independence of $\lesssim_A$ with respect to (Σ, ψ), we have that

(i) together with $a_{S_1} <_{S_1} b_{S_1}$ implies
$$\{a_{S_1}, b_{S_2}, \ldots, b_{S_\ell}\} <_A \{b_{S_1}, b_{S_2}, \ldots, b_{S_\ell}\}. \tag{3.13}$$

By the definition of $\lesssim_{S_2}$, by (i) (for $i = 2$), by (3.12), by (3.13), and by the independence of $\lesssim_A$ with respect to (Σ, ψ), we have

(i) together with $a_{S_1} <_{S_1} b_{S_1}$ for $i = 1$ or $i = 2$
implies $\{a_{S_1}, a_{S_2}, b_{S_3}, \ldots, b_{S_\ell}\} <_A \{a_{S_1}, b_{S_2}, b_{S_3}, \ldots, b_{S_\ell}\}.$

Proceeding in this manner, and using the transitivity of $<_A$, we conclude that (i) and (ii) indeed imply (iii). Moreover, in view of the definition of "independence of $\lesssim_A$ with respect to (Σ, ψ)," a similar ℓ-step argument shows that (i) plus "$a_{S_i} \sim_{S_i} b_{S_i}, i = 1, \ldots, \ell$" implies $a \sim_A b$, that is, that (iv) holds. That completes the proof. ■

3.4 The scope of the independence property in the three illustrative orderings

In the light of the discussion in Section 3.3, Theorem 4 tells us that for each of the three orderings illustrated in Section 3.2 we have independence with respect to (Σ, ψ), where (Σ, ψ) is defined for each ordering as in Section 3.2. Recall, moreover, that

the partitioning set Σ is the same for the first and second orderings but is as large as it can be (it is the set of all partitionings) for the third ordering; moreover, for a given partitioning σ in Σ, the act set $\psi(\sigma)$ is smaller for the second ordering than for the first and is as large as it can be (it is A itself) for the third ordering. (3.14)

To complete the comparison of the three orderings with regard to the scope of the independence property, we need to examine whether for each of the first two orderings independence holds as well with regard to some *other* pair (Σ, ψ) that is (in a suitable sense) "larger" than the pair given for that ordering in Section 3.2. A careful check of the axioms being imposed in each ordering reveals that the answer is no – that the given pair (Σ, ψ) is maximal, in a precise sense, among all pairs with respect to which the ordering is independent. We have the following for the first ordering and the pair (Σ, ψ) given in (a) of Section 3.2, for the second ordering and the pair (Σ, ψ) given in (b) of Section 3.2, and for the third ordering and the pair (Σ, ψ) given in (c) of Section 3.2:

> if $a, b, \hat{a}, \hat{b}$ are acts which, for every partitioning σ in Σ, lie *outside* $\psi(\sigma)$, then violation of the independence property for those acts is consistent with the relevant precalibration axioms (PRS Axiom 4 plus transitivity in the case of the first ordering, Axioms 1–3 of Section 2 in the case of the second ordering, the "independence condition for preferences" plus transitivity in the case of the third ordering). (3.15)

"Violation of the independence property" means that for some set $\Gamma \subset S$, we have

(i) $a(s) = b(s), \hat{a}(s) = \hat{b}(s)$, all $s \in \Gamma$;

(ii) $a(s) = \hat{a}(s), b(s) = \hat{b}(s)$, all $s \notin \Gamma$;

(iii) either $a \leq_A b$ and $\hat{a} >_A \hat{b}$ or $a \sim_A b$ and $\hat{a} <_A \hat{b}$.

The assertion in (3.15) holds vacuously in the case of the third ordering, since there Σ is the set of all partitionings and for every σ in Σ the set $\psi(\sigma)$ is A itself. Statements (3.14) and (3.15), taken together, provide one sense in which the scope of the independence property is wider for the third ordering than the first and wider for the first than the second. But one can also show that the same ranking of the scope of independence holds in another sense. One can show that

(i)   If an act quadruple violates the independence property for the first ordering, then the counterpart of that quadruple must violate independence for the second ordering; it is not true, however, that if an act quadruple violates independence for the second ordering, then every counterpart must violate independence for the first ordering.

(ii) If an act quadruple violates the independence property for the second ordering, then it must violate the independence

property for the third ordering; the converse, however,
is not true. (3.16)

We need the notion of "counterpart" in (i) of (3.16), because the acts in the first ordering are not identical with the acts in the second; acts in the first yield consequences in C, whereas acts in the second yield tickets (which are functions from S to C). If a is an act in the sense of the second ordering, yielding, say, the ticket $t^{a(s)}$ (a function from S to C) for each s, then we call $\tilde{a}$, an act in the sense of the first ordering, the (unique) *counterpart* of a if and only if $\tilde{a}(s) = t^{a(s)}(s)$, for all s in S. If b is an act in the sense of the first ordering, then we call $\tilde{b}$, an act in the sense of the second ordering, a (not necessarily unique) *counterpart* of b if and only if, for all s in S, $\tilde{b}(s)$ is a ticket, say $t^{\tilde{b}(s)}$, for which $t^{\tilde{b}(s)}(s) = b(s)$, all s in S.

Statement (3.16) says that the third ordering imposes the strongest prohibition against independence violations (they are, in fact, totally banned); the first ordering imposes a weaker prohibition, and the second ordering imposes a still weaker prohibition. Returning to the Ellsberg violation of Section 1, it is readily checked that this violation (and indeed the Allais violation, which we have not troubled to present), *although prohibited in the third ordering is permitted in the first and second*. To see this, let $E = \{$Red, Green, Yelow$\}$, let $X^2 = \{x_1^2, x_2^2\} = \{$Heads, Tails$\}$, and let the symbols H, T denote, respectively,

$$X^1 \times \{x_1^2\} \times X^3 \times \cdots \times Y \quad \text{and} \quad X^1 \times \{x_2^2\} \times X^3 \times \cdots \times Y.$$

Then the quadruple $a, b, \hat{a}, \hat{b}$ of the Ellsberg example is the following quadruple of boxes:

a

	H	T
R	W	W
G	L	L
Y	L	L

b

	H	T
R	L	L
G	W	W
Y	L	L

$\hat{a}$

	H	T
R	W	W
G	L	L
Y	W	W

$\hat{b}$

	H	T
R	L	L
G	W	W
Y	W	W

If the acts are those of the first ordering, then the results are L and W, which are consequences in C, as shown. If the acts are those of the second ordering, then L, W have to be replaced by the tickets t_L, t_W. In *both* orderings, $a >_A b$ together with $\hat{a} <_A \hat{b}$ (i.e., the Ellsberg violator's behavior) is permitted. What is *not* permitted in both orderings is $\bar{a} >_A \bar{b}$ together with $\hat{a} <_A \hat{b}$, where $\bar{a}, \bar{b}, \hat{a}, \hat{b}$ are acts like the following:

$\bar{a}$

	H	T
R	L	L
G	W	L
Y	L	W

$\bar{b}$

	H	T
R	L	L
G	L	L
Y	W	W

$\hat{a}$

	H	T
R	L	W
G	W	W
Y	L	L

$\hat{b}$

	H	T
R	L	W
G	L	W
Y	W	L

The common column (the second column) in $\bar{a}, \bar{b}$ is replaced by another common column in order to obtain $\hat{a}, \hat{b}$. One can search for variants of the original Ellsberg violation. So far, such a search has not uncovered any way of turning the prohibition against rankings like $\bar{a} >_A \bar{b}$, $\hat{a} <_A \hat{b}$ into a prohibition against dislike-of-ambiguity rankings of the Ellsberg type.

Exactly analogous statements hold with regard to the Allais violation.

4   Concluding remarks

Returning to our main motivation, honest decision analysis pedagogy requires the frank admission that the independence condition is a vulnerable one. If, however, the admissibility condition is substantially less vulnerable, then it may be pedagogically effective, and is quite consistent with honesty, to base the expected utility rule on an axiom system whose individual axioms place a maximal burden on admissibility and sharply restrict the scope of independence. We have seen that the precalibration axioms of the PRS system do so relative to those of the MR (Savage) system, and those of the system of Section 2 do so still further. The system of Section 2 is, however, cumbersome – with its "tickets" and its long proofs – even if one eliminates the optional-probability-and-utility feature (i.e., $\alpha = A \times A$, Ω is the set of all subsets of E, and $\Lambda = C$). The PRS system, on the other hand, is really not more cumbersome than the MR system (experience suggests that it is just as "teachable"). It is somewhat surprising, therefore, that it seems to have escaped notice that the PRS precalibration axioms are consistent with such behavior as the Ellsberg and Allais violations. The extra clumsiness of the Section 2 system may not be worth the further narrowing of the scope of independence that its precalibration axioms achieve; that becomes a matter of pedagogical choice.

Finally, at the level of theory, a natural question is whether one can go still further in narrowing the scope of independence than do Axioms 1–3 of Section 2. One can conjecture that if a condition is imposed on the ordering, and if that condition, together with transitivity and calibration axioms, implies the expected utility rule, then that condition (plus transitivity) cannot further narrow the scope of independence beyond its scope for Axioms 1–3 of Section 2. [Here "narrowing" could be given the meaning of (3.14), (3.15), or that of (3.16).] I have been unable to confirm or refute a conjecture of this type. There is still more to be learned about the foundations of expected utility.

Appendix: Proof of Theorem 3

For positive integers r, t with $r \leq t$, let the symbol X_{rt} denote the benchmark outcome set $\{x_1^t, \ldots, x_r^t\}$ and let the symbol $\bar{X}_{rt}$ denote the set $\{x_{r+1}^t, \ldots, x_r^t\}$. We can choose integers $n, m_1, \ldots, m_k, \bar{m}_1, \ldots, \bar{m}_\ell$ so that

$$u(c_i) = \frac{m_i}{n}, \quad i = 1, \ldots, k,$$

$$u(d_i) = \frac{\bar{m}_i}{n}, \quad i = 1, \ldots, \ell,$$

(1)

and, without loss of generality,

$$m_1 \geq m_2 \geq \cdots \geq m_{k-2} \geq m_{k-1} \geq m_k.$$

(2)

By the assumption that $c_i \in \Lambda$ ($i = 1, \ldots, k$) and by the definition of u, we have, for $i = 1, \ldots, k$,

$$[a_{c_i}, \gamma(X_{m_i n})] \in \mathcal{C}, \qquad a_{c_i} \sim \gamma(X_{m_i n}).$$

But by Definition 4 and the definition of a_{c_i}, that means also that the tickets t_{c_i} and $\gamma^T(X_{m_i n})$ are comparable for $(\mathcal{C}, \leq)$ and that

$$t_{c_i} \sim_T \gamma^T(X_{m_i n}), \quad i = 1, \ldots, k.$$

(3)

Consider, therefore, the compound[8] act $\tilde{a}_1$ defined by

$$\tilde{a}_1(e, x, y) = \gamma^T(X_{m_i n}) \quad \text{if } e \in E_i, \, i = 1, \ldots, k.$$

In view of equation (3) and Axiom 2 (more precisely, its elementary substitutability implication), we have

$$a \sim \tilde{a}_1.$$

(4)

Now consider the simple act a_1 defined by

$$a_1(e,x,y) = \begin{cases} t_W & \text{if } e \in E_i, \; x^n \in X_{m_i n}, \; i=1,\ldots,k, \\ t_L & \text{if } e \in E_i, \; x^n \in \bar{X}_{m_i n}, \; i=1,\ldots,k. \end{cases}$$

Applying the third part of Axiom 3 k times we obtain

$$\tilde{a}_1 \sim a_1. \tag{5}$$

In view of equation (2), the act a_1 can also be written as in equation (6):

$$a_1(e,x,y) = \begin{cases} t_W & \text{if } x^n \in \{x_1^n,\ldots,x_{m_k}^n\} \text{ and } e \in E_1 \cup E_2 \cup \cdots \cup E_k, \\ \begin{cases} t_W & \text{if } x^n \in \{x_{m_k+1}^n,\ldots,x_{m_{k-1}}^n\} \text{ and } e \in E_1 \cup E_2 \cup \cdots \cup E_{k-1}, \\ t_L & \text{if } x^n \in \{x_{m_k+1}^n,\ldots,x_{m_{k-1}}^n\} \text{ and } e \notin E_1 \cup E_2 \cup \cdots \cup E_{k-1}, \end{cases} \\ \begin{cases} t_W & \text{if } x^n \in \{x_{m_{k-1}+1}^n,\ldots,x_{m_{k-2}}^n\} \text{ and } e \in E_1 \cup \cdots \cup E_{k-2}, \\ t_L & \text{if } x^n \in \{x_{m_{k-1}+1}^n,\ldots,x_{m_{k-2}}^n\} \text{ and } e \notin E_1 \cup \cdots \cup E_{k-2}, \end{cases} \\ \quad\quad\vdots \\ \begin{cases} t_W & \text{if } x^n \in \{x_{m_3+1}^n,\ldots,x_{m_2}^n\} \text{ and } e \in E_1 \cup E_2, \\ t_L & \text{if } x^n \in \{x_{m_3+1}^n,\ldots,x_{m_2}^n\} \text{ and } e \notin E_1 \cup E_2, \end{cases} \\ \begin{cases} t_W & \text{if } x^n \in \{x_{m_2+1}^n,\ldots,x_{m_1}^n\} \text{ and } e \in E_1, \\ t_L & \text{if } x^n \in \{x_{m_2+1}^n,\ldots,x_{m_1}^n\} \text{ and } e \in \bar{E}_1, \end{cases} \\ t_L & \text{if } x^n \in \{x_{m_1+1}^n,\ldots,x_n^n\}. \end{cases} \tag{6}$$

Consider the compound act a_2 defined by equation (7):

$$a_2(e,x,y) = \begin{cases} \gamma^T(E) & \text{if } x^n \in \{x_1^n,\ldots,x_{m_k}^n\}, \\ \gamma^T(E_1 \cup E_2 \cup \cdots \cup E_{k-1}) & \text{if } x^n \in \{x_{m_k+1}^n,\ldots,x_{m_{k-1}}^n\}, \\ \gamma^T(E_1 \cup E_2 \cup \cdots \cup E_{k-2}) & \text{if } x^n \in \{x_{m_{k-1}+1}^n,\ldots,x_{m_{k-2}}^n\}, \\ \quad\quad\vdots \\ \gamma^T(E_1 \cup E_2) & \text{if } x^n \in \{x_{m_3+1}^n,\ldots,x_{m_2}^n\}, \\ \gamma^T(E_1) & \text{if } x^n \in \{x_{m_2+1}^n,\ldots,x_{m_1}^n\}, \\ t_L & \text{if } x^n \in \{x_{m_1+1}^n,\ldots,x_n^n\}. \end{cases} \tag{7}$$

Applying the first part of Axiom 3 k times, we obtain

$$a_1 \sim a_2. \tag{8}$$

Now let $q, r_1,\ldots,r_k, g_1,\ldots,g_k, \bar{g}_1,\ldots,\bar{g}_k$ be integers such that

$$P(E_i) = \frac{g_i}{q}, \quad i=1,\ldots,k; \qquad P(F_i) = \frac{\bar{g}_i}{q}, \quad i=1,\ldots,\ell, \tag{9}$$

$$P(E_1 \cup E_2 \cup \cdots \cup E_j) = \frac{r_j}{q}, \quad j=1,\ldots,k. \tag{10}$$

Thus
$$r_1 = g_1. \tag{11}$$

In view of Theorems 1 and 2, we have
$$r_j - r_{j-1} = g_j, \quad j = 2, \ldots, k, \tag{12}$$
and
$$\begin{aligned} q - r_{k-1} &= (g_1 + g_2 + \cdots + g_k) - (g_1 + g_2 + \cdots + g_{k-1}) \\ &= g_k. \end{aligned} \tag{13}$$

By Remark 5 and (ii) of Axiom 4, the tickets $\gamma^T(E_1 \cup E_2 \cup \cdots \cup E_j)$ and $\gamma^T(\{y_1^q, \ldots, y_{r_j}^q\})$ are (for $j = 1, \ldots, k$) comparable for $\mathcal{C}$, $\leq$ and
$$\gamma^T(E_1 \cup E_2 \cup \cdots \cup E_j) \sim \gamma^T(\{y_1^q, \ldots, y_{r_j}^q\}), \quad j = 1, \ldots, k. \tag{14}$$

Consider, therefore, another compound act, namely a_3, defined by equation (15):

$$\tilde{a}_3(e, x, y) = \begin{cases} \gamma^T(\{y_1^q, \ldots, y_q^q\}) & \text{if } x^n \in \{x_1^n, \ldots, x_{m_k}^n\}, \\ \gamma^T(\{y_1^q, \ldots, y_{r_{k-1}}^q\}) & \text{if } x^n \in \{x_{m_k+1}^n, \ldots, x_{m_{k-1}}^n\}, \\ \gamma^T(\{y_1^q, \ldots, y_{r_{k-2}}^q\}) & \text{if } x^n \in \{x_{m_{k-1}+1}^n, \ldots, x_{m_{k-2}}^n\}, \\ \quad \vdots \\ \gamma^T(\{y_1^q, \ldots, y_{r_2}^q\}) & \text{if } x^n \in \{x_{m_3+1}^n, \ldots, x_{m_2}^n\}, \\ \gamma^T(\{y_1^q, \ldots, y_{r_1}^q\}) & \text{if } x^n \in \{x_{m_2+1}^n, \ldots, x_{m_1}^n\}, \\ t_L & \text{if } x^n \in \{x_{m_1+1}^n, \ldots, x_n^n\}. \end{cases} \tag{15}$$

In view of (14) and Axiom 2 (elementary substitutability again), we have
$$a_2 \sim \tilde{a}_3. \tag{16}$$

Consider the simple act a_3 defined by equation (17):

$$a_3(e, x, y) = \begin{cases} t_W & \text{if } x^n \in \{x_1^n, \ldots, x_{m_k}^n\}, \ y^q \in \{y_1^q, \ldots, y_q^q\}, \\ \begin{cases} t_W & \text{if } x^n \in \{x_{m_k+1}^n, \ldots, x_{m_{k-1}}^n\}, \ y^q \in \{y_1^q, \ldots, y_{r_{k-1}}^q\}, \\ t_L & \text{if } x^n \in \{x_{m_k+1}^n, \ldots, x_{m_{k-1}}^n\}, \ y^q \in \{y_{r_{k-1}+1}^q, \ldots, y_q^q\}, \end{cases} \\ \begin{cases} t_W & \text{if } x^n \in \{x_{m_{k-1}+1}^n, \ldots, x_{m_{k-2}}^n\}, \ y^q \in \{y_1^q, \ldots, y_{r_{k-2}}^q\}, \\ t_L & \text{if } x^n \in \{x_{m_{k-1}+1}^n, \ldots, x_{m_{k-2}}^n\}, \ y^q \in \{y_{r_{k-2}}^q, \ldots, y_q^q\}, \end{cases} \\ \quad \vdots \\ \begin{cases} t_W & \text{if } x^n \in \{x_{m_3+1}^n, \ldots, x_{m_2}^n\}, \ y \in \{y_1^q, \ldots, y_{r_2}^q\}, \\ t_L & \text{if } x^n \in \{x_{m_3+1}^n, \ldots, x_{m_2}^n\}, \ y \in \{y_{r_2+1}^q, \ldots, y_q^q\}, \end{cases} \\ \begin{cases} t_W & \text{if } x^n \in \{x_{m_2+1}^n, \ldots, x_{m_1}^n\}, \ y \in \{y_1^q, \ldots, y_{r_1}^q\}, \\ t_L & \text{if } x^n \in \{x_{m_2+1}^n, \ldots, x_{m_1}^n\}, \ y \in \{y_{r_1+1}^q, \ldots, y_q^q\}, \end{cases} \\ t_L & \text{if } x^n \in \{x_{m_1+1}^n, \ldots, x_n^n\}. \end{cases} \tag{17}$$

By $t+1$ applications of the fifth part of Axiom 3, we have

$$\tilde{a}_3 \sim a_3. \tag{18}$$

Hence, in view of equations (4)-(6), (16), and (18) we have, using Axiom 1 (transitivity)

$$a \sim a_3. \tag{19}$$

The simple act a_3 yields the ticket t_W for some of the nq double benchmark outcomes in the set $X^n \times Y^q$ and it yields the ticket t_L for the rest. The number of double benchmark outcomes of the former sort is, reading directly from (17) and using (9) to (11),

$$m_k + (m_{k-1} - m_k)r_{k-1} + (m_{k-2} - m_{k-1})r_{k-2}$$
$$+ (m_{k-3} - m_{k-2})r_{k-3} + \cdots + (m_2 - m_3)r_2 + (m_1 - m_2)r_1$$
$$= m_k(q - r_{k-1}) + m_{k-1}(r_{k-1} - r_{k-2})$$
$$+ m_{k-2}(r_{k-2} - r_{k-3}) + \cdots + m_3(r_3 - r_2) + m_2(r_2 - r_1) + m_1 r_1$$
$$= \sum_{i=1}^{k} m_i g_i.$$

An exactly analogous argument shows that b is indifferent to a (simple) act that yields t_W for $\sum_{i=1}^{\ell} \bar{m}_i \bar{g}_i$ of the ng double benchmark outcomes in $X^n \times Y^q$. Hence, we have, in view of transitivity and Lemma 1,

$$a \lesssim b \quad \text{if and only if} \quad \sum_{i=1}^{k} m_i g_i \leq \sum_{i=1}^{\ell} \bar{m}_i \bar{g}_i$$

or, since

$$m_i g_i = (nq)u(c_i)P(E_i), \quad i = 1, \ldots, k,$$
$$\bar{m}_i \bar{g}_i = (nq)u(d_i)P(F_i), \quad i = 1, \ldots, \ell,$$

$a \lesssim b$ if and only if $\sum_{i=1}^{n} u(c_i)P(E_i) \leq \sum_{i=1}^{n} u(d_i)P(F_i)$. That completes the proof. ∎

NOTES

1 See Schoemaker (1982) for a recent survey. Among other contributions, Mc-Crimmon and Larsson (1979) and Slovic and Tversky (1974) are particularly relevant for the issues considered here.
2 This sort of difficulty multiplies when acts have "multiattribute" consequences. The attributes have to be independent of each other in a strong sense if the elicited utility function is to have a conveniently separable (e.g., additive) form.

Verifying that the client accepts the required attribute independence is, judging from published decision analysis applications, a hazardous matter. We shall not deal here with the multiattribute complication.

3 Among existing texts, the closest to such a goal is doubtless Raiffa's *Decision Analysis* (1968), which includes discussions of classic axiom violations, namely the Allais violation (pp. 80–86) and (implicitly) the Ellsberg violation (pp. 108–110), together with attempts to dissuade the violators.

4 The whole exercise can also be conducted for Allais violators. We shall not take the space to describe that exercise. The classroom experience with the "coupon" argument in attempting to dissuade Allais violators was very similar to the experience with the attempt to dissuade Ellsberg violators.

5 If the expected utility rule holds, then we have admissibility with respect to *all* subacts (where these are ranked by their conditional expected utility), and that means that independence holds as widely as it can. See Theorem 4.

6 When we use the word *compound* throughout this proof, we use it as an abbreviation for the more accurate description "compound except for the degenerate case in which the ticket-bet in the definition of the act is itself a sure ticket."

7 In its original form the PRS Axiom 4 imposes substitutability alone rather than full admissibility, i.e., it says that if $\bar{a}_{E_i \times X \times Y} \lesssim_{E_i \times X \times Y} \bar{\bar{a}}_{E_i \times X \times Y}$, all i in $\{1, \ldots, \ell\}$, then $\{\bar{a}_{E_1 \times X \times Y}, \ldots, \bar{a}_{E_\ell \times X \times Y}\} \sim_A \{\bar{\bar{a}}_{E_1 \times X \times Y}, \ldots, \bar{\bar{a}}_{E \times X \times Y}\}$. But if one combines the original form of PRS Axiom 4 with PRS Axiom 1b (monotonicity) and Axiom 2b (evaluation of events), then one obtains the modified form presented here.

8 Throughout this proof, just as in the proof of Theorem 2, we use the word *compound* as an abbreviation for a more cumbersome descriptor.

REFERENCES

Fishburn, P. C. (1970), *Utility theory for decision making,* New York: Wiley.

McCrimmon, K. R. and S. Larsson (1979), "Utility theory: Axioms versus paradoxes," in M. Allais and O. Hagen (Eds.), *Expected utility and the Allais paradox,* Dordrecht, Holland: D. Reidel, pp. 333–409.

Machina, M. J. (1982), "Expected utility: Analysis without the independence axiom," *Econometrica,* 50: 277–324.

Marschak, J. and R. Radner (1972), *Economic theory of teams,* New Haven: Yale University Press.

Pratt, J. W., H. Raiffa, and R. Schlaiffer (1964), "The foundations of decisions under uncertainty: An elementary exposition," *Journal of the American Statistical Association,* 59: 373–5.

Raiffa, H. (1968), *Decision analysis: Introduction lectures on choice under uncertainty,* Reading, Mass.: Addison-Wesley.

Savage, L. J. (1954), *The foundations of statistics,* New York: Wiley.

Schoemaker, P. (1982), "The expected utility model: Its variants, purposes, evidence and limitations," *Journal of Economic Literature,* 20: 529–63.

Slovic, P. and A. Tversky (1974), "Who accepts Savage's axioms?," *Behavioral Science,* 19: 368–73.

CHAPTER 6

Univariate and multivariate comparisons of risk aversion: a new approach

Menahem E. Yaari

1   Introduction

A generation ago, Kenneth Arrow (1965) and John Pratt (1964) independently developed a remarkable framework for carrying out comparisons of risk aversion. At the center of this framework lay the construction of risk aversion indices, measuring the degree of concavity of an agent's utility for wealth: The more concave the utility, the more risk averse the agent. [See Machina (1983) for an excellent account.] The Arrow–Pratt framework proved invaluable for comparative statics. For example, in order to show that increased riskiness of future income tends to stimulate present saving, it turned out to be necessary to make assumptions about the behavior of the consumer's indices of risk aversion. Generally speaking, those comparative statics results, which rest upon so-called third derivative conditions, turned out in many cases to be readily and intuitively interpretable in terms of the Arrow–Pratt indices.

The foundation upon which Arrow and Pratt had built was expected utility theory: For agents who evaluate risky prospects by calculating their expected utilities, comparisons of risk aversion can always be stated in terms of the Arrow–Pratt indices (see, for example, Yaari 1969). However, for agents whose evaluation of risky prospects does not involve expected utility, the Arrow–Pratt indices are either undefined or else irrelevant. This is true, for example, for a states-of-nature theory of choice under risk. It is also true for the non-expected-utility theory proposed recently by the present author (Yaari 1985). I know, of course, that is is premature – indeed pretentious – to place the theory that I have proposed alongside expected utility theory and attempt to measure the one against

Work on this paper was carried out under the generous auspices of the International Centre for Economies and Related Disciplines at the London School of Economics.

the other. However, having suggested a so-called dual theory of choice under risk, I have no alternative but to face the question of how, within this theory, comparisons of risk aversion might be carried out, and how these comparisons might enter in an analysis of comparative statics. It is to this question that I wish to devote this chapter.

2   Preliminaries

Here is a brief account of the dual theory proposed in Yaari (1985). Let V be the set of all nonnegative and bounded random variables defined on some probability space. If $v \in V$, then the symbol G_v will be used to denote the *decumulative* distribution function (DDF) of v, that is, $G_v(t) = \Pr\{v \geq t\}$ for $t \geq 0$. Let the set of all DDFs of random variables in V be denoted Γ. A preference relation $\succsim$ is assumed to be defined on V, and it is assumed also that two random variables having the same DDF are always $\succsim$-equivalent.[1] Therefore, the preference relation $\succsim$ induces another preference relation, on Γ, in a natural manner. With the reader's indulgence, the same symbol, $\succsim$, will be used to denote both preference relations, on V and on Γ. The following axioms are enunciated:

Axiom B. $\succsim$ is a complete, nontrivial weak order.

Axiom C. $\succsim$ is continuous, relative to L_1-convergence of distributions.

Axiom D. $G_v(t) \geq G_u(t)$ for all $t \geq 0$ implies that $G_v \succsim G_u$.

Axiom E.[2] Let G_u and G_v belong to Γ, and define $G_u \boxplus G_v$ by

$$(G_u \boxplus G_v)(t) = \begin{cases} G_u(t) & \text{for } 0 \leq t \leq \bar{x}_u, \\ G_v(t - \bar{x}_u) & \text{for } t > \bar{x}_u, \end{cases}$$

where $\bar{x}_u = \sup\{t \mid G_u(t) > 0\}$. If u, v, and w are members of V such that $G_u \boxplus G_w$ and $G_v \boxplus G_w$ both belong to Γ, then

$$G_u \boxplus G_w \succsim G_v \boxplus G_w \quad \text{iff} \quad G_u \succsim G_v.$$

Similarly, if $G_w \boxplus G_u$ and $G_w \boxplus G_v$ both belong to Γ, then

$$G_w \boxplus G_u \succsim G_w \boxplus G_v \quad \text{iff} \quad G_u \succsim G_v.$$

It is shown in Yaari (1985, Theorem 1) that a preference relation $\succsim$ satisfies Axioms B–E if and only if there exists a real function f, defined on the unit interval, which is continuous and nondecreasing and satisfies $f(0) = 0$ and $f(1) = 1$, such that for all u and v in V,

$$u \gtrsim v \quad \text{iff} \quad \int_0^\infty f(G_u(t))\, dt \geq \int_0^\infty f(G_v(t))\, dt \tag{1}$$

and, for all $u \in V$,

$$u \sim \left[\int_0^\infty f(G_u(t))\, dt \right], \tag{2}$$

where $\sim$ denotes indifference and $[x]$ stands for a random variable that assumes the value x with probability 1. The phrase "f represents $\gtrsim$" indicates that equations (1) and (2) hold.

The foregoing assertion provides the foundation for a theory of choice under risk, for an agent whose preferences satisfy Axioms B–E. Such an agent would be viewed as evaluating risky prospects by calculating their "certainty equivalents," as defined in equation (2), using the function f representing the agent's preference order. Given a choice among risky prospects, the agent would then pick a prospect having the greatest certainty equivalent. It follows immediately from equation (2) that, in this theory, *risk neutrality* is characterized by the function f, which represents the agent's preferences, being the identity [i.e., by $f(p) = p$ for all $0 \leq p \leq 1$]. As for *risk aversion*, one gets the following characterization: An agent with a preference relation satisfying Axioms B–E is risk averse if and only if the function f representing $\gtrsim$ is *convex*. [This is Theorem 2 in Yaari (1985).] It seems natural, therefore, to say that one agent is *more risk averse* than another agent if the former's f is more convex than the latter's. But there is also another possibility: Since agents evaluate risky prospects by calculating their certainty equivalents, one is tempted to define the property of one agent being more risk averse than another by saying that the certainty equivalent value assigned to any given risky prospect by the former agent is always lower than that assigned by the latter agent. A moment's reflection, however, reveals that these two definitions do not coincide. The first definition implies the second, but not conversely. A detailed investigation of the relation "more risk averse than . . ." is, therefore, required.

3 Univariate comparisons of risk aversion

Let two decision makers be characterized by their respective preference relations, $\gtrsim_1$ and $\gtrsim_2$, and suppose that, in both cases, Axioms B–E are satisfied. Thus, there exist two real functions, f_1 and f_2, which represent the relations $\succsim_1$ and $\succsim_2$, respectively. What can we say, in terms of f_1 and f_2, to characterize a state of affairs in which the first agent is said to be *more* risk averse[3] than the second? Here are five alternative definitions.

The first agent (with f_1) will be considered more risk averse than the second (with f_2) if and only if...

Definition 1. There exists a convex function g, defined on the unit interval, such that $f_1 = g \circ f_2$, that is, $f_1(p) = g(f_2(p))$ for all p.

Definition 2. For each $v \in V$, let $\bar{x}_v$ be defined by $\bar{x}_v = \sup\{t \mid G_v(t) > 0\}$, that is, $\bar{x}_v$ is the (essential) upper bound of v. Then, for all $v \in V$,

$$[\bar{x}_v, p_1] \sim_1 v \quad \text{and} \quad [\bar{x}_v, p_2] \sim_2 v \quad \text{imply} \quad p_1 \geq p_2.$$

(Here $[x, p]$ is a random variable that takes the values x and 0 with probabilities p and $1 - p$, respectively.) Equivalently, for all $v \in V$, if

$$f_1(p_1) = \frac{1}{\bar{x}_v} \int_0^\infty f_1(G_v(t))\, dt \quad \text{and} \quad f_2(p_2) = \frac{1}{\bar{x}_v} \int_0^\infty f_2(G_v(t))\, dt,$$

then $p_1 \geq p_2$.

Definition 3. For all u and v in V, if

$$\int_0^T f_2(G_u(t))\, dt \geq \int_0^T f_2(G_v(t))\, dt$$

holds for all $T \geq 0$, with equality as $t \to \infty$, then

$$\int_0^\infty f_1(G_u(t))\, dt \geq \int_0^\infty f_1(G_v(t))\, dt.$$

Definition 4. For f_1 and f_2 twice differentiable and strictly increasing, the inequality

$$\frac{f_1''(p)}{f_1'(p)} \geq \frac{f_2''(p)}{f_2'(p)}$$

must hold, for all $0 < p < 1$.

Definition 5. For all $0 \leq p \leq 1$, $f_1(p) \geq f_2(p)$ holds, and consequently

$$\int_0^\infty f_1(G_v(t))\, dt \leq \int_0^\infty f_2(G_v(t))\, dt$$

holds for all $v \in V$.

It seems appropriate to devote a brief comment to each one of these definitions.

Definition 1 characterizes f_1 as being more risk averse than f_2 by the assertion that f_1 is a so-called convex transform of f_2.

In Definition 2, the following question is being presented to the agent: Suppose that, instead of the random variable v, you were offered the *upper bound* of v with probability p and 0 with probability $1 - p$. How high would p have to be to make you indifferent between the two options? It seems quite reasonable to suppose that the more risk averse the agent, the higher will be this critical probability.

Now let us consider Definition 3. This is the analog, for the present framework, of the Diamond–Stiglitz (1974) suggestion that differences in risk aversion be examined by looking at a so-called mean utility-preserving spread. To see this, consider an agent whose preference order, $\succsim$, is represented by the real function f. Given a random variable $v \in V$, we can define a new random variable, $v(f) \in V$, by the requirement that, for each $t \geq 0$,

$$G_{v(f)}(t) = f(G_v(t)) \tag{3}$$

should hold. Under the present theory, the agent is viewed as evaluating a random variable v by calculating the expected value of $v(f)$. Thus, a mean *utility*-preserving spread on v is a *mean*-preserving spread on $v(f)$. [In Diamond and Stiglitz (1974), a mean utility-preserving spread on a random variable v is defined as a mean-preserving spread on $\phi(v)$, where ϕ is the agent's von Neumann–Morgenstern utility.] What Definition 3 says is now clear: f_1 is more risk averse than f_2 if, for each $v \in V$, a mean-preserving spread on $v(f_2)$ can never be f_1-improving.

Definition 4 proposes that the degree of an agent's risk aversion be evaluated locally in terms of a quotient of derivatives, which is the obvious analog of the Arrow–Pratt index of absolute risk aversion.

Finally, in Definition 5, it is suggested that one agent be regarded as more risk averse than another if the amount of money the latter agent is willing to pay to purchase any given gamble is always at least as large as the amount the former agent is willing to pay, for the same gamble.

Theorem 1. Let two preference relations on V, $\succsim_1$ and $\succsim_2$, be represented by the functions f_1 and f_2, respectively, and assume that both f_1 and f_2 are strictly increasing.[4] Consider Definitions 1–5 (D1 to D5), and let the symbol DJ, for $J = 1, \ldots, 5$, stand also for the assertion "$\succsim_1$ is more risk averse than $\succsim_2$ according to Definition DJ." Then,

(a)   D1 ⇔ D2 ⇔ D3;
(b)   D1 ⇔ D4 in the differentiable case;
(c)   D1 ⇒ D5, but not conversely.

Proof: Define a real function g by writing $g = f_1 \circ f_2^{-1}$. Then, g is a continuously increasing function satisfying $g(0) = 0$ and $g(1) = 1$. Consider any $v \in V$ with (essential) upper bound $\bar{x}_v$, and define p_1 and p_2 as in Definition 2. Suppose that g is convex. Then, by Hölder's inequality,

$$f_1(p_1) = \frac{1}{\bar{x}_v} \int_0^\infty g(f_2(G_v(t)))\, dt$$

$$\geq g\left(\frac{1}{\bar{x}_v} \int_0^\infty f_2(G_v(t))\, dt\right)$$

$$= g(f_2(p_2)) = f_1(p_2),$$

and since f_1 is strictly increasing, we conclude that $p_1 \geq p_2$. Conversely, suppose that g is not convex. Then, there exist real numbers q_1, q_2, and λ, all in the unit interval, such that $\lambda g(q_1) + (1-\lambda) g(q_2) < g(\lambda q_1 + (1-\lambda) q_2)$. Without loss of generality, assume that $0 \leq q_1 < q_2 \leq 1$ and $0 < \lambda < 1$. Let $\hat{v} \in V$ be a random variable whose DDF, call it $\hat{G}$, is given by

$$f_2(\hat{G}(t)) = \begin{cases} 1 & \text{for } t = 0, \\ q_2 & \text{for } 0 < t \leq 1 - \lambda, \\ q_1 & \text{for } 1 - \lambda < t \leq 1, \\ 0 & \text{for } t > 1. \end{cases}$$

By the previous argument, we get $p_1 < p_2$ holding for this particular $\hat{v}$. Hence, D1 ⇔ D2.

The equivalence D1 ⇔ D3 is an immediate consequence of Theorem 2 in Yaari (1985), as summarized in Section 2 above. Let $v \in V$. Then,

$$\int_0^\infty f_1(G_v(t))\, dt = \int_0^\infty g(f_2(G_v(t)))\, dt = \int_0^\infty g(G_{v(f_2)}(t))\, dt,$$

where $v(f_2)$ is defined in equation (3). What this formula says is that, for agent 1, the evaluation of v, using f_1, is equivalent to the evaluation of $v(f_2)$ using g. By Theorem 2 in Yaari (1985), mean-preserving spread on $v(f_2)$ will cause its evaluation, using g, to go down for all $v \in V$ if and only if g is convex.

The proof of D1 ⇔ D4, in the case where f_1 and f_2 are twice differentiable, is familiar and I shall not repeat it here.

It is also straightforward to see that D1 ⇒ D5 holds, but not conversely: Recall that g satisfies the conditions $g(0) = 0$ and $g(1) = 1$. Therefore, if g

is convex, then $g(p) \leq p$ holds for all $0 \leq p \leq 1$, but not conversely. This completes the proof of the theorem. ∎

Theorem 1 provides a justification for saying that one agent is more risk averse than another agent if the function f_1 representing the former agent's preferences is *more convex* than the function f_2 representing the latter agent's preferences. This is also the definition that makes "risk averse" synonymous with "more risk averse than a risk-neutral agent," which is clearly a desideratum.

4 The multivariate case

The foregoing analysis is easily extended to the case of multivariate, independently distributed risks. Specifically, let n be a positive integer and write V^n to denote the set of all n-tuples such that $v = (v_1, \ldots, v_n)$ belongs to V^n if and only if each v_i belongs to V (see Section 2) and, for all $i \neq j$, v_i and v_j are independently distributed. We now consider an agent having a preference relation $\succsim$ on V^n, and our objective is to represent this relation numerically, in a manner analogous to what has been done above for $n = 1$. To achieve this, we proceed along a familiar path. For each i, $i = 1, \ldots, n$, let $\succsim_i$ be the preference relation induced by $\succsim$ on the ith coordinate, with the random variables in all the other coordinates being held fixed. In general, of course, $\succsim_i$ depends on the fixed random variables that occupy all but the ith slot, but this dependence will now be assumed away:

Axiom A. For any i, $i = 1, \ldots, n$, let $\succsim_i$ be defined by

$$u \succsim_i v \Leftrightarrow (\bar{v}_1, \ldots, u, \ldots, \bar{v}_n) \succsim (\bar{v}_1, \ldots, v, \ldots, \bar{v}_n).$$
$$\quad\quad\quad\quad\quad \uparrow \quad\quad\quad\quad\quad\quad\quad \uparrow$$
$$\quad\quad\quad\quad\quad i\text{th} \quad\quad\quad\quad\quad\quad\; i\text{th}$$
$$\quad\quad\quad\quad\quad \text{place} \quad\quad\quad\quad\quad \text{place}$$

Then, $\succsim_i$ is the same, for all choices of $\bar{v}_j$, $j \neq i$.

This is the type of independence axiom considered, for example, by Debreu (1960).

The reason for restricting V^n to n-tuples of *independently distributed* random variables is now clear: Axiom A makes no sense whatsoever when preferences are defined over n-tuples of dependent random variables.

With Axiom A in hand, one can proceed to extend the other axioms, namely Axioms B–E of Section 2, to the preference relation $\succsim$ on V^n.

Indeed, to postulate that any of these other axioms holds for $\gtrsim$ will be to require that it should hold for each $\gtrsim_i$ separately, $i = 1, \ldots, n$.

In order to make the theorem about to be stated less cumbersome, let us agree on the following:

(α) If x is a nonnegative real number, then $[x]$ is a degenerate random variable, taking the value x with probability 1.

(β) All references to real functions $f_1, \ldots, f_n$ will be subject to the stipulation that, for all $i = 1, \ldots, n$, f_i is defined on the unit interval, is continuously nondecreasing, and satisfies $f_i(0) = 0$, $f_i(1) = 1$.

(γ) Let $f_1, \ldots, f_n$ be as in (β), and consider a random variable $v \in V$, with DDF G_v. Then, for $i = 1, \ldots, n$, a symbol $F_i(v)$ will be defined, as follows:

$$F_i(v) = \int_0^\infty f_i(G_v(t))\, dt.$$

Theorem 2. Let $\gtrsim$ be a preference relation on V^n. Then $\gtrsim$ satisfies Axioms A–E if and only if there exist n real functions, $f_1, \ldots, f_n$, such that

$$v \sim ([F_1(v_1)], [F_2(v_2)], \ldots, [F_n(v_n)]) \tag{4}$$

holds for every $v = (v_1, \ldots, v_n)$ in V^n. Moreover, suppose that Axioms B and C (order and continuity) are strengthened so as to hold not only in each component separately, but jointly in all components.[5] Then, $\gtrsim$ satisfies Axioms A–E if and only if there exists an increasing and continuous function $U: \mathbb{R}_+^n \to \mathbb{R}$, unique up to a continuously increasing transformation, such that

$$u \gtrsim v \Leftrightarrow U(F_1(u_1), \ldots, F_n(u_n)) \geq U(F_1(v_1), \ldots, F_n(v_n)) \tag{5}$$

holds for all $u = (u_1, \ldots, u_n)$ and $v = (v_1, \ldots, v_n)$ in V^n.

Proof: The proof of equation (4) rests upon Theorem 1 in Yaari (1985), with repeated applications of the independence axiom (Axiom A). The proof of equation (5) rests upon equation (4), in conjunction with Debreu's theorem (1954) on the representation of preferences by a continuous utility. ∎

Note that the function U appearing in the second part of Theorem 2 is an ordinal representation of the agent's preferences over *riskless* multivariate prospects. In other words, U can be any continuous function satisfying the condition

$$U(x_1, \ldots, x_n) \geq U(y_1, \ldots, y_n) \Leftrightarrow ([x_1], \ldots, [x_n]) \gtrsim ([y_1], \ldots, [y_n]). \qquad (6)$$

Theorem 2 thus provides a representation of preferences over multivariate risky prospects in a manner that preserves ordinality and treats risk through the formation of appropriate certainty equivalents. Treating the agent's attitude toward risk does not, in itself, force an abandonment of ordinality.

Given Theorem 2, one is now in a position to introduce the notions of multivariate risk aversion and of comparisons in multivariate risk aversion. Let $\gtrsim$ be a preference relation on V^n and consider the real-valued functions $f_1, \ldots, f_n$ and U ($f_i : [0,1] \rightarrow [0,1]$ for $i = 1, \ldots, n$, $U : \mathbb{R}_+^n \rightarrow \mathbb{R}$). I shall say that $f_1, \ldots, f_n$ and U *represent* the preference relation $\gtrsim$ if equation (5) holds for every u and v in V^n, with $F_1, \ldots, F_n$ defined in (γ) above.

Definition. Let a preference relation $\gtrsim$ on V^n be represented by $f_1, \ldots, f_n$ and U. Then, $\gtrsim$ is said to be risk averse if $f_1, \ldots, f_n$ are convex functions.

Furthermore, let $\gtrsim$ and $\gtrsim'$ be two preference relations on V^n, such that $f_1, \ldots, f_n, U$ represent $\gtrsim$ while $f_1', \ldots, f_n', U'$ represent $\gtrsim'$. Then, $\gtrsim'$ is said to be more risk averse than $\gtrsim$ if there exist n convex functions, $g_1, \ldots, g_n$, such that $f_i' = g_i \circ f_i$ for $i = 1, \ldots, n$.

It should be noted that, in the second part of this definition, the ordinal preferences derived from $\gtrsim$ and $\gtrsim'$ for riskless prospects need not coincide. (That is, there need not exist an increasing function Ψ such that $U' = \Psi \circ U$.) This fact should be viewed in the light of previous treatments of multivariate risk aversion [see, for example, Kihlstrom and Mirman (1974)] where global comparisons of risk aversion could be carried out only among agents whose ordinal preferences over riskless prospects coincide. The usefulness of this added generality in applications is admittedly rather in doubt, because different ordinal preferences over riskless prospects can lead to arbitrary differences in behavior. The theoretical point is, nevertheless, worth making.

The applicability, in comparative statics analysis, of the notions introduced in the foregoing definition will be explored in the remaining sections.

5   Risk and saving

Consider the following very simple choice problem: A consumer, whose present wealth is $w \geq 0$, decides that consumption today shall be at a level

x, $0 \le x \le w$, which produces an amount $w - x$ of savings, to be used in consumption tomorrow. The amount that will actually be consumed tomorrow will be given by $y = w - x + v$, where v is a known random variable, describing the income the consumer expects to receive. (The rate of interest is assumed to be zero, for simplicity.) The set of all feasible consumption pairs (x, y) lies in a subset of V^2, as defined above, whose elements have a degenerate random variable in the first component.[6] Let the consumer's preference order over V^2 be denoted $\succeq$, and assume that Axioms A–E are satisfied. Then, by Theorem 2, there exists two functions, $f: [0, 1] \to [0, 1]$ and $U: \mathbb{R}_+^2 \to \mathbb{R}$, satisfying certain appropriate conditions such that the consumer always evaluates the pair (x, y) by calculating the quantity $U(x, [F(y)])$, where $F(y) = \int f(G_y(t)) \, dt$, with G_y being the DDF of y. The consumer's choice problem may therefore be viewed as picking a savings level s to

$$\text{maximize } U\left(w - s, \left[\int_0^\infty f(G_y(t)) \, dt\right]\right)$$

subject to $0 \le s \le w$ and $y = s + v$. \hfill (7)

The structure of this maximization problem is extremely simple. Note that

$$G_y(t) = \begin{cases} 1 & \text{for } 0 \le t \le s, \\ G_v(t - s) & \text{for } t \ge s. \end{cases}$$

And since $f(1) = 1$, we find

$$\int_0^\infty f(G_y(t)) \, dt = s + \int_0^\infty f(G_v(t)) \, dt.$$

Hence, the maximization problem (7) reduces to the following: Choose two real numbers, x and z, so as to

maximize $U(x, z)$ subject to $0 \le x \le w$, $z \ge 0$, and

$$x + z = w + \int_0^\infty f(G_v(t)) \, dt. \hfill (8)$$

In other words, random income v is replaced by an appropriate certainty equivalent and, from there on, choice proceeds as in the case of certainty, with U serving as the utility function. This leads immediately to the following comparative statics results:

(i)   If the consumer is risk averse and if, in the utility function U, consumption in the first period is a normal good, then an increase in the riskiness of future income always stimulates saving.

(ii) If, in the utility function U, consumption in the first period is a normal good, then an increase in the consumer's risk aversion always stimulates saving.

It is possible, in exactly the same way, to analyze the case where the consumer's savings earn a risky rate of return, but future noninterest income is known with certainty. [This is a celebrated problem, studied, among many others, by Levhari and Srinivasan (1969) and by Selden (1979).] I shall not bother to write down a complete description of the consumer's choice problem in this case. Suffice it to say that, here too, we get two comparative statics results, viz.,

(iii) For a risk-averse consumer, an increase in the riskiness of the rate of return on savings works in the same direction as a decrease in a riskless rate of interest.

(iv) An increase in the consumer's risk aversion works in the same direction as a decrease in a riskless rate of interest.

All four comparative statics statements have obvious counterparts, in terms of *decreases* in the relevant quantities.

It is important to note that no so-called third derivative conditions appear in (i) or in (iii). In other words, the signing of the effect of increased riskiness is achieved on the hypothesis of risk aversion alone, without recourse to any hypotheses on how changes in wealth (or in other parameters) affect the degree of risk aversion. Under expected utility theory, this is not the case. [See Selden (1979) for an extensive discussion of this point.]

On the negative side, the fact must be recorded that the present analysis cannot readily be extended to the study of saving behavior with more than two periods. The reason for this is that, with more than two periods, it is not possible, in general, to analyze savings decisions by means of a preference relation defined over n-tuples of independently distributed random variables.

6   Risky prices

Textbook demand theory begins with the analysis of an allocation problem in which a consumer, operating in a competitive environment, must decide how to allocate a fixed budget. To this, let us now add the following complication: The consumer is not quite sure as to the price levels of the various commodities. From the consumer's point of view, competitive prices are not fixed numerical values but fixed random variables, whose distributions are available to the consumer. How should we modify the familiar consumer allocation problem to take account of this added aspect? Here is one suggestion: Think of an investor in the stock market who instructs his or her broker to sell, say, x dollars' worth of share A, or to buy, say, y dollars' worth of share B. In other words, one way to handle the above-mentioned price uncertainty is to view the consumer as deciding not how much to *buy*, but rather how much to *spend*. This would lead to an allocation process in which the consumer is viewed as selecting n nonnegative real numbers, $y_1, \ldots, y_n$, such that $\sum y_i \leq Y$, where y_i is the amount (say in dollars) to be spent on the ith commodity and Y represents the consumer's total available resources. The consumer's objective is to select $y_1, \ldots, y_n$ so as to maximize preferences. At this point we write p_i for the price of the ith commodity, $i = 1, \ldots, n$, and we assume that $p_1, \ldots, p_n$ are independently distributed positive random variables. The consumer, having selected the amounts $y_1, \ldots, y_n$ to be spent on the various commodities, will end up with the consumption vector $(y_1/p_1, \ldots, y_n/p_n)$, that is, the quantity of the ith commodity that will be available for consumption is given by the random variable y_i/p_i. Every choice of spending levels, $y_1, \ldots, y_n$, determines an n-tuple $(y_1/p_1, \ldots, y_n/p_n)$ of nonnegative, independently distributed random variables, and the consumer's preferences over such n-tuples can be described by a relation $\gtrsim$, defined on V^n. The problem of choosing $y_1, \ldots, y_n$ to maximize preferences, subject to $\sum y_i \leq Y$, is now fully specified. In stating this maximization problem, it is convenient to work with the reciprocals of prices. Accordingly, let $\tilde{G}_i$, for $i = 1, \ldots, n$, be the DDF of $1/p_i$, that is

$$\tilde{G}_i(t) = \Pr\left\{\frac{1}{p_i} \geq t\right\} = \Phi_i\left(\frac{1}{t}\right) \quad \text{for } t > 0,$$
$$\tilde{G}_i(0) = 1,$$

where Φ_i is the *cumulative* distribution function (CDF) of the random variable p_i itself. Furthermore, for $i = 1, \ldots, n$, let the symbol $\tilde{p}_i$ be defined as follows:

$$\frac{1}{\tilde{p}_i} = \int_0^\infty f_i(\tilde{G}_i(t))\,dt, \tag{9}$$

where f_i is some given real function, defined on the unit interval. Equivalently, $\tilde{p}_i$ may be defined by writing

$$\tilde{p}_i = \left[\int_0^\infty \frac{f_i(\Phi_i(s))}{s^2}\,ds\right]^{-1} \tag{10}$$

where, once again, Φ_i is the CDF of p_i. It should be borne in mind that $\tilde{p}_1, \ldots, \tilde{p}_n$ are well defined only after a list of n real functions, $f_1, \ldots, f_n$, has been specified.

Now let a binary relation $\succeq$ be defined on V^n, and assume that Axioms A–E are satisfied. Suppose that $\succeq$ describes the consumer's preferences over risky commodity bundles, as discussed above. Then, by Theorem 2, there exist $n+1$ functions, $f_1, \ldots, f_n, U$, satisfying appropriate conditions, such that the consumer's choice problem is one of selecting nonnegative real numbers $y_1, \ldots, y_n$ so as to

$$\text{maximize } U\left(\frac{y_1}{\tilde{p}_1}, \ldots, \frac{y_n}{\tilde{p}_n}\right) \text{ subject to } \sum_{i=1}^{n} y_i \le Y. \tag{11}$$

It is obvious that this maximization problem (11) can also be stated as follows: Choose n nonnegative real numbers, $x_1, \ldots, x_n$, so as to

$$\text{maximize } U(x_1, \ldots, x_n) \text{ subject to } \sum_{i=1}^{n} \tilde{p}_i x_i \le Y. \tag{12}$$

Formally, (12) is just the consumer's allocation problem in classical demand theory, with the parameters $\tilde{p}_1, \ldots, \tilde{p}_n$ playing the role of market prices and with U playing the role of a utility, representing preferences over deterministic commodity bundles. However, it is important to note that the choice variables, $x_1, \ldots, x_n$, in (12) *do not* stand for quantities to be consumed: After the consumer chooses $x_1, \ldots, x_n$, a price realization $p_1, \ldots, p_n$ reveals itself and the consumer ends up with quantities $\tilde{p}_1 x_1/p_1, \ldots, \tilde{p}_n x_n/p_n$ of the respective commodities available for consumption. The function U, on the other hand, is a genuine utility over deterministic commodity bundles, representing as it does the consumer's preferences over n-tuples of degenerate random variables.

From (12), together with the definition of the $\tilde{p}_i$'s, the following highly intuitive comparative-statics results may immediately be obtained:

(v)   The effect of an increase in the consumer's aversion to risk in the price of the ith commodity is always in the same direction as that of a rise in the price of the ith commodity under certainty.

(vi) Let a *harmonic* mean-preserving spread in a random variable q be defined as an increase in the riskiness of q which keeps $E(1/q)$ constant. Then, a harmonic mean-preserving spread in the price of the ith commodity will cause a risk-averse consumer to adjust in the same direction as would a rise in its price under certainty.

In both of these statements, a second clause could have been added, saying that the effect of a *decrease* of the attribute in question is in the opposite direction.

As might have been expected, a *risk-neutral* consumer will not, in general, remain indifferent when prices undergo a mean-preserving spread.

Rather, risk neutrality is characterized here by the consumer's indifference to a harmonic mean-preserving spread in prices. In the present framework, a risk-neutral consumer is indifferent between facing a risky price and facing its *harmonic* mean with certainty.

NOTES

1 This assumption is sometimes referred to as *ethical neutrality* of random events.
2 This axiom lies at the center of the new theory, and it is discussed at length in Yaari (1985). The statement of the axiom in that paper is different from but equivalent to the statement given here.
3 Throughout this essay, the phrase "more risk averse than. . ." is to be understood in the sense of "at least as risk averse as. . ."
4 A similar but clumsy theorem exists also for the case where the f's are not strictly monotone.
5 Henceforth, I shall assume that Axioms B and C are postulated in this stronger sense.
6 This is quite similar to the framework studied by Selden (1978).

REFERENCES

Arrow, K. J. (1965), *Aspects of the theory of risk-bearing,* Helsinki: Yrjö Jahnssonin Säätiö; see also K. J. Arrow, *Essays in the theory of risk-bearing,* Chicago: Markham, 1971.
Debreu, G. (1954), "Representation of a preference ordering by a numerical function," in R. M. Thrall, C. H. Coombs, and R. L. Davis (Eds.), *Decision processes,* New York: Wiley, pp. 159–65.
Debreu, G. (1960), "Topological methods in cardinal utility theory," in K. J. Arrow, S. Karlin, and P. Suppes (Eds.), *Mathematical methods in the social sciences,* Stanford: Stanford University Press, pp. 16–26.
Diamond, P. A. and J. E. Stiglitz (1974), "Increases in risk and in risk aversion," *Journal of Economic Theory,* 8: 337–60.
Kihlstrom, R. and L. J. Mirman (1974), "Risk aversion with many commodities," *Journal of Economic Theory,* 8: 361–88.
Levhari, D. and T. N. Srinivasan (1969), "Optimal savings under uncertainty," *Review of Economic Studies,* 36: 153–63.
Machina, M. J. (1983), "The economic theory of individual behavior toward risk: Theory, evidence and new directions," IMSSS Technical Report no. 433, Stanford University.
Pratt, J. (1964), "Risk aversion in the small and in the large," *Econometrica,* 32: 122–36.
Selden, L. (1978), "A new representation of preferences over 'certain × uncertain' consumption pairs: The 'ordinal certainty equivalent' hypothesis," *Econometrica,* 46: 1045–60.
Selden, L. (1979), "An OCE analysis of the effect of uncertainty under risk preference independence," *Review of Economic Studies,* 46: 73–82.

Yaari, M. E. (1969), "Some remarks on measures of risk-aversion and on their uses," *Journal of Economic Theory,* 1: 315-29.

Yaari, M. E. (1985), "The dual theory of choice under risk," R.M. No. 65, Center for Research in Mathematical Economics and Game Theory, Jerusalem: The Hebrew University. [Forthcoming in *Econometrica.*]

PART II

Information, communication, and organization

Although Kenneth Arrow is probably best known for his contributions to methods of direct decision making and the theory of ideal market decentralization, he laid much of the groundwork for subsequent discussion on alternative methods of organization. By pointing out and developing the relationships between the competitive allocation mechanism and other planning procedures, he caused us to focus on issues such as information gathering, communication efficiency, and transmission costs in deciding among forms of economic organization.

We think it is fair to say that he set an agenda for the future in his presidential address to the American Economic Association in 1974 and in his Fels lectures (*The limits to organization*) published at roughly the same time. He pointed out the need for a better understanding of information costs and how they should be measured; he suggested that many of the problems faced in understanding the structure and operation of large organizations could be analyzed only by bringing *information* and *communication channels* more directly into the agenda of economists; and he advanced the view that the correct boundaries between *internal* and *market* allocations should be analyzed in those terms.

The contributions in this section explore various aspects of this agenda. Oniki addresses directly the question of how to measure the costs of communication. Drawing on ideas and concepts from information theory, he is able to quantify these costs and perform some suggestive comparisons between centralized and market mechanisms. Gorman motivates a view of the scope of the firm in terms of similarity of purpose and type of operation among production units. Making use of parallels with the theory of aggregation, he demonstrates the "information-saving" features of certain pseudomarket organizational forms.

As soon as we contemplate organizations whose members have conflicting interests, transmission costs become complicated by transmission incentives (as agents attempt to influence the outcome in their favor by altering the message in some advantageous way). This element of the communication problem has generated a voluminous body of research in the past ten years. Chapters by Maskin and by Green and Laffont fall in this category.

Attempts to find general *incentive compatible* allocation mechanisms with desirable welfare properties have generated instead the same types of impossibility theorems alluded to in Volume I of this series in the context of social choice (indeed, it is now known that the two types of problems are intimately related). However, positive results have been obtained for sufficiently restricted contexts. The most significant of these contexts is one in which the *distribution* of unknown characteristics is common knowledge, and realizations are drawn from this distribution independently. Maskin succeeds in broadening this class to allow some degree of dependence in the draws.

Green and Laffont look specifically at problems of information transmission in a *two-party* situation where the two parties may have different information and different objective functions. This type of problem has proved intractable heretofore owing to the discrete nature of pieces of information. However, they develop (in Chapter 10) a new way of thinking about information in a channel that enables them to employ standard methods of analysis. Their approach would appear to be applicable to a wider class of problems. Chapter 11 demonstrates some simple rules of organization that will apply even in the context where information is treated as discrete.

CHAPTER 7

The cost of communication in economic organization: II

Hajime Oniki

1   Introduction

Professor Kenneth Arrow, in his presidential address at the 1973 annual meeting of the American Economic Association, discussed problems in the economics of uncertainty and information. In dealing with the efficiency of the price system, he stated:

> In equilibrium, at least, the [market] system as a whole gives the impression of great economy in the handling of information, presumably because transmission of prices is in some significant sense much cheaper than transmission of the whole set of production possibilities and utility functions ... But what was left obscure is a more definite measure of information and its costs, in terms of which it would be possible to assert the superiority of the price system over a centralized alternative ... if we are going to take informational economy seriously, we have to add to our usual economic calculations an appropriate measure of the costs of information gathering and transmission. (Arrow 1974a, pp. 4–5)

This chapter responds partly to the point raised by Professor Arrow; this is an attempt to find a measure of the cost of internal communication in economic systems.

For the convenience of the reader, we shall first give a brief and informal explanation of this work. We consider the problem of comparing two alternative economic systems, the centralized system and the (decentralized) market mechanism. In this work, each system is composed of a *center* and *agents,* the latter being interpreted to be productive firms. In the centralized system, the center may be considered as the planning board of a socialist state, whereas in the market mechanism it is an *auctioneer,* who runs the system by executing the law of supply and demand.

I owe much to Professors Leonid Hurwicz, Kiyoshi Kuga, Stanley Reiter, and a referee for helpful comments and criticisms.

191

Our strategy is to have each system "solve" an allocation problem and to calculate the cost of internal communication arising from this. For simplicity, we choose a textbook problem of cost minimization.

Suppose that each agent is given a marginal cost schedule to produce an output commodity and that the total output is required to be at a given level. In the centralized economy, this level may be an output target set by the socialist government. In the market system, it may represent a level of inelastic demand for the output commodity. We know, of course, that optimality (or equilibrium) requires equality of marginal costs among all agents.

One can observe that the optimal level of output for each agent is determined from the data of this allocation problem, that is, from the marginal cost schedules and the required level of total output. In other words, the optimal level is a *function* of the given data; the former may be *computed* once the latter is given. We can state, in more general terms, that desired decisions are obtained from data describing a given environment. In this work, we regard each of the two systems, the centralized economy and the market mechanism, as a "computer," that is, an information processing system that can generate what is desired from what is given; this work deals with the *cost* of running such a computer.

From our standpoint, the two systems differ only in the way they handle economic data; otherwise, they are treated equally. In particular, the data given to each system at the beginning of computation are identical. Specifically, we assume that initially, before any computation starts, each agent knows his marginal cost schedule and the center knows the required level of total output. This condition, common to the two systems as remarked above, is called the initial dispersion of information. Further, we require that the computation output from each system be identical; the solution to the given allocation problem obtained by the centralized system must be the same as that obtained by the market mechanism, although the *internal algorithm* in each system may not. Thus, our work is like comparing two (real) computer systems that produce an identical line printer output from an identical card deck.

Computation of desired allocation proceeds as explained below. In the centralized system, each agent transmits to the center the entire marginal cost schedule, and the center, with all the data at hand, calculates the optimal allocation by itself. The decentralized system, on the other hand, simulates a competitive market. The center announces a (tentative) price of the output commodity, and each agent tells the center the quantity of output to be supplied at this price. The center then calculates the total excess demand for the output commodity and revises the price according to the law of supply and demand. The process is continued until an optimal allocation is obtained.

One sees that various kinds of informational activities need to be performed even in the simple process described above; they include observing, gathering, storing, sending, and transforming economic data. (See, e.g., Marschak 1968 for a comprehensive study of informational activities in economic systems.) In this work, however, we deal with internal communication only; the reason for this is that it is the easiest to investigate.

In order to calculate the cost of communication, we must choose a measurement unit. Our strategy for doing this is best explained by comparing communication, which is to move information from one place to another, to transportation, which is to move, say, passengers from one place to another. The amount of passenger transportation is measured by the unit of, say, passenger-kilometer, and the cost of transportation depends on this and the choice of actual means of transportation, which may be characterized by mode (air, auto), route, speed, and so on. For any given means, the greater the amount of transportation expressed by the unit of passenger-kilometer, the higher the cost. Thus, we may state that the amount of transportation is a measure of transportation cost independent of its means.

In this work, we seek to formulate a model in terms of which the amount of information to be transmitted may be obtained independent of the means of information transmission. In communication, we have no common sense unit for measuring information like the unit of passenger-kilometer in transportation. However, information theory fills the gap; in fact, as explained in Section A in the appendix, it provides a universal unit of measuring information, which is independent of the actual content of information and of the channel through which information is transmitted (see also Hess 1983, Chapter 11).

In information theory, "having a piece of information" means that a particular object is designated in a collection of possible objects. For example, the statement "the air temperature is now increasing" may mean that the object *increase* has been selected from the collection of three objects, *increase, decrease,* and *unchanged.* It is essential that this set be specified completely beforehand and its meaning be understood both by the sender and the receiver of information.

Roughly speaking, the amount of information is measured by the *degree of difficulty* to identify an object in the set of possible objects. It depends on the number of objects contained in the set and the probability distribution according to which the object in the set takes place. It does not depend on the interpretation attached to them. As shown in Section A (Appendix), the amount of information is expressed by the expected number of letters (bits) needed to code the objects, which can be approximated by the entropy of the probability distribution.[1]

In Section 2 of this chapter, we use the entropy function to calculate the amount of information to be transmitted in the centralized system and the price mechanism when the optimal allocation is computed. In fact, the author's earlier work (1974) did this by using an elementary combinatorial method. It was found that, in terms of the cost of communication, the price mechanism was more economical than the centralization of information if the required accuracy of resource allocation was not very low; the ratio of the communication cost of the centralized system to that of the price mechanism increases as the required accuracy tends to be high.

This contribution deals with the same problem as summarized above. We shall, however, present an improved formulation of the problem so that the results to be shown will be more accurate and the analysis needed to get them will be much simpler than in the earlier work.

The main difference between the earlier and the present works lies in their formulation. In the earlier work, all the data of the model were discretized, and the entropy function was calculated by combinatorial enumeration. This made the model elementary and easy to understand, but it also made the calculation very cumbersome. In this essay, we shall construct our model by using analytical tools. This will simplify our task greatly, but there is a price for this; the distance between the reality and the model is greater in this work than in the earlier work.

There seems to exist an intrinsic difficulty in formulating models to measure informational costs. As we know, analytical models are simpler than combinatorial ones. For example, differential equations are easier to solve than difference equations, and normal distributions have nice properties not shared by binomials. However, to employ analytical construction, we have to introduce a continuum like the real variables, but this is not directly compatible with the objective of calculating informational costs. The reason is that the cost of identifying an object in a continuous set is infinite (e.g., a real number can only be represented by an infinite decimal sequence). This means that if we use analytical tools with the entropy function to express the informational cost, we must introduce "approximation" into our model and somehow bridge the gap between the continuous and the discrete spheres. In this chapter, this is done by Proposition A6 (Appendix).

2   Complete centralization and the price mechanism

2.1   *Assumptions common to the two systems*

In this section, we construct a model to compare the cost of internal communication in the centralized system and in the price mechanism. First, let us present assumptions that are common to both of the two systems.

We consider a simple problem of resource allocation to be solved by a "center" and agents (producers), each being indexed by i ($i = 1, ..., I$). It is assumed that there is only one commodity, to be denoted by x. The price of the commodity will be expressed by t. Let $T = \{t \mid 0 < t < +\infty\} = (0, +\infty)$ and $X = \{x \mid 0 < x < +\infty\} = (0, +\infty)$ be the price and the quantity spaces, respectively.

The environment to be given to agent i is a supply function (an inverse marginal cost schedule) $g^i(t)$. More precisely, define

$$G = \{g: T \to X \mid g(0) = 0, \ g \text{ is nondecreasing and left continuous}\}$$

to be the set of supply functions, G being common to all agents.

It is assumed that the supply function arises from G subject to what is called the first-passage time distribution of Brownian motions, of which a brief summary is given in Section B (Appendix). In this chapter, we consider the case in which this distribution is identical and independent over all agents. Given $g^i \in G$, let $g^i(t)$ denote the quantity supplied at price $t \in T$. By Proposition B3(i) (Appendix), the random variable $g^i(t)$ has the density function $f(\cdot, t)$ of the one-sided stable distribution with parameter t, which is also explained in Section B (Appendix). Let $z > 0$ be a constant denoting the aggregate demand for the commodity. The objective of the center and the agents is to find a $t^* \in T$ such that the equilibrium condition $\sum g^i(t^*) = z$ be satisfied at least approximately.

We shall assume the following information structure. At the beginning of each period, a state of the world $(g^1, ..., g^I, z)$ obtains. Agent i knows g^i (and g^i only), whereas the center knows z (and z only). The equilibrium price t^* is theoretically determined once the state of the world is given. As explained in Section 1, however, our problem here is to consider adjustment processes (algorithms) that specify the detailed steps leading from the given data describing the state of the world to the equilibrium price and the equilibrium level of output for each agent. In any such process, information about the state of the world, that is, information about $(g^1, ..., g^I, z)$, must be exchanged between the agents and the center.

The cost of communication to execute a process may be calculated by examining how information is transmitted at each step of the process.

As summarized in Section A (Appendix), the cost of communication is determined by the amount of information transmitted, which may be expressed by the expected number of letters needed to code the information to be transmitted.

In order to calculate the amount of information transmitted, we need to impose further assumptions on our model. First, we specify a degree of accuracy required for optimization. Let $\Delta_t > 0$ and $\Delta_x > 0$ denote, respectively, the length of an interval on the price axis and the length of an interval on the quantity axis. In the following, when we consider decision making with approximation, we shall work only with *integer* prices specified by the interval Δ_t (i.e., multiples of Δ_t); a price that is not equal to a multiple of Δ_t will be represented by an integer nearest to it. On the quantity axis, we shall work only with intervals of length Δ_x (i.e., intervals with endpoints that are equal to multiples of Δ_x); any quantity of output commodity will be represented by an interval containing it. (We assume that "ties" are resolved in some way. It will be seen later that the way they are done does not matter.)

When we consider a model in terms of integer prices and quantity intervals, we say that it is *in the approximation mode,* and when we consider a model without approximation, we say that it is *in the theoretical mode.* Decision making in the approximation mode accompanies allocation errors. The length of the intervals Δ_t and Δ_x determines the degree of accuracy for optimization, but it is not necessarily equal to the allocation error (the latter will be considered later). Observe that the cost of informational activities can be considered only in the approximation mode (as long as we use the Shannon measure). We expect that as the accuracy requirements Δ_t and Δ_x tend to be small, the amount of information transmitted will be increased.

Second, we choose a number $M \in T$ so large that the probability for the equilibrium price t^* to lie outside the interval $(0, M)$ may be ignored. It is assumed that all of the adjustments to be considered below are carried out within this interval. Furthermore, for analytical simplicity, we assume that the equations $\Delta_t = 2^{-m}M$ and $\Delta_x = 2^{-n}N$ hold for some positive integers $m > 0$ and $n > 0$ and a number $N > 0$. (See Figure 1.)

Below, we calculate the cost of communication in the centralized system and that in the price mechanism. That is, we calculate the expected number of letters (bits) to be transmitted between the center and the agents for computing the desired allocation to some level of accuracy. For each of the two systems, we explain about the data in the approximation mode to be transmitted between the center and the agents, the maximum allo-

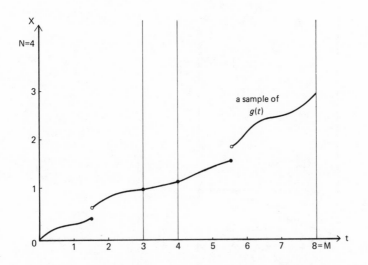

Figure 1. Sample supply function $g(t) \in G$ for the case of $m = 3$, $n = 2$.

cation error that may arise from the adjustment process using the data, and the cost of transmitting the data.

2.2   The centralized system

We first deal with the centralized system. Consider an agent who is given a particular supply function $g(t)$. In order for the center to calculate the equilibrium price in the approximation mode, the center needs to obtain the values of the function $g(t)$ at $t = r\Delta_t$, $(r = 1, 2, ..., 2^m)$. There may be several alternative ways to do this. In this chapter, we assume, for the sake of making our calculation of the communication cost simple, that the agent transmits to the center the quantity interval containing the *increment* of the supply function, that is, it sends the data approximating $\{g(r\Delta_t) - g((r-1)\Delta_t)\}$ for $r = 1, 2, ..., 2^m$ *successively in this order*. (See Figure 2.) The center, having received these data from each agent, obtains information to approximate the aggregate supply curve. It can then compute the optimal solution of the given allocation problem in the approximation mode. The error arising from this depends on the parameters m and n and also on the sample supply functions.

The maximum error that arises from the center's computation of optimum in the approximation mode is determined as follows. Since the agent transmits a quantity interval containing the "true" increment of the

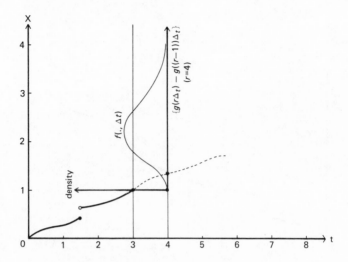

Figure 2. Density of $\{g(r\Delta_t)-g((r-1)\Delta)\}$ given $g((r-1)\Delta_t)$, where $r=4$.

quantity supplied at an integer price, the maximum error arising from this is equal to the length of this interval, that is, Δ_x. In the worst case, this error is accumulated for each increment of the supply function and for each agent; accordingly, the maximum error in estimating the aggregate quantity supplied is equal to $2^m\Delta_x I$, where 2^m is the number of the integer prices and I is the number of the agents. Suppose that we can neglect the probability that the equilibrium price t^* lies outside the interval $(0, M)$ and, in addition, the probability that the aggregate quantity supplied at $t=M$ exceeds N. Then we can state that if $N=2^n\Delta_x$ is much greater than the maximum error $2^m\Delta_x I$, that is, if n is much greater than $m\log_2 I$, the maximum error relative to the aggregate quantity supplied is small. Figures 3(a)-(c) illustrate such a case, whereas Figures 4(a)-(c) illustrate a case in which the relative error is not small. The reader who is not quite satisfied with this result is reminded that the primary objective of this work is to construct a model for comparing economic systems with respect to the cost of communication in a simple setting, not to construct a model

Figure 3. (a) An example of the supply function (parameters: $M=4$, $m=2$, $\Delta_t=1$, $N=32$, $n=5$, $\Delta_x=1$). (b) The quantity intervals of the increments of the supply function in (a) (to be transmitted to the center by the agent). (c) The quantity intervals containing the (true) supply function in (a) (to be reconstructed by the center receiving messages from the agent).

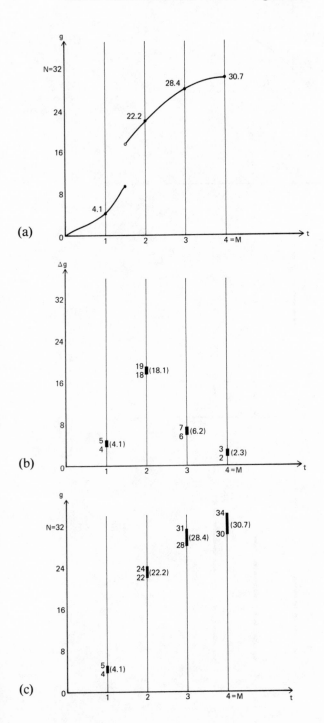

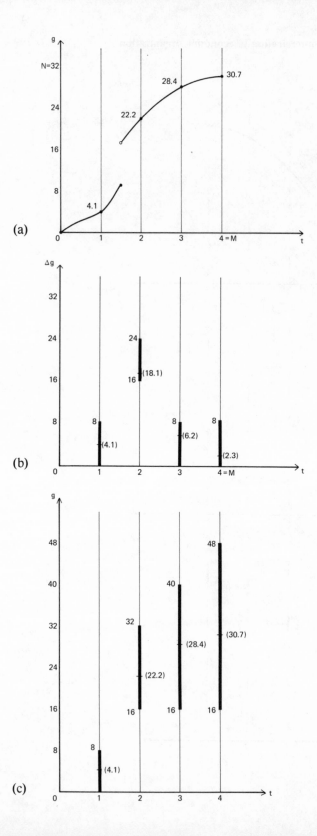

in which the error arising from adjustments in the approximation mode is expressed in a simple form.[2]

Let us now turn to calculating the cost of transmitting the data approximating $\{g(r\Delta_t) - g((r-1)\Delta_t)\}$, for $r = 1, 2, \ldots, 2^m$, from the agent to the center. Proposition B3(ii) (Appendix) states that these data are distributed independently and each of them has the density function $f(\cdot, \Delta_t)$ of the one-sided stable distribution with parameter Δ_t. In other words, the agent is given 2^m random variables distributed independently and identically. (See Figure 2.)

Consider one of these random variables. Since the agent reports to the center a quantity interval of length Δ_x to which the true value of the random variable belongs, the set of messages from which the agent chooses is $S = \{s_1, s_2, \ldots\}$, where s_u denotes the interval $((u-1)\Delta_x, u\Delta_x)$. It is now evident that we can approximate $p_u = \text{Prob}\{s_u\}$ by $f(u\Delta_x, \Delta_t)\Delta_x$.

Proposition A7 (Appendix) allows us to state that the amount of information needed to send a message from the message set S defined above is approximately equal to $\{H(f(\cdot, \Delta_t)) - \log \Delta_x\}$, where $H(\cdot)$ is the entropy function defined by Definition A2 (Appendix). Since there are 2^m such random variables and the number of the agents is I, we may conclude that the communication cost in the centralized system, say C_1, is expressed as

$$C_1 = I \times 2^m \{H(f(\cdot, \Delta_t)) - \log \Delta_x\}. \tag{1}$$

By making use of Proposition B2 (Appendix), we obtain[3]

$$C_1 = I \times 2^m \{(-2m+n)\log 2 + (2\log M - \log N) + K\}, \tag{2}$$

where the constant $K > 0$ is given in Proposition B2.

For simplicity, let us assume that the parameters M, N, m, and n are chosen in such a way that $M^2 = N$ and $2m = n$.[4] We then get

$$C_1 = I \times 2^m K. \tag{3}$$

2.3   The price mechanism

Next, we consider the price mechanism. The center here is an auctioneer and follows the ordinary scheme of price adjustments (i.e., the law of

Figure 4. (a) An example of the supply function (parameters: $M = 4$, $m = 2$, $\Delta_t = 1$, $N = 32$, $n = 5$, $\Delta_x = 8$). (b) The quantity intervals of the increments of the supply function in (a) (to be transmitted to the center by the agent). (c) The quantity intervals containing the (true) supply function in (a) (to be reconstructed by the center receiving messages from the agent; for this case reconstruction is almost impossible).

supply and demand) in order to get to the equilibrium price. In the theoretical mode, the center announces a tentative price, gets the quantity supplied at that price from each agent, and calculates the excess demand. If it is positive, the center will raise the price, whereas if the excess demand is negative, the tentative price will be lowered. In any case, at the following step, the center announces a revised price to the agents and repeats the procedure described above. The adjustment will be terminated when the excess demand becomes zero.

In our model, the adjustment is considered in the approximation mode so that we work only with integer prices and quantity intervals. We assume that, on the price axis, the center adjusts tentative prices in the following way: Let t_j denote the integer price chosen by the center at the jth step of the adjustment procedure. We postulate that the initial price is chosen so that $t_1 = 2^{-1}M$, and, for each $j > 1$, $t_{j+1} = t_j + 2^{-(j+1)}M$ if the excess demand at t_j is positive and $t_{j+1} = t_j - 2^{-(j+1)}M$ if the excess demand at t_j is negative (or zero).

Since, in our model, each agent reports the quantity supplied at a given price by specifying a quantity interval of length Δ_x, the center obtains the aggregate quantity supplied in the form of an *aggregate interval* of length $I \cdot \Delta_x$, where I is the number of the agents. We postulate, for the sake of definiteness, that the center calculates the excess demand at each adjustment step by subtracting the number equal to the midpoint of this aggregate interval from the number equal to the (given) demand for the output commodity.

We assume that, in each case, the center performs exactly m adjustment steps. Since there are 2^m integer prices, this implies that the center obtains information approximating the position of the aggregate supply curve *near the equilibrium price* to the same degree of accuracy as in the centralized system. The allocation error arising from this procedure, which is performed in the approximation mode, depends on the parameters m and n and also on the sample supply functions.[5]

Let us now calculate the cost of communication of this procedure. For simplicity, we ignore the cost attached to the transmission of prices by the center to the agents; we concentrate on the cost attached to the transmission of the quantity by an agent to the center. At the jth step, agent i transmits a message designating the interval containing the value $g^i(t_j)$ of supply function g^i. It is noted that the position of the interval containing $g^i(t_j - 2^{-j}M)$ in the quantity axis is known both to the center and agent i at the jth step, and as stated by Proposition B3(ii) (Appendix), the random variable $g^i(t_j)$ given $g^i(t_j - 2^{-j}M)$ has the probability distribution with the density function $f(\cdot, 2^{-j}M)$. The amount of information that agent i has to transmit at the jth step with the accuracy corresponding to the quantity interval Δ_x is therefore equal to $\{H(f(\cdot, 2^{-j}M)) - \log \Delta_x\}$. Since this expression is independent of i and there are I agents, we may write down the cost of communication in the price system, say C_2, as

$$C_2 = I \sum_{j=1}^{m} \{H(f(\cdot, 2^{-j}M)) - \log \Delta_x\}, \tag{4}$$

which may be simplified by using Proposition B2 (Appendix) as[6]

$$C_2 = Im\{(-m+n-1)\log 2 + (2\log M - \log N) + K\}. \tag{5}$$

If, as in the preceding section, we assume that $M^2 = N$ and $2m = n$, then we get

$$C_2 = Im\{(m-1)\log 2 + K\}. \tag{6}$$

2.4   Summary

To summarize, we state that

$$C_1/C_2 = O(2^m/m^2). \tag{7}$$

In other words, the cost of communication in the centralized system grows linearly in the number of approximation intervals and the cost in the price mechanism is proportional to the square of the logarithm of the number.

It is noted that the results obtained above basically reflect the difference in the number of messages transmitted for adjustments in the two systems. As seen easily, in the centralized system, the agent needs to send to the center 2^m messages to report the quantity supplied at prices $t = r\Delta_t$ $(r = 1, \ldots, 2^m)$. On the other hand, in the market mechanism, the agent needs to send only m messages, since the center revises tentative prices exactly m times.[7] Our estimation of the relative cost of communication in the two systems [i.e., equation (7)] could be obtained by counting the number of messages transmitted in each system (i.e., without relying on information theory). This is because we have used the supply function as the objective of communication both for the centralized system and for the market mechanism. If we formulated a model of centralization in which the production function, not the supply function, were transmitted, then we would not be able to compare communication costs merely by counting the number of messages.

3   Conclusion

From what is stated at the end of the preceding section, the reader may observe that the main reason that, in our model, the once-and-for-all centralization of information is shown to be less efficient than the price mechanism is that the former "wastes" a great deal of information. To solve the allocation problem, some, but *not all,* of the information about the environment of each agent is needed. Which portion of the information about the environment of an agent is relevant to solve the problem depends on the environment of every other agent; it cannot be determined before the problem is actually solved. Thus, if the information about the environment has to be sent to the center before any computation begins there, each agent must send *all* information about the environment (to the required degree of accuracy); for, otherwise, the center might not be able to compute the optimum because of a lack of relevant information. The advantage of the price mechanism over the centralization lies in the fact that at each step of successive adjustments it allows the agent to send only that information relevant to solve the problem at that step, thus making it possible to avoid sending information that will never be used.

The conclusion stated above has been obtained from our model, which is constructed on a number of simplifying assumptions. Whether it holds in a more general setting is, of course, an open question. If, however, we limit our consideration to the case in which the centralized system "simulates" a decentralized algorithm (as in the Lange–Lerner socialist state performing a marketlike adjustment procedure within a computer), then we can assert that the centralization of information is inferior to the decentralized adjustment with respect to the cost of communication for the reason that the former wastes information the latter does not.

This advantage of *decentralizing* information has long been recognized by Lange and Taylor (1938), Hayek (1945), and others in relation to the classical controversy on socialist planning and more recently by Hurwicz (1960, 1971, 1973, 1977), Marschak and Radner (1972), Marschak (1959), Mount and Reiter (1974), Reiter (1977), and others in relation to the problem of designing economic mechanisms satisfying certain performance requirements. The results presented in Section 2 may be regarded as a quantitative confirmation, in terms of the entropy measure of information, of the advantage of decentralizing information for a simple problem of resource allocation.[8]

A question that arises naturally from the foregoing discussion is whether it is possible to explain the existence of centralized information in the real world. A large amount of information is collected and compiled by economic (and other) organizations (e.g., by modern corporations and government institutions) to facilitate their operations. Centralized information in such organizations is stored partly in human beings and partly in various informational devices. One may think of libraries, dictionaries, and data bases as examples of nonhuman means to store centralized information. It is a fact that usually only a fraction of such centralized information is used; the remaining part will never be used and will thus be wasted. There must be factors that make the centralization of information so economical that the disadvantage of wasting information may be offset.

Arrow (1974a, b) has pointed out that one of the major advantages of centralizing information lies in the economies of scale in "handling" information. For example, a particular piece of printed information, once produced, may be copied with a negligible cost and may be distributed widely. It is well known that this property of information likely prevents it from being traded as an ordinary commodity since it is difficult to protect the ownership of information, but it seems less well known that the same property may explain the existence of systems in which information is centralized.

To summarize, we state that centralization of information brings about both advantages and disadvantages. The former comes from scale economies of information handling and the latter from the waste of centralized information. Thus, an *optimal* degree of centralization (or decentralization) may be obtained by weighing these two factors. Whether it is possible to formulate a model explaining this point is an open question.

Appendix

A   *Theorems from information theory*

Here we assemble from information theory definitions and theorems used in the previous sections.

We first define the set of messages (possible objects) and the set of letters (symbols). Let $S = \{s_1, s_2, \ldots\}$ be a countable set of elements s_i ($i = 1, 2, \ldots$), denoting the collection of messages to be transmitted. It is assumed that the message s_i occurs with probability p_i, where $p_i \geq 0$, $\sum p_i = 1$, and $P = (p_1, p_2, \ldots)$. Let $A = \{a_1, \ldots, a_L\}$ be a finite set, denoting the collection of letters (*alphabet*) to be used for coding messages, where the positive integer L denotes the number of letters. Given a positive integer

$K > 0$, let $b_1 b_2 \cdots b_k = (b_1, \ldots, b_K)$ be a sequence of K elements of A, where $b_k \in A$ $(k = 1, \ldots, K)$. Let A^+ be the set of all finite sequences of elements of A:

$$A^+ = \{b_1 \cdots b_K : K \in N, \ b_k \in A \ (k = 1, \ldots, K)\},$$

where N is the set of positive integers.

Definition A1. A *coding* h of the messages S by alphabet A is a one-to-one function $h: S \to A^+$ from S into A^+:

$$s \mapsto h(s) = b_1 \cdots b_K.$$

The value $h(s)$ is the *code* of s, and the *length* $|h(s)|$ of code $h(s) = b_1 \cdots b_K$ is the number K of letters composing the code. The *average length* $|h|$ of coding h of S is given by the weighted sum of all codes:

$$|h| = \sum p_i |h(s_i)|.$$

Definition A2. The entropy of a probability distribution $P = (p_1, p_2, \ldots)$ is

$$H(P) = -\sum p_i \log p_i.$$

Theorem A3 (Shannon 1948; Huffman 1952).

$$H(P) \leq \inf |h| < H(P) + 1,$$

where the infimum is taken over all codings and the base of the logarithm in the entropy function is equal to L, the number of letters available for coding.

Given a positive integer $J > 0$, let $T_J = S \times S \times \cdots \times S$ (J times) be the J-fold Cartesian product of S. To each element $t = (t_1, \ldots, t_J) \in T_J$, $t_j \in S$ $(j = 1, \ldots, J)$, assign the product probability $q = q(t) = q_1 \cdots q_J$ so that $q_j = p_i$ if and only if $t_j = s_i$ $(j = 1, \ldots, J)$. Let $h_J: T_J \to A^+$ be a coding of the messages T_J by A.

Theorem A4 (Shannon 1948).

$$\frac{1}{J} \inf |h_J| \to H(P) \quad \text{as } J \to +\infty,$$

where the infimum is taken over all codings of T_J by A, and the base of the logarithm in the entropy function is equal to L.

Remark A5: The two theorems stated above suggest that the expected number of letters needed to send a message arising from the set S according to a given probability distribution P is approximated by the entropy $H(P)$ of P. If a message is to be coded each time it arises, the average length of a code is equal to a number between $H(P)$ and $H(P)+1$. If one can code a sequence of messages, then the average length of a code per message can be made arbitrarily close to $H(P)$. (Note, however, that the cost and the delay of coding or decoding is not considered in this essay.)

Messages are always transmitted through a channel using some coding. If the channel uses coding from a finite set A (e.g., binary coding using bits 0 and 1; in this case $L=2$), $H(P)$ measures the average length of letters used to transmit a message arising from S. Note that the entropy is invariant in the number of letters L up to multiplication by a positive constant.

The *capacity* of a channel is defined by the number of letters that it can transmit per unit of time. Therefore, if the capacity is denoted by C, then the time needed to transmit information in the amount $H(P)$ is approximately equal to $H(P)/C$. Since the actual means of transmitting infortion is determined by the choice of a channel, we may conclude that the entropy is a measure of communication cost independent of its means.

Furthermore, it is known that what is stated above holds for wider classes of channels: channels using a finite set of letters but with erroneous transmission (noisy channels), channels using "continuous means" like electric or radio waves, and so on. For example, a noisy channel transmits, say, bits with possible errors: 0 as 1 or 1 as 0. If the probability law governing errors in transmission is known, then it is possible to define the capacity from that probability law *only,* so that the relation among the capacity, the amount of information, and the transmission time is exactly the same as in noiseless channels. Hence, we may state that the entropy is a measure of communication costs for a very wide class of channels.

Definition A6. Let $f: R \to R_+$ be a probability density function defined on the reals R, where R_+ denotes the nonnegative reals. The *entropy* $H(f)$ of f is

$$H(f) = -\int_R f(x) \log f(x) \, dx.$$

Proposition A7. Let $f: R \to R_+$ be a probability density function and let a positive number $\Delta > 0$ be given. Let

$$p_i = \int_{i\Delta}^{(i+1)\Delta} f(x)\,dx, \quad i = \ldots, -1, 0, 1, 2, \ldots,$$

$$P = (\ldots, p_{-1}, p_0, p_1, p_2, \ldots).$$

Then

$$H(P) + \log \Delta \to H(f), \quad \text{as } \Delta \to 0.$$

[That is, $H(P)$ may be approximated by $H(f) - \log \Delta$ if Δ is small. Note that $H(f)$ is independent of Δ; P is called a *quantization of f with the interval length* Δ.]

Proof: Let x_i satisfy $i\Delta \le x_i \le (i+1)\Delta$ and $p_i = f(x_i) \cdot \Delta$. (We know from the mean value theorem that such x_i always exists.) We have

$$H(P) = -\sum f(x_i) \cdot \Delta \cdot \log[f(x_i) \cdot \Delta]$$

$$= -\sum [\log f(x_i) + \log \Delta] \cdot \int_{i\Delta}^{(i+1)\Delta} f(x)\,dx$$

$$= -\int_{-\infty}^{\infty} \log[f(v(x))] f(x)\,dx - \log \Delta,$$

where $v(x) = x_i$ if and only if $i\Delta \le x < (i+1)\Delta$. Since $v(x) \to x$ as $\Delta \to 0$, we have $H(P) \to H(f) - \log \Delta$ as $\Delta \to 0$. ∎

B   *The one-sided stable distribution and the first-passage time distribution of Brownian motions*

Given a positive number $t > 0$, let $f: R \to R_+$ be defined by

$$f(x, t) = \begin{cases} (2\pi)^{-1/2} t x^{-3/2} \exp(-t^2/2x), & \text{if } x > 0, \\ 0, & \text{if } x \le 0. \end{cases}$$

The function $f(\cdot, t)$ is the density of the *one-sided stable probability distribution* with parameter t.

Proposition B1 (Feller 1971, pp. 52, 173–5).

(i) $\int_0^y f(x, t) f(y - x, s)\,dx = f(y, t + s),$

where $t > 0$, $s > 0$, and $y > 0$. That is, if X_1 and X_2 are independent random variables with density functions $f(\cdot, t)$ and $f(\cdot, s)$, respectively, then $Y = X_1 + X_2$ has the density function $f(\cdot, t + s)$.

(ii) Let X_i $(i=1,...,I)$ be independent random variables with the common density function $f(\cdot,t)$, where $t>0$. Let $I>0$ be a positive integer. Then the random variable $Y=\sum_{i=1}^{I} X_i$ has the density function $f(\cdot,It)$.

(iii) Let X be a random variable with the density function $f(\cdot,t)$, where $t>0$. Let $I>0$ be a positive number. Then the random variable $Y=IX$ has the density function $f(\cdot,I^{1/2}t)$.

Proposition B2

$$H(f(\cdot,t))=2\log t+K,$$

where

$$K=-\log 2+\frac{1}{2[\log \pi+3\Gamma'(\tfrac{1}{2})\pi^{-1/2}+1]}=3.3245,$$

and $\Gamma'(\tfrac{1}{2})$ is the derivative of the gamma function $\Gamma(\cdot)$ at $\tfrac{1}{2}$.

Proof: Let $f(x,t)=ax^{-3/2}e^{-b/x}$, where $a=t/\sqrt{2\pi}$ and $b=\tfrac{1}{2}t^2$. We have

$$H(f)=-\int_0^\infty f(x,t)\log f(x,t)\,dx$$

$$=-\log a+a\int_0^\infty (\{\tfrac{3}{2}\log x+bx^{-1}\}x^{-3/2}e^{-b/x})\,dx$$

$$=-\log a+\frac{3a}{2\sqrt{b}}\int_0^\infty (\log b\cdot y^{-1/2}\cdot e^{-y}-\log y\cdot y^{-1/2}\cdot e^{-y})\,dy$$

$$+ab\int_0^\infty b^{-3/2}y^{1/2}e^{-y}\,dy \quad \text{(put } y=b/x)$$

$$=-\log a+\frac{3a}{2\sqrt{b}}[\log b\cdot\Gamma(\tfrac{1}{2})-\Gamma'(\tfrac{1}{2})]+abb^{-3/2}\Gamma(\tfrac{3}{2})$$

$$=-\log t+\log \sqrt{2\pi}+\frac{3}{2\sqrt{\pi}}\left[(2\log t-\log 2)\sqrt{\pi}-\Gamma'\left(\frac{1}{2}\right)\right]+\frac{1}{2}$$

$$=2\log t+K,$$

where $\Gamma(\cdot)$ is the gamma function, and

$$K=\frac{1}{2}\left(1-2\log 2+\log \pi-\frac{3}{\sqrt{\pi}}\Gamma'\frac{1}{2}\right)=3.32448,$$

using $\Gamma'(\tfrac{1}{2})=3.480226$, which is computed numerically. ∎

Let $T = X = R_+ = (0, +\infty)$ be the set of positive reals. Let G be the set of left continuous nondecreasing functions $g: T \to X$ from T into X such that $g(0) = 0$. Let $F(x, t)$ be the (cumulative) distribution function of the one-sided stable distribution with the density function $f(x, t)$.

Proposition B3 (Karlin 1966, pp. 276–80). There exists a probability distribution over G satisfying the following properties:

(i)   For any $t > 0$, $\text{Prob}\{g(t) \le y\} = F(y, t)$, $y > 0$.
(ii) For any $t > s > 0$, the random variable $g(t) - g(s)$ is independent of $g(r)$ $(0 < r \le s)$. Furthermore,

$$\text{Prob}\{g(t) - g(s) \le y \mid g(s)\} = F(y, t - s).$$

Remark: The distribution over G introduced in the preceding proposition is called the *first-passage time distribution* (the *FPT distribution*) of Brownian motions (or the inverse-Gaussian process), since the random variable $g(t)$ is the time that the standard Brownian motion passes the given point $t > 0$ for the first time. It is a stochastic process whose sample function is monotone and has finite-dimensional density functions in a closed form. In this chapter, we have exploited the fact that the entropy function of this distribution has a simple form, as shown in Proposition B3, as well as properties similar to those of Brownian motions, as shown in Proposition B1.

NOTES

1   The entropy function is also called the Shannon measure (Shannon 1948), which is a "direct" measure of information in the sense that it focuses on the actual transmission of information and uses bits to measure it. As a measure for comparing resource allocation systems, it is in contrast with the one using the "size" of a space from which information arises (like the dimension of a message space) (see Hurwicz 1977; Mount and Reiter 1974).
2   An obvious alternative way for the agent to transmit the supply function to the center in the approximation mode is to send $g(r\Delta_l)$, $r = 1, 2, \ldots, 2^m$, i.e., to send the values of the quantity supplied at the integer prices rather than their increments. With this assumption, the maximum allocation error would be expressed in a simpler term, but the communication cost would be obtained in a more complicated formula, than with the assumption adopted in the text.
3   $C_1 = I \times 2^m \{2 \log \Delta_l + K - \log \Delta_x\}$
      $= I \times 2^m \{2 \log(2^{-m}M) + K - \log(2^{-n}N)\}$
      $= I \times 2^m \{(-2m + n) \log 2 + 2 \log M - \log N + K\}.$

4 Note that this assumption is consistent with the condition (stated on p. 198) for the relative allocation error to be small.

5 Since each agent transmits a quantity interval exactly m times, the maximum allocation error for this case is equal to $m\Delta_x I$. We have assumed that the center revises output prices according to the rule called *bisectioning* or *dichotomization*. This rule does not minimize the expected number of adjustment steps needed to reach equilibrium unless the equilibrium price is distributed uniformly. Our rule has been chosen here for the sake of simplicity.

6 $$C_2 = I \sum \{2\log(2^{-j}M) + K - \log(2^{-n}N)\}$$
$$= I\{2(\log 2) \sum (-j) + m(2\log M - \log N + n\log 2) + K\}$$
$$= I\{\tfrac{1}{2}[-2(\log 2)m(m+1)] + m(2\log M - \log N + n\log 2) + K\}$$
$$= Im\{(-m+n-1)\log 2 + (2\log M - \log N) + K\}$$

7 In the text, the market mechanism is formulated in such a way that at each step of adjustments the agent sends a message designating the quantity supplied at a price selected according to the bisectioning rule, whereas in the centralized system no bisectioning rule is used; prices are scanned *linearly* from left to right. If in the centralized system the agent sends messages by selecting prices according to the bisectioning rule, then the cost of communication will be equal to

$$C_1' = \sum_{j=1}^{m} \{H(f(\cdot, 2^{-j}M) - \log \Delta_x\} \cdot 2^j$$
$$= 2^{m+1}(2\log 2 + K) - 2\{2(m+1)\log 2 + K\},$$

which is of the same order as C_1 in the text.

8 We point out that this essay may be regarded as a formulation of what Simon (1978) called bounded rationality in resource allocation. In particular, decision making in the approximation mode introduced in this contribution is a way to express the fact that in reality optimization cannot be carried out with perfect accuracy because of the presence of adjustment costs. Further, our work to compare two economic systems with respect to the cost of communication may be considered as a step toward formulating Simon's procedural rationality.

REFERENCES

Arrow, K. J. (1974a), "Limited knowledge and economic analysis," *American Economic Review,* 64(1): 1–10.

Arrow, K. J. (1974b), *The limits of organization,* New York: W. W. Norton.

Arrow, K. J. and L. Hurwicz (1977), *Studies in resource allocation processes,* Cambridge: Cambridge University Press.

Feller, W. (1971), *An introduction to probability theory and its applications,* Vol. 2, 2nd ed., New York: Wiley.

Hayek, F. A. von (1945), "The use of knowledge in society," *American Economic Review,* 35(4): 519–30.

Hess, J. D. (1983), *The economics of organization,* Amsterdam: North-Holland.

Huffman, D. A. (1952), "A method for the construction of minimum redundancy codes," *Proc. IRE,* 40(10): 1098–1101.

Hurwicz, L. (1960), "Optimality and informational efficiency in resource allocation processes," In Arrow, Karlin, and Suppes (Eds.), *Mathematical methods in social sciences,* Stanford: Stanford University Press, pp. 27–46.

Hurwicz, L. (1971), "Centralization and decentralization in economic processes," in A. Eckstein (Ed.), *Comparison of economic systems: Theoretical and methodological approaches,* Berkeley: University of California Press.

Hurwicz, L. (1973), "The design of resource allocation mechanisms," *American Economic Review: Papers and Proceedings,* 58(2): 1–30. Reprinted in Arrow and Hurwicz (1977), pp. 3–37.

Hurwicz, L. (1977), "On the dimensional requirements of Pareto-satisfactory processes," in K. J. Arrow and L. Hurwicz, *Studies in resource allocation processes,* Cambridge: Cambridge University Press, pp. 413–24.

Johnson, N. L. and S. Kotz (1970), *Continuous univariate distributions – 1: Distributions in statistics,* New York: Wiley.

Karlin, S. (1966), *A first course in stochastic processes,* New York: Academic Press.

Lange, O. and F. M. Taylor (1938), *On the economic theory of socialism,* University of Minnesota Press. Reprinted by McGraw-Hill, 1964.

Marschak, J. (1968), "Economics of inquiring, communicating, deciding," *American Economic Review: Papers and Proceedings,* 58(2): 1–18.

Marschak, J. and R. Radner (1972), *Economic theory of teams,* New Haven: Yale University Press.

Marschak, T. (1959), "Centralization and decentralization in economic organizations," *Econometrica,* 27, 399–430.

Mount, K. R. and S. Reiter, "The informational size of message spaces," *Journal of Economic Theory,* 8: 161–92.

Oniki, H. (1974), "The cost of communication in economic organization," *Quarterly Journal of Economics,* 88(4): 529–50.

Reiter, S. (1977), "The (new)² welfare economics," *American Economic Review: Papers and Proceedings,* 67(2): 226–34.

Shannon, C. E. (1948), "The mathematical theory of communication," *Bell System Technical Journal,* 27: 379–423, 623–56; reprinted in C. E. Shannon and W. Weaver, *The mathematical theory of communication,* University of Illinois Press, 1949.

Simon, H. A. (1978), "Rationality as process and as product of thought," *American Economic Review,* 68(2): 1–16.

CHAPTER 8

Assembling efficient organizations?

W. M. Gorman

Introduction

This chapter is a variation on a theme[1] by Arrow (1974), that the limits
of organization are set by the need to economize on information flows,
thought, committee, meetings, and infighting. It is scored for the instru-
ments I can play: duality, profit functions, and, above all, aggregates.

Why *aggregates?* Macroeconomics was invented by Keynes for the
management of natural economies. For that, most economists agree, one
would like to deal in terms of them. Is that a reasonable possibility? Aggregation theorists say no! The condition for them to work perfectly is
that everyone should behave similarly at the margin: Were there to be a
single aggregate for equipment, for instance, a steel firm would change
its production in the same way when given a new blast furnace as a type-
writing agency given enough word processors.[2] That seems altogether too
unrealistic for them to work reasonably well in practice.[3]

God did not make the world, then, for the benefit of macroeconomists.

It is not God but businessmen who make our large firms, commonly by
taking others over, breaking them up, and selling off the pieces they do
not want. Presumably they do so for their own benefit and, in particular, with an eye to ease of control. If countries would be easier to manage
through broad aggregates, were this not misleading, would not large firms
be, too, and would not businessmen bear this in mind in deciding what to
take over and what to sell off?

It would only be one goal, of course, to be traded off against others,
and only important if realistic. Hence the "?" in the title.

The general ideas developed here were discussed in a number of seminars, workshops, and
conferences in the last decade, including Kenneth Arrow's on organization theory. I am
grateful to him, Angus Deaton, James Mirrlees, and John Muellbauer for their comments.

Are appropriate components likely to exist?

The condition that all the firms in a country should behave similarly at the margin requires them to be too alike. Its implications for individual firms are more acceptable. They run in terms of *overheads, variable costs* that are constant per unit over a range of output, *activities* running at levels determined by their relative profitabilities and the equipment available, and, given appropriate convexity, *profit centers*. These, moreover, are consequences of the theory, not assumptions, and the technologies in question are the only ones for which they work perfectly.[4] They are the terms that accountants, statisticians, industrial consultants, and businessmen use, presumably because they fit their experience. The chances are, then, that individual plants commonly are more or less of the appropriate type; the predatory businessman's role is to search out those that are sufficiently similar to each other or to those he already has.[5]

In what sense should the plants be "similar"?

The activities correspond to the aggregates. The implications of similarity is that all firms use the same activities.[6] In the case of capital, the scale at which the corresponding activity runs depends only on the capital equipment it has[7] – similarly for land. In the case of consumer durables, for instance, its *only* outputs are consumer durables, although actual activities use labor and other current inputs – that is, as negative outputs. The latter, at least, is unrealistic. However, industrialists need not think in this way. If they have assembled a number of factories, each using the same activities, into a large firm, it will be quite natural for them to think in terms of the levels at which those activities run, as this theory will predict. In that case, as we will see, each activity may produce or use all the current goods and services, whereas the scale at which it operates depends on its relative profitability and the fixed inputs available. The different plants may vary markedly in their overheads and in the efficiency with which they use their machines to produce "capacity," but given the capacity available to an activity, it operates in the same way in different plants.

Two peculiarities remain.

First, there is the asymmetry between fixed and current inputs. The former affect only the scale at which the various activities operate, not the manner. This reflects in part the history of aggregation theory, initially focused on the differences between capital and other factors. However, the arguments use fixed inputs as shift parameters, to isolate particular firms, and to compare their behavior at the margin. This can be avoided,[8] but at the cost of returning to aggregates specific to particular classes of goods. Its disadvantage here is that the managers of individual factories presumably know the state of their equipment better than those at the center; its advantage is that the latter should presumably decide where investment should go.

Second, economists commonly believe in decentralization via prices, not target quantities. In fact, this is what happens here. The important macrovariables turn out to be the profitabilities of the different activities, price aggregates dual to the scale variables whose value central management has been assumed to set. In fact, it turns out to be more sensible for them to estimate these profitabilities, pass them on to the factory managers, and leave it to each of them to choose the levels at which the various activities should operate in his own factory.

That cancels out the first peculiarity. Note that this, too, is a conclusion, not an assumption.

Two final admissions need to be made. First, ease of control is only one goal, to be traded off against others. This really is a case for bounded rationality, not optimization. Nevertheless, conditions for optimization are what economists know about and often give useful clues for the wider problem. Here, too, one of the goals is monopoly. Now, efficient monopolies presumably do better than inefficient ones and are more likely to last. For efficiency one needs common shadow prices.[9] These replace the perfectly competitive prices of classical aggregation theory, arguably with more justification.[10]

Second, my modeling is distinctly lax. I fix the number of control variables and ask what the operating units should be like for these controls *not to reduce* their efficiency, that is, *not to cause costs to be set against the gains in the collection, dissemination, and processing of information assumed inherent in hierarchical control,* not to speak of possibly monopoly profits. I do not model the central office at all, although the analysis would hold were its costs to depend only on the values of the control variables.[11]

In particular, therefore, I seek perfect aggregates, or control variables, although I am really interested in those that perform reasonably well. The hope, as usual, is that the condition for this is that those for perfect aggregates hold approximately. Since my ultimate aim is approximate, however, I will be content with local results[12] and will feel free to use calculus and rely on the implicit function theorem. (I have not used it since my college days, so that the argument is distinctly clumsy.)

1   Heuristics

Aggregation theorists have traditionally dealt with the short run,[13] in which the *endowments,*

$$u = (u_f)_{f \in F},$$ (1.1)

of fixed inputs are taken as given, where u_f is the *fixed input,* or *endowment, vector* for the firm f; the *net production vector,*

$$x = \sum_{f \in F} x_f,$$ (1.2)

of current goods is chosen from the *short-run production possibility set,* or *technology,*

$$R(u) = \sum_{f \in F} R^f(u_f),$$ (1.3)

whose simple additive structure, reflecting the absence of external economies and diseconomies, is the source of all the results to date and, in particular, explains their close family resemblance. This additive structure is preserved in the *gross profit function*

$$g(p, u) = \sup\{p \cdot x \mid x \in R(u)\} = \sum_f g^f(p, u_f),$$ (1.4)

in an obvious notation, where p is a vector of *efficiency prices,* and in the *production plan*

$$x = g'(p, u) = \sum_f g'^f(p, u_f),$$ (1.5)

where the prime denotes the price gradient[14] of the convex function in question. Since we are dealing with the short run, it is reasonable to assume that the technologies are closed strictly convex bodies, which implies that the gradients in question exist.

Traditional aggregates, whether for capital, land, semiskilled labor, or consumer durables and whether scalars or vectors, can all be presented as quantities of intermediate goods; that is,

$$u \rightarrow v \rightarrow x,$$ (1.6)

so that v looks both ways, if you like, and particular structural assumptions are needed to identify particular components with one side rather than the other, assumptions that reflect the ideas of macroeconomists and are not appropriate here.

Suppose now that $h(p, v)$ is the gross profit function of the *downstream technology* $v \to x$. Then

$$h(p, v) = g(p, u) = \sum_f g^f(p, u_f), \tag{1.7}$$

and hence

$$h'(p, v) = g'(p, u) = \sum_f g'^f(p, u_f), \tag{1.8}$$

either of which may be used to discuss particular problems in aggregation. Equation (1.8) was used to discuss the general problem in the version of this paper read at Kenneth Arrow's workshop in 1980. However, there is no reason to require that control variables be interpreted as intermediate goods. I will therefore revert to an earlier treatment (Gorman 1978) and require only that, given the prices p, they determine the production plan x; that is,

$$x = \theta(p, v) = g'(p, u) = \sum_f g'^f(p, u_f), \tag{1.9}$$

where $\theta(p, v)$ is not necessarily the gradient vector of a potential function $h(p, v)$,[15] much less of an admissible profit function.

In general,

$$v = \phi(p, u), \tag{1.10}$$

so that the central management might have to know the detailed efficiency prices p before making its decisions. One hopes that it will only need to know a few price indices, as indeed it will. In fact, it is these price indices, marginal profitabilities associated with the individual control variables, that turn out to be the valuable controls, allowing the central management to decentralize even broad planning to the individual factories in the short run and confine itself to gathering and processing information and to long-run planning. In fact, (1.10) becomes

$$v = \sum_f v_f = \sum_f \phi^f(a(p), u_f), \text{ say,} \tag{1.11}$$

at least locally, given reasonable smoothness, where

$$a(p) = (a^m(p))_{m \in M}. \tag{1.12}$$

Here M is a minimal set of controls, none of which is specific (see p. 220) to any one factory f, and $a^m(p)$ is the marginal profiability associated with the control m in a convenient normalization. Indeed, we can go further, for there exists a potential function[16]

$$k^f(a(p), u_f), \quad \text{for each } f \in F, \tag{1.13}$$

such that

$$v_f = k'^f(a(p), u_f), \tag{1.14}$$

where the prime represents the gradient with respect to the profitabilities a.

All these functions are conical in the prices or profitabilities, as one would like. When they are convex,[17] too, they correspond to perhaps fictitious technologies. If, for instance, $k^f(\cdot, u_f)$ is convex as well as conical, it corresponds to an *upstream technology* $S^f(u_f)$ for factory f, from which the factory's general manager chooses v_f to maximize profits $a \cdot v_f$ at the shadow prices a set by the central office. In other words, it is run as a profit center. In general, however, $k^f(\cdot, u_f)$ is a potential function; the duty of the general manager is to know it and the state u_f of the factory's equipment and to calculate its gradient $k'^f(a, u_f)$ once he has been told the values of the a's.

That yields v_f. What next?

Here is another wonder. It turns out that

$$g^f(p, u_f) = k^f(a(p), u_f) - b^f(p), \quad \text{for each } f \in F, \tag{1.15}$$

so that

$$x_f = g'^f(p, u_f) = \sum_m k_m^f a'^m(p) - b'^f(p)$$

$$= \sum_m v_{fm} a'^m(p) - b'^f(p), \tag{1.16}$$

in an obvious notation, by (1.14), so that

$$g^f(p, u_f) = p \cdot x_f = \sum_m v_{fm} a^m(p) - b^f(p), \tag{1.17}$$

and

$$g(p, u) = \sum_m v_m a^m(p) - b(p), \quad \text{say,} \quad v_m = \sum_f v_{fm}. \tag{1.18}$$

See why I called the $a^m(p)$ marginal profitabilities? Note, too, that they yield net production patterns $a'^m(p)$ once the prices p are known. These net production patterns are called *activities*. They operate under constant returns, where v_{fm} is the level at which activity m operates in factory f. As we have seen, this level is decided by the general management of the factory in light of the profitabilities a passed on to them by central management. The job of the specialist manager of activity m in factory f is to know $a^m(\cdot)$ and the relevant prices p and then to calculate

$a'^m(p)$ and produce $v_{fm}a'^m(p)$. If $a^m(\cdot)$ is convex as well as conical, and if we have normalized so that $v_{fm} \geq 0$, then there will be a technology A_m associated with $a^m(\cdot)$; the job of the specialist manager will be to choose x_{fm} from $v_{fm}A_m$ so as to maximize the profits $p \cdot x_{fm}$. Hence the specialist manager also would operate a profit center.

Finally, the maintenance managers cover the overheads[18] as cheaply as possible.

The costs of central managers have not been explicitly modeled, so this is metatheory. At that level, their function is first to estimate the macro-prices $a(p)$ for the coming period and then to pass their values to factory management. In the longer run, their function is to direct investment, research, and development and decide what to take over and what to sell off. The latter has already been discussed. To direct the flow of investment, estimates of future profitabilities $a(p)$ and of the general technological structure of their component factories *at the macrolevel,* as defined by $k^f(\cdot)$, are needed. The forms $a^m(\cdot)$ and $k^f(\cdot)$ also give a natural breakdown of research and development into *process research* (to make the individual activities more profitable) and that intended to squeeze more capacity out of existing equipment (to help different factories learn from each other by comparing their performance in that regard and to develop machines directed toward the more profitable activities).[19] Against this, the division between fixed inputs, determining, with $a(p)$, the scale at which activities operate, and the current production plans *within* these activities independent of the equipment available, seems unnatural and yet goes to the heart of the matter.

As mentioned in the Introduction, very similar results were derived by Gorman (1982) in the absence of fixed inputs, using appropriate prices rather than the endowments as the driving parameters, but only so far as the aggregates correspond to distinct classes of goods,[20] which I have already rejected as inappropriate in the present context.

2   The main result

The interest here is in local results and so calculus methods and, in particular, the implicit function theorem will be used. That turns on the rank,

$$\rho = \#M, \tag{2.1}$$

of control variables $m \in M$ needed, of the Jacobian matrix,

$$G(p, u) = [g_{is}(p, u)], \tag{2.2}$$

involved, where

$$g_{is}(p, u) = \partial^2 g / \partial p_i \, \partial u_s,$$

$$= g_{is}^f(p, u_f), \quad s \in f, \tag{2.3}$$

in an obvious notation.

First, I assume that these cross-derivatives *exist and are continuous* – broadly that the corresponding short-run technologies are closed strictly convex bodies and that a small change in the endowment of fixed inputs does not lead to a large change in output[21] – and that the rank ρ of $G(p, u)$ is *constant* throughout an open product set

$$P \times U; \quad U = \prod_f U_f, \tag{2.4}$$

in (p, u) space.

Second, I require that none of the controls be *specific to individual factories f* in the *firm F*. Even if its endowment u_f is held constant, that is, all ρ controls will be needed for the others. Hence the rank of the Jacobian matrix

$$G^{-f}(p, u_{-f}) = [g_{is}^{-f}(p, u_{-f})]_{s \notin f} \tag{2.5}$$

$$= [g_{is}(p, u)]_{s \notin f} \tag{2.6}$$

is ρ throughout $P \times U$, where

$$g^{-f}(p, u_{-f}) = \sum_{g \neq f} g^g(p, u_g) = g(p, u) - g^f(p, u_f) \tag{2.7}$$

is the gross profit function for the remaining factories.

Why is this important?

The basic argument in aggregation theory runs roughly as follows: Fix prices. Having done so, measure v_m, say, by the quasi rents it generates.[22] Increase these by a million dollars by increasing[23] the endowments u_f of a particular *factory f*. Observe the change δx in total output, noting that $p \cdot \delta x = 1$.[24] It has all occurred in f; hence $\delta x_f = \delta x$. Now revert to the previous position and change the endowment u_g of another firm $g \neq f$ instead, again by just enough to increase those quasi rents by a million dollars. The change δx will be the same as before, so that $\delta x_g = \delta x = \delta x_f$. Return to the original position. Increase these quasi rents by two million dollars by giving two successive gifts of new equipment to f, each worth a million dollars in these terms. In each case f will vary its production in the same way as g would have had it been given the million in question. But nothing has happened to g in the meanwhile: Had it been given either gift, it would have raised its output by the same δx_g. Hence both δx_f's equal this δx_g and hence each other. The relevant Engle curve in f, and hence in all the firms, is therefore a straight line; these are parallel to each other at these prices; and that is true at any prices in P. These parallel lines correspond to the activities I have talked about so much.

There are difficulties in this argument. How do we arrange, for instance, that the other aggregates v_n, $n \neq m$, are held constant or, failing that, identify the changes due to the variation in v_m? In traditional theory, where there is a single aggregate for each class of fixed input or current good, this is easily done. Here we have no such simple structure to help us – hence my reliance on calculus methods and search for merely local results.[25] The problem nevertheless remains: Each control must relate to at least two factories.

Let us summarize our assumptions by saying that the *technologies are appropriately convex and smooth* and that *just ρ general*[26] *controls are needed* throughout $P \times U$.

That rank condition can be weakened. If you look over the argument, you will see that I moved one firm at a time, holding the others at the baseline. I threatened to move them, too, but never actually did; if I had, it would have been by one unit only. In a calculus framework, that would be an infinitesimal jump. This suggests the following weaker condition:

> There is a $\bar{u} \in U$ such that $G(p, u_f, \bar{u}_{-f})$ and $G^{-f}(p, \bar{u}_{-f})$ have the same rank $\rho = \#M$, each $p \in P$, $u_f \in U_f$, $f \in F$.

In fact, this too can be considerably weakened, as will be seen in Corollary 3, but I will nevertheless assume it at the outset, together with the existence and continuity of each $g_{is}^f(\cdot)$ in the same region, also oversufficient. Summarize this by saying that the technology is sufficiently convex and smooth and requires just ρ general controls.

I am now in a position to state the main result.

Proposition. If these conditions hold, there exist $\rho = \#M$ functions $a^m(\cdot)$, $2\#F$ functions $k^f(\cdot, u_f)$, $b^f(\cdot)$ about any point $\bar{p} \in P$, and for all $u \in U$, such that

$$g^f(p, u_f) = k^f(a(p), u_f) - b^f(p), \quad \text{for each } f \in F, \tag{2.8}$$

where

$$a(p) = (a^m(p))_{m \in M}, \tag{2.9}$$

Proof: Choose a price vector $\bar{p} \in P$ and a particular firm $h \in F$. Then $G(p, \bar{u})$ has a column basis

$$(g'_m(p, \bar{u}))_{m \in M}, \text{ say}, \tag{2.10}$$

chosen from $G^{-h}(p, \bar{u}_{-h})$ in a neighborhood $N(\bar{p})$ of $\bar{p}$, where the prime still denotes the price gradient. Set

$$a^m(p) = g_m(p, \bar{u}), \quad \text{for each } m \in M; \qquad a(p) = (a^m(p))_{m \in M}, \qquad (2.11)$$

to get

$$g_s'^f(p, u_f) = \sum_m \lambda^{sm} a'^m(p), \quad \text{say}, \quad s \in f \in F, \quad p \in N(\bar{p}). \qquad (2.12)$$

If the level sets

$$P(\alpha) = \{p \in P \mid a(p) = \alpha\} \qquad (2.13)$$

were arc connected on $N(\bar{p})$, we could integrate (2.12) to get

$$g_s^f(p, u_f) = \gamma^s(a(p)), \quad \text{say, for each } s \in f \in F, \qquad (2.14)$$

and would be well on the way to proving the theorem. Unfortunately they need not be on $N(\bar{p})$. However, I will construct a neighborhood $N^*(\bar{p}) \subseteq N(\bar{p})$ of $\bar{p}$ on which they are arc connected, in the Appendix, so that (2.14) holds on it.

Now choose any factory $f \in F$. $G(p, u_f, \bar{u}_{-f})$ and $G^{-f}(p, \bar{u}_{-f})$ have the same rank ρ, each $p \in P$, $u_f \in U_f$. Hence[27]

$$g_s'^f(p, u_f) = \sum_{t \in f} \mu^{st} g_t'^{-f}(p, \bar{u}_{-f})$$

$$= \sum_m \nu^{sm} a'^m(p), \quad \text{for each } s \in f, \quad u_f \in U_f, \quad p \in N^*(\bar{p}), \qquad (2.15)$$

by (2.12). Integrating this in the same manner, we get

$$g_s^f(p, u_f) = k_s^f(a(p), u_f), \quad \text{say},[28] \qquad (2.16)$$

and thus

$$g^f(p, u_f) = k^f(a(p), u_f) - b^f(p), \quad \text{for each } u_f \in U_f, \quad p \in N^*(\bar{p}), \qquad (2.17)$$

because we chose any $f \in F$, for each $f \in F$. That proves (2.8) and the Proposition.

Corollary 1. We can replace the rank condition by

$$R(G(p, u_f, \bar{u}_{-f})) = R(G^{-f}(p, \bar{u}_{-f})) =: \rho^f(p), \qquad (2.18)$$

where R stands for 'rank of', for each $p \in P$, $u_f \in U_f$, $f \in F$, and get similar results.

Hints: Set $u_f = \bar{u}_f$ to get $\rho^f(p) = R(G(p, \bar{u})) = \rho(p)$, say. Since the ρ's are finite integers, $\bar{\rho} = \max\{\rho(p) \mid p \in P\}$ is attained at $\bar{p}$, say, and, since

$G(\cdot, \bar{u})$ is continuous, in a neighborhood $N^{**}(\bar{p})$ of $\bar{p}$. Proceed as above until $P(\bar{\rho}) = \{p \mid \rho(p) = \bar{\rho}\}$ has been exhausted. We now run into difficulty. The rank of a matrix is the order of the largest minor whose determinant does not vanish. Determinants may vanish at isolated points, for instance, or along curves. We have therefore to confine our attention at the outset to *regular points* at and about which $\rho(p)$ is constant and then extend our results to the others by continuity.

Corollary 2. We can choose each $a^m(\cdot), b^f(\cdot), k^f(\cdot, u_f)$ to be conical.

The functions are clearly differentiable. We may take

$$b^f(p) = -g^f(p, \bar{u}_f) \tag{2.19}$$

if we wish; it is then a loss function and hence closed concave, whereas each $a^m(\cdot)$ is then a marginal profit function.

Corollary 3. $g(p, n) = k(a(p), u) - b(p)$, where

$$k(a, u) = \sum_f k^f(a, u_f), \qquad b(p) = \sum_f b^f(p). \tag{2.20}$$

Corollary 4. We can take

$$v = k'(a(p), u) = (\partial k / \partial a^m)_{m \in M}, \tag{2.21}$$

since then

$$x = g'(p, u) = \sum_m k_m a'^m(p) - b'(p),$$

$$= \sum_m v_m a'^m(p) - b'(p). \tag{2.22}$$

Corollary 5. If so,

$$v = \sum v_f, \tag{2.23}$$

where

$$v_f = k'^f(a(p), u_f), \quad \text{for each } f \in F, \tag{2.24}$$

and

$$g^f(p, u_f) = p \cdot x_f = \sum_m a^m(p) v_{mf} - b^f(p), \tag{2.25}$$

$$g(p, u) = \sum_m a^m(p) v_m - b(p). \tag{2.26}$$

The interpretation of v_{fm} as the scale at which activity m is run in factory f is now clear, as is that of $a^m(p)$ as its gross profitability, which is the same in all the factories.

The other main claim in the Introduction was that, given appropriate convexity, these results could be interpreted in the primal in terms of profit centers. I will consider one example. Suppose $k^f(\cdot, u_f)$ is closed convex as well as conical, as in the paragraph following equation (1.14). Define

$$S^f(u_f) = \{v_f \mid a \cdot v_f \le k^f(a, u_f)\};\qquad(2.27)$$

then

$$v_f = k'^f(a, u_f)\qquad(2.28)$$

maximizes $a \cdot v_f$ on $S^f(u_f)$ by the basic theorem of duality. Of course, this is only a local result here, too, because $k^f(\cdot)$ is defined only in a neighborhood $N^*(\bar{p})$ of $\bar{p}$.[29]

3   Some comments and disclaimers

Managers probably take over other firms to increase their sense of power or security and their socially acceptable pay – buccaneers in search of immediate cash to stay in the game. Taking over and selling off are often moves that come to mind to meet immediate contingencies; and once consulted, the experts will naturally see reasons why they might work. That is not just a matter of self-interest: To a cobbler there is nothing like leather. Even under straightforward long-run profit maximization, ease of control is not the only parameter that is important. Nevertheless, ease of control is important; in that context, people often talk in terms of management by objectives and of profit centers. This essay suggests that quantitative objectives are misconceived, at least for the organization as a whole; appropriately normalized, they have shadow prices associated with them, which are better planning tools; and given appropriate convexity, they naturally lead to the location of appropriate profit centers and management structures.

Under imperfect competition, of course, one would have to deal with internal shadow prices instead of observed market prices and probably distinguish between physically identical products in different submarkets.[30] That does not seem to affect the argument, nor, I think, do tax-distorted transfer prices, though I have not looked into that in detail.

That the central office's function in short-run planning should largely be confined to the prediction of market conditions as shown in appropriate broad price indices seems reasonable.[31] That these should relate to the short-run profitabilities of a few basic processes would fall in very well with its long-run role, as in planning investment, where it would concentrate on the investment costs of increasing capacity in different locations and in planning future takeovers and sales.

Firms made up in this way would also accumulate expertise in selecting, appraising, and promoting their managers.

Martin Weitzman has shown how important it may be in practical programming that the right quantities of the right goods should be available in the right place at the right time. This cannot be done by setting a few control variables or their shadow prices, and may require quite a different mode of operation.

Appendix

Lemma. Using the assumptions of the Proposition in Section 2, there is a neighborhood $N^*(\bar{p}) \subseteq N(\bar{p})$ of $\bar{p}$ within which the level sets

$$P(\alpha) = \{p \in P \mid a(p) = \alpha\} \tag{A.1}$$

are arc connected.

Take a row basis I for[32]

$$A(p) = [a_i^m(p)] = [g_{mi}(p, \bar{u})]_{m \in M}, \tag{A.2}$$

and hence for $G(p, \bar{u})$ and each $G^{-f}(p, \bar{u}_{-f})$ in a neighborhood $N^1(\bar{p}) \subseteq N(\bar{p})$, set

$$p_i = \begin{cases} q_i & \text{when } i \in I, \\ r_i & \text{when } i \notin I, \end{cases} \tag{A.3}$$

and solve

$$a(q, r) = a(p) = \alpha \tag{A.4}$$

in a neighborhood $N^2(\bar{p}) \subseteq N^1(\bar{p})$ of $\bar{p}$ to get[33]

$$q = b(\alpha, r). \tag{A.5}$$

Since $b(\cdot)$ is bicontinuous,[33] the set

$$C = \{(\alpha, r) \mid \alpha = a(q, r), \text{ for some } (q, r) \in N^2(\bar{p})\} \tag{A.6}$$

is open. It contains $(\bar{\alpha}, \bar{r})$, where

$$\bar{\alpha} = a(\bar{q}, \bar{r}) = a(\bar{p}). \tag{A.7}$$

Take a rectangular neighborhood $D \subseteq C$ of $(\bar{\alpha}, \bar{r})$ and its image

$$N^*(\bar{p}) = \{(q,r) \mid q = b(\alpha,r) \text{ for some } (\alpha,r) \in D\}$$
$$\subseteq N^2(\bar{p}) \subseteq N^1(\bar{p}). \tag{A.8}$$

Since $b(\cdot)$ is bicontinuous, $N^*(\bar{p})$ is open. Since $N^*(\bar{p})$ contains $\bar{p}$, it is a neighborhood of $\bar{p}$.

I am now ready to show that the level sets $P(\alpha)$ are indeed arc connected in $N^*(\bar{p})$.

To do so, take any $(q^*,r^*) \in N^*(\bar{p})$. Let

$$\alpha^* = a(q^*,r^*). \tag{A.9}$$

Take any $(q^{**},r^{**}) \in N^*(\bar{p})$ such that $a(q^{**},r^{**}) = \alpha^*$, and construct a path

$$r(t) = (1-t)r^* + tr^{**}; \quad q(t) = b(\alpha^*,r(t)), \quad 0 \le t \le 1, \quad (A.10)$$

connecting (q^*,r^*) and (q^{**},r^{**}).

Since $(\alpha^*,r(t)) \in D$, its image $(q(t),r(t)) \in N^*(\bar{p})$. Since $b(\cdot)$ is differentiable, it traces a smooth arc. Since α^* was freely chosen,[34] it is indeed true that the $P(\alpha)$ are arc connected in $N^*(\bar{p})$.

NOTES

1 Of course, there are other themes. The difficulty of getting people to agree on a common aim is also important and can also be regarded as a problem in aggregation. The profit centers that emerge from the analysis may be interpreted in this light.

2 Enough to increase its profits, at the given prices, by the same amount as the blast furnace would the steel firm's. Remember, both are gifts.

3 That is, assuming all the firms do not march step in step, investing and disinvesting together, for instance. Tom Stoker (1982, 1984), in particular, explored cases in which this is not so, as had Henri Theil (1954). One does not need many degrees of freedom to get the results I have quoted, and it is rather easy to see what sort of changes lead to the use of aggregates being badly misleading.

4 Remember, however, that equipment and the like affect only the capacities at which the individual activities are run, not how they are.

5 As it turns out, by using the same activities.

6 At given prices, each activity produces current goods, net, in the same proportions wherever it is used – in the same amounts, indeed, per unit of capacity.

7 Indeed, it is the most convenient measure of that firm f's *capital* or of its excess over that corresponding to a base endowment $\bar{u}_f$.

8 See Gorman (1982) and the last paragraph of Section 1.

9 Of course, the goods have to be carefully defined; if the market for some goods is divided and some factories are only allowed to sell in one part, some in another, we would have to distinguish between those goods according to their market.

10 However, monopolies are pretty robust even when inefficient and may even be defended against takeover bids by monopoly commissions and the like. One should remember Sir John Hick's dictum that the prime gain from monopoly is an easy life for the managers – perhaps not the sort of easy life I have been sketching.

11 Of the form $\psi(p, v)$, where p is the price vector for current goods, and that of the target set by the center. If so, the net demand for i by the central office would be $\psi_i(p, v) = \partial\psi/\partial p_i$ under weak conditions, given v, and this can be subtracted from the right-hand side of equation (1.9).

12 Not approximate. Aggregates that work perfectly in a neighborhood of the point in question. The neighborhood may cover the whole space considered.

13 Charles Blackorby, in particular, has recently published interesting papers on aggregation in intertemporal models (e.g., 1982), and both he (1984) and Frank Fisher (1982) on long-run aggregation. I refer to some unpublished work of my own on the latter below; however, this work does not really affect the point at issue.

14 That is, the vector of price derivatives $g' = (g_i) = \partial g/\partial p_i$. Under the convexity condition, they exist throughout the interior of the function's domain, which is enough for our purposes.

15 By *a potential function* $h(\cdot)$ I merely mean one for which $x = h'$, with no restriction as to shape.

16 Strictly $k^f(\cdot, u_f)$, each $u_f \in U_f$, $f \in F$. See p. 218.

17 Profit functions are closed convex conical and to each such function there corresponds a convex technology for which it is indeed the profit function.

18 $b^f(p) = -g^f(p, \bar{u}_f)$ in a convenient normalization, where $\bar{u}_f$ is a base endowment vector and, therefore, closed concave conical and hence a true cost function.

19 Metaphoric only. Of course, one can double the profits per unit in an activity by rescaling it.

20 I have not investigated the matter fully. It may be possible to get more general results.

21 Because $g_{is} = \partial x_i/\partial u_s$ is assumed to exist. Continuity goes a little further.

22 The quasi rents are the profits over and above those generated by a base equipment vector $\bar{u}$. Read on for some problems.

23 The precise terms I have used are most appropriate for capital aggregation though not really misleading for other aggregates. If we are seeking to increase the amount of skilled labor used at a certain p, it may be appropriate either to increase or decrease the endowment of fixed inputs – "vary" might be a better word.

24 The unit being a million dollars' worth at these prices.

25 The localities – i.e., neighborhoods – may, of course, be large; the results are exact, not approximations.

26 "General" means not specific to any individual factory.

27 The μ and ν below are functions, of course; hence the superscripts. It does not matter what they are functions of.

28 It is trivial that this is a derivative. Call it k^{fs}. Then $k_t^{fs} = g_{st}^f = k_s^{ft}$.

29 I have not extended the technologies beyond the region in question.

30 Physically identical activities in different locations might accordingly be economically different. Their physical identity might, nevertheless, make it easier to predict their distinct marginal profitabilities as well as, of course, simplifying the choice and training of factory and process managers.
31 In the short run, most markets are pretty imperfect. I have not looked into this in any depth; doing so would turn on the extent to which a firm would wish to exploit such imperfections, given the effect on its long-run position.
32 That corresponding to the original nonzero $\rho \times \rho$ determinant.
33 By the implicit function theorem in each case.
34 Here $\alpha^* = a(q^*, r^*)$, (q^*, r^*) freely chosen from $N^*(\bar{p})$, implies (α^*, r^*) freely chosen from D.

REFERENCES

Arrow, K. J. (1974), *The limits of organization,* Fels lectures, New York: Norton.
Blackorby, C. and W. Schworm (1982), "Aggregate investment and consistent intertemporal technologies," *Review of Economic Studies,* 49(4): 545–614.
Blackorby, C. and W. Schworm (1984), "Consistent aggregation in competitive economies," *CORE Discussion Paper* 8446, Louvain.
Fisher, F. M. (1982), "Aggregate production functions revisited: the mobility of capital and the rigidity of thought," *Review of Economic Studies,* 49(4): 615–26.
Gorman, W. M. (1978), "More measures for fixed factors," paper read to Quantitative Economic Workshop at London School of Economics.
Gorman, W. M. (1982), "Aggregation in the short and long run" and "Long run aggregation under constant returns," papers read to James Mirrlees's workshop in Oxford.
Stoker, T. M. (1982), "The use of cross section data to characterize macro functions, *Journal of the American Statistical Association,* 77: 369–80.
Stoker, T. M. (1984), "Completeness, distribution restrictions and the form of aggregate functions," *Econometrica,* 52(4): 887–907.
Theil, H. (1954), *Linear aggregation of economic relations,* Amsterdam: North-Holland.

CHAPTER 9

Optimal Bayesian mechanisms

Eric S. Maskin

Suppose that a population of agents $i = 1, \ldots, n$ have von Neumann–Morgenstern utility functions

$$v_i(d, \theta_i) + t_i,$$

where d is a public decision and t_i is a transfer of a private good to agent i. The parameter θ_i is private information for agent i, and the joint distribution of $(\theta_1, \ldots, \theta_n)$ is given by the cumulative distribution function (c.d.f.) $F(\theta_1, \ldots, \theta_n)$, which is common knowledge. Suppose that $d^*(\theta_1, \ldots, \theta_n)$ solves the problem

$$\max_{d \in D} \sum_{i=1}^{n} v_i(d, \theta_i), \tag{0}$$

where D is the space of possible public decisions [assume a solution to (0) exists]. We shall refer to $d^*(\theta_1, \ldots, \theta_n)$ as the optimal public decision given $\theta_1, \ldots, \theta_n$.

A *mechanism* is a public decision function $d(\mathring{\theta}_1, \ldots, \mathring{\theta}_n)$ and a set of transfers $\{t_i(\mathring{\theta}_1, \ldots, \mathring{\theta}_n)\}$. The interpretation of such a mechanism is that agents announce the values of their parameters (possibly untruthfully) and, on the basis of the announcements $(\mathring{\theta}_1, \ldots, \mathring{\theta}_n)$, the public decision $d(\mathring{\theta}_1, \ldots, \mathring{\theta}_n)$ is taken, and agent i receives transfer $t_i(\mathring{\theta}_1, \ldots, \mathring{\theta}_n)$. In an *optimal Bayesian mechanism*, for all $(\theta_1, \ldots, \theta_n)$,

$$d(\theta_1, \ldots, \theta_n) = d^*(\theta_1, \ldots, \theta_n), \tag{1}$$

$$\mathring{\theta}_i = \theta_i \quad \text{maximizes } E_{\theta_{-i} \mid \theta_i}[v_i(d^*(\mathring{\theta}_i, \theta_{-i}), \theta_i) + t_i(\mathring{\theta}_i, \theta_{-i})], \tag{2}$$

and

$$\sum t_i(\theta_1, \ldots, \theta_n) = 0, \tag{3}$$

This research was supported by the National Science and Sloan Foundations. I thank Louis Gevers and Andreu Mas-Colell for most helpful suggestions.

229

where $E_{\theta_{-i}|\theta_i}$ denotes the expectation operator with respect to θ_{-i} conditional on θ_i. That is, an optimal Bayesian mechanism (a) induces each agent to tell the truth about his or her parameter, assuming that other agents are truthful; (b) chooses the optimal public decision; and (c) balances the budget.

Arrow (1979) and d'Aspremont and Gerard-Varet (1979) (ADG) showed that optimal Bayesian mechanisms exist when the θ_i's are independently distributed. The transfers in these mechanisms take the form

$$t_i(\overset{\circ}{\theta}_1, ..., \overset{\circ}{\theta}_n) = t_{ii}(\overset{\circ}{\theta}_i) - \frac{1}{n-1} \sum_{j \neq i} t_{jj}(\overset{\circ}{\theta}_j), \tag{4}$$

where

$$t_{ii}(\overset{\circ}{\theta}_i) = E_{\theta_{-i}} \sum_{j \neq i} v_j(d^*(\overset{\circ}{\theta}_i, \theta_{-i}), \theta_j).^2 \tag{5}$$

Laffont and Maskin (1979) and Riordan (1984) showed that the independence hypothesis in the ADG proposition can be weakened. Making stronger assumptions about the v_i's and θ_i's, they demonstrated that when, roughly speaking, the θ_i's are nonpositively correlated, optimal Bayesian mechanisms can be found where transfers take the additively separable form (4), although t_{ii} is no longer given by (5).[3]

In this chapter, we present two results. We first provide a proposition in the spirit of the Laffont–Maskin–Riordan results on additively separable transfers (Theorem 1). We then argue (Theorem 2) that if one does not impose the additively separable form and if each θ_i can assume only two values, one can find Bayesian mechanisms regardless of the nature of the correlation across θ_i's.

1   Additively separable transfers

For the purposes of this section *only,* assume that (a) the space of public decisions D is $(0, 1)$; (b) agent i's parameter θ_i is a number in $(0, 1)$, and agent i has a differentiable conditional density function $f_i(\theta_{-i} | \theta_i)$ corresponding to $F(\theta_1, ..., \theta_n)$; (c) the function $v_i(\cdot, \cdot)$ is strictly concave in its first argument, twice continuously differentiable, and satisfies

$$\frac{\partial^2 v_i}{\partial d\, \partial \theta_i} > 0. \tag{6}$$

Suppose first that we attempt to mimic the ADG solution (5). That is, suppose we take

$$t_{ii}(\overset{\circ}{\theta}_i) = E_{\theta_{-i}|\overset{\circ}{\theta}_i} \sum_{j \neq i} v_j(d^*(\overset{\circ}{\theta}_i, \theta_{-i}), \theta_j) =$$

$$= \int \sum_{j \neq i} v_j(d^*(\mathring{\theta}_i, \theta_{-i}), \theta_j) f(\theta_{-1} \mid \mathring{\theta}_i) \, d\theta_{-i} \tag{7}$$

and then define t_i by (4). Then, assuming that other agents are truthful, agent i chooses $\mathring{\theta}_i$ to maximize

$$\int v_i(d^*(\mathring{\theta}_i, \theta_i), \theta_i) f(\theta_{-i} \mid \theta_i) \, d\theta_{-i} + t_{ii}(\mathring{\theta}_i), \tag{8}$$

since $t_{jj}(\mathring{\theta}_j)$, $j \neq i$, does not depend on $\mathring{\theta}_i$. The first derivative of (8) is[4]

$$\int \left[\frac{\partial v_i}{\partial d}(d^*(\mathring{\theta}_i, \theta_{-i}), \theta_i) \frac{\partial d^*}{\partial \theta_i}(\mathring{\theta}_i, \theta_{-i}) f(\theta_{-i} \mid \theta_i) \right.$$

$$+ \sum_{j \neq i} \frac{\partial v_j}{\partial d}(d^*(\mathring{\theta}_i, \theta_{-i}), \theta_j) \frac{\partial d^*}{\partial \theta_i}(\mathring{\theta}_i, \theta_{-i}) f(\theta_{-i} \mid \mathring{\theta}_i)$$

$$+ \left. \sum_{j \neq i} v_j(d^*(\mathring{\theta}_i, \theta_{-i}), \theta_j) \frac{\partial f_i}{\partial \theta_i}(\theta_{-i} \mid \mathring{\theta}_i) \right] d\theta_{-i}. \tag{9}$$

Now, because $d^*(\theta_1, \ldots, \theta_n)$ solves (1),

$$\sum_{j=1}^{n} \frac{\partial v_j}{\partial d}(d^*(\theta_1, \ldots, \theta_n), \theta_j) = 0. \tag{10}$$

Therefore, when $\mathring{\theta}_i = \theta_i$, (9) becomes

$$\int \sum_{j \neq i} v_j(d^*(\mathring{\theta}_i, \theta_{-i}), \theta_i) \frac{\partial f_i}{\partial \theta_i}(\theta_{-i} \mid \theta_i) \, d\theta_{-i}. \tag{11}$$

But unless $\partial f_i / \partial \theta_i = 0$, there is no reason why (11) should vanish. Hence, although truth telling satisfies the first-order conditions for a maximum when the θ_i's are independent, truth telling is not optimal when the θ_i's are correlated. That is why the ADG procedure requires independence.

However, suppose instead that we *define* $t_{ii}(\mathring{\theta}_i)$ so that it satisfies the first-order conditions for a maximum at $\mathring{\theta}_i = \theta_i$. Then, for all $\mathring{\theta}_i$,

$$-\int \frac{\partial v_i}{\partial d}(d^*(\mathring{\theta}_i, \theta_{-i}), \mathring{\theta}_i) \frac{\partial d^*}{\partial \theta_i}(\mathring{\theta}_i, \theta_{-i}) f_i(\theta_{-i} \mid \mathring{\theta}_i) \, d\theta_{-i} = \frac{\partial t_{ii}}{\partial \theta_i}(\mathring{\theta}_i). \tag{12}$$

With $t_{ii}(\cdot)$ defined by (12), the first derivative of agent i's maximand becomes

$$\int \left[\frac{\partial v_i}{\partial d}(d^*(\mathring{\theta}_i, \theta_{-i}), \theta_i) f_i(\theta_{-i} \mid \theta_i) \right.$$

$$- \left. \frac{\partial v_i}{\partial d}(d^*(\mathring{\theta}_i, \theta_{-i}), \mathring{\theta}_i) f_i(\theta_{-i} \mid \mathring{\theta}_i) \right] \frac{\partial d^*}{\partial \theta_i}(\mathring{\theta}_i, \theta_{-i}) \, d\theta_{-i}. \tag{13}$$

Clearly, (13) vanishes at $\mathring{\theta}_i = \theta_i$. Also, in view of (6), $\partial d^*(\mathring{\theta}_i, \theta_i)/\partial \theta_i > 0$. Therefore, to establish that truth telling is optimal, it suffices to show that (13) is nonpositive for $\mathring{\theta}_i > \theta_i$ and nonnegative for $\mathring{\theta}_i < \theta_i$. Now these second-order conditions will not, in general, be satisfied. To ensure that they hold, we must impose stronger conditions on f_i. For any vector θ_{-i}, let $\theta_i^*(\theta_{-i})$ be a value of agent i's parameter such that

$$\frac{\partial v_i}{\partial d}(d^*(\theta_i^*(\theta_{-i}), \theta_{-i}), \theta_i^*(\theta_{-i})) = 0. \tag{14}$$

If $\theta_i^*(\theta_{-i})$ exists, it is unique. To see this, suppose that $\theta_i = \theta_i^*$ satisfies

$$\frac{\partial v_i}{\partial d}(d^*(\theta_i^*, \theta_{-i}), \theta_i^*) = 0. \tag{15}$$

Differentiating $\partial v_i(d^*(\theta_i, \theta_{-i}), \theta_i)/\partial d$ with respect to θ_i, we obtain

$$\frac{\partial^2 v_i}{\partial d^2}(d^*(\theta_i, \theta_{-i}), \theta_i)\frac{\partial d^*}{\partial \theta_i}(\theta_i, \theta_{-i}) + \frac{\partial^2 v_i}{\partial d \partial \theta_i}(d^*(\theta_i, \theta_{-i}), \theta_i). \tag{16}$$

From (10),

$$\frac{\partial d^*}{\partial \theta_i} = \frac{-\partial^2 v_i}{\partial d \partial \theta_i} \bigg/ \sum_{j=1}^n \frac{\partial^2 v_j}{\partial d^2}. \tag{17}$$

Substituting (17) into (16), we obtain

$$\frac{\sum_{j=i}(\partial^2 v_j/\partial d^2)}{\sum_{j=1}^n(\partial^2 v_j/\partial d^2)}\frac{\partial^2 v_i}{\partial d \partial \theta_i}, \tag{18}$$

which is positive. Hence,

$$\frac{\partial v_i}{\partial d}(d^*(\theta_i, \theta_{-i}), \theta_i) \quad \begin{cases} >0 & \text{if } \theta_i > \theta_i^*, \\ <0 & \text{if } \theta_i < \theta_i^*, \end{cases} \tag{19}$$

establishing the uniqueness of $\theta_i^*(\theta_{-i})$. If $\theta_i^*(\theta_{-i})$ fails to exist, set it equal to 1 if $\partial v_i(d^*(\theta_i, \theta_{-i}), \theta_i)/\partial d$ is positive for all θ_i and equal to zero otherwise.

From the definition of d^*,

$$\sum_{j=1}^n \frac{\partial v_j}{\partial d}(d^*(\theta_i, \theta_{-i}), \theta_{-i}) = 0.$$

Thus, $\theta_i^*(\theta_{-i})$ is that value of θ_i that makes the social and individual marginal products of d both zero. In that case, $\theta_i^*(\theta_{-i})$ is the socially *representative* or *average* value of θ_{-i}.

One way of formalizing the idea that θ_i and θ_{-i} are nonpositively correlated is to suppose that as θ_i moves away from the average value of θ_{-i}, the conditional density $f_i(\theta_{-i} \mid \theta_i)$ does not fall. That is,

$$\frac{\partial f_i}{\partial \theta_i}(\theta_{-i} \mid \theta_i) \quad \begin{cases} \geq 0 & \text{if } \theta_i \geq \theta_i^*(\theta_{-i}), \\ \leq 0 & \text{if } \theta_i \leq \theta_i^*(\theta_{-i}). \end{cases} \tag{20}$$

This is the condition we need to establish that truth telling is optimal.

Theorem 1. Under the assumptions we have made about v_i and θ_i in this section, an optimal Bayesian mechanism exists if, for all i, f_i satisfies (20).[5]

Proof: We need only show that the bracketed expression of (13) is nonpositive (nonnegative) for $\mathring{\theta}_i$ greater (less) than θ_i. Consider $\mathring{\theta}_i > \theta_i$.
  Suppose first that

$$\frac{\partial v_i}{\partial d}(d^*(\mathring{\theta}_i, \theta_{-i}), \theta_i) > 0. \tag{21}$$

Then, because d^* is increasing in θ_i and v_i is concave in d,

$$\frac{\partial v_i}{\partial d}(d^*(\theta_i, \theta_{-i}), \theta_i) > 0. \tag{22}$$

Furthermore, from (6),

$$\frac{\partial v_i}{\partial d}(d^*(\mathring{\theta}_i, \theta_{-i}), \mathring{\theta}_i) > \frac{\partial v_i}{\partial d}(d^*(\mathring{\theta}_i, \theta_{-i}), \theta_i) > 0. \tag{23}$$

From (19), (22), and (23), we have

$$\theta_i^*(\theta_{-i}) < \theta_i < \mathring{\theta}_i.$$

Therefore, from (20),

$$f(\theta_{-i} \mid \theta_i) \leq f(\theta_{-i} \mid \mathring{\theta}_i). \tag{24}$$

But (23) and (24) together imply that the bracketed expression in (13) is nonpositive.
  Suppose next that

$$\frac{\partial v_i}{\partial d}(d^*(\mathring{\theta}_i, \theta_{-i}), \theta_i) \leq 0. \tag{25}$$

Then, the bracketed expression is nonpositive unless

$$\frac{\partial v_i}{\partial d}(d^*(\mathring{\theta}_i, \theta_{-i}), \mathring{\theta}_i) < 0. \tag{26}$$

But (26) implies that $\theta_i \le \mathring{\theta}_i \le \theta_i^*(\theta_{-i})$, which in turn means that

$$f(\theta_{-i} \mid \theta_i) \ge f(\theta_{-i} \mid \mathring{\theta}_i). \tag{27}$$

Combining (25)–(27), we conclude once again the the bracketed expression is nonpositive. The argument for $\mathring{\theta}_i < \theta_i$ is similar.   Q.E.D.

If the inequalities in (20) are reversed, then one cannot find a transfer function $t_{ii}(\mathring{\theta}_i)$ that induces agent i to tell the truth. Hence, with positive correlation, there does not exist an optimal Bayesian mechanisms with transfer functions of the form (4).

The conclusion that negative rather than positive correlation makes incentive requirements easier to fulfill accords well with intuition, as Laffont and Maskin (1979) point out. Positive correlation aggravates the free-rider problem. If an agent believes his or her tastes are similar to those of others, the agent can relatively safely leave provision of a public good in their hands.

2   Nonseparable transfers

One limitation of using an additively separable transfer function is that it does not exploit the fact that different values of θ_i correspond to different beliefs about θ_{-i}. If $f_i(\cdot \mid \bar{\theta}_i) \ne f_i(\cdot \mid \bar{\bar{\theta}}_i)$, then an agent of type $\bar{\theta}_i$ views a transfer depending on $\mathring{\theta}_{-i}$ as a different gamble than does an agent of type $\bar{\bar{\theta}}_i$. But these different views are irrelevant to i's maximization problem if the terms of t_i in $\mathring{\theta}_i$ are separable from those in $\mathring{\theta}_{-i}$. Thus additively separable transfer functions reduce our ability to discriminate among types. It may be helpful to illustrate these ideas with an example.

Example. Suppose that there are just two agents and that θ_1 and θ_2 can each assume two values: θ^a and θ^b. Suppose also that $\Pr\{\theta_1 = \theta_2 = \theta^a\} = \Pr\{\theta_1 = \theta_2 = \theta^b\} = \frac{1}{3}$ and $\Pr\{\theta_1 = \theta^a, \theta_2 = \theta^b\} = \Pr\{\theta_1 = \theta^b, \theta_2 = \theta^a\} = \frac{1}{6}$. Assume that regardless of agents' types, the optimal public decision is the same but that, for some other reason (not modeled), it is desirable to elicit agents' preferences. If $t_1(\mathring{\theta}_1, \mathring{\theta}_2)$ takes the form $t_1(\mathring{\theta}_1, \mathring{\theta}_2) = t_{11}(\mathring{\theta}_1) + t_{12}(\mathring{\theta}_2)$, then agent 1, irrespective of parameter value, will choose $\mathring{\theta}_1$ to maximize $t_{11}(\mathring{\theta}_1)$. Hence, agent 1's preferences will not be elicited unless $t_{11}(\theta^a) = t_{11}(\theta^b)$, and even then he or she will be indifferent between lying and telling the truth. If, on the other hand, we set

$$t_1(\mathring{\theta}_1, \mathring{\theta}_2) = \begin{cases} 1 & \text{if } \mathring{\theta}_1 = \mathring{\theta}_2, \\ -1 & \text{if } \mathring{\theta}_1 \ne \mathring{\theta}_2, \end{cases}$$

then agent 1 will be truthful, since if he or she takes $\mathring{\theta}_1 = \theta_1$, the expected transfer is $\frac{1}{3}$, whereas if the agent lies, the expected transfer is $-\frac{1}{3}$.

That the use of nonseparable transfers is a powerful discriminatory device is confirmed by our main result, wherein we drop the special assumptions of Section 1 and revert to the less structured model of the introduction. We assume, however, that agent i's parameter θ_i can assume only two values: $\{\theta^1, \theta^2\}$.

Theorem 2. In the model of the introduction, with the additional hypothesis that parameters take on only the values $\{\theta^1, \theta^2\}$, an optimal Bayesian mechanism exists.

Proof: Because the proof is virtually entirely algebraic manipulation, it will be helpful to consider the simplest possible case to illustrate the ideas as clearly as possible. Accordingly, suppose that there are just two agents. After we go through the argument for this case, it should be apparent how the proof generalizes.

For any $i, j, k, h \in \{1, 2\}$, let

$$v_h^{ijk} = v_h(d^*(\theta^i, \theta^j), \theta^k),$$

and let p^{ij} be the joint probability that $\theta_1 = \theta^i$ and $\theta_2 = \theta^j$. We shall take t^{ij} to be the transfer to agent 1 if $\mathring{\theta}_1 = \theta^i$ and $\mathring{\theta}_2 = \theta^j$. Hence, for balance, the transfer to agent 2 in that event is $-t^{ij}$. Our problem is to find numbers t^{11}, t^{12}, t^{21}, and t^{22} such that

$$\sum_j p^{1j}(v_1^{1j1} + t^{1j}) \geq \sum_j p^{1j}(v_1^{2j1} + t^{2j}), \tag{28}$$

$$\sum_j p^{2j}(v_1^{2j2} + t^{2j}) \geq \sum_j p^{2j}(v_1^{1j2} + t^{1j}), \tag{29}$$

$$\sum_i p^{i1}(v_2^{i11} - t^{i1}) \geq \sum_i p^{i1}(v_2^{i21} - t^{i2}), \tag{30}$$

$$\sum_i p^{i2}(v_2^{i22} - t^{i2}) \geq \sum_i p^{i2}(v_2^{i12} - t^{i1}). \tag{31}$$

We begin by demonstrating several inequalities that follow from the fact that $d^*(\theta_1, \theta_2)$ maximizes $\sum_i v_i(d, \theta_i)$. In particular, we have, for any i, j, k,

$$v_1^{kjk} + v_2^{kjj} \geq v_1^{ijk} + v_2^{ijj}, \tag{32}$$

which can be written as

$$v_2^{kjj} - v_2^{ijj} \geq v_1^{ijk} - v_1^{kjk}. \tag{33}$$

Similarly, we have

$$v_2^{ijj} - v_2^{kjj} \ge v_1^{kji} - v_1^{iji}. \tag{34}$$

Adding (33) and (34), we obtain

$$0 \ge v_1^{ijk} - v_1^{kjk} + v_1^{kji} - v_1^{iji}. \tag{35}$$

Analogously, we have

$$0 \ge v_2^{ikj} - v_2^{ijj} + v_2^{ijk} - v_2^{ikk}. \tag{36}$$

Now, again from the definition of v_h^{ijk}, $h = 1, 2$,

$$v_1^{iji} + v_2^{ijj} \ge v_1^{jii} + v_2^{jij},$$

which can be rewritten as

$$v_1^{iji} + v_2^{ijj} \ge v_1^{iii} + (v_1^{jii} - v_1^{iii}) + v_2^{jjj} + (v_2^{jij} - v_2^{jjj}),$$

or

$$0 \ge (v_1^{iii} - v_1^{iji}) + (v_2^{jjj} - v_2^{ijj}) + (v_1^{jii} - v_1^{iii}) + (v_2^{jij} - v_2^{jjj}). \tag{37}$$

From (33), we have

$$v_2^{jjj} - v_2^{ijj} \ge v_1^{ijj} - v_1^{jjj}, \tag{38}$$

and

$$v_1^{iii} - v_1^{iji} \ge v_2^{iji} - v_2^{iii}. \tag{39}$$

Substituting (38) and (39) in (37) yields

$$0 \ge (v_1^{ijj} - v_1^{jjj}) + (v_2^{iji} - v_2^{iii}) + (v_1^{jii} - v_1^{iii}) + (v_2^{jij} - v_2^{jjj}). \tag{40}$$

Similarly, by permuting indices, we get

$$0 \ge (v_1^{iij} - v_1^{jij}) + (v_2^{iij} - v_2^{jjj}) + (v_1^{jji} - v_1^{iji}) + (v_2^{jji} - v_2^{jii}). \tag{41}$$

We are now ready to solve for the t^{ij}'s. We first rewrite (28)–(31) as

$$\begin{pmatrix} p^{11} & -p^{11} & p^{12} & -p^{12} \\ -p^{21} & p^{21} & -p^{22} & p^{22} \\ -p^{11} & -p^{21} & p^{11} & p^{21} \\ p^{12} & p^{22} & -p^{12} & -p^{22} \end{pmatrix} \begin{pmatrix} t^{11} \\ t^{21} \\ t^{12} \\ t^{22} \end{pmatrix} = \begin{pmatrix} A_1 \\ A_2 \\ A_3 \\ A_4 \end{pmatrix}, \tag{42}$$

and

$$A_1 \ge \sum p^{1j}(v_1^{2j1} - v_1^{1j1}), \tag{43}$$

$$A_2 \ge \sum p^{2j}(v_1^{1j2} - v_1^{2j2}), \tag{44}$$

$$A_3 \geq \sum p^{i1}(v_2^{i21} - v_2^{i11}), \tag{45}$$

$$A_4 \geq \sum p^{i2}(v_2^{i12} - v_2^{i22}). \tag{46}$$

If the matrix of probabilities in (42) were nonsingular, then we could simply invert to solve for the t^{ij}'s. However, the matrix's rows sum to zero, so that it is clearly singular. Accordingly, we fix t^{11} and consider the first three rows of (42):

$$\begin{bmatrix} -p^{11} & p^{12} & -p^{12} \\ p^{21} & -p^{22} & p^{22} \\ -p^{21} & p^{11} & p^{21} \end{bmatrix} \begin{bmatrix} t^{21} \\ t^{12} \\ t^{22} \end{bmatrix} = \begin{bmatrix} A_1 - p^{11}t^{11} \\ A_2 + p^{21}t^{11} \\ A_3 + p^{11}t^{11} \end{bmatrix}. \tag{47}$$

The determinant of the matrix in (47) is

$$\Delta = (p^{21} + p^{11})(p^{11}p^{22} - p^{12}p^{21}).$$

We know from Arrow and d'Aspremont and Gerard-Varet that a solution to (28)–(31) exists if θ_1 and θ_2 are independent, that is, if $p^{11}p^{22} - p^{12}p^{21} = 0$. Accordingly, assume without loss of generality that

$$p^{11}p^{22} - p^{12}p^{21} \neq 0. \tag{48}$$

Then, solving for t^{21}, t^{12}, and t^{22} in (47) using Cramer's rule, we obtain

$$t^{21} = [-A_1(p^{22}p^{21} + p^{11}p^{22}) - A_2(p^{12}p^{21} + p^{11}p^{12})]/\Delta,$$

$$t^{12} = [-A_1((p^{21})^2 + p^{21}p^{22}) - A_2(p^{11}p^{21} + p^{21}p^{12})$$
$$+ A_3(p^{11}p^{22} - p^{12}p^{21})]/\Delta,$$

$$t^{22} = [A_1(p^{21}p^{11} - p^{21}p^{22}) + A_2((p^{11})^2 - p^{12}p^{21})$$
$$+ A_3(p^{11}p^{22} - p^{21}p^{12})]/\Delta.$$

Substituting these values in the fourth row of (42), we obtain

$$(p^{21} + p^{11})^{-1}(A_1(p^{21} + p^{22}) + A_2(p^{11} + p^{12})$$
$$+ A_3(p^{12} + p^{22}) + A_4(p^{21} + p^{11})) = 0. \tag{49}$$

Notice that the t^{11}'s cancel and so do not appear in (49). It remains to show that we can find A_i's that satisfy (43)–(46) and (49). This amounts to showing that

$$\sum_j p^{1j}(v_1^{2j1} - v_1^{1j1})(p^{21} + p^{22}) + \sum_j p^{2j}(v_1^{1j2} - v_1^{2j2})(p^{11} + p^{12})$$

$$+ \sum_i p^{i1}(v_2^{i21} - v_2^{i11})(p^{12} + p^{22}) + \sum_i p^{i2}(v_2^{i12} - v_2^{i22})(p^{21} + p^{11}) \leq 0. \tag{50}$$

But the left side of (50) can be rewritten as

$$p^{11}p^{21}[(v_1^{211}-v_1^{111})+(v_1^{112}-v_1^{212})]+p^{12}p^{22}[(v_1^{221}-v_1^{121})+(v_1^{122}-v_1^{222})]$$

$$+p^{11}p^{12}[(v_2^{121}-v_2^{111})+(v_2^{112}-v_2^{122})]+p^{21}p^{22}[(v_2^{221}-v_2^{211})+(v_2^{212}-v_2^{222})]$$

$$+p^{11}p^{22}[(v_1^{211}-v_1^{111})+(v_1^{122}-v_1^{222})+(v_2^{121}-v_2^{111})+(v_2^{212}-v_2^{222})]$$

$$+p^{12}p^{21}[(v_1^{221}-v_1^{121})+(v_1^{112}-v_1^{212})+(v_2^{221}-v_2^{211})+(v_2^{112}-v_2^{122})]. \qquad (51)$$

From (35), the first two bracketed expressions in (51) are nonpositive. From (36), the second two are nonpositive as well, and from (40) and (41), so are the last two. Hence (50) holds after all.   Q.E.D.

NOTES

1 If f is a function of $\theta_1, \ldots, \theta_n$, the notation $f(\overset{\circ}{\theta}_i, \theta_{-i})$ is shorthand for
$$f(\theta_1, \ldots, \theta_{i-1}, \overset{\circ}{\theta}_i, \theta_{i+1}, \ldots, \theta_n).$$

2 Because the θ_i's are presumed to be independent, the expectation in (5) is unconditional.

3 See also d'Aspremont and Gerard-Varet (1982) for results on the correlated case.

4 Public decision d^* is differentiable because it solves (1) and because v is strictly concave and twice continuously differentiable.

5 Laffont and Maskin (1979) show that, under the hypotheses of Theorem 1, $\overset{\circ}{\theta}_i = \theta_i$ is a *local* maximum when t_{ii} is defined by (12). Riordan (1984) establishes a result related to the theorem when $n = 2$. Although his result is couched in terms of *positive* correlation, he correlates costs and benefits. Therefore, his positive correlation of costs and benefits amounts to negative correlation of benefits.

REFERENCES

Arrow, K. J. (1979), "The property rights doctrine and demand revelation under incomplete information," in M. Boskin (Ed.), *Economics and human welfare*, New York: Academic Press.

d'Aspremont, L. and L. A. Gerard-Varet (1979), "Incentives and incomplete information," *Journal of Public Economics*, 1(1): 25–45.

d'Aspremont, L. and L. A. Gerard-Varet (1982), "Bayesian incentive compatible beliefs," *Journal of Mathematical Economics*, 10: 83–103.

Laffont, J. J. and E. Maskin (1979), "A different approach to expected utility-maximizing mechanisms," in J. J. Laffont (Ed.), *Aggregation and revelation of preferences*, Amsterdam: North-Holland, pp. 289–308.

Riordan, M. (1984), "Uncertainty, information, and bilateral contracts," *Review of Economic Studies*, 51(1): 83–93.

CHAPTER 10

Incentive theory with data compression

Jerry R. Green and Jean-Jacques Laffont

I   Introduction

The economics of information and of incentives has been one of the most active areas of research in economic theory over the past fifteen years. The origin of this work can be traced to the writings of Marschak in the 1920s and, beyond that, to von Hayek and other European authors. During the development of this theory, the nature of the problems studied has steadily evolved. The kinds of informational difficulties in complex organizations that captured the attention of early writers were actually far different from the questions to which modern economic theory has provided interesting answers.

A brief digression on the nature of this evolution will help to define our interests more clearly. In the earliest papers, the issue was the design and evaluation of communication processes. The economy was depicted as continually changing. A good system of communication was one that could quickly and accurately disseminate information about its current state. Writers such as von Hayek (1945) wanted to evaluate the price system in this informational role. Emphasis was primarily on the continued *flow* of new information, and on the transitory character of the state of the economy.

> The sort of knowledge with which I have been concerned is knowledge of the kind which by its nature cannot enter into statistics and therefore cannot be conveyed to any central authority in statistical form. (von Hayek, 1945, p. 524)
>
> ... an essential part of the phenomena with which we have to deal: the unavoidable imperfection of man's knowledge and the consequent need of a process by which knowledge is constantly communicated and acquired. (von Hayek, 1945, p. 530)

Support from the National Science Foundation and the Commissariat au Plan are gratefully acknowledged.

The next stage in the economics of information centered on comparing communication networks. This led naturally to the theory of teams, a subject that was almost twenty years in gestation until the publication of the path-breaking work by Marschak and Radner (1972).[1] The theory of teams dropped the concepts of information flow about a continually changing state in favor of a more static view, with the exception of Chapter 7 in Marschak and Radner (1972). The state of the system was fixed, and team members each possessed different information about it. This was in the tradition of statistical decision theory, where one regards the parameters of a distribution as unknown, and seeks optimal responses to the available information. Marschak and Radner introduced the concept of a team decision rule. One can say that team theory *is* multiplayer statistical decision theory. They tried to study the question of optimal communication structure within the team. However, it is fair to say that most of their results concern the characterization of the optimal decision rule for a fixed communication structure, rather than this comparison.

The final stage, within the last ten years, involved the explicit introduction of differences in objectives among the agents. Communication problems of a technological nature were largely ignored. Instead, most attention was directed at the problem of providing the incentives necessary to make the self-interested agents divulge their information. The idea of a communication network was no longer pursued.

One reason for the rapid acceleration of this type of economic theory is the wide applicability it has found in other areas of economics. Problems of optimal taxation, sorting and screening, adverse selection in insurance, employment contracting, the theory of auctions, among others, have all been shown to be special cases of the general information transmission problem.

To recapitulate this development, we have seen that the ideas of information as a flow and of communication as a complex network design problem have been replaced by a static view of the state of the system and a costless technology for information transmission. This chapter reintroduces the idea of information as a flow to study the interaction of communication constraints and incentives questions.

Section II describes informally the type of principal-agent problem on which we focus. Section III shows how information theory is used to formalize the problem. The solution to the principal–agent problem is given in Section IV. Section V compares the results to those that would be obtained by a social planner.

II   A principal–agent problem with information flows

We consider a two-member organization consisting of a principal and an agent. The agent observes a sequence of realizations of a random process, x_t, and attempts to control a sequence of decisions, y_t. The actual decisions are taken by an obedient subordinate of the agent. The problem is that the agent cannot communicate perfectly with the subordinate because the channel through which this communication is to flow cannot accommodate all the information about x_t. The details of the communication technology will be discussed below. The agent and subordinate use the communication technology as effectively as possible, so as to optimize a common objective: minimizing an expected loss function that depends on x_t and y_t. This objective differs from that of the principal. The principal's only role in this model is to provide and pay for the communication technology for the agent and subordinate. The principal knows that, whatever technology is provided, the agent and subordinate will use it to their best advantage and that this may be different from the principal's.

This chapter studies how the resources devoted by the principal to the communication technology depend on the difference in the objectives and on the characteristics of the source x_t. We compare the amount of resources devoted to communication in this system with those that would be used by a principal who could observe x_t and who could communicate directly to the subordinate. We also compare it to the optimal system, as it would be designed by a social planner to maximize the joint welfare of the principal and the agent, subject to the fact that the agent will observe x_t and will control the use of this communication channel.

The novel feature of this system is the way in which the agent's environment is modeled, particularly the dynamic aspects of his receipt and transmission of information. As this is quite distinct from the usual principal–agent framework, we will now describe it in some detail.

Imagine that the observations x_t are realizations of independent identically distributed random variables taking one of M possible values, and that these realizations are perceived by the agent at the rate of S_0 per unit time. For example, x_t could be the rate of new orders placed at different locations in a distribution system for some manufactured product. Each order consists of a quantity and a place of delivery. Both components arrive at random and are expressed in the message x_t.

The agent has to transmit information about x_t to a subordinate. This is modeled by the agent's ability to send a sequence of pieces of information z_τ to the subordinate. The frequency with which this information z_τ can be transmitted may be different from the rate at which the random inputs x_t arrive. It is for this reason that we denote the times at which the inputs arrive by t and the time at which messages are sent by τ. For example, if inputs arrive each day, but messages can be sent each hour, $t = 1, 2, \ldots$, but $\tau = \frac{1}{24}, \frac{2}{24}, \ldots$. Typically, we imagine that messages are sent at a rate, S_1 per unit time, substantially higher than S_0, but that each z_τ lies in a set with L distinct points, where L is much smaller than M. For example, the transmission might be in Morse code or certain abbreviations and approximations might be used. These qualitative relations are not relevant to the nature of our results. The important point is that the information system may not be able to fully and accurately transmit all the inputs. Information theory gives us one way to model this inability precisely.

The agent's subordinate, having received the sequence z_τ, decodes it as well as possible. The subordinate would, ideally, reconstruct x_t and act upon it. However, unless S_1 is large enough, z_τ will not contain enough information to reconstruct x_t perfectly. Agent and subordinates have the ability to arrange any system of encoding and decoding they desire. Let the best reconstruction of x_t be denoted y_t. The result is that the subordinate will act according to y_t.

We now describe the optimal encoding and decoding further, pursuing the example of orders for delivery of a manufactured product described above. Suppose that the communication technology allows the place of the order to be reconstructed with perfect accuracy, but that the level of the order can only be reconstructed to within 1,000 units. Any more accurate reconstruction of orders would require more transmissions of z_τ per unit time than the channel could handle. Were the agent and subordinate to attempt this with the current channel, it would take too much time and unfilled orders would pile up without bound. We assume that a fixed delay between x_t and y_t, due to the time taken in the encoding, transmission, and decoding process, can be tolerated without loss. But orders must be processed *at the same rate* as they arrive.

The essential difference between this model and the usual principal-agent models can now be described. The most important difference is the idea that the information received by the agent is arriving as a flow over time. It is this idea that allows us to treat the communication technology available to the agent as a continuous variable – the rate per unit time at which messages can be sent.

In the usual principal–agent model, the agent receives some information and is allowed to act on it at will, perhaps subject to a limitation on the set of possible actions. In this static context, the literature on the principal–agent problem has modeled the difficulties encountered by the agent in actually implementing his desired choice by employing a *dimension counting* approach. The random variable x_t lies in a space of fixed dimension, the agent's action is constrained to span a space of lower dimension, but the selection of this action is still in the hands of the agent.[2] Such an approach is technically very messy, and its "integer" nature makes it hard to study by analytical means the principal's choice of a space to provide for the agent. In environments where enough informational resources exist to achieve a fully efficient economic allocation, Mount and Reiter (1974) and Reichelstein (1983) have characterized the minimum dimensionality of the space in which messages must be allowed to vary. At present, a "second-best" approach to these problems along "dimensionality" lines – that is, asking how many dimensions are necessary to achieve a given, suboptimal, efficiency criterion – has not been attempted. This chapter addresses such second-best issues by modeling informational resources as the continuous variable speed of transmission available between the agent and subordinate, instead of the integer-valued dimensionality measure.

III   Detailed model of agent's behavior and information theory

The precise model of the agent's behavior that we will use below needs some justification and explanation. In the process of offering it, we will explain some related ideas in information theory.

As described above, the agent receives x_t and can transmit z_τ. The way in which x_t should be coded into z_τ depends on the statistical distribution of x_t and on the ratio of the speed of input arrival to the speed of the transmission. For example, in English, certain letters such as q and x are very rare relative to e and s. Therefore their Morse code symbols are longer strings of dots and dashes – four such symbols instead of one or two. If the letters in English were arriving at the rate of one per second, and were encoded in Morse code, we would need to send about 2.4 Morse code symbols per second to transmit at the required rate. If S_1/S_0 were below 2.4, we would either have to tolerate some mistakes or we would have to find a more efficient code. Mistakes might be, for instance, that certain rarely used letters could be assigned the same code. Thus, q and x might not be distinguishable upon decoding. Hopefully this would not cause too much of a loss.

One of the main ideas of information theory has been to find the most efficient method for encoding. It has asked whether, for a given transmission speed, some code can be found that will allow for error-free decoding. The solution to this problem is to code long strings of letters into long "code words." For example, instead of coding each letter in English into a Morse code sequence of from one to four letters, longer sequences of input letters, say ten at a time, might be encoded into longer strings of dots and dashes, say strings of ten to twenty such symbols. Such codes are called block codes.

One of the most powerful results of information theory[3] concerns the maximal amount of compression that can be achieved as more and more complex block codes are allowed. For any $\epsilon > 0$, perfect encoding, transmission, and decoding of a stationary source, x_t sending S_0 characters of the source per second, is possible using a language with L symbols, if the speed of transmission of z_τ is $S_0 H + \epsilon$ where H is the entropy of the source (log base L) and if a sufficiently long block-code is used. Conversely, if $S_1 < S_0 H$, then some error must be tolerated no matter how complex the code.

The relationship between the average error and the transmission rate depends of course on the loss function that is used to measure the error. For any loss function we define the *rate distortion function* as the infimum of the transmission rate S_1 of channels that can be used, together with some block code, so as to achieve the indicated average loss. This average loss is called the *distortion D* and the rate distortion function is written $R(D)$.

This is the model of the agent's information transmission problem that we use below. The principal gives the agent a channel with transmission speed S_1. The agent and subordinate arrange to use this channel in the most effective manner possible.

Let us look further into the nature of the decisions that the agent and subordinate can achieve in this way. Suppose, as much of information theory does, that the loss associated with each x_t depends only on the associated y_t. In our example with orders arriving at random, we would be assuming that a mistake in filling the order x_t engenders a loss for the agent if $y_t \neq x_t$. The magnitude of the loss depends on the nature of x_t and y_t. But any other $y_{t'}$ is irrelevant to this loss. For instance, if x_t represents an order for 5,000 units in New York, and y_t is "send 4,000 units to Topeka," there is a loss. And if $y_{t'}$ ($t' > t$) is "send 3,000 units to New York," that does not mitigate the loss incurred by the mistake already incurred at t. In information theory such loss functions are called *single-letter fidelity criteria*.

Suppose a particular value of x_t is received. What will be the magnitude of the loss conditional on this event? After encoding, transmission, and decoding, there will be a value of y_t. But the y_t that results from x_t depends on the code word, which will typically be very long, in which x_t is imbedded. Different occurrences of the same realization of x_t will often be decoded differently, when a complex code is used. Therefore, the optimal code induces a transition probability $q(y_t | x_t)$ which is not degenerate. For expected loss computations, it is this transition probability and the process x_t that are relevant.

The main result of information theory cited above can be reinterpreted in terms of the realized transition probabilities $q(y_t | x_t)$. A transition probability $q(\cdot | \cdot)$ is attainable by an information system (a block code and a channel with a given transmission rate) if and only if the *average mutual information* of y_t and x_t, $I(y, x)$, is less than this transmission rate. The average mutual information is defined as

$$I(y, x) = \int_Y \int_X p(x) q(y | x) \log \frac{q(y | x)}{q(y)} \, dx \, dy,$$

where $p(x)$ and $q(y)$ are the marginal distributions of x and y, X and Y being the range of x and y.

Therefore, neglecting the approximation involved in the need to use arbitrarily long block codes to achieve the transmission rate, we can look upon the agent's decision problem as the minimization of the expected value of the loss function $w(x, y)$ by choosing a family of conditional distributions $q(\cdot | x)$ such that the average mutual information of x and y is below the transmission rate of the channel. This is a convex programming problem, whose solution can be found by means of constrained optimization methods.

It is important to realize that the randomness in y_t given x_t is not a "bad" thing. One can, with simpler codes, make y_t nonstochastic given x_t. In doing so, however, the problem is that many x_t will generally be coded as the same y_t and the average loss will be higher. Random y_t are a necessary by-product of block codes. And block codes are the key method through which limited channels achieve their best performance. Thus, when we optimize over $q(\cdot | y)$, we are implicitly incorporating the choice of a good code into the agent's design problem. We do not have to construct the code explicitly; indeed, the construction of such codes is itself a highly complex numerical problem. Its existence is guaranteed by the results of information theory cited above.

Any finite-length code that would transform blocks of x_t into a finite set of possible z_τ would therefore generate only a discrete set of decoded y_t. However, as we consider longer and longer code words, with an optimal encoding procedure, the regenerated y_t converge to a continuous distribution. Thus, since we have already accepted this limiting operation when we take the constraint $I(x, y) \leq R$, it does not represent any new assumption to treat the transitions $q(\cdot \mid \cdot)$ as a family of continuous distributions.

The principal knows the agent's preferences and therefore can compute conditional distributions $q_R(\cdot \mid y_t)$ that the agent would choose if given a channel with transmission rate R. The principal can choose R and must pay for its cost of installation (and maintenance). For simplicity, we assume that this cost is linear in the transmission rate. Therefore, the principal's problem is

$$\max \int_Y \int_X u(x, y) q_R(y_t \mid x_t) p(x) \, dy \, dy - cR,$$

where the expectation is taken over (x, y) with the exogenous process x and with y distributed according to the agent's chosen transition rule $q_R(\cdot \mid \cdot)$ as described above.

In order to have a tractable form of this problem, we need a stationary process x_t and a single-letter fidelity criterion $w(y_t, x_t)$ for the agent such that the resulting $q_R(\cdot \mid x_t)$ takes a sufficiently simple form.[4] Although the basic properties of $R(D)$ hold for very general processes and fidelity criteria, the resulting $q_R(\cdot \mid x_t)$ usually cannot be computed in closed form. This makes evaluation and optimization by the principal impossible to carry out analytically.

The only case in which $q(\cdot \mid x_t)$ takes a simple form is where x_t is Gaussian and $w(x_t, y_t)$ is quadratic. This is the model of the agent that we study below. For the principal, we assume that $u(x_t, y_t) = -(y_t - ax_t)^2$.

The use of a continuous input and a continuous output requires a little comment because the discussion above was specifically directed to the case of a discrete set of inputs, strings of which could be encoded into strings of code letters. When the input is continuous, any encoding into a discrete set of code letters necessitates some error. An infinite transmission sequence would be necessary to send even one number with perfect accuracy. Nevertheless, the concept of a rate distortion function and the relationship of this function to the mutual information of x and y is still valid. The only qualification is that it must be possible to define a partition of the values of x into a family of sets with the cardinality of the code letters such that the average distortion within each element of the partition is finite. For the case of x normally distributed and the squared error fidelity criterion, this qualification is clearly satisfied (see Gallager 1968, Section 9.6, pp. 470–5).

IV   The solution to the principal–agent problem

We assume that the stationary source x is Gaussian with mean 0 and variance σ^2, and we denote its density by $p(x)$. The agent maximizes expected utility under the given channel constraint by solving

$$\max - \int_Y \int_X (y-x)^2 p(x)q(y\,|\,x)\,dx\,dy \quad \text{subject to}$$

$$\int_Y \int_X p(x)q(y\,|\,x)\log\frac{q(y\,|\,x)}{q(y)}\,dx\,dy \le R. \tag{1}$$

From Gallager (1968) we know that the value of the agent's program at optimum is

$$u_A^* = -\sigma^2 e^{-2R}. \tag{2}$$

Moreover, this value is achieved by choosing a message y that has a conditional distribution

$$q^*(y\,|\,x) \rightsquigarrow \mathfrak{N}(\rho x, \rho\sigma^2 e^{-2R}), \tag{3}$$

where

$$\rho = 1 - e^{-2R}. \tag{4}$$

The optimal distortion has the appearance of a contraction toward the origin and the addition of a Gaussian noise with variance $\rho\sigma^2 e^{-2R}$.

The principal has a different objective function

$$u_P = -\int_Y \int_X (y-ax)^2 p(x)q(y\,|\,x)\,dx\,dy - cR, \tag{5}$$

where the cost of the channel R is supposed to be cR. The principal knows that the agent is maximizing his own objective leading to equations (3) and (4). Therefore, he looks for the best channel capacity R by maximizing equation (5) subject to equations (3) and (4).

Substituting equations (3) and (4) into (5) we rewrite the optimization program:

$$\max_{R \ge 0} - [e^{-2R}(2a-1) + (a-1)^2]\sigma^2 - cR. \tag{6}$$

A straightforward solution to this problem is characterized by the following relations. If $a \le \frac{1}{2} + c/4\sigma^2$, the optimal channel capacity is $R^* = 0$; the utility level of the principal is then $u_P^* = -a^2\sigma^2$ and the utility level of the agent is $u_A^* = -\sigma^2$. If $a > \frac{1}{2} + c/4\sigma^2$, then

$$R^* = \frac{1}{2} \log \frac{2(2a-1)\sigma^2}{c},$$

$$u_P^* = -(a-1)^2\sigma^2 + \frac{c}{2}\left(1 + \log \frac{2(2a-1)\sigma^2}{c}\right),$$

and

$$u_A^* = -\frac{c}{2(2a-1)} - \sigma^2.$$

Note that if $c = 0$, the principal either provides a channel of capacity that leads the agent to choose a constant action $x = 0$ (which is also the principal's best decision without any information) or provides an infinite channel to let the agent achieve his first best.

If there were no incentives problem, the principal could achieve

$$\max_{R \ge 0, q(\cdot \mid \cdot)} -\int_Y \int_X (y - ax)^2 p(x) q(y \mid x) \, dx \, dy - cR$$

$$\text{subject to } \int_Y \int_X p(x) q(y \mid x) \log \frac{q(y \mid x)}{q(y)} \, dx \, dy \le R, \tag{7}$$

which yields

$$q^{**}(y \mid x) \rightsquigarrow \mathfrak{N}(\rho a x, \rho a^2 \sigma^2 e^{-2R}); \tag{8}$$

$$p = 1 - e^{-2R}; \tag{9}$$

$$R^{**} = \begin{cases} \frac{1}{2} \log(2a^2\sigma^2/c) & \text{if } 2a^2\sigma^2 \ge c, \\ 0 & \text{if } 2a^2\sigma^2 < c; \end{cases} \tag{10}$$

$$u_P^{**} = \begin{cases} -\frac{c}{2}[1 + \log(2a^2\sigma^2/c)] & \text{if } 2a^2\sigma^2 \ge c, \\ -a^2\sigma^2 & \text{if } 2a^2\sigma^2 < c. \end{cases} \tag{11}$$

The additional loss suffered by the principal due to the presence of an agent whose objective function differs from his own is plotted in Figure 1.

Given a cost function for the communication technology, the loss due to incentives increases monotonically with the amount of information to be transmitted. This result can be contrasted with results obtained in Green and Laffont (1982), where the loss due to incentives was not monotonic in the amount of information to be transmitted.

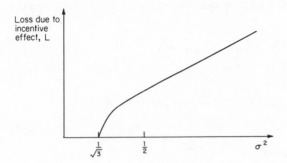

Figure 1. $L = 1 + \log 3\sigma^2 - 3\sigma^2$ if $\dfrac{1}{\sqrt{3}} < \sigma^2 \le \dfrac{1}{2}$

$\qquad\qquad\quad = \sigma^2 + \log \dfrac{3}{4}$ if $\sigma^2 > \dfrac{1}{2}$

V   Social planning

A utilitarian social planner whose objective incorporated both the agent and principal and who could fully control the agent's behavior would solve

$$\max_{q(\cdot\,|\,\cdot),\,R} \int_Y \int_X [(y - ax)^2 + (y - x)^2]\, p(x)q(y\,|\,x)\, dx\, dy - cR \qquad (12)$$

such that

$$\int_Y \int_X p(x)q(y\,|\,x) \log \frac{q(y\,|\,x)}{q(y)}\, dx\, dy \le R.$$

Note that

$$(y - ax)^2 + (y - x)^2 = 2[y - \tfrac{1}{2}(a+1)x]^2 + \tfrac{1}{2}x^2(a-1)^2.$$

Using the change of variable, $v = \tfrac{1}{2}(a+1)x$, the problem becomes

$$\max_{q(\cdot\,|\,\cdot),\,R} -2 \int_Y \int_X (y - v)^2 p(v)q(y\,|\,v)\, dv\, dy - \tfrac{1}{2}(a-1)^2\sigma^2 - cR \qquad (13)$$

such that

$$\int_Y \int_X p(v)q(y\,|\,v) \log \frac{q(y\,|\,v)}{q(y)}\, dv\, dy \le R,$$

where $p(v)$ is the density function of v, that is, Gaussian with mean 0 and variance $[\tfrac{1}{2}(a+1)]^2\sigma^2$.

From Gallager (1968) we know that the optimal solution with respect to $q(\cdot\,|\,\cdot)$ is

$$q^*(y\,|\,v) \leadsto \mathfrak{N}(\rho v, \rho[\tfrac{1}{2}(a+1)]^2\sigma^2 e^{-2R}), \tag{14}$$

$$\rho = 1 - e^{-2R}, \tag{15}$$

and that the value of $\int_Y \int_X (y-v)^2 p(v) q(y\,|\,v)\, dv\, dy$ is

$$[\tfrac{1}{2}(a+1)]^2\sigma^2 e^{-2R}. \tag{16}$$

The optimization reduces to

$$\min_R -\{[\tfrac{1}{2}(a+1)]^2\sigma^2 e^{-2R} - \tfrac{1}{2}(a-1)^2\sigma^2 - cR\}, \tag{17}$$

yielding

$$R^{**} = \begin{cases} \tfrac{1}{2}\log[(a+1)^2\sigma^2/c] & \text{if } (a+1)^2\sigma^2 \ge c, \\ 0 & \text{if } (a+1)^2\sigma^2 < c; \end{cases} \tag{18}$$

and a social welfare

$$u^{**} = \begin{cases} -\tfrac{1}{2}(a-1)^2\sigma^2 - \tfrac{c}{2}(1+\log[(a+1)^2\sigma^2/c]) & \text{if } (a+1)^2\sigma^2 \ge c, \\ -\tfrac{1}{2}(a-1)^2\sigma^2 & \text{if } (a+1)^2\sigma^2 < c. \end{cases} \tag{19}$$

Consider now what this social planner can achieve under the further constraint that the agent cannot be fully controlled, but rather that the agent will use the available channel to his own best advantage.

From Section IV we know that the agent chooses according to equations (3) and (4). The planner's objective function is then

$$-2a\sigma^2 e^{-2R} - [\tfrac{1}{2}(a-1)]^2\sigma^2 - cR, \tag{20}$$

yielding

$$R^* = \begin{cases} \tfrac{1}{2}\log(4a\sigma^2/c) & \text{if } 4a\sigma^2 \ge c, \\ 0 & \text{if } 4a\sigma^2 < c; \end{cases} \tag{21}$$

and a social welfare

$$u^* = \begin{cases} -\tfrac{1}{2}(a-1)^2\sigma^2 - \tfrac{c}{2}[1+\log(4a\sigma^2/c)] & \text{if } 4a\sigma^2 \ge c, \\ -\tfrac{1}{2}(a-1)^2\sigma^2 & \text{if } 4a\sigma^2 < c. \end{cases} \tag{22}$$

The additional social loss due to incentive problems is

$$L = \begin{cases} \tfrac{c}{2}\log[(a+1)^2/4a] & \text{if } \sigma^2 \ge c/4a, \\ \tfrac{c}{2}\log[(a+1)^2\sigma^2/c] & \text{if } c/(a+1)^2 < \sigma^2 < c/4a, \\ 0 & \text{if } \sigma^2 \le c/(a+1)^2. \end{cases} \tag{23}$$

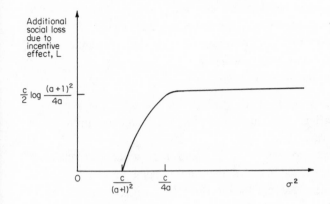

Figure 2

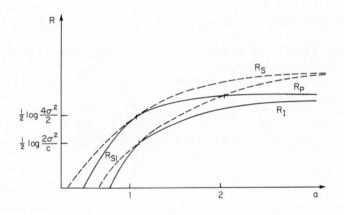

Figure 3

Here again the additional loss due to incentives is increasing mono-tonically in the information to be transmitted (see Figure 2).

We show in Figure 3 the optimal channel capacity or optimal expen-ditures on communication incurred in the various cases studied in this chapter:

R_P Principal–agent problem without incentives constraints
R_{PI} Principal–agent problem with incentives constraints
R_S Social planner problem without incentives constraints
R_{SI} Social planner problem with incentives constraints

Figure 3 is constructed under the assumption that $c/\sigma^2 < 2$. It is natural to focus on this case because in the opposite case the cost of the channel is so high that the principal would not like to use the channel even if the agent shared his objective function.

We observe the following results:

1. In both the principal–agent problem and the social planning problem, incentives constraints lead to a reduction in communication expenditures.
2. Under incentives constraints, expenditures in the principal–agent problem are always smaller than in the social planner's problem. Without incentives constraints this relationship continues to hold unless a becomes very large.

NOTES

1   However, Marschak (1971) attempted to bridge economics and information theory.
2   In Green and Laffont (1982), we study this interaction when communication constraints are expressed as constraints on the dimensionality of the Euclidean spaces used by economic units to communicate their messages. See also Green (1982), Reichelstein (1983).
3   This theory was developed by Shannon (1948, 1959). Berger (1971) provides the most comprehensive treatment.
4   An algorithm due to Blahut (1972) could be used to solve these problems numerically.

REFERENCES

Berger, T. (1971), *Rate distortion theory: A mathematical basis for data compression,* Englewood Cliffs, N.J.: Prentice-Hall.
Blahut, R. (1972), "Computation of channel capacity and rate distortion functions," *IEEE Transactions on Information Theory,* 4: 460–70.
Gallager, R. (1968), *Information theory and reliable communication,* New York: Wiley.
Green, E. J. (1982), "Decentralizability of truthful revelation and other decision rules," California Institute of Technology, Discussion Paper No. 419.
Green, J. and J.-J. Laffont (1982), "Limited communication and incentive compatibility," Harvard Institute of Economics Research Discussion Paper No. 919, to appear in volume in honor of L. Hurwicz.
Marschak, J. (1971), "Economics of information systems," *Journal of the American Statistical Association,* 66: 192–219.
Marschak, J. and R. Radner (1972), *Economic Theory of Teams,* New Haven: Yale University Press.

Mount, K. and S. Reiter (1974), "The informational size of message spaces," *Journal of Economic Theory,* 8(2): 161–92.

Reichelstein, S. (1983), "Incentive compatibility and informational requirements," Center for Research in Management Science and Economics Working Paper No. IP-314, Berkeley.

Shannon, C. (1948), "A Mathematical theory of communication," *Bell System Technical Journal,* 27: 379–423, 623–56.

Shannon, C. (1959), "Coding theorems for a discrete source with a fidelity criterion," *IRE National Convention Records,* XX: 142–63.

von Hayek, F. A. (1945), "The use of knowledge in society," *American Economic Review,* 35: 519–30.

CHAPTER 11

Alternative limited communication systems: centralization versus interchange of information

Jerry R. Green and Jean-Jacques Laffont

1   Introduction

This chapter is a contribution to the study of optimal organizational design, a subject of interest to economists for many years but one in which little actual progress has been made. Organizations function by communicating information and coordinating the actions of their members. Both of these activities require the establishment and use of channels for transmitting information between members. The pattern of these communication links is called the organizational structure, or design.

More complex designs allow a fuller sharing of information and a more precise implementation of the desired collective decision. Neglecting the costs of the design and the communication, the more elaborate designs can achieve a higher expected payoff for the organization. Comparing organizational designs requires the computation of the costs of communication itself. It is at this point that economic theory has failed to provide a basis for the analysis, and it is for this reason that the literature on organizational design has not yielded rigorous theoretical results.

Costs of an organizational structure should include all the basic activities in which the organization is involved: collection, storage, retrieval, transmission, and processing of both quantitative and nonquantitative information. The only cost that economists have dealt with, to date, is the cost of transmission. And even here, the metrics in which costs are reckoned are terribly simple. It is in general assumed that each real number transmitted costs the same. The questions typically addressed have been of the form: How many transmissions are needed in order to achieve a particular desired standard of performance? Usually, an efficiency criterion such as Pareto optimality has been the standard.

Financial support from National Science Foundation and Commissariat au Plan (Paris) is gratefully acknowledged.

This approach to organizational design is quite different from what the early writers had in mind.[1] They wanted to judge different designs against each other in order to measure the benefits from additional resources devoted to the organization's internal network. But without a theory of the costs of alternative design, this program was not feasible.

The primary framework used to date to study the organization design problem on a rigorous basis has been the theory of teams. As set forth in *The Economic Theory of Teams* (Marschak and Radner 1972), the goal of this theory is to be able to compare alternative designs by a two-step method. First, for each given design, we find the optimal mode of functioning for the organization. Second, the cost of operating the communication process is to be subtracted from the optimized objective function of each design, and their net values compared. *The Economic Theory of Teams* did not actually carry out this program. It did set up some useful definitions, and it provided some important results on the first of these steps. But the second step, cost assessment and comparison, was not really attemped, despite a clear view of the problem. Marschak and Radner (1972) are led to the following types of assumptions to validate their analysis. When they compare information structures based on fixed or variable partitions of the team's members into groups, they assume that costs of information depend only upon the average group size. When they compare error in instruction with error in observation, they assume that costs depend upon the ratio of the variance of the error to the variance of the message.

The more recent literature on economic organization has proceeded in two other directions, but has likewise neglected the design problem. Conflicting objectives among the organization's members have been introduced, giving rise to the extensive literature on incentives and the economics of information. And the asymptotic behavior of certain decision rules has been studied as the size of organization grows larger.

In this chapter we return to the original goal in the spirit of Marschak and Radner's Chapter 8. We compare organizational designs that use the *same* resources, thus circumventing the problem of measuring the cost of these resources. We retain the number of communication links in the organization as the measure of the resources needed. In particular, we will assume that the costs of coding and decoding are identical and do not involve increasing returns. This is well in the tradition of team theory. As stressed by Kenneth Arrow (1982): "Team theory assumes a fixed amount of communication in fixed channels. The costs of communication are modelled by scarcity."

We compare two forms of a two-member organization. Each form requires that two pieces of information be sent and received. They differ in that in the first, which we call centralization, one member sends two pieces of information to the other. In the second, which we call interchange, they each send and receive a single piece of data. Thus, under interchange, neither member is as well informed as the receiving agent would be under centralization.

Our results concern the choice between these two communication systems as the team's objective function and its stochastic environment vary. If the costs of malcoordination of the team members' actions are sufficiently high, the member with the more accurate observation on each exogenous variable should send it to the other. This results in centralization if one agent is the better observer of all variables, and in interchange otherwise. *Thus, the superiority of the communication system called centralization requires, in this model, both superiority of information by one player and relatively high costs of malcoordination.*

In Section 2 we describe the basic model to be used. Sections 3 and 4 give analyses of the optimal utilization of interchange and centralization, respectively. Section 5 derives analytical results on their comparative efficiency, which are supplemented by numerical calculations.

2   The model

We study a team, that is, a group of agents with a common objective and to each of whom is assigned a specific set of choice variables relevant to the team's payoff. Although centralizing these choices might be desirable on informational grounds, we regard it as technologically infeasible. Thus, the problem we study is a by-product of the dispersions of actions and of information. More specifically, it is due to the fact that some agents have information relevant to other agents' decisions.

We consider a two-member organization that must take four decisions. Agent 1 controls x_1 and y_1, and agent 2 controls x_2 and y_2. The organization operates in an uncertain environment with two unknown parameters a and b. Information is dispersed. Each agent observes both a and b with error. Specifically, agent i sees α_i and β_i, where

$$\alpha_i = a + \epsilon_i,$$
$$\beta_i = b + \eta_i.$$

We assume that a, b, ϵ_1, ϵ_2, η_1, and η_2 are all Gaussian mean zero independently distributed random variables.

The organization's goal is to minimize the expectation of the loss function

$$L = (x_1 + x_2 - a)^2 + (y_1 + y_2 - b)^2 + \lambda(x_1 - x_2)^2 + \mu(y_1 - y_2)^2, \quad (1)$$

where $\lambda, \mu \geq 0$ are fixed constants. The first two terms express the objective of taking collective actions that approximate the targets a and b. The third and fourth terms represent the costs incurred due to the imperfectly coordinated individual actions.

We take the decentralization of actions across team members as immutable. The problem studied in this chapter is the design of the communication system that agents use to share their information. The actions of the agents can be based on the observations they receive directly and on whatever additional information they receive through the chosen communication system.

We are interested in comparing the efficiency of forms of communication that use the same number of messages transmitted. To share all information completely would require four messages to be sent – each would have to send both observations to the other. This would achieve the first-best results.

The possible *forms* of communication for fewer than four messages can be represented in the following diagrams:

$\alpha_1 \longrightarrow$

$\beta_1 \longrightarrow$
Agent 1 $\longrightarrow$ Agent 2
$\longleftarrow \alpha_2$

$\longleftarrow \beta_2$

A. One message sent

$\alpha_1 \longrightarrow$

$\beta_1 \longrightarrow$
Agent 1 $\longrightarrow\!\!\longrightarrow$ Agent 2
$\longleftarrow \alpha_2$

$\longleftarrow \beta_2$

B. Two messages sent by the same agent

$\alpha_1 \longrightarrow$

$\beta_1 \longrightarrow$
Agent 1 $\longrightarrow$ $\longleftarrow$ Agent 2
$\longleftarrow \alpha_2$

$\longleftarrow \beta_2$

C. Two messages: one sent by each agent

$\alpha_1 \longrightarrow$

$\beta_1 \longrightarrow$
Agent 1 $\Longrightarrow$ $\longleftarrow$ Agent 2
$\longleftarrow \alpha_2$

$\longleftarrow \beta_2$

D. Three messages sent: one by one agent and two by the other

The arrows in these diagrams represent a single real number transmitted in the indicated direction. Notice that in every case there is another communication structure in which the direction of the transmission is reversed.

In this simple model, it is only in the case of exactly two messages being sent that there is a *real choice of structural form* in the pattern of communication – B versus C. B models a centralized organization while C describes a more symmetric type of interchange of information between the players.[2] Consequently, the focus of the formal analysis below is limited to these two cases.

The choice of communication structure is based on the team's a priori beliefs about its environment as well as on the information available to its members. Using the principle of person-by-person optimality (Marschak and Radner 1972, Chapter 5, Section 3), the best team decision rule involves each agent computing his posterior beliefs based on all the information available, and then optimizing the team's objective function. We concentrate on the case in which the available information greatly reduces the a priori uncertainty of each agent about the parameters a and b. We therefore derive asymptotic results that apply as the variances of the prior distributions of a and b, respectively σ_a^2 and σ_b^2, become very large. These results are much sharper than what would be obtained in the general case of an optimal Bayesian decision rule with an informative prior.

3   Interchange of information

The form of communication in diagram C will be termed *interchange,* as it involves having the agents send messages to each other. Each agent then controls two variables based on three inputs, the two observations seen personally and the message received from the other. We restrict attention to transmissions that are linear combinations of the observations each player receives. Actually, without loss of generality we can consider convex combinations, which are denoted

$$z_1 = c\alpha_1 + (1-c)\beta_1, \qquad z_2 = d\alpha_2 + (1-d)\beta_2.$$

The decisions of agent 1 are

$$x_1 = ez_2 + f\alpha_2 + g\beta_1, \qquad y_1 = hz_2 + k\alpha_1 + \ell\beta_1.$$

Note, however, that g and k must both be zero. Information about b contained in β_1 is completely irrelevant to the choice of x_1 since a and b are independent. Likewise $k = 0$ would make y_1 dependent on a, and hence would introduce noise in the objective function. Similar considerations apply to agent 2.

Therefore we let the decisions be given by

$$x_1 = ez_2 + f\alpha_1, \qquad y_1 = hz_2 + \ell\beta_1,$$
$$x_2 = mz_1 + n\alpha_2, \qquad y_2 = qz_1 + s\beta_2.$$

Substituting the communication and decision rules into (1), we find that the coefficients of σ_a^2 and σ_b^2 are, respectively,

$$(ed + f + mc + n - 1)^2 + (hd + qc)^2 + \lambda(ed + f - mc - n)^2 + \mu(hd - qc)^2,$$

$$(2)$$

and

$$[e(1-d) + m(1-c)]^2 + [h(1-d) + \ell + q(1-c) + s - 1]^2$$
$$+ \lambda[e(1-d) - m(1-c)]^2 + \mu[h(1-d) + \ell - q(1-c) - s]^2. \tag{3}$$

Setting each of the eight squared expressions above to zero[3] gives the relationships

$$ed + f = \tfrac{1}{2}, \qquad mc + n = \tfrac{1}{2},$$
$$hd = 0, \qquad qc = 0,$$
$$e(1-d) = 0, \qquad m(1-c) = 0, \tag{4}$$
$$h(1-d) + \ell = \tfrac{1}{2}, \qquad q(1-c) + s = \tfrac{1}{2}.$$

The simplest way to solve the overall minimization problem is to consider c and d as choice variables and to let the other eight variables be determined by the above. Because of the multiplicative form of the restrictions (4), we have several cases to consider. The cases are divided according to whether c and d are zero, one, or something in between. This would produce nine cases in all. However, only the four in which c and d have an extreme value will be of interest.

To see why the other five cases can be eliminated, consider for example the restrictions implied by equation (4) when c and d are both between zero and one. Here we have directly that

$$h = q = e = m = 0, \qquad f = n = \ell = s = \tfrac{1}{2}.$$

The meaning of these restrictions is that any information received from the other agent is ignored in the decision rule. The agents behave in an entirely decentralized fashion, setting x_i and y_i at one-half of the mean of the distributions of a and b, respectively.

In general, whenever one agent chooses to transmit a mixed signal, the restrictions of equation (4) imply that the transmission is not used by the other agent. Intuitively, a mixed signal cannot be interpreted by the receiver who cannot decompose the signal into a piece relevant for action x and a piece relevant for action y.

Thus, we concentrate on the four remaining cases:

Case 1. $c = 0$, $d = 0$; interchange of information on b implying the following constraints:

$$
\left.\begin{aligned} e &= 0 \\ f &= \tfrac{1}{2} \end{aligned}\right\} \quad \begin{aligned} &\text{agent 1 uses only private information} \\ &\text{on } a \text{ to make } x \text{ decision} \end{aligned}
$$

$$
\left.\begin{aligned} m &= 0 \\ n &= \tfrac{1}{2} \end{aligned}\right\} \quad \begin{aligned} &\text{agent 2 uses only private information} \\ &\text{on } a \text{ to make } x \text{ decision} \end{aligned} \tag{5}
$$

$$
\left.\begin{aligned} h + \ell &= \tfrac{1}{2} \\ q + s &= \tfrac{1}{2} \end{aligned}\right\} \quad \begin{aligned} &\text{weights of own and exchanged information} \\ &\text{to make } y \text{ decision must sum to } \tfrac{1}{2} \end{aligned}
$$

Case 2. $c = 0$, $d = 1$; agent 1 transmits information on b, agent 2 transmits information on a, implying the following constraints:

$$
e + f = \tfrac{1}{2} \quad \text{agent 1 uses both information to set } x_1
$$

$$
\left.\begin{aligned} m &= 0 \\ n &= \tfrac{1}{2} \end{aligned}\right\} \quad \begin{aligned} &\text{agent 2 uses only private information} \\ &\text{on } a \text{ to make } x \text{ decision} \end{aligned}
$$

$$
\left.\begin{aligned} h &= 0 \\ \ell &= \tfrac{1}{2} \end{aligned}\right\} \quad \begin{aligned} &\text{agent 1 uses only private information} \\ &\text{on } b \text{ to make } y \text{ decision} \end{aligned} \tag{6}
$$

$$
q + x = \tfrac{1}{2} \quad \text{agent 2 uses both information to set } y_2
$$

Case 3. $c = 1$, $d = 0$; agent 1 transmits information on a, agent 2 transmits information on b, implying the following constraints:

$$
e = 0, \qquad f = \tfrac{1}{2},
$$

$$
h + \ell = \tfrac{1}{2}, \qquad m + n = \tfrac{1}{2}, \tag{7}
$$

$$
q = 0, \qquad s = \tfrac{1}{2}.
$$

Case 4. $c = 1$, $d = 1$; interchange of information on a, implying the following constraints:

$$
e + f = \tfrac{1}{2}, \qquad h = 0,
$$

$$
\ell = \tfrac{1}{2}, \qquad m + n = \tfrac{1}{2}, \tag{8}
$$

$$
q = 0, \qquad s = \tfrac{1}{2}.
$$

Now, to minimize the expectation of the loss function in each case, we substitute the conditions derived above into equation (1) and minimize the remaining expression. Having set equations (2) and (3) to zero because we consider the asymptotic case of large prior uncertainty, the remaining expression in the minimand involves only the four error variances $\sigma_{\epsilon_1}^2$, $\sigma_{\epsilon_2}^2$, $\sigma_{\eta_1}^2$ and $\sigma_{\eta_2}^2$.

It turns out that in each case the objective function is convex. For example, in case 1, the optimum is given by

$$q = \ell = \frac{1}{2} \frac{\sigma_{\eta_2}^2}{\sigma_{\eta_1}^2 + \sigma_{\eta_2}^2} \tag{9}$$

with the other parameters determined directly from equation (4). The value of the loss function at this optimum is

$$L_{11} = \frac{1}{4}(1+\lambda)(\sigma_{\epsilon_1}^2 + \sigma_{\epsilon_2}^2) + \frac{\sigma_{\eta_1}^2 \sigma_{\eta_2}^2}{\sigma_{\eta_1}^2 + \sigma_{\eta_2}^2}. \tag{10}$$

Before considering the other cases, the economic interpretation of these conditions should be discussed.

As information about b has been transmitted, the full state of knowledge about b is perceived in common by the two agents. The decision rule is set up to produce $y_1 = y_2$ at the value of one-half the conditional mean of b given both observations. Indeed, this eliminates the cost of malcoordination because taking the best action is conditional on all the information about b. As no information about a is available, other than the direct observation of each agent, the organization is at risk with respect to errors both of estimation and of malcoordination. Each agent's own error of estimation contributes separately to the former, as there is no reduction due to pooling of observations. Each agent bases his or her action x on personal information about a, neglecting the cost of malcoordination. This occurs because σ_a^2 is very large. An attempt to coordinate should be based on the prior information, which is too negative for this course of action to be worth it.

Case 2 is somewhat different in structure. The parameters should be chosen at

$$f = \frac{\sigma_{\epsilon_2}^2}{\sigma_{\epsilon_1}^2 + \sigma_{\epsilon_2}^2}\left(\frac{1}{1+\lambda}\right), \qquad s = \frac{\sigma_{\eta_1}^2}{\sigma_{\eta_1}^2 + \sigma_{\eta_2}^2}\left(\frac{1}{1+\mu}\right). \tag{11}$$

The value of the loss function is

$$L_{12} = \sigma_{\epsilon_2}^2\left(1 - \frac{\sigma_{\epsilon_2}^2}{(1+\lambda)(\sigma_{\epsilon_1}^2 + \sigma_{\epsilon_2}^2)}\right) + \sigma_{\eta_1}^2\left(1 - \frac{\sigma_{\eta_1}^2}{(1+\mu)(\sigma_{\eta_1}^2 + \sigma_{\eta_2}^2)}\right). \tag{12}$$

In this case, agent 1's information about b is transmitted to agent 2 and agent 2's information about a is transmitted to agent 1. Therefore agent 1 is in a good position to control x, having the better information ex post. On the other hand, to the extent that agent 2 does not choose the same level of x_2 as agent 1 chooses for x_1, they are at risk for the coordination loss, and increasingly so as λ becomes large. Equation (11) shows that as λ becomes large agent 2 uses less and less of his or her own information to avoid malcoordination.

These considerations can be useful in deriving an upper bound on the loss in this mode. This loss is achieved by using a decision rule that we call the *mimic strategy*, which eliminates the risk due to malcoordination of the x and y decisions.

With respect to the information relevant to the choice of x_1 and x_2, as the decision rules are common knowledge, the agent can choose $x_1 = x_2$ identically. For finite λ this will not be optimal, but as $\lambda \to \infty$, the agent ignores his or her own information and sets $x_1 = \frac{1}{2}z_2 = \frac{1}{2}\beta_2$.

Precisely the same considerations apply, of course, for player 2 and the y decisions.

As this "mimic" strategy is always available, the worst that can happen under case 2 is to use player 2's information about a to choose $x_1 = x_2$ and player 1's information about b to choose $y_1 = y_2$, while ignoring 2's information about b and 1's information about a. Algebraically, the loss L_{12} is at most

$$\sigma_{\eta_1}^2 + \sigma_{\epsilon_2}^2. \tag{13}$$

Case 3 parallels case 2. The loss is

$$L_{13} = \sigma_{\epsilon_1}^2 \left(1 + \frac{\sigma_{\epsilon_1}^2}{(1+\lambda)(\sigma_{\epsilon_1}^2 + \sigma_{\epsilon_2}^2)}\right) + \sigma_{\eta_2}^2 \left(1 - \frac{\sigma_{\eta_2}^2}{(1+\mu)(\sigma_{\eta_1}^2 + \sigma_{\eta_2}^2)}\right). \tag{14}$$

Case 4 parallels case 1; the loss is

$$L_{14} = \frac{1}{4}(1+\mu)(\sigma_{\eta_1}^2 + \sigma_{\eta_2}^2) + \frac{\sigma_{\epsilon_1}^2 \sigma_{\epsilon_2}^2}{\sigma_{\epsilon_1}^2 + \sigma_{\epsilon_2}^2}. \tag{15}$$

For any combination of parameters, the optimal use of the interchange mode will be determined by which of the four cases achieves the minimum loss.

If λ (or μ) equals zero, the above method does not apply. It is easy to see that the first best is then achievable by the following strategy. Since $\lambda = 0$, there is no cost in malcoordination of the actions x_1 and x_2 and the optimal predictor of a is

$$\frac{\sigma_{\epsilon_2}^2}{\sigma_{\epsilon_1}^2 + \sigma_{\epsilon_2}^2}\alpha_1 + \frac{\sigma_{\epsilon_1}^2}{\sigma_{\epsilon_1}^2 + \sigma_{\epsilon_2}^2}\alpha_2, \tag{16}$$

which is linear in α_1 and α_2 and can be reached in a decentralized way at no cost. That is, agent i sets x_i equal to the corresponding term of equation (16), that is,

$$x_1 = \frac{\sigma_{\epsilon_2}^2}{\sigma_{\epsilon_1}^2 + \sigma_{\epsilon_2}^2}\alpha_1 \quad \text{and} \quad x_2 = \frac{\sigma_{\epsilon_1}^2}{\sigma_{\epsilon_1}^2 + \sigma_{\epsilon_2}^2}\alpha_2.$$

The two channels of communication can then be used to pool all available information about b. Thus, as all information is then common knowledge, each agent can choose one-half of the optimal predictor, causing no loss of coordination. The expected loss is

$$L = \frac{\sigma_{\epsilon_1}^2 \sigma_{\epsilon_2}^2}{\sigma_{\epsilon_1}^2 + \sigma_{\epsilon_2}^2} + \frac{\sigma_{\eta_1}^2 \sigma_{\eta_2}^2}{\sigma_{\eta_1}^2 + \sigma_{\eta_2}^2}.$$

When $\lambda \neq 0$, $\mu \neq 0$, as seen above, the cost of malcoordination forces the team to use the predictor

$$\tfrac{1}{2}(\alpha_1 + \alpha_2). \tag{17}$$

This is because we are considering the asymptotic case where σ_a^2 goes to infinity. If σ_a^2 is finite, the optimal action would be a combination of equations (16) and (17).

4   Centralization of information

We consider centralization of information in the hands of agents 1 and 2, which we refer to as cases 1 and 2 of the centralization mode. In case 1, where agent 2 sends two messages to agent 1, he or she will obviously send two observations,

$$\alpha_2 = a + \epsilon_2, \qquad \beta_2 = b + \eta_2.$$

Using the principle of person-to-person optimality in Marschak and Radner [(1972) Chapter 5, Section 3] we can set

$$x_2 = \tfrac{1}{2}\alpha_2, \qquad y_2 = \tfrac{1}{2}\beta_2. \tag{18}$$

Substituting equation (18) in the loss function of the team we have:

$$L = [x_1 + \tfrac{1}{2}(\epsilon_2 - a)]^2 + [y_1 + \tfrac{1}{2}(\eta_2 - b)]^2$$
$$+ \lambda[x_1 - \tfrac{1}{2}(a + \epsilon_2)]^2 + \mu[y_1 - \tfrac{1}{2}(b + \eta_2)]^2.$$

In view of the independence of the errors, the decision rule of agent 1 is of the form

$$x_1 = e\alpha_1 + f\alpha_2, \qquad y_1 = g\beta_1 + h\beta_2. \tag{19}$$

Substituting equation (19) in the loss function and maximizing the expected value of the loss given the information $(\alpha_1, \alpha_2, \beta_1, \beta_2)$ yields

$$e = \frac{\sigma_{\epsilon_2}^2}{(1+\lambda)(\sigma_{\epsilon_1}^2 + \sigma_{\epsilon_2}^2)}, \qquad g = \frac{\sigma_{\eta_2}^2}{(1+\mu)(\sigma_{\eta_1}^2 + \sigma_{\eta_2}^2)},$$

$$f = \tfrac{1}{2} - e, \qquad h = \tfrac{1}{2} - g.$$

The value of the expected loss in case 1 is

$$L_{C1} = \sigma_{\epsilon_2}^2\left(1 - \frac{\sigma_{\epsilon_2}^2}{(1+\lambda)(\sigma_{\epsilon_1}^2 + \sigma_{\epsilon_2}^2)}\right) + \sigma_{\eta_2}^2\left(1 - \frac{\sigma_{\eta_2}^2}{(1+\mu)(\sigma_{\eta_1}^2 + \sigma_{\eta_2}^2)}\right). \tag{20}$$

Symmetrically (case 2) if agent 1 transmits both observations to agent 2, we find an optimal expected value of the loss

$$L_{C2} = \sigma_{\epsilon_1}^2\left(1 - \frac{\sigma_{\epsilon_1}^2}{(1+\lambda)(\sigma_{\epsilon_1}^2 + \sigma_{\epsilon_2}^2)}\right) + \sigma_{\eta_1}^2\left(1 - \frac{\sigma_{\eta_1}^2}{(1+\mu)(\sigma_{\eta_1}^2 + \sigma_{\eta_2}^2)}\right). \tag{21}$$

5 Comparison of communication forms

When λ and μ are very large, cases 1 and 4 of interchange become irrelevant because they provide no way of avoiding the costs of malcoordination. The reason is that they specialize exchange of information on either b (or a), obliging the agents to take the x decision (y decision) on the basis of their diverse private information. Since σ_a^2 is large, they cannot rely on a common prior.

As λ and μ go to infinity, the asymptotic loss in the centralization mode is

$$\inf(\sigma_{\epsilon_1}^2 + \sigma_{\eta_1}^2, \sigma_{\epsilon_2}^2 + \sigma_{\eta_2}^2).$$

For example, if $\sigma_{\epsilon_1}^2 + \sigma_{\eta_1}^2 < \sigma_{\epsilon_2}^2 + \sigma_{\eta_2}^2$, that is, agent 1 is a better observer, there must be centralization in the hands of agent 2. Then, both agents can take the same decisions (to avoid the costs of malcoordination) based on the best common information structure that is possible given the informational constraints.

Similarly, in the interchange mode the asymptotic loss is

$$\inf(\sigma_{\epsilon_1}^2 + \sigma_{\eta_2}^2, \sigma_{\epsilon_2}^2 + \sigma_{\eta_1}^2).$$

The best mode depends on what is the best combination of good information in terms of the sum of the variances.

The optimal form of communication is then easily derived from the best observers. If one agent is the best observer of both parameters (e.g., $\sigma^2_{\epsilon_1} < \sigma^2_{\epsilon_2}$, $\sigma^2_{\eta_1} < \sigma^2_{\eta_1}$) we have centralization (in the hands of the bad observer). If each agent is the best observer in one parameter, we have interchange, in which for each parameter the transmission is made by the good observer. *The most accurate observer of each parameter should transmit his observation to the other agent.*

On the other extreme, when $\lambda = 0$ (or $\mu = 0$) the first best is achieved by the interchange mode case 1 (or case 4). The optimal predictor of a (respectively, b) is achieved in a decentralized way without worrying about malcoordination of x (respectively, y) and full exchange of information is possible on b (respectively, a) so that the optimal predictor of b (respectively, a) is also achieved but here with $y_1 = y_2$ (respectively, $x_1 = x_2$) which avoids any cost of malcoordination.

In this case the centralization mode cannot reach the first best. For example, if agent 1 transmits information, action y_1 will have to be based only on partial information and a loss will be incurred. The best form of centralization depends on the relative values of μ, $\sigma^2_{\epsilon_1}$, $\sigma^2_{\epsilon_2}$, $\sigma^2_{\eta_1}$, and $\sigma^2_{\eta_2}$, in the case $\lambda = 0$ as seen in equations (20) and (21). Table 1 illustrates the domination of the interchange mode 1 (because $\lambda = 0$) and gives in each case the best form of centralization.

When λ and μ are finite, we are in a case intermediary between the two extremes described above and the comparison is more subtle, as seen in Tables 2 and 3. A necessary condition for centralization to win is that the information of an agent be better than the information of the other agent concerning both variables. But this is not sufficient. This dominance ensures the superiority of centralization to cases 2 and 3 of the interchange mode but not necessarily to cases 1 and 4, if λ and μ are small enough.

A typical entry in the tables is as follows:

centralization loss	
	optimal case
interchange loss	
	optimal case

Table 1. $\sigma_{\epsilon_1}^2 = 1$, $\lambda = 0 = \mu = 10$.

$\sigma_{\epsilon_2}^2 = 1$

$\sigma_{\eta_1}^2$ \ $\sigma_{\eta_2}^2$	1	5	9
1	1.46 (2) / 1.00 (1)	1.49 (2) / 1.33 (1)	1.49 (1) / 1.40 (1)
5	1.49 (2) / 1.33 (1)	5.27 (2) / 3.00 (1)	5.34 (2) / 3.71 (1)
9	1.49 (2) / 1.40 (1)	5.34 (2) / 3.71 (1)	9.09 (2) / 5.00 (1)

$\sigma_{\epsilon_2}^2 = 5$

$\sigma_{\eta_1}^2$ \ $\sigma_{\eta_2}^2$	1	5	9
1	1.75 (1) / 1.33 (1)	1.82 (1) / 1.67 (1)	1.82 (1) / 1.73 (1)
5	1.82 (2) / 1.67 (1)	5.61 (1) / 3.33 (1)	5.67 (1) / 4.05 (1)
9	1.82 (2) / 1.73 (1)	5.67 (2) / 4.05 (1)	9.42 (2) / 5.33 (1)

$\sigma_{\epsilon_2}^2 = 9$

$\sigma_{\eta_1}^2$ \ $\sigma_{\eta_2}^2$	1	5	9
1	1.86 (2) / 1.40 (1)	1.89 (1) / 1.73 (1)	1.89 (1) / 1.80 (1)
5	1.89 (2) / 1.73 (1)	5.67 (2) / 3.40 (1)	5.74 (2) / 4.11 (1)
9	1.89 (2) / 1.80 (1)	5.74 (2) / 4.11 (1)	9.49 (2) / 5.40 (1)

Table 2. $\sigma^2_{\epsilon_1} = 1$, $\lambda = \mu = 2$.

$\sigma^2_{\epsilon_2} = 1$

$\sigma^2_{\eta_1}$ \ $\sigma^2_{\eta_2}$		1	5	9
1		1.67_1	1.78_2	1.80_3
		1.67_2	1.78_2	1.80_2
5		1.78_1	5.00_1	5.24_2
		1.78_3	4.00_1	4.71_1
9		1.80_1	5.24_2	8.33_1
		1.80_3	4.71_1	6.00_1

$\sigma^2_{\epsilon_2} = 5$

$\sigma^2_{\eta_1}$ \ $\sigma^2_{\eta_2}$		1	5	9
1		1.78_2	1.89_2	1.91_2
		1.78_3	4.56_3	4.58_2
5		4.56_1	5.11_2	5.35_2
		1.89_3	5.11_1	7.71_1
9		4.58_1	8.02_1	8.44_2
		1.91_3	5.35_3	8.44_3

$\sigma^2_{\epsilon_2} = 9$

$\sigma^2_{\eta_1}$ \ $\sigma^2_{\eta_2}$		1	5	9
1		1.80_2	1.91_2	1.93_2
		1.80_3	4.58_3	7.27_3
5		4.58_2	5.13_2	5.37_2
		1.91_3	5.13_3	8.04_3
9		7.27_2	8.04_2	8.47_2
		1.93_3	5.37_3	8.47_3

Table 3. $\sigma_{\epsilon_1}^2 = 1$, $\lambda = 1 = \mu = 10$.

$\sigma_{\epsilon_2}^2 = 1$

$\sigma_{\eta_1}^2$ \ $\sigma_{\eta_2}^2$	1	5	9
1	1.71 (1)	1.74 (2)	1.74 (2)
	1.50 (1)	1.74 (2)	1.74 (2)
5	1.74 (1)	5.52 (1)	5.59 (2)
	1.74 (3)	3.50 (1)	4.21 (1)
9	1.74 (1)	5.59 (1)	9.34 (1)
	1.74 (3)	4.21 (1)	5.50 (1)

$\sigma_{\epsilon_2}^2 = 5$

$\sigma_{\eta_1}^2$ \ $\sigma_{\eta_2}^2$	1	5	9
1	1.87 (2)	1.90 (2)	1.90 (2)
	1.87 (3)	3.83 (1)	3.90 (1)
5	3.90 (1)	5.69 (2)	5.75 (2)
	1.90 (3)	5.50 (1)	6.21 (1)
9	3.91 (1)	7.75 (1)	9.51 (2)
	1.90 (3)	5.75 (3)	7.50 (1)

$\sigma_{\epsilon_2}^2 = 9$

$\sigma_{\eta_1}^2$ \ $\sigma_{\eta_2}^2$	1	5	9
1	1.91 (2)	1.94 (2)	1.94 (2)
	1.91 (3)	5.57 (3)	5.90 (1)
5	5.57 (2)	5.72 (2)	5.79 (2)
	1.93 (3)	5.72 (3)	8.21 (1)
9	5.94 (1)	9.42 (2)	9.54 (2)
	1.94 (3)	5.79 (3)	9.50 (1)

NOTES

1 The earlier literature includes theoretical papers by Hurwicz (1951), Beckman (1953), Marschak (1954) as well as experimental papers by Bavelas (1951). See also the more recent work of Miyasawa (1967), Oniki (1974) and Groves and Radner (1972).

2 As stressed in the introduction, implicitly, we assume that the costs of coding and decoding are identical and without increasing returns. In mode B, agent 1 encodes two messages and agent 2 decodes two messages. In mode C, each agent encodes one message and decodes one message.

3 We are assuming here that $\lambda \neq 0$, $\mu \neq 0$. See below the treatment of the cases where $\lambda = 0$ or $\mu = 0$.

REFERENCES

Arrow, K. (1982), "Team theory and decentralized resource allocation: An example," IMSSS No. 371, Stanford University.

Bavelas. A. (1951), "Communication patterns in task oriented groups," in H. D. Lasswell and D. Lerner (Eds.), *Policy Sciences,* Stanford: Stanford University Press.

Beckman, M. (1953), "On Marschak's model of an arbitrage firm," *Econometrica,* 21: 347.

Groves, T. and R. Radner (1972), "Allocation of resources in terms," *Journal of Economic Theory,* 3: 415–41.

Hurwicz, L. (1951), "Theory of economic organization," *Econometrica,* 19: 54.

Marschak, J. (1954), "Towards an economic theory of organization and information," in R. M. Thrall, C. H. Coombs, and R. L. Davis (Eds.), *Decision processes,* New York: Wiley.

Marschak, J. and R. Radner (1972), *Economic theory of teams,* New Haven: Yale University Press.

Miyasawa, K. (1967), "A Bayesian approach to team decision problems," in M. Shubik (Ed.), *Essays in mathematical economics in honor of O. Morgenstern,* Princeton: Princeton University Press.

Oniki, H. (1974), "The cost of communication in economic organization," *Quarterly Journal of Economics,* 88: 529–50.

Publications of Kenneth J. Arrow

BOOKS

1951. *Social choice and individual values.* New York: Wiley.

1958 (with S. Karlin and H. Scarf). *Studies in the mathematical theory of inventory and production.* Stanford: Stanford University Press.

1958 (with L. Hurwicz and H. Uzawa). *Studies in linear and non-linear programming.* Stanford: Stanford University Press.

1959 (with M. Hoffenberg and the assistance of H. Markowitz and R. Shephard). *A time series analysis of interindustry demands.* Amsterdam: North Holland.

1963. *Social choice and individual values,* 2nd ed. New Haven: Yale University Press.

1965. *Aspects of the theory of risk bearing.* Helsinki, Finland: Yrjö Jahnssonin Säätiö.

1970 (with M. Kurz). *Public investment, the rate of return, and optimal fiscal policy.* Baltimore: The Johns Hopkins University Press.

1971. *Essays in the theory of risk-bearing.* Chicago: Markham. Amsterdam: North Holland. 278 pp.

1971 (with F. H. Hahn). *General competitive analysis.* San Francisco: Holden-Day. Edinburgh: Oliver & Boyd.

1974. *The limits of organization.* New York: Norton.

1976 (with S. Shavell and J. Yellen). *The limits of the market economy* (in Japanese). Memorandum for Ministry of International Trade and Industry, Japan.

1976. *The viability and equity of capitalism.* E. S. Woodward lecture, Department of Economics, University of British Columbia.

1977 (with L. Hurwicz). *Studies in resource allocation processes.* Cambridge: Cambridge University Press.

1983. *General equilibrium.* Collected Papers, Vol. 2. Cambridge, Mass.: Belknap.

1983. *Social choice and justice.* Collected Papers, Vol. 1. Cambridge, Mass.: Belknap.

1984. *Individual choice under certainty and uncertainty.* Collected Papers, Vol. 3. Cambridge, Mass.: Belknap.

1984. *The economics of information.* Collected Papers, Vol. 4. Cambridge, Mass.: Belknap.

1985. *Applied economics.* Collected Papers, Vol. 6. Cambridge, Mass.: Belknap.

1985. *Production and capital.* Collected Papers, Vol. 5. Cambridge, Mass.: Belknap.

BOOKS EDITED

1960 (with S. Karlin and P. Suppes). *Mathematical methods in the social sciences, 1959: Proceedings of the first Stanford symposium.* Stanford: Stanford University Press.

271

1962 (with S. Karlin and H. Scarf). *Studies in applied probability and management science.* Stanford: Stanford University Press.

1969 (with T. Scitovsky). *Readings in welfare economics.* Homewood, Il.: Richard D. Irwin. American Economic Association Series of Republished Articles in Economics, Vol. XII.

1971. *Selected readings in economic theory from Econometrica.* Cambridge, Mass.: M.I.T. Press.

1978 (with S. J. Fitzsimmons and R. Wildenmann). *Zukunftsorientierte Planung und Forschung für die 80er Jahre.* Köningstein/Ts., W. Germany: Athenaum Verlag.

1981 (with C. C. Abt and S. J. Fitzsimmons). *Applied research for policy: The United States and The Federal Republic of Germany compared.* Cambridge, Mass.: Abt Books.

1981 (with M. D. Intriligator). *Handbook of mathematical economics.* New York: North Holland.

1985 (with S. Honkapohja). *Frontiers of economics.* Oxford: Blackwell.

PAPERS

1949. On the use of winds in flight planning. *Journal of Meteorology,* 6: 150–9.

1949 (with D. Blackwell and M. A. Girshick). Bayes and minimax solutions of sequential decision problems. *Econometrica.* 17: 213–44.

1950. Homogeneous systems in mathematical economics: A comment. *Econometrica.* 18: 60–2.

1950. A difficulty in the concept of social welfare. *Journal of Political Economy.* 58: 328–46.

1951. Alternative proof of the substitution theorem for Leontief models in the general case. In T. C. Koopmans (ed.), *Activity analysis of production and allocation.* New York: Wiley, Chapter IX.

1951 (with T. E. Harris and J. Marschak). Optimal inventory policy. *Econometrica.* 19: 250–72.

1951. Alternative approaches to the theory of choice in risk-taking situations. *Econometrica.* 19: 404–37.

1951. Little's critique of welfare economics. *American Economic Review.* 41: 923–34.

1951. Mathematical models in the social sciences. In D. Lerner and H. D. Lasswell (eds.), *The policy sciences.* Stanford: Stanford University Press, pp. 129–54.

1951. An extension of the basic theorems of classical welfare economics. In J. Neyman (ed.), *Proceedings of the second Berkeley symposium on mathematical statistics and probability.* Berkeley and Los Angeles: University of California Press, pp. 507–32.

1952. The determination of many-commodity preference scales by two-commodity comparison. *Metroeconomica.* IV: 107–15.

1952. Le principe de rationalité dans les choix collectifs. *Economie Appliqué.* V: 469–84.

1953. Le rôle des valeurs boursières pour la répartition la meilleure des risques. *Econometrie.* Colloques Internationaux du Centre National de la Recherche Scientifique, Vol. XI, pp. 41–47.

1953 (with E. W. Barankin and D. Blackwell). Admissible points of convex sets. *Contributions to the theory of games,* Vol. II. Princeton: Princeton University Press, pp. 87–91.

1954 (with G. Debreu). Existence of equilibrium for a competitive economy. *Econometrica.* 22: 265–90.

1954. Import substitution in Leontief models. *Econometrica.* 22: 491–2.

1956 (with L. Hurwicz). Reduction of constrained maxima to saddle-point problems. In J. Neyman (ed.), *Proceedings of the third Berkeley symposium on mathematical statistics and probability.* Berkeley and Los Angeles: University of California Press, Vol. V, pp. 1–20.

1956 (with A. C. Enthoven). A theorem on expectations and the stability of equilibrium. *Econometrica.* 24: 288–93.

1957 (with L. Hurwicz). Gradient methods for constrained maxima. *Operations Research,* 5: 258–65.

1957. Statistics and economic policy. *Econometrica.* 25: 523–31.

1957. Decision theory and operations research. *Operations Research.* 5: 765–74.

1958. Utilities, attitudes, choices: a review note. *Econometrica.* 26: 1–23.

1958. Tinbergen on economic policy. *Journal of the American Statistical Association.* 53: 89–97.

1958. The measurement of price changes. In Joint Economic Committee, *The relationship of prices to economic stability and growth.* Washington, DC: U.S. Government Printing Office, pp. 77–88.

1958 (with M. Nerlove). A note on expectations and stability. *Econometrica.* 26: 297–305.

1958 (with A. Alchian and W. M. Capron). *An economic analysis of the market for scientists and engineers,* RM 2190-RC. Santa Monica: The RAND Corporation.

1958 (with M. McManus). A note on dynamic stability. *Econometrica.* 26: 448–54.

1958 (with L. Hurwicz). On the stability of the competitive equilibrium, I. *Econometrica.* 26: 522–52.

1959. Toward a theory of price adjustment. In M. Abramovitz et al., *The allocation of resources.* Stanford: Stanford University Press, pp. 41–51.

1959 (with M. M. Capron). Dynamic shortages and price rises: the engineer-scientist case. *Quarterly Journal of Economics.* 63: 292–308.

1959. Rational choice functions and orderings. *Economica.* N.S. 26: 121–7.

1959 (with H. D. Block and L. Hurwicz). On the stability of the competitive equilibrium, II. *Econometrica.* 27: 82–109.

1959. Functions of a theory of behavior under uncertainty. *Metroeconomica.* 11: 12–20.

1960 (with L. Hurwicz). Competitive stability under weak gross substitutability: the "Euclidean distance" approach. *International Economic Review.* 1: 38–49.

1960. Optimization, decentralization, and internal pricing in business firms. In *Contributions to scientific research in management.* Western Data Processing Center, Graduate School of Business Administration, University of California, Los Angeles, pp. 9–18.

1960. Decision theory and the choice of a level of significance for the *t*-test. In I. Olin et al. (eds.), *Contributions to probability and statistics.* Stanford: Stanford University Press, pp. 70-8.

1960. The work of Ragnar Frisch, econometrician. *Econometrica.* 28: 175-92.

1960. Price-quantity adjustments in multiple markets with rising demands. In K. J. Arrow, S. Karlin, and P. Suppes (eds.), *Mathematical methods in the social sciences, 1959.* Stanford: Stanford University Press, pp. 3-16.

1960 (with L. Hurwicz). Decentralization and computation in resource allocation. In R. W. Pfouts (ed.), *Essays in economics and econometrics.* Chapel Hill: University of North Carolina Press, pp. 34-104.

1960 (with L. Hurwicz). Stability of the gradient process in *n*-person games. *Journal of the Society for Industrial and Applied Mathematics.* 8: 280-94.

1960 (with L. Hurwicz). Some remarks on the equilibria of economic systems. *Econometrica.* 28: 640-6.

1961. Additive logarithmic demand functions and the Slutsky relations. *Review of Economic Studies.* 28: 176-81.

1961 (with H. B. Chenery, B. Minhas, and R. M. Solow). Capital-labor substitution and economic efficiency. *Review of Economics and Statistics.* 43: 225-50.

1961 (with L. Hurwicz and H. Uzawa). Constraint qualifications in maximization problems. *Naval Research Logistics Quarterly.* 8: 175-91.

1961 (with A. C. Enthoven). Quasi-concave programming. *Econometrica.* 29: 779-800.

1962. Case Studies: Comment. In National Bureau of Economic Research, *The rate and direction of inventive activity: Economic and social factors.* Princeton: Princeton University Press, pp. 353-58.

1962. Economic welfare and the allocation of resources for invention. Ibid., pp. 609-25.

1962. Optimal capital adjustment. In K. J. Arrow, S. Karlin, and H. Scarf (eds.), *Studies in applied probability and management science.* Stanford: Stanford University Press, pp. 1-17.

1962 (with M. Nerlove). Optimal advertising policy under dynamic conditions. *Economica.* N.S. 29: 129-42.

1962. The economic implications of learning by doing. *Review of Economic Studies.* 29: 155-73.

1962 (with L. Hurwicz). Competitive stability under weak gross substitutability: nonlinear price adjustment and adaptive expectations. *International Economic Review.* 3: 233-55.

1963. Conference Remarks. In M. Astrachan and A. S. Cahn (eds.), *Proceedings of RAND's Demand Prediction Conference,* January 25-26, 1962. Santa Monica, CA: The RAND Corporation, RM-3358-RP, pp. 125-34.

1963. Utility and expectation in economic behavior. In S. Koch (ed.), *Psychology: a Study of a Science,* Vol. 6. New York: McGraw-Hill, pp. 724-52.

1963. The economic cost to Western Europe of restricted availability of oil imports: a linear programming computation. In H. Lubell, *Middle East oil crises and Western Europe's energy supplies.* Baltimore, Md.: Johns Hopkins University Press, Appendix D, pp. 214-220.

1963. Comment on Duesenberry's "The Portfolio Approach to the Demand for Money and Other Assets." *Review of Economics and Statistics*. 45: pp. 24-7.

1963. Uncertainty and the welfare economics of medical care. *American Economic Review*. 53: 941-73.

1963-4. Control in large organizations. *Management Science*. 10: 397-408.

1964. Optimal capital policy, the cost of capital, and myopic decision rules. *Annals of the Institute of Statistical Mathematics*. 16: 21-30.

1964. Research in management controls: a critical synthesis. In C. P. Bonini, R. K. Jaedicke, and H. M. Wagner, *Management controls: New directions in basic research*. New York: McGraw-Hill, Chapter 17, pp. 317-27.

1965. Connaissance, productivite et pratique. *Bulletin SEDEIS*, Etude No. 909 Supplement.

1965. *Statistical requirements for Greek economic planning*. Athens, Greece: Center of Planning and Economic Research, Lecture Series No. 18.

1965. Uncertainty and the welfare economics of medical care: reply (The Implications of Transaction Costs and Adjustment Lags). *American Economic Review*. 55: 154-8.

1965. Criteria for social investment. *Water Resources Research*. 1: 1-8.

1965. The economic context. In S. T. Donner (ed.), *The future of commercial television*, 1965-75 (privately printed), pp. 116-39.

1966. Discounting and public investment criteria. In A. V. Kneese and S. C. Smith (eds.), *Water research*. Baltimore, Md.: Johns Hopkins University Press, pp. 13-32.

1967. Values and collective decision-making. In P. Laslett and W. G. Runciman (eds.), *Philosophy, politics and society*, Third series. Oxford: Blackwell, Chapter 10, pp. 215-232.

1967. The place of moral obligation in preference systems. In S. Hook (ed.), *Human values and economic policy*. New York: New York University Press, Part II, 3, pp. 117-19.

1967. Samuelson collected. *Journal of Political Economy*. 85: 506-13.

1968. Economic equilibrium. In *International Encyclopedia of The Social Sciences*. New York: Macmillan and the Free Press, Vol. 4, pp. 376-86.

1968. Meyer A. Girshick. In *International Encyclopedia of The Social Sciences*. New York: Macmillan and the Free Press, Vol. 6, pp. 191-3.

1968. The economics of moral hazard: further comment. *American Economic Review*. 58: 537-9.

1968 (pseudonym of Archen Minsol; joint with H. B. Chenery, B. S. Minhas, and R. M. Solow). Some tests of the international comparisons of factor efficiency with the CES production function: a reply. *Review of Economics and Statistics*. 50: 477-9.

1968. Optimal capital policy with irreversible investment. In J. N. Wolfe (ed.), *Value, capital, and growth*. Edinburgh: Edinburgh University Press, pp. 1-20.

1968. Applications of control theory to economic growth. In American Mathematical Society, *Mathematics of the decision sciences*, Part 2. Providence: American Mathematical Society, pp. 85-119.

1969. Classificatory notes on the production and transmission of technological knowledge. *American Economic Review Papers and Proceedings*. 59: 29-35.

1969. The organization of economic activity: issues pertinent to the choice of market versus nonmarket allocation. In Joint Economic Committee, U.S. Congress, *The analysis and evaluation of public expenditures: The PPB system,* Vol. 1. Washington, DC: Government Printing Office, pp. 47–66.

1969 (with M. Kurz). Optimal consumer allocation over an infinite horizon. *Journal of Economic Theory.* 1: 68–91.

1969. Tullock and an existence theorem. *Public Choice.* VI: 105–12.

1969 (with M. Kurz). Optimal public investment policy and controllability with fixed private savings ration. *Journal of Economic Theory.* 1: 141–177.

1969 (with D. Levhari). Uniqueness of the internal rate of return with variable life of investment. *Economic Journal.* 79: 560–6.

1969. The social discount rate. In G. G. Somers and W. D. Woods (eds.), *Cost-Benefit Analysis of Manpower Policies.* Kingston, Ontario: Industrial Relations Centre, Queen's University.

1970. The effects of the price system and market on urban economic development. In K. J. Arrow et al., *Urban processes as viewed by the social sciences.* Washington, DC: The Urban Institute, pp. 11–20.

1970 (with M. Kurz). Optimal growth with irreversible investment in a Ramsey model. *Econometrica.* 38(2): 331–4.

1970. New ideas in pure theory: discussion. *American Economic Review, Papers and Proceedings.* 60: 462–3.

1970 (with R. C. Lind). Uncertainty and the evaluation of public investment decisions. *American Economic Review.* 60: 364–78.

1970. Criteria, institutions, and function in urban development decisions. In A. H. Pascal (ed.), *Thinking about cities.* Belmont, Calif.: Dickenson.

1970. Induced technical change and patterns of international trade: comment. In R. Vernon (ed.), *The technology factor in international trade.* New York: National Bureau of Economic Research, pp. 128–32.

1971. The firm in general equilibrium theory. In R. Marris and A. Wood (eds.), *The corporate economy: growth, competition, and innovative potential.* London: Macmillan. Cambridge, Mass.: Harvard University Press, pp. 68–110.

1971. A utilitarian approach to the concept of equality in public expenditures. *Quarterly Journal of Economics.* 85: 409–15.

1971. Exposition of the theory of choice under uncertainty. In C. B. McGuire and R. Radner (eds.), *Decision and organization.* Amsterdam: North Holland, pp. 19–55.

1971. The value of and demand for information. In C. B. McGuire and R. Radner (eds.), *Decision and organization.* Amsterdam: North Holland, pp. 19–55.

1972 (with L. Hurwicz). An optimality criterion for decision-making under ignorance. In C. F. Carter and J. L. Ford (eds.), *Uncertainty and expectations in economics: Essays in honour of G. L. S. Shackle.* Oxford: Blackwell, pp. 1–11.

1972 (with R. C. Lind). Uncertainty and the evaluation of public investment decisions: reply. *American Economic Review.* 62: 171–2.

1972. Problems of resource allocation in United States medical care. In R. M. Kunz and H. Fehr (eds.), *The challenge of life.* Basel and Stuttgart: Birkhauser, pp. 392–408.

1972. Models of job discrimination. In A. H. Pascal (ed.), *Racial Discrimination in Economic Life*. Lexington, Mass.: Heath, Chapter 2, pp. 8–102.

1972. Some mathematical models of race in the labor market. Ibid., Chapter 6, pp. 187–204.

1972. Gifts and exchanges. *Philosophy and public affairs*. 1: 343–62.

1972 (with D. Levhari and E. Sheshinski). A production function for the repairman problem. *Review of Economic Studies*. 39: 241–9.

1973. Some ordinalist-utilitarian notes on Rawls's theory of justice. *Journal of Philosophy*. 70: 245–63.

1973 (with D. Starrett). Cost- and demand-theoretical approaches to the theory of price determination. In J. R. Hicks and W. Weber (eds.), *Carl Menger and the Austrian school of economics*. Oxford: Clarendon Press, Chapter 7, pp. 129–48.

1973. Higher education as a filter. *Journal of Public Economics*. 2: 193–216.

1973. General economic equilibrium: purpose, analytic techniques, collective choice. In *Les Prix Nobel en 1972*. Stockholm: The Nobel Foundation, pp. 206–31.

1973. Social responsibility and economic efficiency. *Public Policy*. 21: 303–18.

1973. Formal theories of social welfare. In P. P. Wiener (ed.), *Dictionary of the history of ideas*, Vol. IV. New York: Scribner, pp. 276–84.

1973. *Information and economic behavior*. Stockholm: Federation of Swedish Industries (Lecture).

1973. The theory of discrimination. In O. Ashenfelter and A. Rees (eds.), *Discrimination in labor markets*. Princeton, NJ: Princeton University Press, pp. 3–33.

1973 (with F. J. Gould and S. M. Howe). A general saddle point result for constrained optimization. *Mathematical Programming*. 5: 225–34.

1973. Rawls's principle of just saving. *Swedish Journal of Economics*. 75: 323–35.

1974. The measurement of real value added. In P. A. David and M. W. Reder (eds.), *Nations and households in economic growth*. New York: Academic Press, pp. 3–19.

1974. Stability independent of adjustment speed. In G. Horwich and P. A. Samuelson (eds.), *Trade, stability, and macroeconomics*. New York: Academic Press, pp. 181–202.

1974. Capitalism, for better or worse. In L. Silk (ed.), *Capitalism: The moving target*. New York: Quadrangle/New York Times Company, pp. 105–13.

1974. Unbounded utility functions in expected utility maximization: response. *Quarterly Journal of Economics*. 88: 136–8.

1974. Limited knowledge and economic analysis. *American Economic Review*. 64: 1–10.

1974. Optimal insurance and generalized deductibles. *Scandinavian Actuarial Journal*. 1974: 1–42.

1974 (with A. C. Fisher). Environmental preservation, uncertainty, and irreversibility. *Quarterly Journal of Economics*. 88: 312–19.

1974. On the agenda of organizations. In R. Marris (ed.), *The corporate society*. New York: Wiley, pp. 214–34.

1974. The combination of time series and cross-section data in interindustry flow analysis. *European Economic Review*. 5: 25–32.

1974. Government decision making and the preciousness of human life. In L. R. Taneredi (ed.), *Ethics of health care*. Washington, DC: National Academy of Sciences, Chapter II, pp. 33–47.

1974. On the agenda of organizations. In R. Marris (ed.), *The Corporate Society*. New York and Toronto: Wiley, pp. 214–34.

1974. The combination of time series and cross-section data in interindustry flow analysis. *European Economic Review*. 5: 25–32.

1975. Vertical integration and communication. *The Bell Journal of Economics*. 6: 173–83.

1975. Thorstein Veblen as an economic theorist. *The American Economist*. 19: 5–9.

1975. On a theorem of Arrow: comment. *Review of Economic Studies*. 62: 487.

1975. Economic development: the present state of the art. Papers of the East-West Communication Institute, No. 14.

1976. Economic dimensions of occupational segregation: Comment I. *Signs*. 1(3): 233–7, Part 2.

1976. Quantity adjustments in resource allocation: a statistical interpretation. In R. E. Grierson (ed.), *Public and urban economics*. Lexington, Mass.: Lexington Books, pp. 3–11.

1976. *Theoretical issues in health insurance*. The University of Essex, Noel Buxton lecture for 1973.

1976. Welfare analysis of changes in health coinsurance rates. In R. N. Rossett (ed.), *The role of health insurance in the health services sector*. New York: National Bureau of Economic Research, Chapter 1, pp. 2–23.

1976. Evaluation of social experiments: discussion. In C. G. Abt (ed.), *The evaluation of social programs*. Beverly Hills, Calif.: Sage, pp. 49–54.

1976. The rate of discount for long-term public investment. In H. Ashley, R. L. Rudman, and C. Whipple (eds.), *Energy and the environment: A risk–benefit approach*. New York: Pergamon, pp. 113–40.

1977. The genesis of dynamic systems generated by Metzler matrices. In R. Henn and O. Moeschlin (eds.), *Mathematical economics and game essays in honor of Oskar Morgenstern*. New York: Springer-Verlag, pp. 629–44.

1977. Extended sympathy and the possibility of social choice. *American Economic Review, Papers and Proceedings*. 67(1): 219–25.

1977. Current developments in the theory of social choice. *Social Research*. 44: 607–22.

1978. The future and the present in economic life. *Economic Inquiry*. 16: 157–70.

1978. Nozick's entitlement theory of justice. *Philosophia*. 7: 265–79.

1978. Risk allocation and information: some recent theoretical developments. *The Geneva papers on risk and insurance*, No. 8, June 1978 (Association Internationale pour l'Etude de l'Economie de l'Assurance).

1979. The Trade-off between Growth and Equity. In H. I. Greenfield, A. M. Levenson, W. Hamovitch, and E. Rotwein (eds.), *Theory for economic efficiency: Essays in honor of Abba P. Lerner*. Cambridge, Mass.: MIT Press, pp. 1–11.

1979 (with J. P. Kalt). Petroleum price regulation: should we decontrol? Studies in energy policy. *AEI Studies* 256.

1979 (with R. Radner). Allocation of Resources in Large Teams. *Econometrica.* 47(2): 361–85.

1979. Pareto efficiency with costly transfers. *Economic Forum.* 1: 1–13.

1979. The property rights doctrine and demand revelation under incomplete information. In M. Boskin (ed.), *Economics and human welfare.* New York: Academic Press, pp. 23–39.

1980. Real and nominal magnitudes in economics. In *The crisis in economic theory, Public interest special issue.* New York: National Affairs.

1980. Real and nominal magnitudes in economics. *Journal of Financial and Quantitative Analysis.* 15(4): 773–83.

1981. Optimal and voluntary income distribution. In S. Rosefield (ed.), *Economic welfare and the economics of Soviet socialism: Essays in honor of Abram Bergson.* Cambridge: Cambridge University Press, pp. 267–88.

1981. Medicine and moral philosophy. In M. Cohen, T. Nagel, and T. Scanlon (eds.), *Philosophy and public affairs.* Princeton, NJ: Princeton University Press, p. xi, 308 pp.

1981 (August). Evaluation of the UNITAR project, technology, domestic distribution and North–South relations. New York: UNITAR.

1981 (with L. Pesotchinsky and M. Sobel). On partitioning a sample with binary-type questions in lieu of collecting observations. *Journal of the American Statistical Association.* 76(374): 402–9.

1982. Risk perception in psychology and economics. *Economic Inquiry.* 20: 1–9.

1982. Optimal pricing, use, and exploration of uncertain natural resource stocks. *Journal of Environmental Economics and Management.* 9(1): 1–10.

1984. Permanent and transitory substitution effects in health insurance experiments. *Journal of Labor Economics.* 2(2): 259–67.

COLLECTIVE STUDIES

1975 (as member of Climatic Impact Committee of the National Research Council, National Academy of Sciences, National Academy of Engineering). *Environmental impact of stratospheric flight.* Washington, DC: National Academy of Sciences.

1977 (as member of Nuclear Energy Policy Study Group; S. M. Keeny, Jr., et al.). *Nuclear power issues and choices.* Cambridge, Mass.: Ballinger.

1979 (as member of a study group sponsored by the Ford Foundation and administered by Resources for the Future; Hans H. Landsberg, chairman). *Energy, the next twenty years: Report.* Cambridge, Mass.: Ballinger.

Author index

281